How This Book Can Help You

A Note from the Author

The eighth edition of *EasyWriter* comes to you at a critical moment, when the country and the world continue to recover from a pandemic that has cost millions of lives and to grapple with the devastating effects of climate change on communities everywhere. It also comes at a time of ongoing struggle against systemic racism and a deep divisiveness fueled by the onslaught of misinformation and false and misleading news. And finally, it arrives when students (and teachers) are still experiencing the effects of altered learning conditions and all the challenges associated with them.

These times call—perhaps more than ever before—for all of us not to retreat or give up but to make our voices heard even as we listen respectfully and carefully to the voices of others. In short, this situation calls on all of us to be *engaged*—as writers, as speakers, as thinkers, as contributors to an open and fair society. And *EasyWriter* is here to help you achieve that goal—to get engaged with your own writing and ideas, engaged with other people, and engaged with the world around you.

This kind of engagement calls on you to examine your own values and to be aware of your own biases or ways of seeing—*and* to become a strong critical reader who can check facts like a pro and distinguish whether information is true, false, or manipulated (see Chapters 8 and 13 on reading and evaluating texts). Constructive engagement also calls on you to listen openly to a wide range of perspectives, to understand that sometimes you might be wrong, to be open to changing your mind, and to practice ethical and empathetic communication (see Chapter 1, "A Writer's Opportunities"). This new edition of *EasyWriter* will guide you as you practice expressing yourself clearly, persuasively, and ethically. In this book, you'll find helpful advice about how to be an effective listener, writer, speaker, and reader—all in a small package that we've worked hard to make friendly and easy to use. In Achieve, the new digital platform, you'll be an active and engaged learner who will see progress over time as you read and write and interact with others.

v

Being an effective communicator means taking a rhetorical approach to learning, one that focuses on understanding and connecting to audiences across a wide spectrum of differences. The major tool we have for such communication is language, and in particular the English language. *EasyWriter* will remind you that there are many forms and dialects of English, many based on regional or ethnic varieties, and that all forms of English are vital and valid. Expressing your ideas in Black English, Cajun English, the English of the Pacific Northwest, or some other form is a decision you will make based on purpose, audience, genre, and message. One form of English, sometimes called American Standard and referred to in this text as standardized English, is one that no one grows up speaking. Standardized English is not a traditional dialect like the one you use in your home community, but a set of patterns that have been sanctioned over time—that is, *made standard*—by schools, government, business, and other institutions and that call for common communication across differences. Where you go to school, your instructors may expect you to write and speak in standardized English.

That doesn't mean you shouldn't think critically about these expectations. As linguist Max Weinreich pointed out long ago, such a "standard" language is a "dialect with an army and a navy." That is to say, standardized English is the language of the powerful. However, it is important to understand how such a "dialect with an army and a navy" has worked to empower and privilege some and to disempower and silence others. That has certainly been the case in the United States, from the efforts of the earliest colonists—white people from Europe—who founded colleges to teach English to the indigenous peoples and force them to speak it, to the attempts to withhold literacy from enslaved peoples, to the dismissal of regional, ethnic, and even occupational dialects as "substandard." Anyone who has been penalized or made fun of for the way they speak has felt this bias.

EasyWriter respects the validity and beauty of all forms of English, and is itself written in what I hope is a fairly informal, user-friendly version of "standardized" English—that is, a version characterized by features that can be understood by speakers of a wide range of dialects and languages. But the text aims to be inclusive, to promote language awareness, and to welcome and value all voices and all audiences. Part 5, "Style: Effective Language,"

Quick Start Menu

Find your assignment, and then start with the advice and examples listed here.

✳ indicates content only in Achieve with *EasyWriter*.

What Are You Writing?	Get Advice	See Student Models
Annotated bibliography	**13h** Creating an annotated bibliography	**13i** Annotated bibliography entries
Argument	**9** Arguing Ethically and Persuasively	**9g** Argument essay (L.J. Bryan)
Blog	**7b** Types of low-stakes assignments **10d** Choosing genres for public writing	✳ Reflective blog post (Thanh Nguyen)
Film analysis	**8e** Analyzing **9e** Making an argument	✳ Film analysis (Amrit Rao)
Job application	**2c** Considering audiences **4b** Choosing appropriate formats **9e** Making an argument	✳ Cover letter (Nastassia Lopez) ✳ Résumé (Megan Lange)
Lab report	**10a** Recognizing expectations of academic disciplines **10c** Adapting genre structures	**10e** Chemistry lab report (Allyson Goldberg)
Literary analysis	**8** Reading and Listening Analytically, Critically, and Respectfully **10** Writing in a Variety of Disciplines and Genres **16** MLA Style	**10e** Excerpts from a close reading of poetry (Bonnie Sillay)
Multimodal project	**4** Making Design Decisions **10** Writing in a Variety of Disciplines and Genres	**10e** Samples in a variety of disciplines and genres [Poster, web page, comic]
Personal reflection	**6c** Reflecting on your own work	**6d** Reflection (James Kung)
Portfolio	**4** Making Design Decisions **6b** Creating a portfolio	✳ **6d** Portfolio cover letter (James Kung)

What Are You Writing?	Get Advice	See Student Models
Poster	**4c** Choosing visuals and media **4d** Using visuals and media ethically **10d** Choosing genres for public writing	**10e** Poster (Hebron Warren)
Presentation	**11** Creating Presentations	✳ **11h** Excerpts from a presentation (Shuqiao Song)
Proposal	**9** Arguing Ethically and Persuasively	✳ Pitch package (Deborah Jane and Jamie Burke) ✳ Research proposal (Tara Gupta)
Research essay or project	**9** Arguing Ethically and Persuasively **12–15** Research **16** MLA Style (composition and literature) **17** APA Style (social sciences) **18** *Chicago* Style (history and the arts) **19** CSE Style (sciences)	**9g** Research-based argument essay in MLA style (L.J. Bryan) **16f** Research essay in MLA style (Julia Sakowitz) **17e** Research essay in APA style (Martha Bell) **18d** Research essay (excerpt) in *Chicago* style (Amanda Rinder) ✳ Complete papers in history and science
Rhetorical analysis	**8d** Summarizing **8e** Analyzing **9e** Making an argument	**8f** Rhetorical analysis (Cameron Hauer)
Social media or website	**1b** Using social media wisely **4** Making Design Decisions **10d** Choosing genres for public writing	**10e** Fundraising web page (Justin Dart)
Summary	**8d** Summarizing	✳ Summary of an assigned reading (Samyuktha Comandur)
Visual	**4c** Choosing visuals and media **4d** Using visuals and media ethically	**10e** Samples in a variety of disciplines and genres [Poster, web page, comic]

EIGHTH EDITION

easy writer

with Exercises

Andrea A. Lunsford

STANFORD UNIVERSITY

Coverage for multilingual writers with

Paul Kei Matsuda
ARIZONA STATE UNIVERSITY

Christine M. Tardy
UNIVERSITY OF ARIZONA

bedford/st.martin's
Macmillan Learning

Boston | New York

FOR BEDFORD/ST. MARTIN'S

Vice President, Humanities: Leasa Burton
Program Director, English: Stacey Purviance
Senior Program Manager: Laura Arcari
Senior Executive Editor: Michelle M. Clark
Assistant Editor: Aislyn Fredsall
Director of Content Development: Jane Knetzger
Director of Media Editorial: Adam Whitehurst
Media Editor: Dan Johnson
Marketing Manager: Vivian Garcia
Senior Director, Content Management Enhancement: Tracey Kuehn
Senior Managing Editor: Michael Granger
Senior Digital Content Project Manager: Ryan Sullivan
Lead Digital Asset Archivist and Senior Workflow Manager: Jennifer Wetzel
Production Coordinator: Brianna Lester
Director of Design, Content Management: Diana Blume
Interior Design: Claire Seng-Niemoeller
Cover Design: William Boardman
Director of Rights and Permissions: Hilary Newman
Permissions Editor: Allison Ziebka-Viering
Photo Researcher: Krystyna Borgen, Lumina Datamatics, Inc.
Director of Digital Production: Keri deManigold
Media Project Manager: Elizabeth Dziubela
Copyeditor: Julie Dock, Lumina Datamatics, Inc.
Indexer: Christine Hoskin, Lumina Datamatics, Inc.
Composition: Lumina Datamatics, Inc.
Printing and Binding: RR Donnelley

Library of Congress Control Number: 2021943297

ISBN: 978-1-319-39334-2

Printed in China.

1 2 3 4 5 6   26 25 24 23 22 21

ACKNOWLEDGMENTS

Text acknowledgments and copyrights appear below. Art acknowledgments and copyrights appear on the same page as the art selections they cover.

"Music Instruction Aids Verbal Memory" [press release]. Copyright © 2003 American Psychological Association. Reproduced with permission. All rights reserved.

includes a new chapter on language and identity and new examples that experiment with language. And Chapters 22 and 36 present more inclusive guidelines for pronouns. The entire book is stronger thanks to a number of very generous advisers (see p. xiv) who have shared so much of their knowledge and wisdom with me.

The eighth edition of *EasyWriter* can help you to use language and rhetoric responsibly, ethically, and effectively—and to become the engaged writer and citizen you want to be. In challenging and changing times, *EasyWriter* aims to be a friendly guide that helps you find and *use* your voice in order to, in the words of civil rights icon John Lewis, "[s]tand up, speak up, speak out" for what you believe in.

Andrea A. Lunsford

New to This Edition

Readers who are familiar with previous editions of *EasyWriter* will notice the following changes.

Achie✓e is an exciting and comprehensive set of inter-connected teaching and assessment tools. It integrates the most effective elements from the Bedford/St. Martin's digital content you may be familiar with (LaunchPad and LearningCurve) with writing tools built for engagement and based on research—all in a powerful, easy-to-use platform that works for face-to-face, remote, and hybrid learning scenarios.

- **Superior content you trust.** Andrea Lunsford's approach and advice are evident in the interactive e-book, engaging video tutorials, adaptive quizzes, and more—all designed to deliver a coherent learning experience and to make prep, practice, and review easy.

- **Writing tools that keep writing and revision at the center of your course.** Achieve with *EasyWriter* gives teachers deeper visibility into students' writing processes to target instruction and feedback and help writers grow across drafts, across assignments, and across courses. Students do the work of the course

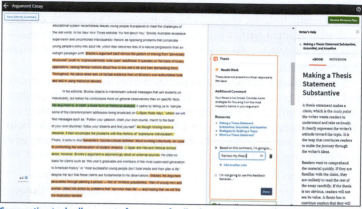

Commenting tools allow you to focus your feedback on Draft Goals and link to relevant e-book content.

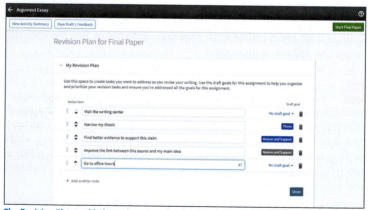

The Revision Plan tool helps writers turn feedback into concrete revision strategies.

in a contained and active writing space that promotes revision, reflection, and review.

- **Assignments that make your life easier.** A flexible assignment building tool allows you to assign ready-made writing prompts— all customizable—or create your own. You can tailor the following assignments to fit your needs: Analysis, Annotated bibliography, Argument, Narrative, Reflection, and Research.

- **Diagnostics and study plans that give students ownership.**
  Diagnostic tests for reading and sentence skills establish a baseline for student performance, promote personalized learning,
  and point students to actionable study plans that build skills and
  confidence.

- **Source Check plagiarism prevention that teaches.** This tool
  helps students become more responsible and ethical research
  writers. It allows students to scan their work for potential
  plagiarism *before* they submit it for review, allowing students to
  learn academic habits and citation practices in the context of
  their own writing.

- **Reports and insights that inform your teaching.** An innovative dashboard highlights student engagement, opportunities
  for intervention, and both whole-class and individual progress
  toward goals.

Advisory Board for Diversity, Equity, and Inclusion (DEI) To
meet the moment—and especially the calls for social and linguistic justice that echoed throughout 2020—we worked with a board
of advisers (see p. xiv), writing teachers from two- and four-year
schools who helped us ensure that students from all backgrounds
can see themselves and their experiences represented in their handbook. This generous group shared their expertise from the classroom,
from scholarship, and from lived experience and made suggestions
for changes throughout the book. Their mighty and meaningful
efforts helped us to promote critical language awareness, respect,
and inclusion in the eighth edition and to fight racism, linguicism,
and discrimination in course materials for college students.

Emphasis on being an open-minded learner Based on new
research with college writers and teachers of writing, a new Chapter 1,
"A Writer's Opportunities," provides a framework for developing the
habits of open-minded readers, writers, listeners, and speakers. A new
approach invites students to expect and engage difference and provides
strategies for communicating respectfully with others.

**New strategies for lateral reading, critical thinking, and fact-
checking** Writing with sources is a foundational skill for college, and too many students arrive with little experience in finding

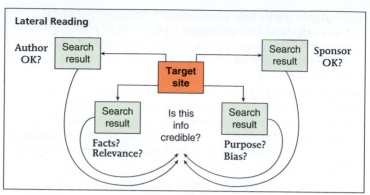

Lateral reading is a smart new way to evaluate sources (see 13c).

sources, questioning the sources they read online, and approaching them with skepticism. New advice for lateral reading and evaluating sources and revised tips for fact-checking (see Chapter 8 and sections 13a–d) help students respond to the information and misinformation in news sources and in social media—and help them balance open-mindedness and skepticism as they evaluate sources. New advice in 12d and e encourages students to seek out sources they might have otherwise overlooked.

Broader presentation of language use Grounded in an understanding of "standardized" English as the traditional language of power and access in the United States, *EasyWriter* coaches students in following, experimenting with, and sometimes even resisting conventions—and in respecting English in all of its forms and dialects. A **new chapter on Language and Identity** (Chapter 20) helps students think more openly and carefully about the language we claim as our own and about language used to label us and others. A **revised chapter on Language Varieties** (Chapter 23) fosters a new openness to translingual composition—with excerpts from student writing. Attention to **gender-neutral pronoun use** (22b, 36b) raises awareness about writing to include rather than to exclude.

New visual help for writers and new student essay models
Two new graphic organizers for argument writing help visual learners plan and execute essays (9f). New student-written analysis, argument, and research essays (8f, 9g, and 16f) provide useful models and annotations that teach.

New resource for corequisite composition A new workbook for developing writers in support or corequisite composition sections provides a wide range of activities to help students practice the skills and habits they need to be success-

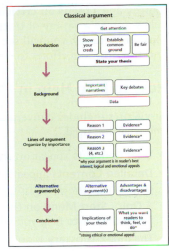

ful academic writers. *A Student's Companion to Lunsford Handbooks* is designed specifically to help underprepared students improve their reading and writing performance—with material on time management and etiquette, substantial coverage of reading strategies, graphic organizers for visual learners, and more than sixty exercises on writing, research, and grammar.

What Hasn't Changed

In the eighth edition, you can still count on **rhetorical grounding** and an emphasis on writers' choices about purpose, audience, topic, and style; advice for writing in different **contexts, disciplines, and genres**; unique coverage of language and style that helps you think about where others are "coming from" in the choices they make and about how you can communicate across differences; **attention to the challenges of research**, especially evaluating and citing

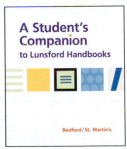

A new resource for corequisite composition

sources; and a **focus on critical thinking and argument** that will help you read a variety of texts and compose effective arguments. Most importantly, you will see our signature **respect for learners and learning** and efforts to empower writers, always.

How to Find Help in the Book

EasyWriter includes convenient menus and features to help you find what you need.

- **Brief Contents** appear on the inside front cover of the book.
- **Detailed Contents** appear on pages 445–46 and the inside back cover and show subsections within chapters.
- A **Quick Start Menu** on the first book page points you to advice and examples to help you with a specific writing project.
- The **Index/Glossary** is an alphabetical list of every topic or concept that's covered in the book—with definitions of key terms. Any **bold** term you see in the book is defined in the index.
- **Lists of citation examples** help you cite your sources responsibly. Each style (MLA, APA, *Chicago*, and CSE) has its own color-coded section; look for lists of examples within each section to find models you can follow. **Source maps** illustrate the process of citing common types of sources.
- **"Language, Culture, and Context" boxes** promote language awareness and offer help for speakers of all kinds of English, and from all educational and cultural backgrounds.
- The **Glossary of Usage** begins on page 395 and can help you with commonly confused and misused words.

Welcome, then, to *EasyWriter,* Eighth Edition. We hope it will be a faithful companion on your journey through college—and beyond.

Bedford/St. Martin's Puts You First

From day one, our goal has been simple: to provide inspiring resources that are grounded in best practices for teaching reading and writing. For forty years, Bedford/St. Martin's has partnered with the field, listening to teachers, scholars, and students about the support writers need. We are committed to helping every writing instructor make the most of our resources in any learning scenario.

How can we help *you*?

- Our editors can align our resources to your outcomes through correlation and transition guides for your syllabus. Just ask us.

- Our sales representatives specialize in helping you find the right materials to support your course goals.

- Our learning solutions and product specialists help you make the most of the digital resources you choose for your course.

- Our curriculum solutions team can help you design a custom product to meet your needs and even deliver a royalty to your department. You can choose from trade title excerpts with our MAP program, brief skills chapters from our ForeWords content, or add original content.

- Our *Bits* blog on the Bedford/St. Martin's English Community (**community.macmillan.com**), which features more than one hundred posts by Andrea Lunsford, publishes fresh teaching ideas weekly. You'll also find easily downloadable professional resources such as *Teaching with Lunsford Handbooks* and links to author webinars on our community site.

Contact your Bedford/St. Martin's sales representative or visit **macmillanlearning.com** to learn more.

Ordering Information

Digital

Achieve with *EasyWriter* (six-month access) ISBN 978-1-319-39327-4

- To order Achieve packaged with the print version of *EasyWriter*, use ISBN 978-1-319-45879-9

- To order Achieve packaged with the print version of *EasyWriter with Exercises*, use ISBN 978-1-319-45881-2

Popular e-book formats   For details about our e-book partners, visit **macmillanlearning.com/ebooks**.

Inclusive Access   Enable every student to receive their course materials through your LMS on the first day of class. Macmillan Learning's Inclusive Access program is the easiest, most affordable way to ensure all students have access to quality educational resources. Find out more at **macmillanlearning.com/inclusiveaccess**.

Print

- *EasyWriter*, Eighth Edition ISBN 978-1-319-24422-4
- *EasyWriter with Exercises*, Eighth Edition ISBN 978-1-319-39334-2
- *A Student's Companion to Lunsford Handbooks*
  ISBN 978-1-319-33328-7

Contact your Bedford/St. Martin's sales representative for additional pricing and packaging information.

Meet Our Advisory Board for Diversity, Equity, and Inclusion

The following fellow teachers of writing worked with us to make sure students can see themselves and their experiences represented in the eighth edition, to review terminology, to promote critical language awareness, to promote inclusion and openness, and to develop a resource that can be part of the antiracist teaching of writing. We are grateful to them for sharing themselves with us.

Kendra N. Bryant, North Carolina Agricultural and Technical State University

Javier Dueñas, Miami Dade College, North

Symmetris Jefferson Gohanna, Calhoun Community College

David F. Green, Howard University

Jamila Kareem, University of Central Florida

Esther Milu, University of Central Florida

Kristin vanEyk, University of Michigan

See our catalog page for *EasyWriter* to learn more about our board members.

Thank You, Reviewers and Student Writers

Reviewers   Mindy Helen Adams, Texas State University; Mark Baker, University of California–Santa Cruz; Rob J. Brault, Winona State University; Maya Brown, American University; Sandra Cooper, College of Central Florida; William Donohue, Lincoln University of Pennsylvania; Kegan Doyle, Kwantlen Polytechnic University; Michael Garcia Juelle, Florida International University; Brian C. Graves, University of North Carolina, Asheville; Cantice Greene, Clayton State University; Wanda Grimes, Volunteer State Community College; Donald Hettinga, Calvin College; Craig Hulst, Grand Valley State University; Alexandra Kay, Orange County Community College; Danielle Lanigan, Cape Fear Community College; Leslie Layne, Lynchburg College; David Leight, Reading Area Community College; Amy Leonard, De Anza College; James McWard, Johnson County Community College; Dominic Micer, Loyola University Maryland; Kelly Ormsby, Volunteer State Community College; Paul J. Patterson, St. Joseph's University; Lynn Raymond, University of North Carolina, Charlotte; Sorina Riddle, Coker College; Paul Roberts, St. Joseph's University; Cristie Roe, Phoenix College; Rita Rozzi, Xavier University; Nina V. Salmon, Lynchburg College; Jenny Spinner, St. Joseph's University; Lori Ann Stephens, Southern Methodist University; Theresa Stowell, Siena Heights University; John Sullivan, San Bernardino Valley College; Thomas Sura, West Virginia University; Sabrina Vargas Ortiz, Park University; Julie R. Voss, Lenoir-Rhyne University; Emily Wierszewski, Seton Hill University; Brittany Wilson, Salisbury University; Nancy Wilson, Texas State University

Student writers   Martha Bell, L.J. Bryan, Jamie Burke, Tony Chan, Samyuktha Comandur, Justin Dart, Paola García-Muñiz, Allyson Goldberg, Tara Gupta, Cameron Hauer, Joanna Hays, Deborah Jane, Zack Karas, James Kung, Megan Lange, Nastassia Lopez, Thanh Nguyen, Amrit Rao, Amanda Rinder, Julia Sakowitz, Bonnie Sillay, Shuqiao Song, Nandita Sriram, Hebron Warren, Shravan Yandra

Join Our English Community

community.macmillan.com

Author Andrea Lunsford posts to the Community's **Bits blog** regularly, offering teaching tips, reading suggestions, observations about everyday rhetoric, and multimodal moments to trigger your creativity and transform your teaching.

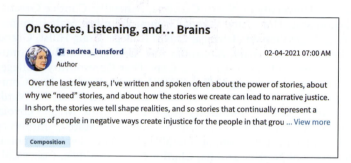

On Stories, Listening, and... Brains

🎵 **andrea_lunsford**
Author   02-04-2021 07:00 AM

Over the last few years, I've written and spoken often about the power of stories, about why we "need" stories, and about how the stories we create can lead to narrative justice. In short, the stories we tell shape realities, and so stories that continually represent a group of people in negative ways create injustice for the people in that grou ... View more

Composition

Resources for teachers don't stop at the *Bits* blog, however. Visit the English Community

- for professional resources and webinars
- for information about **Achieve**, our powerful online platform that includes writing, feedback, and peer review tools
- to learn about our Bedford New Scholars — an advisory board of graduate teaching assistants who share assignments, approaches, and observations about teaching and learning

Bedford Bibliography of Online Writing

Resources for online writing instruction.

Virtual Learning Resources

See all of our content to help you transition to online teaching.

English Webinars On Demand

See our archived, latest, and upcoming webinars.

Bedford New Scholars

Learn more about the Bedford New Scholars.

easy
writer

with Exercises

Writing Processes

1   **A Writer's Opportunities**   2

2   **A Writer's Choices**   7

3   **Exploring, Planning, and Drafting**   10

4   **Making Design Decisions**   17

5   **Reviewing, Revising, and Editing**   24

Top 20   **Top Twenty Tips for Editing Your Academic Writing**   27

6   **Sharing and Reflecting on Your Writing**   38

1   A Writer's Opportunities

What does it mean to be a college student? It means becoming the self and the thinker and the writer you most want to be. It means engaging with challenging new ideas and with people who are different from you in many ways. It means not only opening your books but also opening your mind.

In a time when many writers find themselves in the echo chambers provided by social media—those "bubbles" in which they encounter only ideas and views like their own—being open-minded seems especially necessary in order to engage in the kind of respectful civil discourse you can practice as a college writer, speaker, and thinker.

1a   Being open to and engaging difference

Whether you go to college in the North, South, East, or West; whether you attend a predominantly white university, a Hispanic-serving institution, an HBCU, or a Tribal College or University—or a two-year college, a small liberal arts college, or a technical college; whether you come from a conservative or liberal background—or somewhere in between—you will meet people who come from very different places, who display a range of cultures and values, who speak different languages and dialects, and who have ideas different from your own.

Being open is one way to get the most out of college and learn from people who are different from you. In fact, openness is one of eight key abilities the authors of *The Framework for Success in Post-secondary Writing* identify as "habits of mind" that support success in college: openness, curiosity, engagement, creativity, persistence, responsibility, flexibility, and reflection.

1b   Using social media wisely

Social connections today involve so much writing that you probably write more out of class than in class. On Twitter, for example, you can compose short bursts of 140 or 280 characters, tagging content, tweeting at groups and individuals, and pointing toward links to start discussions, participate in ongoing conversations, and invite others to join you. But you can also encounter bots and trolls, mean-spirited "haters," even stalkers. That's why Steve Kerr, head coach of the Golden State Warriors, suggests paying careful attention to what you write and to whom and always remembering that there's a person on the other side of that message who deserves fairness and respect. And think twice about information you get from social media: spreading rumors and false information is as easy—and as dangerous—as a retweet. Most of all, keep in mind that being an ethical writer, reader, and thinker calls for being responsible for what you post, being skeptical of what you read on social media, and making sure any information you pass on or retweet is reliable and honest. Be careful not to spread what might be rumor, libel, or lies.

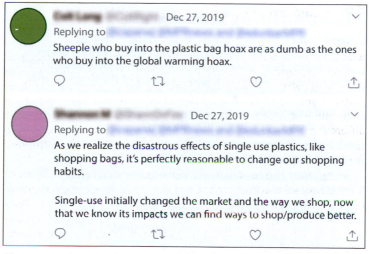

Disagreements are common on social media; some users insult and point fingers while others use reason.

1c Positioning yourself as an academic writer

You may not be as familiar with academic writing as you are with social media writing, and perhaps you aren't used to writing lengthy texts or carrying out extensive research. College writing will require you to face new challenges—you may be asked to create a persuasive website or infographic or to research, write, and deliver an argument that you then transform into a multimedia presentation. And if you grew up speaking and writing in other languages, the transition to producing college work in the dominant standardized English dialect can pose opportunities as well as challenges.

Authority   To establish authority, assume that your well-reasoned opinions and your lived experience count and that your audience expects you to present them fairly. Show your familiarity with the ideas and works of others, both from the assigned course reading and from good points your instructor and classmates have made.

 Checklist

Expectations for U.S. Academic Writing

While there is certainly no one single "correct" style of communication, and what is considered "good" writing differs from field to field, several features are often associated with U.S. standardized or academic English, a variety of the language that comes from and privileges Western European practices.

✔ Considers purpose and audience carefully, making sure that the topic is appropriate to both. (2a–c)

✔ States a claim or thesis explicitly, and supports it with evidence and authorities of various kinds. (3b)

✔ Carefully documents all sources, including visual ones. (Chapters 16–19)

✔ Makes explicit links between ideas. (3e)

✔ Uses the level of formality that is appropriate for the audience and purpose. (24a)

✔ Uses formats favored by scholars in academic genres. (Chapter 10)

✔ Uses widely accepted conventions of grammar, spelling, punctuation, and mechanics. (Chapters 31–48)

✔ Uses an easy-to-read type size and typeface and conventional margins. For print projects, double-spaces text. Considers those who may use screen readers. (4b)

Directness and clarity   Research for this book confirms that readers depend on writers to organize and present their material—using sections, paragraphs, sentences, arguments, details, and source citations—to aid understanding. Traditional academic writing offers a clear **thesis**, prepares readers for what is coming next, provides definitions, and includes topic sentences.

To achieve directness in your writing, try the following strategies:

- State your main point early and clearly. Academic writing may call for an explicit **claim** or thesis (3b and 9e).

- Avoid overqualifying your statements. Instead of writing *I think the facts reveal*, come right out and say *The facts reveal.*

- Avoid unnecessary digressions. When you use an anecdote or example from personal experience, be sure it relates directly to the point you are making.

- Use appropriate evidence and authorities of various kinds to support each point you make (3c). Carefully document all of your sources, including visuals and media.

- Make explicit links between ideas (3e). The first sentence of a new paragraph should reach back to the paragraph before and then look forward to what comes next.

- Follow clear, easy-to-follow organizational patterns.

While these features of academic style will most often be expected by your instructors, remember that they are not "better" than other styles you might choose. Indeed, the academic styles and practices of other cultures are not only valid but also powerful and can be used appropriately and effectively.

Active, respectful reading and listening   Your instructors will expect you to be an active reader, one who is curious and talks back to texts and topics. They will also expect you to be an active and attentive listener who respects the perspectives of others and is open to new and challenging ideas. And remember that stating your own informed opinions doesn't mean you are combative: just as you listen respectfully to others, they will be expected to listen respectfully to you. So try to understand what others are saying before drawing conclusions about what they have said, and remember to practice empathy by looking at the issue from the other person's or author's point of view, trying to understand where they are coming from and why they are making certain points. Indeed, as inclusion of perspectives and experiences from many cultures is increasingly important, you may find that you want to go beyond primarily white American and European scholars and authors to seek out the expertise of people from many different backgrounds and cultures.

EXERCISE 1.1 Answer the following questions about expectations for college writing.

1. How do you define good college writing? Make a list of the characteristics you come up with. Then make a list of what you think your instructors' expectations are for good college writing, and note how they may differ from yours. Do you need to alter your ideas about good college writing to meet your instructors' expectations? Why, or why not?

2. Research for this book suggests that many students today define good writing as "writing that makes something happen." That is, they see writing as *active and performative,* as *doing something.* Would that match your definition or that of your instructors? What might account for the differences—and the similarities—between students' and instructors' definitions and lists?

1d Collaborating with others

Student writers are collaborating more and more with other writers, for class assignments as well as for writing online and on the job. Since you will need to work well with others not only during college but also in your work life, pay attention to what makes for successful collaboration. Here are some strategies:

- Make sure every writer has an equal opportunity—and responsibility—to contribute.

- Exchange contact information, and plan face-to-face meetings (if any).

- Pay close attention to each writer's views. Expect disagreement, and remember that the goal is to listen to each view fairly and to discuss all possibilities.

- Pay close attention to each writer's style of communication, and expect differences: silence may not necessarily mean lack of engagement or interest but rather very close attention;

speaking in loud tones can mean intense interest rather than hostility.

- If you are preparing a document collaboratively, divide up the drafting duties and set reasonable deadlines. Work together to iron out the final draft, aiming for consistency of tone. Proofread together, and have one person make corrections.

- Take advantage of free software such as Google Drive to share files, edit documents collaboratively, and track changes.

- Give credit where credit is due: acknowledge all members' contributions as well as any help you receive from outsiders.

2 A Writer's Choices

As a college writer (in and out of class), you are responsible for the messages you send and the projects, reports, summaries, reviews, and other assignments you produce. And part of that responsibility calls for recognizing the full context in which any piece of writing or message exists, often called its **rhetorical situation**. Once you explore the rhetorical situation—the audience and purpose; your own stance as author; the genre, media, and particular formats—of a piece of writing, you are in a much better position to make choices that will allow you to shape the message and get it across to those you want to reach.

2a Considering the assignment and purpose

For writing you do for personal reasons or for work, you may have a clear purpose in mind. But even in those instances, analyzing what you want to accomplish and why can help you communicate more effectively.

An academic assignment may explain why, for whom, and about what you are supposed to write, or it may seem to come out of the blue. In any case, comprehending the assignment is crucial to your success, so make every effort to understand what your instructor expects.

- What is the primary purpose of your writing—to persuade? to explain? to entertain? something else?

- What purpose did the instructor want to achieve—to test your understanding? to evaluate your thinking and writing abilities? to encourage you to think outside the box?

- What, exactly, does the assignment ask you to do? Look for words such as *analyze*, *explain*, *prove*, and *survey*. Remember that these words may differ in meaning from discipline to discipline and from job to job.

2b   Choosing a topic

Experienced writers say that the best way to choose a topic is to let it choose you. Look to topics that compel, puzzle, or pose a problem for you: these are likely to engage your interests and hence produce your best writing.

- Can you focus the topic enough to write about it effectively in the time and space available?

- What do you know about the topic? What else do you need to learn?

- What seems most important about it?

- What do you expect to conclude about the topic? (Remember, you may change your mind.)

For information on exploring a topic, see 3a.

2c   Considering audiences

Every communicator can benefit from thinking carefully about who the audience is, what the audience already knows or thinks, and what the audience needs and expects to find out. As an effective communicator, you'll want to be able to write for a variety of audiences, using language, style, and evidence appropriate to particular readers, listeners, or viewers. Even if your text can theoretically reach people all over the world, focus your analysis on those you most want or need to reach and those likely to take an interest.

- What audience do you most want to reach—people who are already sympathetic to your views? people who disagree with you? If you are writing or speaking to people who disagree with you, make sure that you attend carefully, openly, and respectfully to their views.

- In what ways are the members of your audience different from you? from one another? What do you know about their abilities/disabilities that might have an effect on how they receive and understand your message?

- What assumptions can you legitimately make about the audience? What might they value—brevity, originality, deference, honesty, wit? How can you understand and appeal to their values?

- What sorts of information and evidence will your audience find most compelling—quotations from experts? stories or narratives? personal experiences? statistical data? images?

- How can you build common ground with your audience? How can you make clear what you want your audience to think, feel, or do?

EXERCISE 2.1 Write a brief description of a college course for three different audiences: a best friend, your parents, and some high schoolers attending an open house at your college. Then describe how the differences in audience led you to different choices in content, organization, and wording.

2d Considering stance and tone

Knowing your own stance (where you are coming from) can help you connect effectively with your audience. What is your overall attitude toward the topic—approval? disapproval? curiosity? What social, political, religious, or other factors account for your attitude? Be especially aware of any preconceptions about your topic that may affect your stance.

Your purpose, audience, and stance will help to determine the tone your writing should take. Should it be humorous? serious? impassioned? Think about ways to show that you are knowledgeable and trustworthy. Remember, too, that visual and audio elements can influence the tone of your writing as much as the words you choose.

Considering stance and tone often requires you to examine your own assumptions and biases, or characteristic ways of looking at the world. It's impossible not to have biases, since it's impossible to see all points of view or every angle of every argument. We may be able to stand on the shoulders of giants, but our view will still be partial and limited. It's particularly important to watch out for *confirmation bias*—the tendency to favor or find credible information that we already agree with or that confirms what we already believe. In your writing in college, take every opportunity to try to view things with as little bias as possible.

2e Considering time, genre, medium, and format

Many other elements of your context for a particular writing project will shape the final outcome.

- How much time will you have for the project? Do you need to do research or learn unfamiliar technology? Allow time for revision and editing.

- What **genre** does your purpose call for—a review? an argument essay? a lab report? a blog post? Study examples to learn the conventions of the genre.

- In what medium will the text appear—on the open Internet? on a password-protected website? in a print essay? in a presentation? Will you use images, video, or audio?

- What kind of organization should you use?

- How will you document your sources? Will your audience expect a particular documentation style (see Chapters 16–19)? Should you embed links?

3 Exploring, Planning, and Drafting

One student I know defines drafting as the time in writing "when the rubber meets the road." As you explore your topic, decide on a thesis, organize materials to support that central idea, and sketch out a plan, you have already begun the drafting process.

3a Exploring a topic

Among the most important parts of the writing process are choosing a topic (2b), exploring what you know about it, and determining what you need to find out. The following strategies can help you choose and explore your topic:

- Use the language or dialect most familiar and useful to you during your exploration.

- When you get to choose your topic, look for one that grabs and holds your interest; writing about topics that are of great interest to you usually results in better writing.

- Brainstorm. Write key words and phrases about the topic and see what they prompt you to think about further. Then try out these ideas on friends or your instructor.

- Freewrite without stopping for ten minutes to see what insights or ideas you come up with. You can also "freespeak" by recording your thoughts on your phone or another device.

- Draw or make word pictures about your topic.

- Try clustering—writing your topic on a sheet of paper and then writing related thoughts near the topic idea. Circle each idea or phrase, and draw lines to show how ideas are connected.

- Ask questions about the topic: *How is it defined? What caused it? What is it like or unlike? What larger system is the topic a part of? What do people say about it?* Or choose the journalist's questions: *Who? What? When? Where? Why? How?*

- Browse sources to find out what others say about the topic.

3b Developing a working thesis

Academic and professional writing in the United States often contains an explicit **thesis statement**. You should establish a working thesis early on: while your final thesis may eventually be very different, this working thesis focuses your thinking and research and helps keep you on track.

A working thesis should have two parts: a topic, which indicates the subject matter of the writing, and a comment, which makes an important point about the topic.

▶ In the graphic novel *Fun Home*, images and words combine to make meanings that are subtler than either words alone or images alone could convey.

Language, Culture, and Context

Stating a Thesis

In some cultures, people consider it rude to state an opinion out-right, preferring a more indirect approach. In the United States, however, most academic and business practices expect writers to make key positions explicitly clear.

A successful working thesis has three characteristics:

1. It is potentially *interesting* to the intended audience.
2. It is as *specific* as possible.
3. It limits the topic enough to make it *manageable*.

You can evaluate a working thesis by checking it against each of these characteristics, as in the following examples:

▶ **Graphic novels combine words and images.**

INTERESTING?   The topic of graphic novels could be interesting, but this draft of a working thesis has no real comment attached to it—instead, it states a bare fact, and the only place to go from here is to more bare facts.

▶ **In graphic novels, words and images convey interesting meanings.**

SPECIFIC?   This thesis is not specific. What are "interesting meanings," exactly? How are they conveyed?

▶ **Graphic novels have evolved in recent decades to become an important literary genre.**

MANAGEABLE?   This thesis would not be manageable for a short-term project because it would require research on several decades of history and on hundreds of novels from all over the world.

3c Gathering credible evidence and doing research

Where can you go to locate **evidence** that is credible and trustworthy, that avoids misinformation and lies, and that is instead based on facts and valid interpretation? What kinds of evidence will be most persuasive to your audience and most effective in the field in which you are working—historical precedents? expert testimony? statistical data? experimental results? personal experience? narratives or stories? Knowing what kinds of evidence count most in a particular field will help you make appropriate choices.

If the evidence you need calls for research, determine what research you need to do:

- Make a list of what you already know about your topic.
- Keep track of where information comes from so you can return to your sources later.
- Check your source information for accuracy and credibility.
- Determine what else you might need to know and where you might find other credible sources of information (library resources, online sources, field research).

For more on research and evaluating sources, see Chapters 12–15.

3d Planning and drafting

Sketch out a rough plan for organizing your writing, perhaps simply beginning with your thesis. Then review your notes, research materials, and media, and list all the evidence you have to support the thesis. One informal way to organize your ideas is to figure out what belongs in your introduction, body paragraphs, and conclusion. You may also want to make (or be required to make) an informal outline, which can help you see exactly how the parts of your writing fit together. (For a sample formal outline, see 15e.)

Thesis statement

I. First main idea
    1. First supporting detail or point
    2. Second supporting detail, and so on

II. Second main idea
  1. First supporting detail
  2. Second supporting detail, and so on
III. Third main idea
  1. First supporting detail
  2. Second supporting detail

Storyboarding—working out a narrative or argument in visual form—can also help you come up with an organizational plan. You can create your own storyboard by using note cards or sticky notes, taking advantage of different colors to keep track of threads of argument, subtopics, and so on. Move the cards and notes around, trying out different arrangements, until you find an organization that works well for your writing situation.

 Checklist

Drafting

✔ **Set up a folder or file for your essay.** Give the file a clear and relevant name, and save to it often. Date your drafts. If you decide to try a new direction, save the file as a new draft, but keep all previous drafts.

✔ **Have all your information close at hand** and arranged according to your organizational plan. Stopping to search for a piece of information can break your concentration or distract you.

✔ **Try to write in stretches of at least thirty minutes.** Writing can provide momentum, and once you get going, the task becomes easier.

✔ **Don't let small questions bog you down.** Make a note of them in brackets or caps—or make a tentative decision and move on.

✔ **Remember: first drafts aren't perfect.** Use the language or dialect that's most comfortable for you, and concentrate on getting your ideas down.

✔ **Stop writing at a place where you know exactly what will come next.** Doing so will help you start easily when you return to the draft.

No matter how good your planning, investigating, and organizing have been, chances are you will need to do more work as you draft. The first principle of successful drafting is to be flexible. If you see that your plan is not working, alter it. If some information now seems irrelevant, or perhaps unreliable, leave it out. Very often you will continue planning, investigating, and organizing throughout the writing process.

3e Developing paragraphs

Three qualities essential to most effective paragraphs are unity, development, and coherence.

Unity   In most college writing, an effective paragraph focuses on one main idea. You can achieve unity by stating that main idea clearly in one sentence—the topic sentence—and relating all other sentences in the paragraph to that idea. Like a thesis (see 3b), the topic sentence includes a topic and a comment on that topic. A topic sentence often begins a paragraph, but it may come at the end—or be implied rather than stated directly.

Development   In addition to being unified, a good paragraph holds readers' interest and explores its topic fully, using whatever details, evidence, and examples are necessary. Without such development, a paragraph may seem lifeless and abstract.

Most good academic writing backs up general ideas with specifics. Shifting between the general and the specific is especially important at the paragraph level. If a paragraph contains nothing but specific details, its meaning may not be clear to readers—but if a paragraph makes only general statements, it may seem boring or unconvincing.

Coherence   A paragraph has **coherence**—or flows—if its details fit together in a way that readers can easily follow. The following methods can help you achieve paragraph coherence:

- A general-to-specific or specific-to-general organization helps readers move from one point to another.
- Repetition of key words or phrases links sentences and suggests that the words or phrases are important.
- Returning to your thesis throughout the paragraph, a variation of call and response, helps ensure consistency and coherence.

- Parallel structures help make writing more coherent (see Chapter 29).

- **Transitions** such as *for example* and *however* help readers follow the progression of one idea to the next.

The same methods that you use to create coherent paragraphs can be used to link paragraphs so that a whole piece of writing flows smoothly. You can create links to previous paragraphs by repeating or paraphrasing key words and phrases and by using parallelism and transitions.

The following sample paragraph from Julia Sakowitz's research project (16f), which identifies a topic and a comment on the topic and then develops the topic with detailed evidence in support of the point, achieves unity by linking each sentence to the main topic. It also achieves coherence with a general-to-specific organization, repetition of key terms and ideas, and transitions that relate this paragraph to the preceding one and relate sentences to one another.

Transition from preceding paragraph

Topic sentence— sticks to this main idea throughout

Supporting evidence

Repetition of key words and ideas (highlighting)

Another equally important issue stemming from tourism is commercial gentrification, the phenomenon of large chain stores and boutiques replacing stores that serve the poor (Zukin et al. 48). Such changes have long been viewed as positive. A low-income neighborhood often lacks necessary retail infrastructure, instead featuring businesses like used merchandise outlets, check cashing operations, liquor stores, or job training and family services (Hoffman 288). Tourism can encourage middle-class economic activity like supermarkets, commercial banks, and legal and accounting services, which are as much needed by low-income residents as wealthier ones (Hoffman 288). But boutique stores and chain stores can replace services that might still be needed by the poor, leaving low-income residents feeling unwelcome (Zukin et al. 48). Economic gain from new businesses also bypasses most Harlem residents: fewer than half of new retail entrepreneurs are residents, and even those entrepreneurs who are residents overwhelmingly come from the newly arrived middle class (Zukin et al. 59).

Checklist

Strong Paragraphs

Most readers of English have certain expectations about how paragraphs work:

✔ Paragraphs begin and end with information that is important for the reader.

✔ The opening sentence is often the topic sentence that tells what the paragraph is about.

✔ The middle of the paragraph develops the idea.

✔ The end may sum up the paragraph's contents, closing the discussion of an idea and anticipating the paragraph that follows.

✔ A paragraph makes sense as a whole; the words and sentences are clearly related.

✔ A paragraph relates to other paragraphs around it.

4 Making Design Decisions

When millions of messages vie for attention, effective design is especially important: the strongest message may not get through to its audience if it is presented and designed in a bland or boring way. In fact, because writers today must also be designers, you will want to understand and use effective design to make sure you get and keep your audience's attention.

4a Considering design principles

In designer Robin Williams's *Non-Designer's Design Book*, she identifies four simple principles that are a good starting point for making any print or digital text more effective.

Contrast Begin with a focal point—a dominant visual or text that readers should look at first—and structure the flow of other information from that point. Use color, boldface or large type, white space, and so on to set off the focal point.

Alignment   Horizontal or vertical alignment of words and visuals gives a text a cleaner, more organized look. In general, wherever you begin aligning elements—on the top or bottom, on the right or left, or in the center—stick with it throughout the text.

Repetition   Readers are guided in large part by the repetition of key words or design elements. Use color, type, style, and other visual elements consistently throughout a document.

Proximity   Parts of a text that are related should be physically close together (*proximate* to each other).

These principles can help you create the appropriate overall impression or mood for your text. For an academic essay, you will probably make fairly conservative choices that strike a scholarly tone. In a newsletter for a campus group, you might choose attention-getting images. In a website designed to introduce yourself to future employers, you might favor a mix of material drawn from your current résumé, including writing, embedded video or links to digital content that relates to your skills and goals, and at least one image of yourself—all in a carefully organized and easy-to-comprehend structure.

4b   Choosing appropriate formats

Think about the most appropriate way to format a document to make it inviting and readable for your intended audience.

White space   Empty space, called "white space," guides the reader's eyes to parts of a page or screen. Consider white space at the page level (margins), paragraph level (spacing between paragraphs or sections), and sentence level (space between lines and between sentences). You can also use white space around particular content, such as a graphic or list, to make it stand out.

Color   Choose colors that relate to the purpose(s) of your text and its intended audience.

- Use color to draw attention to elements you want to emphasize—such as headings, bullets, boxes, or visuals—and be consistent in using color throughout your text.

- For academic work, use color sparingly to avoid a jumbled or informal look.

- Make sure the colors you choose are readable in the format you're using. A color that looks clear onscreen may be less legible in print or projected on a screen.

Do keep in mind that not everyone will see color as you do. Some individuals do not perceive color at all.

Type   Choose an easy-to-read type size and typeface, and be consistent in the styles and sizes of type used throughout your project. For most college writing, 11- or 12-point type is standard. And although unusual fonts may seem attractive at first glance, readers may find them distracting and hard to read over long stretches of material.

Spacing   Final drafts of any printed academic writing should be double-spaced, with the first line of paragraphs indented one-half inch. Other documents, such as memos, letters, and web texts, are usually single-spaced, with a blank line between paragraphs and no paragraph indentation. Some kinds of documents, such as newsletters, may call for multiple columns of text.

Headings   Consider organizing your text with headings that will aid comprehension. Some genres have standard headings that readers expect.

- Distinguish levels of headings using indents along with type. For example, you might center main headings and align lower-level headings at the left margin.

- Look for the most succinct and informative way to word your headings. You can state the topic in a single word (*Toxicity*); in a noun phrase (*Levels of Toxicity*) or gerund phrase (*Measuring Toxicity*); in a question to be answered in the text (*How Can Toxicity Be Measured?*); or in an imperative that tells readers what to do (*Measure the Toxicity*). Structure all headings of the same level consistently.

4c Choosing visuals and media

Choose visuals and media that will help make a point more vividly and succinctly than words alone. Consider carefully what you want visuals, audio, or video to do for your writing. What will your audience want or need you to show? Choose visuals and media that will enhance your credibility, allow you to make points more emphatically, and clarify your overall text. (See pp. 21–22 for advice on which types of visuals to use in particular situations.)

Effective media content can come from many sources—your own drawings or recordings you make, as well as audio or video materials created by others. If your document will be on the web, you can insert clips that readers can watch and listen to as they read your text. Such inserts can make powerful appeals: if you are writing about an ongoing migrant crisis in Europe, for example, a link to a video clip of people barely surviving in border "camps" may make the point better than you can do in words. Include such links as you would other visuals, making sure to provide a caption as well as a lead-in to the clip and a commentary after it if appropriate. If you are using media created by someone else, be sure to give appropriate credit and to get permission before making it available to the public as part of your work.

Position and identification of visuals and media Position visuals alongside or after the text that refers to them. In academic and other formal writing, number your visuals (number tables separately from other visuals), and provide informative captions. In some instances, you may need to give readers additional data such as source information in the caption. Consider using alt-text to make sure visuals are accessible to all readers.

Consult the sample student texts in Part 4 to see how visuals are placed and formatted in MLA, APA, *Chicago*, and CSE styles.

Type of Visual	When to Use It
Pie Chart 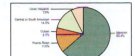	Use *pie charts* to compare parts to the whole.
Bar Graph 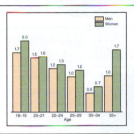	Use *bar graphs* or *line graphs* to compare one element with another, to compare elements over time, or to show correlations and frequency.
Table 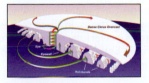	Use *tables* to draw attention to detailed numerical information. U.S. CENSUS BUREAU
Diagram	Use *diagrams* to illustrate textual information or to point out details of places or objects described. NATIONAL WEATHER SERVICE
Photograph 	Use *photographs* to show particular people, places, objects, or situations described in the text to help readers understand certain content. LIBBY WELCH/ALAMY

Map	Lands of federally recognized tribes in the western U.S. 	Use *maps* to show geographical locations and to emphasize spatial relationships. U.S. DEPARTMENT OF THE INTERIOR INDIAN AFFAIRS
Audio or Video		Use *links to audio or video material* to help readers see and hear a point you are making.

🌐 Language, Culture, and Context

Using Visuals

In some cultures, visual elements carry more prominence than words in many communication situations. In these contexts, the visual elements communicate as powerfully or even more so than the words—and the relationship between visual and textual media is key to getting the message across.

4d Using visuals and media ethically

Technical tools available today make it easy to manipulate or "doctor" images in deceptive ways. As you would with any source material, carefully assess any visuals and video or audio files you find for accuracy as well as effectiveness, appropriateness, and validity.

- Check the context in which the visual appears. Is it part of an official government, school, or library site?

- Does the information you find about the visual or media source seem believable? If not, be skeptical.
- Carry out a reverse image search using Google Images or TinEye to help you discover whether an image has been altered or manipulated.
- If the visual is a chart, graph, or diagram, are the numbers and labels in it explained? Are the sources of the data given? Will the visual representation help readers make sense of the information, or could it mislead them?
- Is biographical and contact information for the designer, artist, or photographer given?

At times, you may make certain changes to visuals and media that you use, such as cropping an image to show the most important detail, enhancing sound quality, or brightening a dark image. To ensure that your alterations to images are ethical, follow these guidelines:

- Never mislead readers. Show things as accurately as possible.
- Tell your audience what changes you have made.
- Include information about the original visual or media file, including the source.

 Checklist

Using Visuals and Media Ethically and Effectively

✔ Use visuals and media files as a part of your text, not just as decoration.

✔ Tell the audience explicitly what the visual or media file demonstrates, especially if it presents complex information. Do not assume readers will "read" the material the way you do; your commentary on it is important.

✔ Number and title all of your visuals. Number tables and figures separately.

✔ Refer to each visual or media file before it actually appears in your text.

✔ Follow established conventions for documenting sources, and ask permission for use if someone else controls the rights. (14d)

✔ Get responses to your visuals and media in an early draft. If readers can't follow them or are distracted by them, revise accordingly.

✔ If you alter a visual or media file, be sure to do so ethically.

5   Reviewing, Revising, and Editing

After giving your draft a rest, make time to review it by yourself and with others, to revise, and to edit. Becoming an astute critic of your own writing will pay off as you get better and better at taking a hard look at your drafts, revising them thoughtfully, and editing them with care.

5a   Reviewing

Reviewing calls for reading your draft with a critical eye and asking others to look over your work. Ask classmates or your instructor to respond to your draft, answering questions like these:

- What do you see as the major point, claim, or thesis?
- How convincing is the evidence? What can I do to support my thesis more fully?
- What points are unclear? How can I clarify them?
- How easy is it to follow my organization? How can I improve?
- What could I do to make my introduction grab the attention of my audience?
- What could I do to make my conclusion stronger?
- What can I do to make my draft more interesting?

5b   Revising

Approach comments from peer reviewers or from your instructor in several stages. First, read straight through the comments. Take a few minutes to digest the feedback and get some distance from your work. Then make a revision plan in order to prioritize the changes you need to make as you revise.

Focus on comments about your thesis or point, your audience, your support, and your organization. Leave any changes to sentences, words, punctuation, and format for later in your process; your revision of big-picture issues comes first.

- Make sure that your thesis states the topic clearly and makes a point about the topic. Revise if your point is unclear or unfocused. If you revise your thesis, revise the rest of the draft accordingly.

- Make sure that each paragraph relates to or supports the thesis statement and includes enough detail to support the point you are making. Eliminate unnecessary material; identify where you need more examples or explanation.

- Make sure your writing progresses logically from point to point. Look for confusing leaps or gaps, and revise to add transitions if they would make the writing easier to follow.

EXERCISE 5.1 Answer the following questions about your reviewing and revising process.

1. How did you begin reviewing your draft?

2. What kinds of comments on or responses to your draft did you receive? How helpful were they, and why?

3. How long did revising take? How many drafts did you produce?

4. What kinds of changes did you tend to make? For example, did you make changes in organization, paragraphs, sentence structure, wording, or adding or deleting information? Did you revise the use of visuals?

5. What gave you the most trouble as you were revising?

6. What pleased you most? What is your favorite sentence or passage in the draft, and why?

7. What would you most like to change about your process of revising, and how do you plan to go about doing so?

5c Editing and proofreading

Once you are satisfied with your revised draft's big picture, edit your writing to make sure that every detail is as correct as you can make it for the readers you plan to share it with (6a).

- Read your draft aloud to "hear" how smoothly it flows and to find typos.

- Are your sentences varied in length and in pattern or type?

- Have you used active verbs, vivid word images, and effective figurative language?

- Are all sentences complete and correct (unless you are trying for an effect!)?

- Do any sentences begin with "It is . . ." or "There was . . ."? If so, revise to delete these "filler" words.

- Have you used the spell checker—and double-checked its recommendations?

- What tone do you establish and how does it reflect your stance?

- Have you checked for language that might offend or confuse readers? for the use of **gender-neutral pronouns**? (36b)

- Have you chosen an effective design and used fonts, white space, headings, and color appropriately?

- Have you proofread one last time, going word for word?

For more on troubleshooting your writing, see "Top Twenty Tips for Editing Your Academic Writing" on the following pages.

EXERCISE 5.2   Answer each of the following questions about your own editing and proofreading process.

1. What do you look for when editing? What kinds of changes do you tend to make?

2. What decisions are most difficult in editing your work?

3. What patterns of problems, if any, do you tend to notice when you edit your own work? If you have not yet started an editing and proofreading checklist, consider beginning one now.

Top Twenty Tips for Editing Your Academic Writing

As the poet Nikki Giovanni says, "Mistakes are a fact of life." So it is with writing: everyone makes mistakes; some don't make much difference, but others keep people from understanding what you're saying or don't reflect your best work. Even writing teachers don't mark every little mistake and usually concentrate only on ones that are distracting or confusing. On top of that, people differ on what constitutes a "mistake": research for this book shows that some instructors view certain mistakes as serious errors and some view them as stylistic choices and that, in fact, what count as "errors" changes over time. And on top of *that*, what is considered correct in one variety of English is not considered correct in another.

Such differing opinions and changes don't mean that there is no such thing as correctness in writing—only that *correctness is always highly contextual*, always depends on whether the choices you make are appropriate to your audience, your purpose, and your topic.

Of course, all writers want to be considered competent, careful, and compelling. If you are using the dialect of standardized English most often practiced in college courses, sometimes referred to as the "language of power" in the United States, you will want to understand and use the conventions of grammar, punctuation, and so on associated with that dialect—even though such conventions are constantly and subtly changing. You will also want to understand how this particular version of English has been used to silence some groups while privileging others—and you may want to resist or challenge this form of language, pushing to create other powerful ways of communicating effectively. (See Chapter 23.)

Which of these conventions seem most troublesome to student writers today? To find out, we've analyzed thousands of pieces of first-year student writing from all across the country to answer that question and to develop the following Top Twenty Tips. For each one, we provide brief examples, shown with hand corrections and cross-references to other places in this book where you will find more detailed information and examples. And the best news is that if you learn to use these tips to edit your writing, you'll take care of many of the mistakes that can dent your credibility as a writer. Remember, though, that language conventions of "correctness" are always changing and that these, like any others, are not set in stone.

✔ **Checklist**

Top Twenty Tips for Editing Your Academic Writing

1	Check for wrong words	*p. 29*
2	Use a comma after an introductory element	*p. 29*
3	Make sure documentation is complete	*p. 30*
4	Check pronoun reference	*p. 30*
5	Check for spelling (including homonyms)	*p. 31*
6	Use quotation marks conventionally	*p. 31*
7	Avoid unnecessary commas	*p. 31*
8	Check for capitalization	*p. 32*
9	Look for missing words	*p. 32*
10	Look for confusing sentence structures	*p. 32*
11	Use commas with nonrestrictive elements	*p. 33*
12	Avoid unnecessary shifts in verb tense	*p. 33*
13	Use a comma between clauses in a compound sentence	*p. 33*
14	Check apostrophes (including *its/it's*)	*p. 33*
15	Look for fused (run-on) sentences	*p. 34*
16	Look for comma splices	*p. 34*
17	Check for pronoun-antecedent agreement	*p. 34*
18	Integrate quotations smoothly	*p. 35*
19	Check for missing or unnecessary hyphens	*p. 35*
20	Check for sentence fragments	*p. 35*

1 Check for wrong words

▶ Religious texts, for some, take ~~prescience~~ *precedence* over other kinds of sources.

Prescience means "foresight," and *precedence* means "priority."

▶ The child suffered from a severe ~~allegory~~ *allergy* to peanuts.

Allegory is a spell checker's replacement for a misspelling of *allergy*.

▶ The panel discussed the ethical implications ~~on~~ *of* the situation.

Wrong-word errors can involve using a word with the wrong shade of meaning, using a word with a completely wrong meaning, or using a wrong **preposition** or another wrong word in an idiom. Selecting a word from a thesaurus without knowing its meaning or allowing a spell checker to correct spelling automatically can lead to wrong-word errors, so use these tools with care. If you have trouble with prepositions and idioms, memorize the standard usage. (See Chapter 24 on word choice and Chapter 37 on prepositions and idioms.)

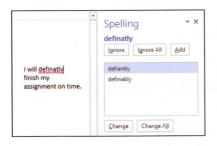

The writer means *definitely,* but the spell checker suggests wrong words.

2 Use a comma after an introductory element

▶ Determined to get the job done, we worked all weekend.

▶ Although the study was flawed, the results may still be useful.

Readers usually need a small pause—signaled by a comma—between an introductory word, **phrase**, or **clause** and the main part of the

sentence. Use a comma after every introductory element. When the introductory element is very short, you don't always need a comma, but including it is never wrong. (See 40a.)

3   Make sure documentation is complete

▶ Satrapi says, "When we're afraid, we lose all sense of analysis
(263).
and reflection/"
^

This quotation comes from a source with page numbers, so a page number is needed.

▶ Some experts agree that James Joyce wrote two of the five best
("100 Best Novels").
novels of all time/
^

The source of this information should be identified. The title is given for a source with no page numbers.

Cite each source you refer to in the text, following the guidelines of the documentation style you are using. (The preceding examples follow MLA style—see Chapter 16; for other styles, see Chapters 17–19.) Omitting documentation can result in plagiarism. (See Chapter 14.)

4   Check pronoun reference

POSSIBLE REFERENCE TO MORE THAN ONE WORD

▶ The best way to improve elections is to communicate to voters
elections
that ~~they~~ matter.
^

In the original sentence, *they* could refer to the elections or to the voters.

REFERENCE IMPLIED BUT NOT STATED

a policy
▶ The company prohibited smoking, ~~which~~ many employees resented.
^

What does *which* refer to? The editing clarifies what employees resented.

A **pronoun** should refer clearly to the word or words it replaces (called the **antecedent**) elsewhere in the sentence or in a previous sentence. If more than one word could be the antecedent, or if no specific antecedent is present, edit to make the meaning clear. (See Chapter 36.)

5 Check for spelling (including homonyms)

▶ Ronald ~~Regan~~ ^{Reagan} won the election in a landslide.

▶ ~~Every where~~ ^{Everywhere} we went, we saw crowds of tourists.

The most common misspellings today are those that spell checkers cannot identify. The categories that spell checkers are most likely to miss include homonyms, compound words incorrectly spelled as separate words, and proper **nouns**, particularly names. After you run the spell checker, proofread carefully for errors such as these—and be sure to run the spell checker to catch other kinds of spelling mistakes.

6 Use quotation marks conventionally

▶ "I grew up the victim of a disconcerting confusion,"/ Rodriguez says (249).

The comma should be placed *inside* the quotation marks.

Follow conventions when using quotation marks with commas (40h), colons, and other punctuation. Always use quotation marks in pairs, and follow the guidelines of your documentation style for block quotations. Use quotation marks for titles of short works (44b), but use italics for titles of long works (48a).

7 Avoid unnecessary commas

BEFORE CONJUNCTIONS IN COMPOUND CONSTRUCTIONS THAT ARE NOT COMPOUND SENTENCES

▶ This conclusion applies to the United States/ and to the rest of the world.

No comma is needed before *and* because it is joining two phrases that modify the same verb, *applies*.

WITH RESTRICTIVE ELEMENTS

▶ Many parents/ of gifted children/ do not want them to skip a grade.

No commas are needed to set off the restrictive phrase *of gifted children*, which is necessary to indicate which parents the sentence is talking about.

Do not use commas to set off **restrictive elements** that are necessary to the meaning of the words they modify. Do not use a comma before a **coordinating conjunction** (*and, but, for, nor, or, so, yet*) when the conjunction does not join parts of a compound sentence (error 13, p. 33). Do not use a comma before the first or after the last item in a series, between a **subject** and **verb**, between a verb and its **object** or complement, or between a **preposition** and its object. (See Chapter 40.)

8   Check for capitalization

▶ Some ~~Traditional~~ ^{traditional} Chinese ~~Medicines~~ ^{medicines} containing ~~Ephedra~~ ^{ephedra} remain legal. ^

Capitalize proper nouns and proper adjectives, the first words of sentences, and important words in titles, along with certain words indicating directions and family relationships. Do not capitalize most other words. When in doubt, check a dictionary. (See Chapter 46.)

9   Look for missing words

▶ The site foreman discriminated ^{against} women and promoted men with less experience. ^

Proofread carefully for omitted words, including prepositions (37a), parts of two-part verbs (37b), and **correlative conjunctions**. Be particularly careful not to omit words from quotations.

10   Look for confusing sentence structures

▶ ~~The information which high~~ ^{High} school athletes are presented with ^
~~mainly includes~~ information on what credits ~~needed~~ ^{they} to graduate, ^
~~and thinking about the college~~ which ~~athletes are trying~~ ^{colleges to try} to play ^
for, ^{how to} and apply. ^

A sentence that starts with one kind of structure and then changes to another kind can confuse readers. Make sure that each sentence contains a subject and a verb, that subjects and **predicates** make sense together (26b), and that comparisons have clear meanings

(26c). When you join elements (such as subjects or **verb phrases**) with a coordinating conjunction, make sure that the elements have parallel structures (see Chapter 29).

11 Use commas with nonrestrictive elements

▶ Marina, who was the president of the club, was first to speak.

The clause *who was the president of the club* does not affect the basic meaning of the sentence: Marina was first to speak.

A **nonrestrictive element** gives information not essential to the basic meaning of the sentence. Use commas to set off a nonrestrictive element (40c).

12 Avoid unnecessary shifts in verb tense

▶ Priya was watching the great blue heron. Then she ~~slips~~ slipped and ~~falls~~ fell into the swamp.

Verbs that shift from one **tense** to another with no clear reason can confuse readers (30a).

13 Use a comma between clauses in a compound sentence

▶ Meredith waited for Samir, and her sister grew impatient.

Without the comma, a reader may think at first that Meredith waited for both Samir and her sister.

A compound sentence consists of two or more parts that could each stand alone as a sentence. When the parts are joined by a coordinating conjunction, use a comma before the conjunction to indicate a pause between the two thoughts (40b).

14 Check apostrophes (including *its/it's*)

▶ Overambitious parents can be very harmful to a ~~childs~~ child's well-being.

▶ The car is lying on ~~it's~~ its side in the ditch. ~~Its~~ It's a white 2020 Passat.

To make a noun **possessive**, add an apostrophe and an -*s* (*Ed's book*) or an apostrophe alone (*the boys' gym*). Do *not* use an apostrophe in the possessive pronouns *ours*, *yours*, and *hers*. Use *its* to mean *belonging to it*; use *it's* to mean *it is* or *it has*. (See Chapter 43.)

15 Look for fused (run-on) sentences

▶ Klee's paintings seem simple, ^{but} they are very sophisticated.

▶ ~~She~~ ^{Although she} doubted the value of meditation, she decided to try it once.

A **fused sentence** (also called a *run-on*) joins clauses that could each stand alone as a sentence with no punctuation or words to link them. Fused sentences must either be divided into separate sentences or joined by adding words or punctuation. (See Chapter 38.)

16 Look for comma splices

▶ I was strongly attracted to her, ^{for} she was beautiful and funny.

▶ We hated the meat loaf_/ ^{that} the cafeteria served ~~it~~ every Monday.

A **comma splice** occurs when only a comma separates clauses that could each stand alone as a sentence. To correct a comma splice, you can insert a semicolon or period, connect the clauses with a word such as *and* or *because*, or restructure the sentence. (See Chapter 38.)

17 Check for pronoun-antecedent agreement

▶ Each of the proposals has ~~their~~ ^{its} merits.

▶ ~~Every student~~ ^{All students} must provide their own ~~uniform.~~ ^{uniforms.}

In formal academic writing, pronouns agree with their antecedents both in gender (male or female) and in number (singular or plural). Traditionally, **indefinite pronouns** such as *every*, *everyone*, and *each* have been treated as singular antecedents and have required singular pronouns such as *his or her*, *his*, *her*, or *its*. Many writers choose to rewrite such sentences as plural, as in the second example. However, the use of *they/their/them* is acceptable with singular indefinite pronouns—to include people who do not identify as *he/his* or *she/her*. (See 36b.)

▶ Everyone should check their passport's expiration date before the trip.

18   Integrate quotations smoothly

▶ Schlosser cites a 1970s study that *showed how color affects taste:* "Once it became apparent that the steak was actually blue and the fries were green, some people became ill" (565).

▶ *According to Lars Eighner,* "Dumpster diving has serious drawbacks as a way of life" (~~Eighner~~ 383). Finding edible food is especially tricky.

Quotations should all fit smoothly into the surrounding sentence structure. They should be linked clearly to the writing around them (usually with a signal phrase) rather than dropped abruptly into the writing. (See 14b.)

19   Check for missing or unnecessary hyphens

▶ This paper looks at fictional and real-life examples.
  A compound adjective modifying a noun that follows it requires a hyphen.

▶ The buyers want to fix/up the house and resell it.
  A two-word verb should not be hyphenated.

A compound **adjective** that appears before a noun needs a hyphen. However, be careful not to hyphenate two-word verbs or word groups that serve as subject complements. (See Chapter 48.)

20   Check for sentence fragments

NO SUBJECT

▶ Marie Antoinette spent huge sums of money on herself and her favorites. *Her extravagance* ~~And~~ helped bring on the French Revolution.

6   Sharing and Reflecting on Your Writing

Once you have completed a piece of writing, share it! You've worked hard on a topic that's important to you, and there's a good chance others will care about it, too. Sharing and talking about a piece of writing that you've finished are also good steps toward reflecting on the entire writing experience and assessing what you learned from it.

6a   Sharing with audiences

Chances are, you already share your writing with family, friends, and others via social media (1b). So why not go ahead and share your academic writing with others you think will be interested? And if you invite them, you may well start a conversation that will keep going.

- Can you find interested readers through social media sites like Twitter?
- Should you keep a blog to share your writing, using a free site such as Weebly?
- Would your work find audiences on YouTube, Instagram, or other visual platforms?
- Could you submit your writing to student publications or organizations on your campus?

You can also share your ideas by joining conversations started by others. You might contribute to Wikipedia or other wikis; comment on online newspaper or magazine articles, editorials, or videos; write reviews for books and other products on Amazon; post to fan fiction sites; or find other public sites where you can participate in producing content and responding to what others have written. As a writer today, you have nearly limitless possibilities for interaction with other readers and writers.

6b   Creating a portfolio

One especially good way to share your writing is by developing a portfolio that showcases your abilities and experience. Most instructors who assign portfolios as a culmination of a course will give you advice about what to include, such as a cover letter, a personal reflection, and several polished pieces of your writing. You may also want to keep a portfolio throughout your college career, adding outstanding examples of your work from year to year.

6c   Reflecting on your own work

Thinking back on what you've learned helps make that learning stick. Whether or not your instructor requires you to write a formal reflection on a writing course or piece of writing, make time to think about what you have learned from the experience. Student Thanh Nguyen created a political poster for a course on immigration. On his personal blog, he posted the image of his poster with some reflections about what he had learned:

REFLECTIVE BLOG POST (EXCERPT)

It's not too obvious what I was trying to get at in this poster, which is my own fault. I replaced the cherubs and angels from Michelangelo's *Creation of Adam* with ICE agents and politicians to comment on anti-immigrant practices. I could have gotten my point across in a better and less confrontational way!

The following questions can help you to think critically about your writing and to develop a reflective statement:

- What lessons have you learned from the writing? How will they help you with future writing?
- What about your writing are you most confident of? What needs additional work?
- What confused you during your writing? How did you resolve your questions?
- How has this piece of writing helped you clarify your thinking or extend your understanding?
- Identify a favorite passage of your writing. What pleases you about it? Can you apply what you learn from this analysis to other writing situations?

- How would you describe your development as a writer?
- How might you organize a formal reflection on your writing? Will you begin by describing your writing at the beginning of your course and then tracing changes and improvements? By summing up what you have learned about writing and then "flashing back" to examples of how you learned those lessons?

6d A sample reflection (excerpt)

Student James Kung wrote a reflective cover letter as part of a portfolio for his first-year writing course. Part of that letter appears here.

Dear Professor Ashdown:

Reflects on improvement

"Writing is difficult and takes a long time." You have uttered this simple yet powerful statement so many times in our class that it has essentially become our motto. In just ten weeks, my persuasive writing skills have improved dramatically, thanks to many hours spent writing, revising, polishing, and (when I wasn't writing) thinking about my topic. The various drafts, revisions, and other materials in my course portfolio clearly show this improvement.

Analyzes overall strengths and weaknesses

I entered this first-quarter Writing and Rhetoric class with both strengths and weaknesses. I was strong in the fundamentals of writing: logic and grammar. I have always written fairly well-organized essays. However, despite this strength, I struggled throughout the term to narrow and define the various aspects of my research-based argument.

The rest of the letter analyzes specific pieces of writing

The first aspect of my essay that I had trouble narrowing and defining was my major claim, or my thesis statement. In my first writing assignment for the class . . .

Contexts for Writing, Reading, and Speaking

7   **Learning from Low-Stakes Writing**   42

8   **Reading and Listening Analytically, Critically, and Respectfully**   44

9   **Arguing Ethically and Persuasively**   51

10   **Writing in a Variety of Disciplines and Genres**   67

11   **Creating Presentations**   81

7   Learning from Low-Stakes Writing

Professor Peter Elbow differentiates between "high-stakes writing"—which you do for formal graded assignments and exams—and "low-stakes writing"—informal writing that is often ungraded but that helps you think about, learn, and remember course material and stay engaged with your classes. So a very good way to put your writing to work is to use it as a way to learn and to retain that learning. This kind of writing is always helpful, but it is particularly effective when you are engaged in online learning. It provides a chance for you to mull over what you got from an online class, to synthesize the ideas you took away from the session, to sum up things that confused you or were ignored, and to spend some time reviewing and reflecting on these lessons.

7a   The value of low-stakes writing

Sometimes referred to as "writing to learn," low-stakes writing is powerful because it gives you a chance to figure out what you know and don't know about a topic, and it can help you watch your own mind at work—all without having to be judged or graded. Research shows that reflecting on your own thinking, writing, and learning style can contribute significantly to your development as a critical thinker. Your instructor may assign such low-stakes writing throughout the term; if so, take advantage of it. If not, do some informal writing yourself and see how it helps improve both your understanding of course material and your grades.

7b   Types of low-stakes assignments

Quickwrites   A good way to get mental gears going, quickwrites are prompts—usually open-ended questions about a topic of study—to which writers respond in short bursts of two to eight minutes. Instructors often use quickwrites to get class discussion started and focused, but you can use them on your own to get your thinking about a subject down in words.

Freewrites   Like quickwrites, freewrites ask you to write about a topic without stopping, usually for ten minutes. Freewrites let you explore your thinking without worrying about correctness, grades, and so on. For quickwrites or freewrites, use the language or variety of language that is most comfortable and familiar to you—and don't worry about anything except capturing your ideas.

 Checklist

Participating in Class Blogs, Wikis, Zooms, and Other Forums

✔ If you are participating in discussions through video apps like Zoom, be sure to check your microphone and camera before the session and make sure you are presentable(!). Look into the camera when you are speaking and mute yourself when you are not.

✔ Take advantage of opportunities to engage with others about the course material—even if you're a little nervous about being onscreen—and sum up your views in writing; doing so will help you internalize the information.

✔ Be polite and professional when contributing to an online forum.

✔ Avoid unnecessary criticism of others; the point of these activities is to have productive exchanges about what you are learning. Rather than criticize, simply ask for clarification (*Are you saying that . . .?*) or offer what you take to be correct information.

✔ If others criticize you, give them the benefit of the doubt and reply with courtesy and patience.

✔ For email threads, decide whether to reply off-list to the sender of a message or to the whole group, and be careful to use REPLY or REPLY ALL accordingly to avoid potential confusion.

✔ Remember that many class forums are archived, so more people than you think may read your messages.

Thought pieces   Some instructors assign thought pieces—pieces of writing that sum up background information and your own opinions and analyses of a subject. They can help you see how much you know—and how much more you need to know—about your topic.

Reading responses   These may be the most frequently assigned type of low-stakes writing. In reading responses, you sum up your understanding of an assigned reading and evaluate its effectiveness. Whether or not your instructor assigns such responses, you will profit by setting up a reading log file on your computer and recording your responses and critical evaluations there.

Class discussion forums   Whether your classes are online, in person, or some blend of the two, most instructors will set up online spaces for discussion forums—on a local course management system, a series of Zoom sessions, a class blog or wiki, or a class page on Facebook or other social media site—as a place to talk about the reading, writing, and speaking you are doing in the class. Active participation in these forums will allow you to get your views out there for others to respond to and help you understand the viewpoints of others.

8   Reading and Listening Analytically, Critically, and Respectfully

In a time of 24/7 newsfeeds, misinformation, and fake news, critical reading demands *defensive* reading strategies that will help protect you from being manipulated by the texts you read. But critical reading also calls on you to engage with, understand, and respect messages from people who may hold views very different from your own. So while it's important to remain skeptical until you know a text is accurate, it's also important to remember that there are real people on the other side of the screen, with feelings of their own. In any case, most important to critical reading is *attention*, focusing intently and purposefully on any text you approach.

8a Reading collaboratively

Especially for difficult or high-stakes reading, there's nothing better than tackling the task with others. Researchers tell us, in fact, that if you read and take notes on a reading in small groups, understanding of the text improves, as do test scores based on the material. So why not ask a couple of classmates to form a group and set up a shared folder on Google Drive where you can share notes and annotations and responses to what you are reading. Doing so will help you gain various perspectives on the text and try out your own ideas about it.

8b Previewing

Find out all you can about a **text** before beginning to read or listen to it analytically and critically, considering its context, author, subject, genre, and design.

- Where have you encountered the work? Is it in its original context? What can you infer about its intended audience and purpose?

- What information can you find about the author, creator, or sponsor of the text? What purpose, expertise, and possible agenda might you expect this person to have?

- What do you know about the subject of the text? What opinions do you have about it, and why? What more do you want to learn about it?

- What does the title (or caption or other heading) indicate?

- What role does the medium play in achieving the purpose and connecting to the audience?

- What is the genre of the text? Is it a letter? a report? an essay? What can it tell you about the intended audience or purpose?

- How is the text presented? What do you notice about its language, style, design, and general appearance?

8c Annotating

As you read or listen to a text for the first time, begin analyzing it by marking it up or taking notes. Make note of the author's main ideas and key terms, considering content, author, intended audience, genre, and design. Write questions you'd like to ask the writer, and talk back to the text throughout, noting where you agree and disagree—and why.

- Are you sure you are really hearing what the text is saying rather than rushing to conclusions about it? Are you open to the ideas in the text and respectful of the writer's right to hold them?

- What's confusing or unclear about the text? Who can you ask for more information—your instructor? classmates? someone else?

- What are the key terms and ideas or patterns? What key images stick in your mind?

- What sources or other works does this text refer to? Are they reliable and trustworthy—should you fact-check them (see 13a)?

- Which points do you agree with? Which do you disagree with? Why?

- Do the authors or creators present themselves as you anticipated?

- For what audience was this text created? Are you part of its intended audience?

- What underlying assumptions can you identify in the text?

- Are the medium and genre appropriate for the topic, audience, and purpose?

- Is the design appropriate for the subject and genre?

- Does the organization help you see what is more and less important in the text?

- How effectively do words, images, sound, and other media work together?

- How would you describe the style of the text? What contributes to this impression—word choice? references to research or popular culture? formatting? color? something else?

8d Summarizing

A summary *briefly* captures the main ideas of a text in your own words and omits information that is less important for the reader. Try to identify the key points in the beginning, middle, and end of the text, along with the major support for those points. Use transitions to connect your summary points in order of occurrence and explain the points concisely and fairly, so that a reader unfamiliar with the original text can make sense of it all. Deciding what to leave out can make summarizing a tricky task. To test your understanding—and to avoid unintentional plagiarism—put the text aside while you write your summary.

8e Analyzing

You can learn many good lessons about how to make appropriate and effective choices in your own writing by identifying and studying the choices other writers have made. You may want to begin the process of analysis by asking several key questions: What are the text's main points and claims? Are they implied or explicitly stated? Which points do you agree with? Which do you disagree with? Why?

✔ Checklist

Analyzing and Fact-Checking Texts

✔ What cultural contexts inform the text—the time and place the argument was written; the economic, social, and political events surrounding the argument; and so on? What do they tell about where the writers, creators, or sponsors are coming from and what choices they have had to make?

✔ What emotional, ethical, or logical appeals has the writer chosen to use in the text? Are the appeals reasonable, fair, and honest?

✔ Does the writer have a particular "slant" on the topic? A site like allsides.com labels articles on it as leaning left, leaning right, or center—where might the text you are analyzing fit in?

✔ What are other sources saying about this text? If you are reading the text online, open another browser and search for the author and/or title of the text or the sponsor of the site and see what other sites say about it and about its credibility. (Find out more about this kind of "lateral reading" in 13c.)

✔ What strategies has the writer chosen to establish credibility?

✔ What assumptions does the writer make? Are those assumptions valid?

✔ Are alternative perspectives included and treated respectfully? Are some perspectives left out, and if so, how does this exclusion affect the argument?

✔ What sources does the author use to inform the text? How can you tell that they are current, reliable, and trustworthy? ▶

✔ What kinds of evidence does the text offer to support its claims—examples? facts, statistics, and other data? analogies? personal experience? expert testimony? What other evidence should have been included?

✔ How convincing is the evidence to you? Have you checked facts, looking for false or misinformation, incomplete information, or extreme bias? Do other reliable sources corroborate the facts? (See 13a for more about evaluating and fact-checking sources.)

✔ How has the writer or creator chosen visuals and design to support the main ideas? How well do words and images work together to make a point?

✔ What surprises, intrigues, puzzles, or irritates you about the text? Why?

✔ What overall impression does the text create?

✔ Do the authors achieve their purpose? Why, or why not?

EXERCISE 8.1

1. Think about the last film you watched for fun. What did you know about it before you watched it? What did you feel and learn as you watched? What have you told others about the film, both in terms of summarizing the story and of analyzing what the overall experience of viewing the film meant to you?

2. Write a paragraph describing how you might use previewing, summarizing, and analyzing the next time you are asked to read a text.

3. Search for a topic or text using two different search engines—choose from Google, Bing, Yahoo, DuckDuckGo. Because each has a different algorithm, the results you get in response to your search terms will differ. What do you learn about web searching from this activity?

8f Rhetorical analysis

STUDENT WRITER

Cameron Hauer

For a class assignment, Cameron Hauer was assigned to analyze the rhetorical choices and the emotional, ethical, and logical appeals in a *New York Times* op-ed article in which columnist Nicholas Kristof argues that American public lands are being threatened.

Hauer 1

Cameron Hauer
Professor Walters
Writing and Rhetoric 1
7 March 2019

Appeal, Audience, and Narrative in Kristof's Wilderness

Growing up in the Pacific Northwest instilled a love of the
outdoors in me. As an adolescent, I spent practically every weekend in
the pristine wilderness of Washington, Idaho, and Montana. Alpine ski
trips and weeklong backpacking treks were a big part of my life. I owe
a lot of personal development and fond memories to the vast public
wilderness of the United States, the value of which Nicholas Kristof
captures stirringly in his *New York Times* op-ed column, "Fleeing to the
Mountains." He warns, however, that this wilderness is under attack.

> Uses personal experience to help establish ethos

To strengthen his case for the specialness of wildlands in the
US, Kristof relies on ethical and emotional appeals: a lively account of
his family's backpacking trips and the ways they free people from the
buzz and hum of modern life. Kristof's style here ranges from breezy
and playful (the wilderness is "heaven with blisters") to awestruck
and reverent (it is "our inheritance and shared playground"). He also
offers personal testimony; having spent time in wild places, Kristof is
well positioned to describe their virtues. He invites readers to share
this ethic, to see the joy of open spaces, and to regard them as a
sacred inheritance.

> Provides an overview of Kristof's argument

> States Kristof's claims

Halfway through the column, Kristof shifts his focus to address
threats facing the US wilderness. He lays blame on those in power, like
members of the administration, who, Kristof alleges, "see this heritage
as an opportunity for development" and are "systematically handing
over America's public lands for private exploitation in ways that will
scar the land forever." He moves to using logos rather than the ethos
and pathos of the earlier sections. Whereas earlier he tries to evoke
a particular feeling and ethic, his present goal is to marshal facts—
including the administration's lifting of a moratorium on new mining

> Transitions to Kristof's discussion of threats to wilderness

> Focuses on Kristof's use of appeals

Hauer 2

**Shows how
Kristof
engages his
audience**

leases and the opening up of new lands to fossil fuel extraction—to
convince readers that public lands in the US are under threat. Kristof
lessens the abruptness of this shift in appeal by maintaining his
narrative of wilderness as an inheritance.

**Analyzes
Kristof's
intended
audience**

Several elements of Kristof's argument give insight into
his context and audience. The place of Donald Trump in Kristof's
narrative is significant. The policies Kristof describes are simply the
implementation of long-standing Republican priorities and have little
to do with Trump himself. But in Kristof's rhetorical context—a left-of-
center newspaper in 2017—choosing Trump as an anti-environmental
symbol is a strong, if obvious, rhetorical move. The mention of the
sitting president invites Kristof's liberal readership to adopt a pro-
wilderness platform as one plank of a broader anti-Trump agenda.

**Practices
critical
reading to
point out
Kristof's
omissions**

There are some notable omissions in Kristof's argument. In his
framing, wildlands are either public and devoted to use by the people
or privatized for resource extraction and for "ranches for the rich."
To a liberal already inclined to value publicly owned resources, this
framework may be convincing, but conservatives often view public
ownership of natural resources with suspicion. Kristof portrays public
ownership as a means of providing equal access for all US residents,

**Considers
opposing
viewpoints**

but rural conservatives may view it as a way that valuable resources
are turned into playgrounds for yuppies. They may also resist Kristof's
portrayal of private ownership as promoting degradation and waste,
viewing it instead as a way for hardworking people to make a living
off the land.

**Questions
Kristof's key
assumption**

Another evasion in Kristof's argument, one that may stand out
sharply to left and right, is his characterization of public lands as "a
bastion of equality." This is true in a sense—most public lands are
open to everyone, free of charge; but in practical terms, access to
wilderness requires a salary and paid time off, among other things.
In a country where millions struggle to make ends meet, frequent
recreational use of US wildlands remains out of reach.

Hauer 3

    These evasions and omissions may indicate Kristof's biases
and his own rhetorical stance, but they are not damning. An op-ed
article is, after all, crafted for a particular audience. To address the
concerns of staunch conservatives would require Kristof to adopt
different rhetorical strategies. Kristof's readers are likely a self-
selected group of liberal-minded people already sympathetic to his
views. His rhetorical goal is not to convince a group of adversaries
of his position but to persuade a group of amenable readers that this
particular issue—and this particular ethic—is one that they should
adopt as their own.

Underscores Kristof's major purpose

Hauer 4

Work Cited

Kristof, Nicholas. "Fleeing to the Mountains." *The New York Times,*
12 Aug. 2017, www.nytimes.com/2017/08/12/opinion/sunday
/hiking-pacific-crest-trail.html. Op-ed.

Follows MLA style

9   Arguing Ethically and Persuasively

If you wonder whether one person's argument can make a difference, consider recent college grad Kennedy Mitchum, who wrote an
email message to the editors of the Merriam-Webster dictionary,
arguing that their definition of "racism" needed to be revised and
updated:

Racism is not only prejudice against a certain race due to the color
of a person's skin, as it states in your dictionary. It is both prejudice combined with social and institutional power. It is a system of
advantage based on skin color.

After careful consideration, the editors agreed, saying that Mitchum's argument was convincing and that they would revise their definition accordingly. Learning how to compose your own persuasive and ethical arguments will serve you well not just in college but far beyond.

9a Listening (and reading) purposefully and openly

The arguments you make are often in response to something others have written or said, so in a very important sense, your own arguments depend on how well you have attended to the conversation surrounding the topic you are addressing. As you do research and reading on your topic, make sure you are doing so carefully, purposefully, and openly: what you take in about your topic from others can help you craft an effective argument, but you need to make sure that you are giving respectful attention to those sources that inform your work and considering sources that others might have ignored.

9b Identifying basic appeals in an argument

Emotional appeals Emotional appeals stir our feelings and remind us of deeply held values. In analyzing any text, look carefully to see how the writer has chosen to use emotional appeals to rouse the audience's pride, fear, anger, grief, or other emotions.

Ethical appeals Ethical appeals support the credibility, moral character, and goodwill of the argument's creator. To identify these appeals, ask how knowledgeable, credible, and trustworthy the author is about the topic. What words, phrases, or examples show that knowledge, credibility, and trustworthiness?

Logical appeals Recent scientific research demonstrates that most people make decisions based on emotion more than anything else, but logical appeals are still important to Western audiences. As some say, "The facts don't lie" (though as you know, even facts can be manipulated, taken out of context, or presented in unfair ways). In addition to carefully checking the facts of any text, then, look for firsthand evidence drawn from observations, interviews, surveys or question-naires, experiments, and personal experience, as well as secondhand evidence from authorities, precedents, the testimony of others, sta-tistics, and other research sources. As you evaluate these sources, ask how trustworthy they are and whether all terms are clearly defined.

9c Analyzing the elements of an argument

According to philosopher Stephen Toulmin's framework for analyz-ing arguments, most arguments contain common features: a **claim** (or claims); reasons for the claim; stated or unstated assumptions that underlie the argument (Toulmin calls these **warrants**); **evi-dence** such as facts, authoritative opinion, examples, and statistics; and qualifiers that limit the claim in some way.

Suppose you read a brief argument about abolishing the Electoral College, often a hot topic. The diagram that follows shows how you can use the elements of argument for analysis.

Elements of Toulmin Argument

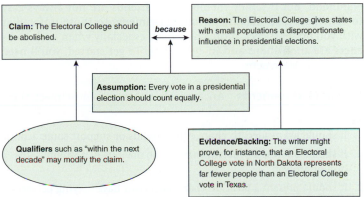

9d Arguing purposefully

Since all language is in some sense argumentative, the purposes of argument vary widely.

Arguing to win   In the most traditional purpose of academic argument, arguing to win, you aim to present a position that prevails over the positions of others.

Arguing to convince   A frequent goal of argument is to convince others to change their minds about an issue. To convince, you must provide reasons so compelling that the audience willingly agrees with your conclusion.

Arguing to understand   Rogerian argument (named for psychologist Carl Rogers) and invitational argument (named by researchers Sonja Foss and Cindy Griffin) both call for understanding as a major goal of arguing. Your purpose in many situations will be to share information and perspectives in order to make informed political, professional, and personal choices.

9e   Making an argument

Chances are you've been making convincing arguments since early childhood. But if family members and friends are not always easy to convince, then making effective arguments to those unfamiliar with you presents even more challenges, especially when such audiences are anonymous and in cyberspace. To get started, you'll need an arguable statement.

Arguable statements   An arguable statement must meet three criteria:

1. It should ask readers to change their minds or support some action.
2. It should address a problem that has no obvious or absolute solution or answer.
3. It should present a position that readers can have varying perspectives on.

ARGUABLE STATEMENT	Playing violent video games leads to violent behavior.
UNARGUABLE STATEMENT	Video games earn millions of dollars every year.

EXERCISE 9.1 Using the three criteria just listed, decide which of the following sentences are arguable and which are not. Example:

One of the best health decisions a person can make is to become a vegetarian. arguable

1. Humans were never intended to eat meat, and we would all live longer, healthier lives if we stopped eating it.

2. Health experts agree that vegetarians tend to have lower blood pressure and a lower mortality rate from heart disease than meat eaters do.

3. Killing animals for food is cruel, unethical, and unnecessary.

4. During World War I, the U.S. government encouraged citizens to eat vegetarian diets one day per week—on "Meatless Tuesdays"—to conserve meat for the troops.

5. Nothing is more disgusting than the way animals in slaughterhouses are killed for their meat.

Argumentative thesis or claim To make the move from an arguable statement to an argumentative thesis, begin with an arguable statement:

ARGUABLE STATEMENT Pesticides should be banned.

Attach at least one good reason.

REASON Pesticides endanger the lives of farmworkers.

You now have a working argumentative thesis.

ARGUMENTATIVE THESIS Because they endanger the lives of farmworkers, pesticides should be banned.

Develop the underlying assumption that supports your argument.

ASSUMPTION Farmworkers have a right to a safe working environment.

Identifying this assumption will help you gather evidence in support of your argument. Finally, consider whether you need to qualify your claim in any way.

Ethical appeals Ethical appeals support the writer's credibility, moral character, and goodwill using words, phrases, and examples to show knowledge and trustworthiness. Here are some ways to use ethical appeals effectively:

- Demonstrate that you are knowledgeable about the issues and topic.
- Show that you respect the views of your audience and have their best interests at heart.
- Demonstrate that you are fair and evenhanded by showing that you understand alternative or opposing viewpoints and can make a reasonable and fair counterargument.

Remember that the language you use can also help establish credibility. You may choose to use standardized English, another dialect of English, or another language to connect most effectively with a particular audience. Finally, remember that visuals can also make ethical appeals. Just as you consider the impressions your LinkedIn profile photo or the photos you share on Instagram make on your audience, you should think about what kind of case you're making when you choose images and design elements for your argument.

Logical appeals   Audiences almost always want proof—logical reasons that back up an argument. Remember, though, that all of the evidence you present must be trustworthy and accurate—and must seem so to your audience. You can create good logical appeals in the following ways:

A Visual That Makes a Logical Appeal

- Provide strong examples that are representative and that clearly support your point.
- Introduce precedents—particular examples from the past—that support your point.
- Use narratives or tell stories in support of your point.
- Cite authorities and their testimony, as long as each authority is timely and is genuinely qualified to speak on the topic.
- Establish that one event is the cause—or the effect—of another.

Visuals that make logical appeals can be useful in arguments, since they present factual information that can be taken in at a glance. Consider how long it would take to explain all the information in the map on p. 56 by using words alone.

Emotional appeals   Emotional appeals stir our feelings and remind us of what we value. You can appeal to the hearts as well as to the minds of your audience with the ethical use of strong emotional appeals:

- Introduce a powerful and credible quotation or image that supports your point.
- Use personal interest stories, your own or others', to make your point.
- Use concrete nouns, active verbs, and details to make your points more vivid.
- Use figurative language—metaphors, similes, analogies, and so on—to make your point both lively and memorable.

Visuals that make powerful emotional appeals can add substance to your argument as long as you test them with potential readers to check whether they interpret the visual the same way you do.

9f   Organizing an argument

Although there is no universally "ideal" organizational framework for an argument, the following patterns, first for Classical argument and then Rogerian argument, may give you some ideas about how to proceed. You can also use the elements of a Toulmin argument as an organizational framework (see 9c).

In any organizational pattern you choose, remember that there is seldom anything more powerful in appealing to audiences than a good story. In fact, a powerful story can serve as the major organizing principle for an argument, so don't forget to put narratives to work for you.

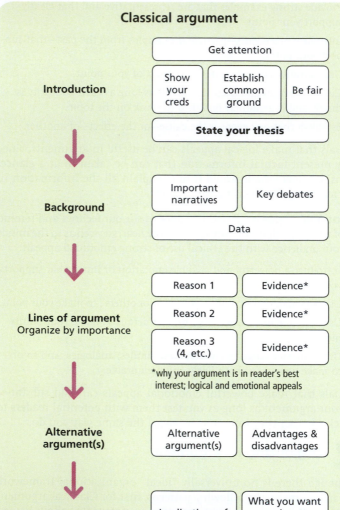

Classical argument

Introduction	Get attention
	Show your creds / Establish common ground / Be fair
	State your thesis
Background	Important narratives / Key debates / Data
Lines of argument Organize by importance	Reason 1 / Evidence* Reason 2 / Evidence* Reason 3 (4, etc.) / Evidence*
	*why your argument is in reader's best interest; logical and emotional appeals
Alternative argument(s)	Alternative argument(s) / Advantages & disadvantages
Conclusion	Implications of your thesis / What you want readers to think, feel, or do*
	*strong ethical or emotional appeal

Rogerian/invitational argument

	Describe the problem/issue

First
Aim to understand

Establish connection	Show respect

Recognize a variety of perspectives

Then
Consider all points
of view

Discuss alternative perspectives

Be fair	Be thorough

Next
Share your perspective
or story

Your perspective	Explain why it's valid

Show how it responds to or includes other perspectives

Show how your position offers mutual benefits to all

Finally
Extend thanks and invite
fuller discussion

Focus on common ground and understanding

9g   An argument essay

STUDENT WRITER

L.J. Bryan

In this essay, student L.J. Bryan argues that low voter turnout threatens democracy in the United States and is fueled by lack of knowledge, distrust of the government, and voter suppression.

Bryan 1

L.J. Bryan

Professor Clements

English Composition 1

10 October 2020

Title includes a topic and comment

Opens with a memorable, provocative quotation

Low Voter Turnout: A Lesion in the Land of the Free

Civil rights icon John Lewis once said, "The right to vote is the most powerful nonviolent tool we have in a democracy." This sentiment rings true for many democratic nations; however, in the United States, many citizens lack a basic trust in this tool, resulting in a dismal voter turnout rate: US elections represent only around sixty percent of the population's opinions (DeSilver). Because this fundamental element of trust is missing, many Americans are choosing not to participate in elections without realizing how the denial of this powerful right can affect their lives. Americans who can understand how ignorance, distrust, and voter suppression cause the low voter turnout rate will be better equipped to call for changes that protect and promote democracy.

Thesis establishes purpose

First claim related to thesis

Clarification establishes ethos (credibility)

Ignorance about politics is one of the leading contributors to the low voter turnout rate, but it might also be the easiest to mend. To be clear, when I say *ignorance*, I do not mean to imply that US citizens are unwilling or unable to learn, only that many

have been inadequately educated on the government and its
political systems. In fact, most schools do not even have entry-
level civics classes, and according to a survey by the Center for
American Progress, only twenty-six percent of American citizens
can name each branch of government (Brown and Shapiro). The
Center argues that "[w]ithout an understanding of the structure
of government; rights and responsibilities; and methods of public
engagement, civic literacy . . . will continue to plague American
democracy." The use of the word *plague* is especially fitting in this
circumstance since if many people within a population are ignorant,
that ignorance will continue to spread. But writer and former librarian
Pat Scales emphasizes that this is not a failing of the citizens
themselves, but rather of the education system. Because so many
people have not been properly educated about government, many do
not realize the importance of voting or feel entitled to make political
decisions. If the United States made civics a priority in public
education, more citizens would be empowered to vote.

> **Cites authorita-tive source in support of claim**

> **Metaphor underscores the serious-ness of the claim**

> **Presents reason in support of claim**

   Unfortunately, there are some who believe that the uneducated
should have less of a voice. Jason Brennan, a professor of public
policy at Georgetown University, argues that democracy in the US
should be replaced with epistocracy, which gives more voting power
to those with more knowledge. Brennan explains, "An epistocracy
might deny citizens the franchise unless they can pass a test of basic
political knowledge . . . and submit their demographic information."
He argues, "With such data, any statistician could calculate the
public's 'enlightened preferences,' that is, what a demographically
identical voting population *would* support if only it were better
informed." This way of thinking can have dangerous ramifications.
Though the intent may be pure, there are glaring concerns about
where this could lead, with the most notable precedent being the
literacy tests that wrongfully suppressed people of color from voting

> **Alternative argument presented fairly**

> **Rebuttal shows weakness of alternative argument**

Bryan 3

decades ago. Similarly, claims of what the public's "enlightened preferences" are would simply be assumptions and could easily be used to silence the voices of communities that already struggle to be heard. If something like this were to occur, it would become extremely difficult for the US to maintain its moniker as the land of the free because many citizens would be left under the subjugation of the "elites" like the livestock of *Animal Farm* or the proles of *1984*. More effort should be spent attempting to inform the public instead of silencing those who may be less informed.

Transition to second claim

Example supports claim and makes emotional appeal

While ignorance is a major and easily addressable reason for low voter turnout, distrust of the government is a more complex issue. When a person looks at the countless incidents of police brutality or the statistics that show how people of color routinely receive a worse punishment than their white peers despite committing similar offenses, it is easy to see how some might lose trust in the government and choose to distance themselves from these institutions. While this might seem illogical because it leaves important decisions in the hands of others, this thinking is difficult to overcome because once people feel distrust, they get caught up in a cyclical state of mind that reinforces their notions about the government. Unfortunately, the action of not voting based on one's distrust in the government does nothing but harm the potential voter's chances of creating positive change. If forty percent of potential voters aren't casting ballots, there is no way of knowing if the majority's voice is truly being heard. This is why it is imperative to encourage citizens to use their voices and votes to create change.

Transition to third claim

Presents example that supports claim

Even after the hurdles of ignorance and distrust are overcome, voter suppression cuts a path through the electoral process in a variety of ways. Voter ID laws are just one of these ways, culling out around 21 million potential voters each election cycle ("Voter ID"). Voter ID laws require individuals to provide identification to participate in elections. Upon first glance, this seems benign,

Bryan 4

but "[a]ccessing a photo ID is much more challenging for the young, the elderly, people of color, and people with low incomes" ("Voter ID"). If the United States wants to empower all people's voices, then there should be as few barriers to the voting process as possible. Many continue to advocate for voter ID laws, citing how easily its abolition could lead to voter fraud. However, this notion has already been disputed: one study found only thirty-one credible incidents of voter impersonation out of more than one billion ballots cast between 2000 to 2014, whereas in only four states during this same time period "more than 3,000 votes (in general elections alone) have reportedly been affirmatively rejected for lack of ID" (Levitt). Studies like these highlight both the uselessness and the harm of voter ID laws.

Additional logical appeals and support for the claim

In addition to voter ID laws, some voters are held up by prohibitively long lines, seen in figure 1, and mishandling of polling procedures. The Democratic Party of Georgia even sued the state during the 2020 primary election for this exact scenario, where voters were forced to wait in line for over four hours to cast their ballots and multiple voting machines broke down without sufficient backup paper ballots, despite the state's spending more than $100 million on their voting system (Cassady; Gallagher et al.). In the lawsuit, the Party claimed that "the myriad problems voters encountered . . . were 'directly traceable' to election officials" (Cassady). The Secretary of State placed the blame on the COVID-19 pandemic and inadequate training (Gallagher et al.), but others saw this as an attempt to suppress voters, especially voters of color, since voting districts with a higher population of people of color saw the longest lines.

Use of a visual provides emotional appeal

Presents and counters alternative perspective

Even when citizens are able to vote successfully, gerrymandering can suppress and effectively negate people's votes. Gerrymandering is the redrawing of voting districts in order to manipulate the vote to favor a specific party. For example, in the 2018 state Senate election

Bryan 5

Fig. 1. Ethan Miller. *Five States Hold Primaries as Pandemic Continues in America.* 9 June 2020. *Getty Images,* www.gettyimages.com/detail/news-photo/people-who-are-registering-to-vote-or-who-need-a-ballot-news-photo/1248635497.

in North Carolina, which took place after lines were redrawn, "Democrats received 50.5 percent of the vote, but Republicans won 57.9 percent of the seats" (Tausanovitch and Root). Gerrymandering continues this cycle of voter suppression that undermines the entire idea of democracy and in turn helps to feed the seeds of distrust that cause many to lose faith in the US political system. However, it is that very political system that has the power to create change and stop voter suppression.

Conclusion reiterates thesis and calls for action

Many obstacles stand in the path of a true democracy; however, in spite of all of this, the voter turnout rate in the United States can improve if the country makes an effort to combat the lack of basic political knowledge, distrust of the government, and voter suppression. As a collective, US residents must face these issues head

Bryan 6

on and effectively call for change, bettering education, government, and the voting system. This ensures the well-being of not only the country's democracy, but the lives of its citizens for generations to come. While the task may seem daunting, it is something that must be done in order to preserve our most powerful democratic tool.

Closing lines echo opening quotation

Bryan 7

Works Cited

Brennan, Jason. "The Right to Vote Should Be Restricted to Those with Knowledge." *Aeon*, 29 Sept. 2016, aeon.co/ideas/the-right -to-vote-should-be-restricted-to-those-with-knowledge.

Brown, Catherine, and Sarah Shapiro. "The State of Civics Education." *Center for American Progress*, 21 Feb. 2018, www.americanprogress.org/issues/education-k-12/reports/ 2018/02/21/446857/state-civics-education.

Cassady, Daniel. "Democrats Sue Georgia Election Officials over Long Lines during Primary Election." *Forbes*, 6 Aug. 2020, www .forbes.com/sites/danielcassady/2020/08/06/democrats-sue -georgia-election-officials-over-long-lines-during-primary -election.

DeSilver, Drew. "U.S. Trails Most Developed Countries in Voter Turnout." *Pew Research Center*, 21 May 2018, www.pewresearch .org/fact-tank/2018/05/21/u-s-voter-turnout-trails-most -developed-countries.

Gallagher, Dianne, et al. "Polls Closed in Georgia after a Day Marked by Voters Waiting for Hours to Cast Their Ballots." *CNN*, 10 June 2020, www.cnn.com/2020/06/09/politics/georgia-primary -election-delays/index.html.

Levitt, Justin. "A Comprehensive Investigation of Voter Impersonation Finds 31 Credible Incidents out of One Billion Ballots Cast." *The Washington Post*, 6 Aug. 2014, www .washingtonpost.com/news.

Lewis, John. "The right to vote is the most powerful nonviolent tool we have in a democracy. . . ." *Facebook,* 25 Feb. 2013, www .facebook.com/RepJohnLewis/posts/the-right-to-vote-is -the-most-powerful-nonviolent-tool-we-have-in-a-democracy -i-/473010132753004.

Scales, Pat. "Weighing In: Trouble, Folks." *Book Links*, vol. 26, no. 1, Sept. 2016, p. 40. *EBSCOhost*, ebscohost.com.

Bryan 8

Tausanovitch, Alex, and Danielle Root. "How Partisan Gerrymandering
Limits Voting Rights." *Center for American Progress*, 8 July
2020, www.americanprogress.org/issues/democracy/reports
/2020/07/08/487426/partisan-gerrymandering-limits-voting
-rights.

"Voter ID 101: The Right to Vote Shouldn't Come with Barriers."
Indivisible, 23 July 2020, indivisible.org/resource/voter-id-101
-right-vote-shouldnt-come-barriers.

10 Writing in a Variety of Disciplines and Genres

One of your goals as a writer will be to learn to enter the conversations going on in different academic disciplines—learning to "talk the talk" and "walk the walk" in each one. You will begin to get a sense of such differences as you prepare assignments for courses in the humanities, social sciences, and natural sciences. You are also likely to write in other, more public contexts with the goal of making a difference in the world, and you will need to make choices about how to reach your intended audience.

10a Recognizing expectations of academic disciplines

It's frustrating to know that there is no one single "correct" style of communication in any discipline. In addition, effective written and **multimodal** styles differ from effective oral styles (Chapter 11), and what is considered good writing in one field of study may not be viewed as appropriate in another. Even the variety of English often referred to as "standard" or "standardized" covers a wide range of styles (Chapter 23). In each discipline you study, you can learn how to use different sets of conventions, strategies, and resources.

Even though disciplinary expectations differ, you can begin figuring them out by becoming a bit of a sleuth, looking very closely at examples of good writing from any discipline and seeing what makes them tick.

Study disciplinary vocabulary   A good way to enter into the conversation of a field or discipline is to study its vocabulary. Highlight key terms in your reading or notes to help you distinguish any specialized terms. Mark any disciplinary jargon or technical terms that aren't familiar to you and ask for clarification from the instructor or fellow students. And pay careful attention to your textbook's vocabulary: try to master unfamiliar terms by checking to see if the textbook has a glossary, by asking your instructor questions, and by looking up key words or phrases.

Study disciplinary style   Here are some questions that will help you identify a discipline's stylistic features:

- How would you describe the overall tone of the writing—serious? scholarly? matter-of-fact? Do writers in the field usually strive for an objective stance (2d)? Are they aggressive or argumentative?

- Is the level of writing highly formal, highly technical, aimed at a general audience, or more informal and conversational?

- Do they use the first person (*I*) or prefer such terms as *one* or *the investigator*? What is the effect of this choice?

- In general, how long are the sentences and paragraphs?

- Are verbs generally active or passive—and why? (See 31f.)

- How many and what kinds of examples seem to be featured? What kinds of evidence seem to be valued?

- How does the writing integrate visual elements—graphs, tables, charts, photographs, or maps—or include video or sound?

- How is the writing organized? Does it typically include certain features, such as an abstract, a discussion of methods, headings, or other formatting elements?

Study the use of evidence   As you grow familiar with any area of study, you will develop a sense of what it takes to prove a point in that field. As you read assigned materials, consider the following questions about evidence:

- How do writers in the field use precedent, authority, and evidence? How are stories or narratives or personal experience used in this field? What kinds of evidence do writers in this field seem to ignore and why?

- What kinds of quantitative data (items that can be counted and measured) and qualitative data (items that can be systematically observed) are used—and why?

- How is logical reasoning used? How are definition, cause and effect, analogy, and example used in this discipline?

- What are the primary materials—the firsthand sources of information—in this field? What are the secondary materials—the sources of information derived from others? (See 12c.)

- How is research (by others, or by the authors) used and integrated into the text?

- What documentation style is typically used in this field? (See Chapters 16–19.)

Evidence in the humanities   Evidence for assignments in the humanities may come from a primary source you are examining closely, such as a poem, a philosophical treatise, an artifact, or a painting. For certain assignments, secondary sources such as journal articles or reference works can also provide useful evidence. Ground your analysis of each source in key questions about the work you are examining that will lead you to a thesis.

Evidence in the social sciences   You will need to understand both the quantitative and qualitative evidence used in your sources as well as other evidence you may create from research you conduct on your own. Summarizing and synthesizing information drawn from sources will be key to your success.

Evidence in the natural and applied sciences   You will probably draw on two major sources of evidence: research—including studies, experiments, and analyses—conducted by credible scientists, and research you conduct by yourself or with others. Each source should provide a strong piece of evidence for your project.

10b Understanding and using genres

Early on in your writing in any discipline, consider the **genre** or kind of text the instructor expects you to produce: a lab report for biology, for example, or a review of the literature for psychology, or a proposal for political science. If you are not sure what kind of text you are supposed to write, ask for clarification from your instructor, and check to see if your school's writing center has examples of such genres as well. You can ask your instructor to recommend examples of the kind of writing you will do in the course, and you can also take a look at major scholarly journals to find other examples of the genre you are aiming to write. You may also gather multiple examples to get a sense of how different writers approach the same genre. Then ask what genres seem to be most prevalent in your discipline: what is their major purpose?

Consider organization Genres often use a generally agreed-upon organizational plan. A typical laboratory report, for instance, follows a fairly standard framework (often the "introduction, methods, results, and discussion" format known as IMRAD) and uses these as major headings in the report. Ask:

- How exactly is the text organized in this genre?
- What are its main parts?
- Are the parts labeled with headings?

Consider format Genres sometimes have an agreed-upon format. Also ask:

- Is a title page called for? If so, what should be on it?
- What size and shape does the genre call for? a trifold layout? or double-columned or double-sided? Does it feature information in boxes or sidebars?
- Does an abstract precede the main text? If so, how long is it?
- What kind of spacing is used? What are typical fonts?
- Does the genre seem to call for the use of color?
- Does the genre call for use of visuals or other illustrations?
- Does the genre seem to have a typical way of beginning or ending?

10c **Adapting genre structures**

Learning to borrow and adapt transitional devices and pieces of sentence structure from other writing in the genre in which you are working is one way to help you learn the conventions of that discipline. Avoid copying the whole structure, however, or your borrowed sentences may seem plagiarized (Chapter 14). Find sample sentence structures from similar genres but on different topics so that you borrow a typical structure (which does not belong to anyone) rather than the idea or the particular phrasing. Write your own sentences first, and look at other people's sentences just to guide your revision.

ABSTRACT FROM A SOCIAL SCIENCE PAPER

Using the interpersonal communications research of J. K. Brilhart and G. J. Galanes, along with T. Hartman's personality assessment, I observed and analyzed the group dynamics of my project collaborators in a communications course. Based on results of the Hartman personality assessment, I predicted that a single leader would emerge. However, complementary individual strengths and gender differences encouraged a distributed leadership style.

EFFECTIVE BORROWING OF STRUCTURES

Drawing on the research of Deborah Tannen on conversational styles, I analyzed the conversational styles of six first-year students at DePaul University. Based on Tannen's research, I expected that the three men I observed would use features typical of male conversational style and the three women would use features typical of female conversational style. In general, these predictions were accurate; however, some exceptions were also apparent.

EXERCISE 10.1   Consider some of the genres that you have encountered as a student, jotting down answers to the following questions and bringing them to class for discussion.

1.   What are some genres that you read but don't usually write?
2.   What are some genres that you are generally assigned by teachers?
3.   What are some genres that you write to or with other students?

4. What are some genres that you will likely encounter in your major or in your career?

5. How are some of the genres you listed different from those you encountered in high school?

10d Choosing genres for public writing

At some point during your college years or soon after, you are highly likely to create writing that is not just something you turn in for a grade but writing that is important to you because it tries to make something good happen. Public writing has a very clear purpose, is intended for a specific audience, and addresses that audience directly, usually in straightforward, everyday language. It uses the genre most suited to its purpose and audience (a poster, a newsletter, a brochure, a letter to the editor), and it appears in a medium (print, online, or both) where the intended audience will see it. For example, if you want to convince your neighbors to pool time, effort, and resources to build a local playground, you might decide that a print flyer delivered door-to-door and posted at neighborhood gathering places would work best. If you want to create a flash mob to publicize ineffective security at chemical plants near your city, on the other hand, an easily forwarded message—text, tweet, or email—will probably work best.

10e STUDENT WRITING Samples in a variety of disciplines and genres

The following pages show examples of some of the many forms academic and public writing can take.

Student writing in academic disciplines

Close reading of poetry The following excerpt is taken from student Bonnie Sillay's close reading of two poems by E. E. Cummings, an assignment for her second-year American Literature seminar. This excerpt includes the introduction to the essay and Bonnie's reading of the first poem, "since feeling is first," in which she uses evidence from the poem to create her own interpretation. Note that she uses MLA style for her documentation (see Chapter 16).

Bonnie Sillay
Instructor Angela Mitchell
English 1102
4 December 2019

"Life's Not a Paragraph": The Triumph of Emotion in
the Poetry of E. E. Cummings

Throughout his poetry, E. E. Cummings leads readers deep into a
thicket of scrambled words, missing punctuation, and unconventional
structure. Within Cummings's poetic bramble, ambiguity leads the reader
through what seems at first a confusing and winding maze. However, this
confusion actually transforms into a path that leads the reader to the
center of the thicket where Cummings's message lies: readers should not
allow their experience to be limited by reason and rationality. In order to
communicate his belief that emotional experience should triumph over
reason, Cummings employs odd juxtapositions, outlandish metaphors,
and inversions of traditional grammatical structures that reveal the illogic
of reason. Indeed, by breaking down such formal boundaries, Cummings's
poems "since feeling is first" and "as freedom is a breakfastfood" suggest
that emotion, which provides the compositional fabric for our experience
of life, should never be defined or controlled.

In "since feeling is first," Cummings urges readers to reject
attempts to control emotion, using English grammar as one example
of the restrictive conventions present in society. Stating that
"since feeling is first / who pays any attention / to the syntax of
things" (lines 1–3), Cummings suggests that emotion should not be
forced to fit into some preconceived mold. He carries this message
throughout the poem by juxtaposing images of the abstract and the
concrete—images of emotion and grammar. Cummings's word choice
enhances his intentionally strange juxtapositions, with the poet using
grammatical terms that suggest regulation. For example, in the line
"And death i think is no parenthesis" (16), Cummings uses the idea
that parentheses confine the words they surround in order to warn
the reader not to let death confine life or emotions.

Present tense for poetry

Foreshadows discussion of work to come

Introductory paragraph ends with thesis statement

Sillay 2

Transition sentence connects the previous paragraph to this one

The structure of the poem also rejects traditional conventions. Instead of the final stanzas making the main point, Cummings opens his poem with his primary message, that "feeling is first" (1). Again, Cummings shows that emotion rejects order and structure. How can emotion be bottled in sentences and interrupted by commas, colons, and spaces? To Cummings, emotion is a never-ending run-on sentence that should not be diagrammed or dissected.

Quotation introduced effectively

Metaphor captures the spirit of Cummings's point

In the third stanza of "since feeling is first," Cummings states his point outright, noting "my blood approves, / and kisses are a better fate / than wisdom" (7–9). Here, Cummings argues for reveling in the feeling during a fleeting moment such as a kiss. He continues, "the best gesture of my brain is less than / your eyelids' flutter" (11–12). Cummings wants the reader to focus on a pure emotive response (the flutter of an eyelash)—on the emotional, not the logical—on the meanings of words instead of punctuation and grammar.

Cummings's use of words such as *kisses* and *blood* (8, 7) adds to the focus on the emotional. The ideas behind these words are difficult to confine or restrict to a single definition: kisses mean different things to different people, blood flows through the body freely and continually. The words are not expansive or free enough to encompass all that they suggest. Cummings ultimately paints language as more restrictive than the flowing, powerful force of emotion.

Paragraph reiterates Cummings's claim and sums up his argument

The poet's use of two grammatical terms in the last lines, "for life's not a paragraph / And death i think is no parenthesis," warns against attempts to format lives and feelings into conventional and rule-bound segments (15–16). Attempts to control, rather than feel, are rejected throughout "since feeling is first." Emotion should be limitless, free from any restrictions or rules.

Clear and explicit transition from discussion of first poem

While "since feeling is first" argues that emotions should not be controlled or analyzed, "as freedom is a breakfastfood" suggests the difficulty of defining emotion. In this poem, Cummings uses deliberately far-fetched metaphors such as "freedom is a breakfastfood" and "time is a tree" (1, 26). . . .

Sillay 5

Works Cited

Cummings, E. E. "as freedom is a breakfastfood." *E. E. Cummings: Complete Poems 1904–1962*, edited by George J. Firmage, Liveright, 1991, p. 511.

---. "since feeling is first." *E. E. Cummings: Complete Poems 1904–1962*, edited by George J. Firmage, Liveright, 1991, p. 291.

Sources cited according to MLA style

Psychology research essay For a psychology class, student Martha Bell was assigned to write a research essay that follows the conventions of social science writing in this genre. She chose to analyze evidence that suggests a range of choices for—as well as a robust debate about—treatments for Lyme disease. To read her paper, see 17e.

Chemistry lab report Student Allyson Goldberg prepared a lab report on an experiment she was assigned as part of her chemistry class. The excerpt that follows includes the Introduction, Materials and Methods, and Results sections of the report. Not included are the title page, which comes first in such reports, the discussion section, and the conclusion.

Goldberg 2

Introduction
explains
purpose
of lab
and gives
overview of
results

Introduction

The purpose of this investigation was to experimentally determine the value of the universal gas constant, R. To accomplish this goal, a measured sample of magnesium (Mg) was allowed to react with an excess of hydrochloric acid (HCl) at room temperature and pressure so that the precise amount and volume of the product hydrogen gas (H_2) could be determined and the value of R could be calculated using the ideal gas equation, $PV=nRT$.

**Materials
and meth-
ods section
explains lab
setup and
procedure**

Materials & Methods

Two samples of room temperature water, one about 250mL and the other about 400mL, were measured into a smaller and larger beaker, respectively. 15.0mL of HCl was then transferred into a side arm flask that was connected to the top of a buret (clamped to a ringstand) through a 5/16" diameter flexible tube. (This "gas buret" was connected to an adjacent "open buret," clamped to the other side of the ringstand and left open to the atmosphere of the laboratory at its wide end, by a 1/4" diameter flexible tube. These two burets were adjusted on the ringstand so that they were vertically parallel and close together.) The HCl sample was transferred to the flask such that none came in contact with the inner surface of the neck of the flask. The flask was then allowed to rest, in an almost horizontal position, in the smaller beaker.

The open buret was adjusted on the ringstand such that its 20mL mark was horizontally aligned with the 35mL mark on the gas buret. Room temperature water was added to the open buret until the water level of the gas buret was at about 34.00mL.

**Passive
voice
throughout
is typical
of writing
in natural
sciences**

A piece of magnesium ribbon was obtained, weighed on an analytical balance, and placed in the neck of the horizontal side arm flask. Next, a screw cap was used to cap the flask and form an airtight seal. This setup was then allowed to sit for 5 minutes in order to reach thermal equilibrium.

Goldberg 3

After 5 minutes, the open buret was adjusted so that the menisci on both burets were level with each other; the side arm flask was then tilted vertically to let the magnesium ribbon react with the HCl. After the brisk reaction, the flask was placed into the larger beaker and allowed to sit for another 5 minutes.

Next, the flask was placed back into the smaller beaker, and the open buret was adjusted on the ringstand such that its meniscus was level with that of the gas buret. After the system sat for an additional 30 minutes, the open buret was again adjusted so that the menisci on both burets were level.

This procedure was repeated two more times, with the exception that HCl was not again added to the side arm flask, as it was already present in enough excess for all reactions from the first trial.

Results and Calculations

Trial #	Lab Temp. (°C)	Lab Pressure (mbar)	Mass of Mg Ribbon Used (g)	Initial Buret Reading (mL)	Final Buret Reading (mL)
1	24.4	1013	0.0147	32.66	19.60
2	24.3	1013	0.0155	33.59	N/A*
3	25.0	1013	0.0153	34.35	19.80

*See note in Discussion section.

Trial #	Volume of H_2 (L)	Moles of H_2 Gas Produced	Lab Temp. (K)	Partial Pressure of H_2 (atm)	Value of R (L atm/ mol K)	Mean Value of R (L atm/ mol K)
1	0.01306	6.05×10^{-4}	298	0.970	0.0704	0.0728
2	N/A	N/A	N/A	N/A	N/A	
3	0.01455	6.30×10^{-4}	298	0.968	0.0751	

Table 1 Experimental results

Data is organized in a table

Student writing in more public contexts

Poster Student Hebron Warren won first place in the New York City Police Department's contest for posters encouraging victims to report campus sexual assaults to the police. Hebron's eye-catching design focuses on the action he wants audiences to take: "Speak up!" He uses visual symmetry to emphasize that assaults happen to both men and women, and includes simple statistics to persuade the audience that too few of these crimes are reported. The message is concise and simple enough to be understood quickly by passersby.

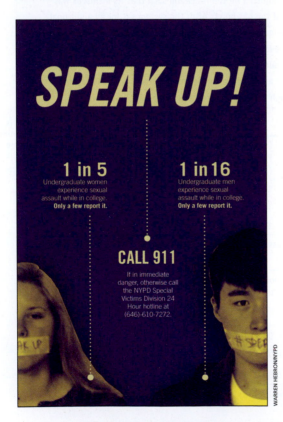

Fundraising web page Student Justin Dart created this fundraising web page with a very clear purpose: to crowd-source the funding to help Jey, a young street vendor in Accra, Ghana, get a college education. Using the Indiegogo template, Justin posted a video spelling out the background and purpose of his fundraiser, a short written description of the project, and a list of perks for donors at various levels. Other tabs offered updates from Justin on his progress, comments from donors, photos, and more. To reach as many people as possible, Justin shared this page with his friends and acquaintances and urged them to share it on social media outlets. Justin ended up raising enough to pay for Jey's university tuition for his college career, as well as housing and incidentals.

JUSTIN DART

Web comic Student Zack Karas worked with a team of classmates on an assignment to do field research in a public space. His group chose a local coffee shop, and after conducting observations of the environment and the interactions among people there, they presented a critical analysis of the coffee-drinking scene to the rest of the class.

Zack then used his team's coffee shop experience as the basis for a comic, which he posted on a blog created to host his artwork. The final panels include a twist: Zack's comic avatar fails to recognize that he, like many of the customers, is also a "post-ironic hipster . . . with facial hair, a hoodie, and an iPhone." Turning the report into a comic allowed Zack to reach an audience beyond his classmates—readers who share his interest in humor, online comics, and the critique of the coffee-culture demographic.

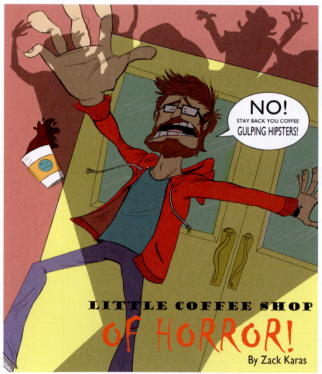

11 Creating Presentations

It's a good idea to jump at every opportunity you can to make presentations, since this form of creating and sharing knowledge is getting more and more prominent in almost all fields. This chapter will help you put your best foot forward as you do so.

11a Considering task, purpose, and audience

Think about how much time you have to prepare; where the presentation will take place and how long it will be; whether you will use written-out text or note cards; whether visual aids are called for; and what equipment you will need. If you are making a group presentation, divide duties and practice with your classmates.

It's important to start by answering a few questions. What's the purpose of your presentation—to lead a discussion? teach a lesson? give a report? make a proposal? present research? Also, who's your audience? What do they know about your topic, what opinions and values do they have about it, and how can you help them follow your presentation and perhaps accept your point of view?

11b Writing a memorable introduction and conclusion

Listeners tend to remember beginnings and endings most readily. Make yours memorable by using a surprising statement, opinion, or question; a vivid anecdote; or a powerful quotation or image. Make sure that at the end, the audience gets the main takeaway.

11c Using explicit structure and signpost language

Organize your presentation clearly and give an overview of your main points up front. Then pause between major points, and use signpost language to move from one idea to the next: *The second crisis point in the breakup of the Soviet Union came hard on the heels of the first* instead of *Another thing about the Soviet Union's problems.* . . . Signposts also include repeating key words and ideas. Finally, avoid complicated sentences, and use as many concrete verbs, nouns, and examples as possible.

11d   Preparing a script for ease of presentation

If you decide to speak from a script, use a large double- or triple-spaced print. End each page with the end of a sentence so you won't have to pause to turn a page. Whether you speak from a full text, a detailed outline, note cards, or points on flip charts or slides, mark the places where you want to pause, and highlight the words you want to emphasize.

11e   Planning visuals

Think of your visuals not as add-ons but as a major means of getting your points across. Many speakers use presentation software (such as Google Slides or Prezi) to help keep on track and to guide the audience. And posters, flip charts, or interactive whiteboards can also help you make strong visual statements.

When you work with visuals for your presentation, they must be large enough to be easily read—even if you are sharing your screen during a Zoom or other online presentation. Be sure the information is simple, clear, and easy to understand. Do *not* read from your visuals or, if it's a live presentation, turn your back on your audience as you refer to them. Most important, make sure your visuals help listeners understand rather than distract from your message. Try out each visual on classmates or friends: if they don't grasp the meaning and purpose of the visual, scrap it and try again.

Slides   Here are some guidelines for preparing effective slides:

- Keep information on each slide minimal; simple words or a picture can make a point.
- Avoid more than five bullet points (or forty words) on a slide, and never read the slides to your audience. Instead, say something to explain or emphasize what's on the slide.

Checklist

Reviewing Your Presentation

Before your instructor or another audience evaluates your presentation, do a review for yourself:

✔ Does your presentation have a clear thesis, a compelling introduction and conclusion, and a simple, clear structure?

✔ Do you use sources to support your points and demonstrate your knowledge? Do you include a works cited slide at the end of the presentation?

✔ Is your use of media (posters, slides, video clips, and so on) appropriate for your topic and thesis? If you are using slides, will they appeal to your audience and make your points effectively?

✔ Do you use clear signpost language and effective repetition?

✔ Have you thought about your delivery—tone and projection of voice, pacing, and stance?

- Use light backgrounds in a darkened room, dark backgrounds in a lighted one. In an online presentation, a light background with dark type is best.

- Make sure that audio or video clips with sound are clearly audible and captioned.

- Use only images large and sharp enough to be clearly visible to your audience, and remember to describe the images as you present them.

Handouts   You may also want to prepare handouts for your audience: pertinent bibliographies, for example, or text too extensive to be presented otherwise. Unless the audience will need the handout as you speak, share it after the presentation.

11f **Practicing**

Set aside enough time to practice your presentation at least twice. Record your rehearsals, or practice with friends who can comment on content and style. Timing your run-throughs will tell you whether you need to cut (or expand) material to make the presentation an appropriate length.

11g Delivering the presentation

To calm your nerves and get off to a good start, know your material thoroughly and use the following strategies to good advantage before, during, and after your presentation:

- Visualize your presentation with the aim of feeling comfortable during it.
- If possible, stand: speakers make a stronger impression standing rather than sitting.
- Face your audience (know where the camera is on your laptop!), and make eye contact whenever possible.
- Allow time for questions, and thank the audience at the end of the presentation.

11h STUDENT WRITING Excerpts from a presentation

Here's the opening of the script student writer Shuqiao Song prepared for her presentation, "The Residents of a Dys*FUN*ctional *HOME*: Text and Image."

> Welcome! I'm Shuqiao Song and I'm here to talk about "The Residents of a Dys*FUN*ctional *HOME*." We meet these characters in a graphic memoir called *Fun Home,* which later became a hit Broadway musical. [Here Song showed a three-second video clip of author Bechdel saying, "I love words, and I love pictures. But especially, I love them together—in a mystical way I can't even explain."]
>
> That was Alison Bechdel, author of *Fun Home*. In that clip, she conveniently introduces the topics of my presentation today: Words. Pictures. And the mystical way they work together.

Note that Shuqiao opens with a play on words ("Dys*FUN*ctional *HOME*"), to which she returns later on, and with a short video clip that sums up her main topic. Also note the use of short sentences and fragments, special effects that act like drumbeats to get and hold the audience's attention.

For her presentation, Shuqiao developed a series of very simple slides aimed at underscoring her points and keeping her audience focused on them. She began by introducing the work, showing the book cover on an otherwise black slide. Throughout the presentation, she used very simple visuals—a word or two, or a large image from the book she was discussing—to keep her audience focused on what she was saying.

In her presentation, Shuqiao Song uses simple visuals to focus her audience on her analysis.

Research

12 **Conducting Research** 88

13 **Evaluating Sources and Taking Notes** 96

14 **Integrating Sources and Avoiding Plagiarism** 113

15 **Writing a Research Project** 120

12   Conducting Research

Whether you're figuring out the best software to use for a project or investigating ways to earn money while going to school, you are doing research. And in college, you are part of a research community—one that values the work of researchers and knows that the results of research can lead to important breakthroughs. Research can help you earn a good grade, of course, and it can also help you make your mark—make something good happen in the world around you.

12a   Understanding challenges to research today

You'd think that research should be easier than ever to conduct, with so much information instantly available through technology. But more doesn't always or even often mean better: today, dis- and misinformation, fake news, outright lies, and conspiracy theories can overwhelm credible, trustworthy information. As a result, you need to recognize the challenges that face you and read *defensively* and skeptically rather than simply accepting what sources say. That's what two University of Washington science professors are doing with a course that teaches students to recognize how statistics and visual representation of data (especially "big" data) can be used to misinform and confuse. And it's what researchers everywhere are doing when they fact-check and triangulate sources—or, in other words, when they look at the evidence from several different standpoints. Finally, ethical researchers never rely solely on social media as a main source. You'll be wise, then, to stick with fully credible sources you can access through library databases and reliable, ethical websites. (See 12d.) As a researcher, you want to be able to vouch for your sources, to make sure that they are accurate, credible, and trustworthy.

12b   Beginning the research process

Once you have your skeptical/critical hat on and have a topic that's assigned to you or that you have chosen, move on to analyze the assignment, articulate a research question to answer, and form a hypothesis. Then, after your preliminary research is complete, you can refine your hypothesis into a working thesis (see 3b) and begin your research in earnest.

Considering context   Ask yourself what the *purpose* of your research project is—perhaps to describe, survey, analyze, persuade, explain, classify, compare, or contrast. Then consider your *audience.* Who will be most interested, and what will they need to know? What assumptions and values might they hold? What response do you want from them? Also examine your own *stance* or *attitude* toward your topic (see 2d). Do you feel curious, critical, confused, or something else entirely? What influences have shaped your stance? What biases may you have about this topic?

Then consider how many and what *kinds of sources* you need to find. What kinds of evidence will help your audience understand or agree with your position? Where will you be most likely to find evidence that will speak directly to your audience, including stories and narratives, personal experience, and information from sources you have not considered before or that have been ignored? What visuals might you need? Would it help to do field research, such as surveys, observations, interviews, or more informal conversations? Finally, consider how long your project will be, how much time it will take, and when it is due.

Formulating a research question and hypothesis   After analyzing your project's context, work from your general topic to a research question and a hypothesis.

TOPIC	How tourism affects residents/ neighborhoods
NARROWED TOPIC	How tourism in Harlem affects its residents
ISSUE	Many types of tourism business are operating in historic Harlem, not all of which bring benefits to residents.
RESEARCH QUESTION	What type of tourism business is more beneficial to residents of Harlem, a small locally owned business or an outside tour company?

HYPOTHESIS	Small locally owned businesses may benefit residents of Harlem more than those that come in from outside of Harlem.

After you have explored sources to test your hypothesis and sharpened it by reading, writing, and talking with others, you can refine it into a working thesis (3b).

WORKING THESIS	Although economic initiatives have favored big tourism companies from outside, research shows that small locally owned and culturally relevant companies provide more economic and social benefits to residents of Harlem.

Planning research   Once you have formulated your hypothesis, determine what you already know about it and where you found this information. Think hard about the kinds of sources you expect to consult—articles, print or digital books, specialized reference works, experts on your own campus, and so on—and the number you think you will need, how current they should be, and where you might find them.

12c   Choosing among types of sources

Keep in mind some important differences among types of sources.

Primary and secondary sources   **Primary sources** provide you with firsthand knowledge, while **secondary sources** report on or analyze the research of others. Primary sources are basic sources of raw information, including your own field research; films, works of art, or other objects you examine; literary works you read; and eyewitness accounts, photographs, news reports, and historical documents. Secondary sources are descriptions or interpretations of primary sources, such as researchers' reports, reviews, biographies, and encyclopedia articles. What constitutes a primary or secondary source depends on the purpose of your research. A film review, for instance, serves as a secondary source if you are writing about the film but as a primary source if you are studying the critic's writing.

Scholarly and popular sources   Nonacademic sources like magazines can be helpful, and you should draw on them, especially if they are well known to your audience. In addition, you will want to look to scholarly journals, authorities in a field, whose articles have been vetted by other experts. Here are some tips for distinguishing between scholarly and popular sources:

SCHOLARLY	POPULAR
Title often contains the word *Journal*	*Journal* usually does not appear in title
Source is available (for free) mainly through your library databases	Source is generally available at newsstands or on the free web
Few or no commercial advertisements	Many advertisements
Authors are identified with academic credentials	Authors are usually journalists or reporters hired by the publication, not academics
Summary or abstract appears on first page of article; articles are fairly long	No summary or abstract; articles are fairly short
Articles cite sources and provide bibliographies	Articles may include quotations but rarely cite sources or provide bibliographies

Older and more current sources   Most projects can benefit from both older, historical sources and more current ones. Some older sources are classics; others are simply dated.

Personal experience and narratives   Remember that your own experience can serve as an important source, one you can call on during your research. What in your experience illustrates or explains something about your topic? In addition, how might you use narratives or stories—either from your own experience or from the experiences of others—as powerful sources to support and exemplify your topic or claim? Pay special attention to narratives or stories from those who have often been ignored or misrepresented—they may offer particularly compelling evidence for your topic and audience.

12d Using web and library resources

To find scholarly, popular, primary, secondary, and other sources, you will most often turn to the web or to your college library.

Starting with online searches Writers today often begin research by turning to Google, so remember that a quick search can give you an overview of what's out there. Wikipedia also offers a good place to begin research: the entries are relatively short, clearly written, and well organized and can point to themes or issues you can then pursue on sites like Google Scholar. Because Wikipedia articles can and do change often, you may not want to use them for formal citations.

Finding authoritative sources on the open web The Internet will let you enter virtual libraries that allow access to some collections in libraries other than the one at your school. Collections available through government sites can be especially useful: see, for instance, the Library of Congress (www.loc.gov); the National Institutes of Health (www.nih.gov); or the U.S. Census Bureau (www.census .gov). Online versions of reputable newspapers such as the *Black Star News*, *Washington Post*, *El Nuevo Herald*, or the *Wall Street Journal* or sites like C-SPAN can provide sources of current news. In addition, general interest magazines (including Slate and Salon) are published only on the web, and many other reputable publications, like *Newsweek*, *Ebony*, *The New Yorker*, or *The New Republic*, make some of their content available online for free. Finally, media networks such as ABC, NPR, and Telemundo regularly post online content.

Consulting your library's staff Your library's staff—especially reference librarians—can be a valuable resource. You can talk with a librarian about your research project and get specific recommendations about databases and other helpful places to begin your research. Many libraries also have online tours and chat rooms where students can ask questions.

Catalogs Library catalogs show whether a book is housed in the library and, if so, offer a call number that helps you find the book on the shelf. Because books are organized by subject, browsing through books near the one you've found in the catalog can

Checklist

Effective Search Techniques

You can access online catalogs, databases, and websites without going to the library. And you can search the web by using carefully chosen keywords to limit the scope of your search and refine a search.

✔ Advanced search tools let you focus your search more narrowly—by combining terms with AND or eliminating them with NOT, by specifying dates and media types, and so on—so they may give you more relevant results.

✔ Adding *site:.org* or *site:.edu* to a search term can help limit results to nonprofit sites or university-sponsored sites.

✔ If you don't see an advanced search option, start with keywords. Check the first page or two of results. If you get many irrelevant options, think about how to refine your keywords to get more targeted results.

✔ Most college libraries classify material using the *Library of Congress Subject Headings*, or LCSH. When you find a library source that seems especially relevant, be sure to use the subject headings for that source as search terms to bring up all the entries under each heading.

help locate other works related to your topic. Catalogs also indicate where to find a particular periodical, either in print or in an online database, at the library.

Indexes and databases   Remember that most college libraries subscribe to a large number of indexes and databases that you can access online for free, and these sources contain much information that you will not have access to in a general Google search. Some databases include the full text of articles from newspapers, magazines, journals, and other works; some offer only short abstracts (summaries), which give an overview so you can decide whether to spend time finding and reading the whole text. Indexes of reviews provide information about a potential source's critical reception.

Check with a librarian for discipline-specific indexes and databases or those related to your specific topic, such as the International

Index to Black Periodicals, the Hispanic American Periodicals Index, the LGBT Magazine Archive, American Indian History and Culture, Scottish Women Poets, and many others.

Reference works General reference works, such as encyclopedias, biographical resources, almanacs, digests, and atlases, can help you get an overview of a topic, identify subtopics, find more specialized sources, and identify keywords for searches.

Bibliographies Bibliographies—lists of sources—in books or articles related to your topic can lead you to other valuable resources. Ask a librarian whether your library has more extensive bibliographies related to your research topic.

Other resources Your library can help you borrow materials from other libraries (this can take time, so plan ahead). Check with reference librarians, too, about audio, video, multimedia, and art collections; government documents; and other special collections or archives.

12e Doing field research

For many research projects, you will need to collect field data. Consider *where* you can find relevant information, *how* to gather it, and *who* might be your best providers of information. You may also want to talk with your instructor about any field research you plan to do, to make sure your research will not violate your college's guidelines for doing research that involves people.

Interviews Some information is best obtained by asking direct questions of other people. If you can talk with an expert—in person, on the telephone, or online—you may get information you cannot obtain through any other kind of research. Think carefully, therefore, about what kind of interviewees will be able to provide you with the most useful and reliable information.

- Determine your exact purpose; make sure it relates to your research question and your hypothesis.
- Set up the interview well in advance. Specify how long it will take, and if you wish to record the session, ask permission to do so.

- Prepare a written list of factual and open-ended questions. If the interview proceeds in a direction that seems fruitful, don't feel that you have to ask all of your prepared questions.

- Record the subject, date, time, and place of the interview.

- Thank those you interview, either in person or in a letter or email.

Alternatives to formal interviews Formal, structured interviews will not be appropriate in every situation. In some cultures, the kind of direct questions used in such interviews can even be offensive. Indigenous researchers often prefer more informal, unobtrusive methods of gathering information. For example, they may prefer to meet informally in a comfortable setting where they can join together in some activity, to share their own experiences, to leave quiet time and to respect the other person's silences, and not to ask direct questions, preferring to let the conversation develop naturally.

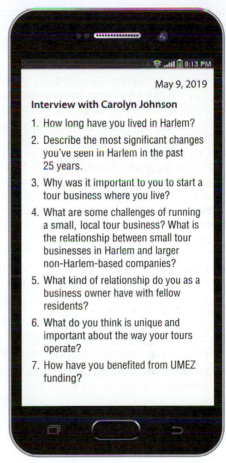

May 9, 2019

Interview with Carolyn Johnson

1. How long have you lived in Harlem?

2. Describe the most significant changes you've seen in Harlem in the past 25 years.

3. Why was it important to you to start a tour business where you live?

4. What are some challenges of running a small, local tour business? What is the relationship between small tour businesses in Harlem and larger non-Harlem-based companies?

5. What kind of relationship do you as a business owner have with fellow residents?

6. What do you think is unique and important about the way your tours operate?

7. How have you benefited from UMEZ funding?

Sample questions for a personal interview

Observation Trained observers report that making a faithful record of an observation requires intense concentration and mental agility.

- Determine the purpose of the observation, how it relates to your research question and hypothesis, and what you think you may find.

- Brainstorm about what you are looking for, but don't be rigidly bound to your expectations.

- Develop an appropriate system for recording data. Consider using a split notebook or page: on one side, record your observations directly; on the other, record your thoughts or interpretations.

- Record the date, time, and place of observation.

Opinion surveys   Surveys usually depend on questionnaires. On any questionnaire, the questions should be clear and easy to understand and designed so that you can analyze the answers without difficulty. Questions that ask respondents to say *yes* or *no* or to rank items on a scale are easiest to tabulate.

- Write out your purpose, and determine the kinds of questions to ask.

- Figure out how to reach respondents—either online via email, apps, or social media; over the phone; or in person.

- Draft questions that call for short, specific answers.

- Test the questions on several people, and revise questions that seem unfair, ambiguous, or too hard or time-consuming.

- Draft a cover letter or invitation email. Be sure to state a deadline.

- If you are using a print questionnaire, leave adequate space for answers.

- Proofread the questionnaire carefully.

 13   Evaluating Sources and Taking Notes

All research builds on the careful and sometimes inspired use of sources—that is, on research done by others. Since you want the information you glean from sources to be reliable and persuasive, evaluate each potential source carefully.

13a Checking facts

Especially with online sources, practice what media analyst Howard Rheingold calls "crap detection," which means identifying information that is faulty or deceptive. Rheingold recommends finding three separate credible online sources that corroborate the point you want to make. Here are some tips for becoming a good fact-checker:

- Consider the facts carefully. Are any taken out of context? Can you find them corroborated in other sources? If not, be suspicious. How thoroughly documented is each source?

- Become familiar with nonpartisan fact-checkers that can help you, like PolitiFact, FactCheck.org, and AmericanPressInstitute.org. Snopes.com is also useful for fact-checking general rumors and Internet memes.

- Be on the lookout for claims that are unsubstantiated, for quotations or statistics that are not attributed to a reliable source, for clickbait headlines or titles, and for nonstandard URLs—those that have, for instance, a ".co" ending. (NYTimes.com.co is not the *New York Times*.)

- Also be attentive to the tone with which facts are presented or represented: if it is sensationalistic or highly exaggerated, take special care that the facts are not also exaggerated.

13b Reading vertically

When you are considering online sources, judging credibility can be especially tricky. One good, basic way to evaluate a source is to examine it closely, top to bottom, front to back, really drilling down on it to make sure you understand not only its content but also its stance, where it's coming from. The following guidelines will help you do this kind of vertical reading to begin assessing each source.

- **Your purpose.** How does the source add to your research project? Does it help you support a major point? demonstrate that you have researched the topic fully? help establish your credibility?

- **Relevance.** Is the source closely related to your research question? Read beyond the title and opening paragraph to check for relevance.

- **Name of the author and sponsor or publisher.** Is it obvious who composed the material? Is the author's name included? Are credentials or an area of expertise listed? Can you tell who sponsors or publishes the site? Often you can visit an "About" page for such information.

- **Date of publication.** Recent sources are often more useful than older ones, particularly in fields that change rapidly. However, the most authoritative works may be older ones. The publication dates of Internet sites can often be difficult to pin down. And even for sites that include the dates of posting, remember that the material posted may have been composed sometime earlier.

- **Stance of source.** Identify the source's point of view or rhetorical stance, and scrutinize it carefully. Does the source present facts that you can verify? Does it interpret or evaluate them, and if so, is this interpretation overly biased? If it presents facts, what is included and what is omitted, and why? If it interprets or evaluates information that is not disputed, the source's stance may be obvious, but at other times you will need to think carefully about the source's goals. What does the author or sponsoring group want—to convince you of an idea? sell you something? call you to action in some way?

- **Level of specialization.** General sources can be helpful as you begin your research, but you may then need the authority or currency of more specialized sources. On the other hand, extremely specialized works may be very hard to understand.

- **Audience of source.** Was the source written for the general public? specialists? advocates or opponents? a group with a particular bias or ideology?

Vertical reading will go a long way toward helping you evaluate sources, but often not far enough because it keeps you focused only on the source itself. Especially with web-based sources that can so easily be made to *appear* to be trustworthy and credible, smart researchers move beyond the source itself. Combining vertical reading with lateral reading (13c) is the best way to judge whether a source is credible and will be useful for your project.

Vertical Reading

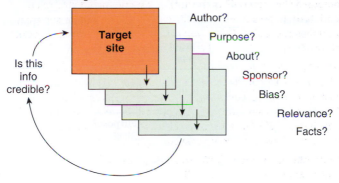

13c   Reading laterally

When a group of Stanford researchers asked historians, undergraduates, and professional fact-checkers to examine two websites and determine which was the more authoritative, they found that the historians and undergraduates did not do very well while the fact-checkers were 100 percent correct. What was their secret? Rather than reading vertically—that is, staying within a website to determine whether or not it is credible—the fact-checkers immediately left the websites in question, opened new tabs, visited new sites, and checked what other sources had to say about the sponsors of the websites under examination. They used external sites as lenses for evaluating their "target" site. The researchers refer to this as *lateral reading*, and it's a practice you can take up as you evaluate sources, especially those you find online. Here are a few guidelines that can help you begin reading laterally.

- For any website, first check the "about" or "about us" tab, which may tell you what groups the site is associated with or sponsored by.

- Make sure the site/source is clearly *relevant* to your research project.

- Open new browser tabs and search for the *sponsor* or *publisher* to see what others have had to say about their credibility, trustworthiness, political leanings or *bias*, and so on. Don't simply click on the

Lateral Reading

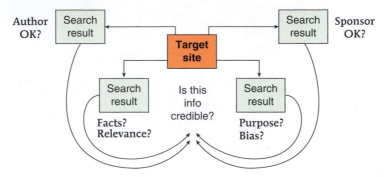

first search result that pops up; rather, search for the most reputable, reliable one. And don't settle for just one opinion—see if you can corroborate, or confirm, what the search result site is saying about your "target" site.

- Do the same kind of lateral searching for information about the *author* of the source. What can you learn about the author's *credentials*?

- Search for what other sources have to say about the major *claims* your source or site is making. Do other sources confirm the claim or call it into question?

- Do fact-checking to corroborate any *facts* presented by the source.

- Practice what the Stanford researchers call "click restraint": see what you can tell about a source's reliability before clicking on it.

13d Reading and analyzing sources

After you have determined that a source is potentially useful, read it carefully and critically (see Chapter 8), asking yourself the following questions about how this research fits your writing project:

- How relevant is this material to your research question and hypothesis?

- What claim(s) does the source make and how is each supported?

- Does the source include counterarguments that you should address?

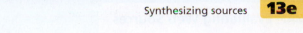

- How credible and persuasive is the evidence? Does it represent alternative views fairly? Will it convince your audience?

- Will you need to change your thesis to account for this information?

- What quotations from this source might you want to use?

As you read and take notes on your sources, keep in mind that you will need to present data and sources clearly to other readers so that they can understand your point.

13e Synthesizing sources

Analysis requires you to take apart something complex (such as an article in a scholarly journal) and look closely at each part to understand how the parts fit together (or don't!). Academic writing also calls for **synthesis**—grouping similar pieces of information together and looking for patterns and themes, or similarities and differences—so you can put your sources and your own knowledge together in an original argument. Synthesis is the flip side of analysis: you assemble the parts into a new whole.

To synthesize sources for a research project, try the following tips, which continue on page 106:

- **Don't just grab a quotation and move on.** Rather, read the material carefully (see Chapter 8). A national study of first-year college writing found that student writers often used sources they hadn't read carefully enough to realize they were not really relevant to their point. Another study showed that some students tended to use quotations *only* from the first one or two pages of a source, suggesting that they may not really know how relevant it is.

- **Understand the purpose of each source.** Make sure the source is relevant and necessary to your argument.

- **Determine the important ideas in each source.** Take notes on each source (13f). Identify and summarize the key ideas.

- **Formulate a position.** Figure out how the pieces fit together. Look for patterns and themes, similarities and differences. Consider multiple perspectives on the topic before deciding what you want to say.

1 Determine the **sponsor or publisher** of the source. See what information you can get from the URL. The domain names for government sites may end in *.gov* or *.mil* and for educational sites in *.edu*. The ending *.org* may—but does not always—indicate a nonprofit organization. Also check the header and footer, which may identify the sponsor. The web page on p. 103 is a *.org* site sponsored by The American College of Pediatricians with a publication date of 2020.

2 Look for an **About page** or a link to a home page for background information on the sponsor. Is a mission statement included? What are the sponsoring organization's purpose and point of view? Is the mission statement balanced? What is the purpose of the site (to inform, to persuade, to advocate, to advertise, or something else)?

3 Conduct a new search to **read laterally**. Search for the author, publisher, or sponsor to see what others say about the **credibility** and **accuracy** of the target site. A web search may lead you to a list of results that call the organization into question. In the example on p. 103, articles by the Southern Poverty Law Center (a civil rights group), Wikipedia, and *Psychology Today* point out the conservative bias and anti-LGBTQ positions of the target site.

4 Follow links to read more, gather a fuller perspective, **confirm (or reject) claims**, and **check facts** presented on the target site. From the search result sites, what can you tell about the target source's point of view, **stance, goals,** and **target audience**?

Return to the target site and weigh what you have learned from your lateral reading; then determine whether the target site fits your purpose and goals and meets high standards for credibility.

Target Site

2 **About Page**

1 **Sponsor or Publisher**

3 **Search Results**

4 **Search Result Site**

SOURCE MAP: Evaluating Articles

Determine the relevance of the source.

1 Look for an **abstract** or summary of the article. Is this source directly related to your research? Does it provide useful information and insights? Will readers consider it persuasive support?

Determine the credibility of the publication.

2 Consider the **title**. Words such as *Journal*, *Review*, and *Quarterly* may indicate that the periodical is a scholarly source (see 12c). Most research projects rely on authorities in a particular field, whose work usually appears in scholarly journals.

3 Try to determine the **publisher or sponsor**. The journal on p. 105 is published by the University of Illinois. Academic presses such as this one generally review articles carefully before publishing them. Also do a web search to see what others are saying about this article, publisher, or sponsor. For more on lateral reading, see 13c.

Determine the credibility of the author.

4 Evaluate the **author's credentials**. In this case, they are given in a note that indicates the author is a college professor.

Determine the currency of the article.

5 Look at the **publication date**, and think about whether your topic and your credibility depend on your use of very current sources.

Determine the accuracy of the article.

6 Look at the **sources cited** by the author of the article. Here, they are listed in a bibliography. Ask yourself whether the works the author has cited seem credible and current. Are any of these works cited in other articles you've considered?

In addition, consider the following questions:

- What is the article's stance or point of view? What are the author's goals? What does the author want you to know or believe?

- How does this source fit in with your other sources? Does any of the information it provides contradict or challenge other sources?

ELIZABETH TUCKER

Changing Concepts of Childhood: Children's Folklore Scholarship since the Late Nineteenth Century

1 Abstract

This essay examines children's folklore scholarship from the late nineteenth century to the present, tracing key concepts from the Gilded Age to the contemporary era. These concepts reflect significant social, cultural, political, and scientific changes. From the "savage child" to the "secret-keeping child," the "magic-making child," the "cerebral child," the "taboo-breaking child," the "monstrous child," and others, scholarly representations of young people have close connections to the eras in which they developed. Nineteenth-century children's folklore scholarship relied on evolutionism; now evolutionary biology provides a basis for children's folklore research, so we have re-entered familiar territory.

407

SINCE 1977, WHEN THE American Folklore Society decided to form a new section for scholars interested in young people's traditions, I have belonged to the Children's Folklore Section. It has been a joy to contribute to this dynamic organization, which

which mentions

's and my studies lthough my word pact on children

).

Abrahams, Roger. 1976. The Complex Relations of Simple Forms. *Folklore Genres*, ed. Dan Ben-Amos, pp. 193–214. Austin: University of Texas Press.
Anglund, Joan Walsh. 2003. *Little Angels' Alphabet of Love*. New York: Simon and Schuster.
Aries, Philippe. 1962. *Centuries of Childhood: A Social History of Family Life*. New York: Vintage.
Beresin, Anna R. 2010. *Recess Battles: Playing, Fighting, and Storytelling*. Jackson: University Press of Mississippi.
Berres, Allen. 2002. "Everybody Is Their Enemy": Goths, Spooky Kids, and the American School Shooting Panic. *Children's Folklore Review* 24(1–2):43–54.

children's folklore scholarship took shape, I consider ours and to be light years away from nineteenth-century scholars' research but may find, when reading nineteenth-century works, that we have stayed fairly close to our scholarly "home base."

Before examining concepts of childhood that have developed, I will offer a working definition of childhood and trace the beginning of childhood studies. I will also summarize children's folklore scholarly work during the past thirty-four years. According to the *OED*, childhood means "the state or stage of life of a child; the time during which one is a child; the time from birth to puberty" (2011). Scholars of childhood tend to draw a line between childhood and adolescence, which begins at puberty and follows pre-adolescence. The folklore

Childhood and

Press.

Appleton.

Lake City:

re Review

ore Society. Chil-

's Folklore Review

niversity Press of

2 Title of Publication

Journal of American Folklore

4 Author's Credentials

ELIZABETH TUCKER is Professor of English at Binghamton University

Journal of American Folklore 125(498):389–410

3 Publisher

Board of Trustees of the University of Illinois

5 Publication Date

2012

6 Sources Cited

ial Sciences

ts and Cul-

Macmillan. ponsibility.

and Humanities 3:145–60.

Carpenter, Carole H. 2011. Why Children's Studies? ca/pdf/papers/Carole.Carp
Francis. 1896. *The Child and*
Fay. 1990. *Parenting with* Pinon Press.
Conrad, JoAnn. 2002. The War on Youth: A Modern Oedipal Tragedy. *Children's Folklore Review* 24(1–2):33–42.
Crandall, Bryan Ripley. 2009. *Cow Project*. bryanripleycrandall.files.wordpress.com/2009/05/slbscow-project.pdf.
Darwin, Charles. 1859. *On the Origin of Species by Means of Natural Selection, or the Preservation of Favoured Races in the Struggle for Life* (1st edition). London: John Murray.
Dégh, Linda. 2001. *Legend and Belief*. Bloomington: Indiana University Press.
Dorson, Richard M. 1968. *The British Folklorists: A History*. Chicago: University of Chicago Press.
Douglas, Norman. [1916] 1968. *London Street Games*. Detroit: Singing Tree Press.

- **Gather evidence to support your position.** Consider using paraphrases, summaries, or direct quotations from your sources as evidence (13g), and don't forget your own personal experience or prior knowledge.

- **Consider alternative viewpoints.** Recognize and respect valid perspectives that differ from yours, and try to understand them fully before explaining why you don't accept them.

- **Identify patterns and themes** that run through several or even all of your sources. What do these patterns suggest about your topic? Where do your sources agree—and where do they disagree, and why?

Write out a page or two in which you answer the questions above and show how your sources, taken together, can add to and/or support your argument. Be careful to avoid simply summarizing all of your research. Try to weave the various sources together rather than discuss each of your sources one by one.

Even after you have fully evaluated a source, take time to look at how well the source works in your specific rhetorical situation. (If you change the focus of your work after you have begun doing research, be especially careful to check whether your sources still fit.)

13f Keeping track of sources

Because sources are so readily available, it's sometimes hard to keep them under control, and you end up with snippets, bits and pieces, and links that you no longer remember or can identify. You will save time in the long run, then, if you have a system for keeping careful track of sources you want to use in your research.

- Not many researchers print out their sources. Often you can use the "save page as PDF" function in your browser to save a web-based source. You will want to annotate the source to identify key passages and vocabulary and ask critical questions. Avoid just copying and pasting passages from online sources into a Word or Google doc unless you also copy accurate publication information.

- If you take notes on a source, record the author, title, place and date of publication, volume and issue, and page number. You will need this information for your bibliography or list of works cited, so getting the information down will save you a lot of time later on.

- For online resources, make sure you have the accurate URL so you can find the source again easily.

- Set up a special computer file for your sources, and arrange them in a way most convenient to you—alphabetically by author, according to topics or points in your research essay, and so on.

13g Working with quotations, paraphrases, and summaries

Whatever method you use to capture and annotate your sources, you should make sure that for each one you (1) record enough information to help you recall the major points of the source; (2) put the information in the form in which you are most likely to incorporate it into your project, whether a quotation, paraphrase, or summary; and (3) note all information you will need to cite the source accurately. Keep a working bibliography that includes citation information for each source in a file or another format that you can rearrange and alter as your project takes shape. Doing so will simplify the process of documenting sources for your final project. For every note or entry you make, be sure to include the author's name, the title, and a page number (if available).

Quoting   Quoting involves bringing a source's exact words into your text. Limit your use of quotations to those necessary to your thesis or memorable for your readers. To guard against unintentional plagiarism, photocopy or print out sources and identify the needed quotations right on the page.

- If you need to copy a quotation into your notes, make sure that all punctuation, capitalization, and spelling are exactly as in the original.

- Enclose the quotation in quotation marks (44a).

- Use brackets if you introduce words of your own into the quotation or make changes in it (45b). Use ellipses if you omit words from the quotation (45f). If you later incorporate the quotation into your research project, copy it from the note precisely, including brackets and ellipses.

Quotation-Style Note

Running a socially conscious business •———— Subject heading

Church, "The Wave of Social Entrepreneurship" •———— Author and
Stanford University (online podcast)   short title of
                                                 source (no page
"Social entrepreneurs look at their businesses   number for
as nine parts cause, one part business. In the   online source)
beginning, it needs to be nine parts business,
one part cause, because if the business doesn't
stay around long enough because it can't make
it, you can't do anything about the cause."

                                                Indication that
(Quotation) •———— note is direct
                                                quotation

Paraphrasing   When you paraphrase, you're putting brief material from an author (including major and minor points, usually in the order they are presented) into *your own words and sentence structures.*

- Include all main points and any important details from the original source in the same order in which the author presents them, but in your own words. Put the original source aside to avoid following the wording too closely.

- If you want to include any language from the original, enclose it in quotation marks.

- Save your comments, elaborations, or reactions for another note.

- Recheck to be sure that the words and sentence structures are your own and that they express the author's meaning accurately.

- Finally, identify this note as a paraphrase.

The following examples of paraphrases resemble the original material either too little or too much.

ORIGINAL

Just in the last ten or fifteen years, nearly everyone started to carry a little device called a smartphone on their person all the time that's suitable for algorithmic behavior modification. A lot of us are also using related devices called smart speakers on our kitchen counters or in our car dashboards. We're being tracked and measured constantly, and receiving engineered feedback all the time. We're being hypnotized little by little by technicians we can't see, for purposes we don't know. We're all lab animals now. . . . This book argues in ten ways that what has become suddenly normal—pervasive surveillance and constant, subtle manipulation—is unethical, cruel, dangerous, and inhumane. Dangerous? Oh yes, because who knows who's going to use that power, and for what?

—Jaron Lanier, *Ten Arguments for Deleting Your Social Media Accounts Right Now* (pp. 5, 7–8)

UNACCEPTABLE PARAPHRASE: STRAYING FROM THE AUTHOR'S IDEAS

Lanier argues that today our many digital devices are controlling and manipulating how we act. The constant use of these devices allows them to gather data on much of what we do and say without our even knowing it. But this constant surveillance is damaging and harmful. In addition, these devices could even affect our brains in negative ways.

This paraphrase starts off well enough, but in the last sentence veers off into the writer's own ideas about the danger devices pose to the brain.

UNACCEPTABLE PARAPHRASE: USING THE AUTHOR'S WORDS

Lanier argues that in recent years almost everyone has a smartphone and other devices that control us and modify our behavior, tracking us constantly. Yet we don't even realize that we are being hypnotized and treated like animals in labs. Lanier offers ten ways in which this new normal is actually unethical and dangerous.

Because the underlined phrases are either borrowed from the original without quotation marks or changed only superficially, this paraphrase plagiarizes.

UNACCEPTABLE PARAPHRASE: USING THE AUTHOR'S SENTENCE STRUCTURES

Lanier argues that the constant presence of cell phones and other digital devices controls and manipulates us through tracking our words and movements though we don't even know it. <u>We're mesmerized one step at a time by people we don't know, for uses we can't explain.</u> Lanier offers ten ways in which such control is unethical and dangerous.

Here the second sentence uses the same structure as the fourth sentence in the original passage.

ACCEPTABLE PARAPHRASE: IN THE STUDENT WRITER'S OWN WORDS

Jaron Lanier argues that most people today have cell phones and other digital devices that control and manipulate them without their knowledge, gathering data on our movements, our thoughts, and our words. Lanier illustrates this problem, which he sees as severe, by describing in detail ten reasons to show that the current situation is untenable, unacceptable, and a chilling misuse of power.

Summarizing   A **summary** is a significantly shortened version of a passage or even a whole chapter, article, film, or other work that captures main ideas *in your own words.* Unlike a paraphrase, a summary uses just enough information to record the points you wish to emphasize.

- Put the original aside to write your summary. If you later decide to include language from the original, enclose it in quotation marks. Label your work "summary."

- Recheck to be sure you have captured the author's meaning and that the words are entirely your own.

Language, Culture, and Context

Identifying Sources

While some language communities and cultures expect audiences to recognize the sources of important documents and texts, thereby eliminating the need to cite them directly, academic conventions for writing in the United States call for careful attribution of any quoted, paraphrased, or summarized material. When in doubt, explicitly identify your sources.

Summary Note

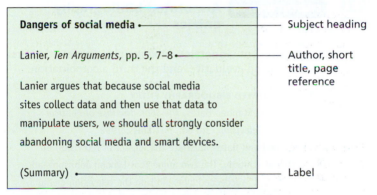

Dangers of social media ●	Subject heading
Lanier, *Ten Arguments*, pp. 5, 7–8 ●	Author, short title, page reference
Lanier argues that because social media sites collect data and then use that data to manipulate users, we should all strongly consider abandoning social media and smart devices.	
(Summary) ●	Label

13h Creating an annotated bibliography

You may want to annotate your working bibliography, or your instructor may ask you to submit some annotated bibliography entries as part of your research project. Annotating sources can help you understand and remember what the source says. Here are some tips for doing so:

- Decide whether you will prepare a descriptive or an evaluative annotated entry. A descriptive one sticks to a clear, concise summary of the source's content; an evaluative one adds your assessment of the source's usefulness.

- Decide if the source is worth annotating—that is, whether you will use it in your research project. If so, read the source carefully, being open and fair but also critical. Identify the major points the author makes and what evidence is offered in support. Also check out the author(s) to make sure that they are reliable and credible.

- Write a brief, succinct descriptive summary of the source's content, in your own words. Include major points and claims.

- If you are writing an evaluative entry, add your assessment of the source's usefulness.

13i **STUDENT WRITING** Annotated bibliography entries

Here are three student annotated bibliography entries—the first descriptive, the second evaluative, and the third a combination:

DESCRIPTIVE ANNOTATED BIBLIOGRAPHY ENTRY

Diamond, Edwin, and Stephen Bates. *The Spot: The Rise of Political Advertising on Television.* 3rd ed., MIT Press, 1992.

> Diamond and Bates illustrate the impact of television on political strategy. The two argue that Lyndon Johnson's ad "Daisy Girl" succeeded by exploiting the television medium, using violent images and sounds and the words "nuclear bomb" to sway viewers' emotions. Emphasizing Johnson's control over the production of the ad, the authors illustrate the role the ad played in portraying Goldwater as a warmonger.

EVALUATIVE ANNOTATED BIBLIOGRAPHY ENTRY

Pearson, Taylor. "Why You Should Fear Your Toaster More Than Nuclear Power." *Everything's an Argument with Readings,* 7th ed., by Andrea A. Lunsford and John J. Ruszkiewicz, Bedford/St. Martin's, 2016, pp. 174–79.

> The author argues that since the dangers of nuclear power, such as waste, radiation, and death, are less than those of

energy sources we rely on today, nuclear plants represent the most practical way to generate power while still reducing greenhouse gases. The article is well written and provides facts and examples related to nuclear energy, but it doesn't identify its sources. As a result, I will need to corroborate the facts with information from other sources.

COMBINED DESCRIPTIVE AND EVALUATIVE ANNOTATED BIBLIOGRAPHY ENTRY

Dávila, Arlene. "Empowered Culture? New York City's Empowerment Zone and the Selling of El Barrio." *The Annals of the American Academy of Political and Social Science*, vol. 594, no. 1, July 2004, pp. 49–64. *JSTOR*, www.jstor.org/stable/4127693.

> NYU sociology professor Arlene Dávila explains that programs designed to stimulate tourism in Harlem have ignored Latino/a residents of East Harlem, known as *El Barrio*. Rather than blaming leaders of Harlem's Black neighborhoods, which she suggests are seen as more marketable to tourists, she questions the anti-Latino bias of the economic policies of the Upper Manhattan Empowerment Zone. Dávila calls for debate about the problems that come with treating culture as a commodity. Although the article is older, Dávila's argument is valuable. She provides a counterpoint to the idea that economic initiatives have benefited all Harlemites.

14 Integrating Sources and Avoiding Plagiarism

As a writer and thinker, you have been influenced by what you have already read and experienced—and this includes your sources. So you will need to know how best to integrate and acknowledge the work of others in your own research. Integrating sources seamlessly into your writing means not letting them take over your writing or drown out your voice but rather using them to add support to your own good ideas. And to acknowledge your sources fully calls on you to understand current definitions of plagiarism (which have changed over time and differ from culture to culture) as well as the concept of intellectual property—works protected by copyright or by alternatives such as a Creative Commons license—so you can give credit where credit is due. An age of instant copying and linking may someday lead to revised understandings in the United States about who can "own" a text. But in college today, you should cite your sources carefully and systematically to avoid plagiarism, the use of someone else's words and ideas as if they were your own.

14a Using sources ethically

If you've ever had your words taken out of context or twisted in some way that doesn't represent what you really said, then you know how it feels to have a source (in this case, you!) used unethically. As you begin to work with your sources, keep these tips in mind:

- Have respect for the author's intentions; don't misrepresent them.
- Don't ignore sources that disagree with you; rather, take them into consideration.
- Don't take the author's words out of context, and be careful not to lead readers to interpret the source favorably or unfavorably. For example, use neutral language such as "the author states" rather than "the author badgers" or "the author falsely claims."
- Avoid "selective" quoting that chooses only phrases or passages that agree with your point of view while ignoring others that oppose your perspective.
- Finally, never use an author's words or ideas as if they were your own: that's plagiarism.

14b Integrating quotations, paraphrases, and summaries

Integrate source materials into your writing with care to ensure that the integrated materials make grammatical and logical sense and that your readers understand which words and ideas came from your sources.

Quotations Because your research project is primarily your own work, limit your use of quotations to those necessary to your thesis or especially memorable for your readers. Use an author's exact words when those words are so memorable or express a point so well that you cannot improve or shorten it without weakening it, when the author is an authority whose opinion supports your ideas, or when an author disagrees profoundly with others in the field.

Short quotations should run in with your text, enclosed by quotation marks. Longer quotations should be set off from the text (44a). Integrate all quotations into your text so that they flow smoothly and clearly into the surrounding sentences. Be sure that the sentence containing the quotation is grammatically complete, especially if you incorporate a quotation into your own words.

Signal phrases Introduce the quotation with a signal phrase or signal **verb**, such as those underlined in these examples.

- As Eudora Welty notes, "Learning stamps you with its moments. Childhood's learning," she continues, "is made up of moments. It isn't steady. It's a pulse" (9).
- In her essay, Haraway strongly opposes those who condemn technology outright, arguing that we must not indulge in a "demonology of technology" (181).

Choose a signal verb that is appropriate to the idea you are expressing and that accurately characterizes the author's viewpoint. Other signal verbs include words such as *acknowledges, agrees, asserts, believes, claims, concludes, describes, disagrees, explains, objects, offers, reports, reveals, says, suggests,* and *writes.*

When you follow Modern Language Association (**MLA**) style, used in the examples in this chapter, put verbs in signal phrases in the **present tense**. For *Chicago* style, use the present tense (or use the **past tense** to emphasize a point made in the past).

If you are using American Psychological Association (**APA**) style to describe research results, use the past tense or the **present perfect tense** (*the study showed* or *the study has shown*) in your signal phrase. Use the present tense to explain implications of research (*for future research, these findings suggest*).

When using the Council of Science Editors (**CSE**) style, in general use the present tense for research reports and the past tense to describe specific methods or observations, or to cite published research.

Brackets and ellipses In direct quotations, enclose in brackets any words you change or add, and indicate any deletions with ellipsis points.

▶ "There is something wrong in the [Three Mile Island] area," one farmer told the Nuclear Regulatory Commission after the plant accident ("Legacy" 33).

▶ Economist John Kenneth Galbraith pointed out that "large corporations cannot afford to compete with one another. . . . In a truly competitive market someone loses" (Key 17).

Be careful that any changes you make in a quotation do not alter its meaning. Use brackets and ellipses sparingly; too many make for difficult reading and might suggest that you have removed some of the context for the quotation.

Paraphrases and summaries Introduce paraphrases and summaries clearly, usually with a signal phrase that includes the author of the source, as the underlined words in this example indicate.

▶ Professor of linguistics Deborah Tannen illustrates how communication between women and men breaks down and then suggests that a full awareness of "genderlects" can improve relationships (297).

EXERCISE 14.1 Read the brief original passage that follows. Then decide which attempts to quote or paraphrase it are acceptable and which are not.

> The strange thing about plagiarism is that it's almost always pointless. The writers who stand accused, from Laurence Sterne to Samuel Taylor Coleridge to Susan Sontag, tend to be more talented than the writers they lift from.
>
> — Malcolm Jones, "Have You Read This Story Somewhere?"

1. According to Malcolm Jones, writers accused of plagiarism are always better writers than those they are supposed to have plagiarized.

2. According to Malcolm Jones, writers accused of plagiarism "tend to be more talented than the writers they lift from."

3. Plagiarism is usually pointless, says writer Malcolm Jones.

4. Those who stand accused of plagiarism, such as historian Stephen Ambrose, tend to be better writers than those whose work they use.

5. According to Malcolm Jones, "plagiarism is . . . almost always pointless."

14c Integrating visuals and media

Choose your visuals and media wisely, whether you use video, audio, photographs, illustrations, charts and graphs, or any other kinds of images. Integrate all visuals and media smoothly into your text.

- **Does each visual or media file make a strong contribution to the message?** Purely decorative visuals and media may weaken the power of your writing.
- **Is each fair to your subject?** An obviously biased perspective may seem unfair to your audience.
- **Is each appropriate for your audience?**
- **Have you made sure not to alter or manipulate the visual in any way?**

While it is considered "fair use" to use such materials in an essay or other project for a college class, once that project is published on the web, you might infringe on copyright protections if you do not ask the copyright holder for permission to use the visual or media file. If you have questions about whether your work might infringe on copyright, ask your instructor for help.

Like quotations, paraphrases, and summaries, visuals and media need to be introduced and commented on in some way.

- Refer to the visual or media element in the text *before* it appears: . . . *as figure 3 illustrates.*
- Explain or comment on the relevance of the visual or media file. This explanation can appear *after* the visual.
- Check the documentation system you are using to make sure you label and caption visual and media elements appropriately; MLA, for instance, asks that you number (***Table 1***) and title (*Average Rainfall by Region*) all tables and figures.
- If you are posting your work publicly, make sure you have permission to use any copyrighted visuals.

14d Knowing which sources to acknowledge

As you do your research, remember the distinction between materials that require acknowledgment (in in-text citations, footnotes, or endnotes; and in the list of works cited or bibliography) and those that do not.

While you need to prepare accurate and thorough citations in most formal academic assignments, much of the writing you do outside of college will not require formal citations. In writing on social media, for example, or even in highly respected newspapers and magazines like *The New York Times, Black Enterprise,* or *The Atlantic*, providing a link is often the only "citation" the authors need. So learn to be flexible: use formal citations when called for in formal college work, and weave in and acknowledge your sources more informally in most out-of-college writing.

Materials that do not require acknowledgment   You do not usually need to cite a source for the following:

- Common knowledge—facts that most readers are already familiar with

- Facts available in a wide variety of sources, such as encyclopedias, almanacs, or textbooks

- Your own findings from field research. You should, however, acknowledge people you interview as individuals rather than as part of a survey.

Materials that require acknowledgment   You should cite all of your other sources to be certain to avoid plagiarism. Follow the documentation style required (see Chapters 16–19), and list the source in a bibliography or list of works cited. Be especially careful to cite the following:

- Sources for quotations, paraphrases, and summaries that you include

- Facts not widely known or arguable assertions

- All visuals from any source, including your own artwork, photographs you have taken, and graphs or tables you create from data found in a source

- Any help provided by a friend, an instructor, or another person

14e   Avoiding plagiarism

Academic integrity enables us to trust those sources we use and to demonstrate that our own work is equally trustworthy. Plagiarism is especially damaging to one's academic integrity, whether it involves inaccurate or incomplete acknowledgment of one's sources in citations—sometimes called unintentional plagiarism—or deliberate plagiarism that is intended to pass off one writer's work as another's.

Whether or not it is intentional, plagiarism can have serious consequences. Students who plagiarize may fail the course or be expelled. Others who have plagiarized, even inadvertently, have had degrees revoked or have been stripped of positions or awards.

Unintentional plagiarism   If your paraphrase is too close to the wording or sentence structure of a source (even if you identify the source); if after a quotation you do not identify the source (even if you include the quotation marks); or if you fail to indicate clearly the source of an idea that you did not come up with on your own, you may be accused of plagiarism even if your intent was not to plagiarize. This inaccurate or incomplete acknowledgment of one's sources often results either from carelessness or from not learning how to borrow material properly.

Take responsibility for your research and for acknowledging all sources accurately. To guard against unintentional plagiarism, photocopy or print out sources and identify the needed quotations right on the copy. You can also insert footnotes or endnotes into the text as you write.

Deliberate plagiarism   Deliberate plagiarism—such as handing in an essay written by a friend or purchased or downloaded from an essay-writing company; cutting and pasting passages directly from

 Language, Culture, and Context

Thinking about Plagiarism as a Cultural Concept

Many cultures, such as those of China and Japan, do not recognize Western notions of plagiarism, which rest on a belief that language and ideas are property that can be owned. Indeed, in many cultures and communities, using the words and ideas of others without attribution is considered a sign of deep respect as well as an indication of knowledge. In academic writing in the United States, you should credit all materials except those that are common knowledge, that are available in a wide variety of sources, or that are your own creations or your own findings from field research.

source materials without marking them with quotation marks and acknowledging their sources; failing to credit the source of an idea or concept in your text—is what most people think of when they hear the word *plagiarism.* This form of plagiarism is particularly troubling because it represents dishonesty and deception: those who intentionally plagiarize present someone else's hard work as their own and claim knowledge they really don't have, thus deceiving their readers.

Deliberate plagiarism is also fairly simple to spot: your instructor will be well acquainted with your writing and likely to notice any sudden shifts in the style or quality of your work. In addition, by typing a few words from a project into a search engine, your instructor can identify "matches" very easily.

15 Writing a Research Project

When you are working on a research project, there comes a time to draw the strands of your research together and articulate your conclusions in writing.

15a Drafting your text, including illustrations

Once you have all the information you think you'll need, try arranging your notes and visuals to identify connections, main ideas, and possible organization. You may also want to develop a working outline, a storyboard, or an idea map. And don't forget to figure out where you will place illustrations such as visual images, video clips, and so on.

For almost all research projects, drafting should begin well before the deadline in case you need to gather more information or do more drafting. Begin drafting wherever you feel most confident. If you have an idea for an introduction, begin there.

Working title and introduction   The title and introduction set the stage for what is to come. Ideally, the title announces the subject in an intriguing or memorable way. The introduction should draw readers in and provide any background they will need to understand your discussion. Consider opening with a question, a vivid image, or a provocative statement.

Language, Culture, and Context

Asking Experienced Writers to Review a Thesis

You might find it helpful to ask one or two classmates who have more experience with the particular type of academic writing you are doing to look at your explicit thesis statement. Ask if the thesis is as direct and clear as it can be, and revise accordingly.

Conclusion   A good conclusion helps readers know what they have learned. One effective strategy is to begin with a reference to your thesis and then expand to a more general conclusion that reminds readers why your discussion is significant. Try to conclude with something that will have an impact—but avoid sounding preachy.

15b   Reviewing and revising a research project

Once you've completed your draft, reread it slowly and carefully. As you do so, reconsider the project's purpose and audience, your stance and thesis, and the evidence you have gathered. Then, ask others to read and respond to your draft. (For more on reviewing and revising, see Chapter 5.)

15c   Preparing a list of sources

Once you have a final draft with your source materials in place, you are ready to prepare your list of sources. Create an entry for each source used in your final draft, consulting your notes and working bibliography. Then double-check your draft to make sure that you have listed every source mentioned in the in-text citations or notes and that you have omitted any sources not cited in your project. (For guidelines on documentation styles, see Chapters 16–19.)

15d   Editing and proofreading

When you have revised your draft, check grammar, usage, spelling, punctuation, and mechanics. Proofread the final version of your project, and carefully consider the advice of spell checkers and grammar checkers before accepting it. (For more information on editing, see 5c.)

15e STUDENT WRITING Outline of a research project

Student writer Julia Sakowitz drew up a working outline of her ideas as she was conducting research about tourism in Harlem. She thought this simple structure would help her focus on the information she still needed to find.

Thesis statement: Although there is no simple solution for tourism in Harlem, small locally owned tourist businesses have the potential to more directly and widely benefit the community while causing fewer social and economic problems.

I. Tourism growth

    A. Description of Upper Manhattan Empowerment Zone (UMEZ)

    B. How has UMEZ encouraged tourism in Harlem?

II. Benefits and disadvantages of tourism

    A. Economic benefits (statistics)

    B. Research "gentrification"

III. Tour companies

    A. Harlem-based vs. outside tour companies

    B. Interviews with company owners

Documentation

16 **MLA Style** 124

List of examples: In-text citations in MLA style 130

List of examples: Works cited in MLA style 136

17 **APA Style** 174

List of examples: In-text citations in APA style 178

List of examples: References in APA style 182

18 *Chicago* **Style** 212

List of examples: Notes and bibliographic entries in
Chicago style 216

19 **CSE Style** 235

List of examples: References in CSE style 238

16 MLA Style

Many fields in the humanities ask students to follow Modern Language Association (MLA) style to format essays and to document various kinds of sources. This chapter introduces MLA guidelines. For further reference, consult the *MLA Handbook*, Ninth Edition (2021).

16a Understanding MLA citation style

Why does academic work call for very careful citation practices when writing for the general public may not? The answer is that readers of your academic work expect source citations for several reasons:

- Source citations demonstrate that you've done your homework on your topic and that you are a part of the conversation surrounding it. Careful citation shows your readers what you know, where you stand, and what you think is important.

- Source citations show your readers that you understand the need to give credit when you make use of someone else's intellectual property. Especially in academic writing, when it's better to be safe than sorry, include a citation for any source you think you might need to cite. (See 14d.)

- Source citations give explicit directions to guide readers who want to look for themselves at the works you're using.

The guidelines for MLA style help you with this last purpose, giving you instructions on exactly what information to include in your citation and how to format that information.

16b Considering the context of your sources

New kinds of sources crop up regularly. As the *MLA Handbook* confirms, there are often several "correct" ways to cite a source, so you will need to think carefully about *your own context* for using the source so you can identify the pieces of information that you should emphasize or include and any other information that might be helpful to your readers.

Elements of MLA citations The first step is to identify elements that are commonly found in most works that writers cite.

Author and title The first two elements, both of which are needed for many sources, are the author's name and the title of the work. Each of these elements is followed by a period.

> **Author. Title.**

Even in these elements, your context is important. The author of a novel may be obvious, but who is the "author" of a television episode? Is it the director? The writer? The show's creator? The star? The answer may depend on the focus of your own work. If an actor's performance is central to your discussion, then MLA guidelines ask you to identify the actor as the author. If the plot is your focus, you might name the writer of the episode as the author.

Container The next step is to identify elements of what the MLA calls the "container" for the work. The context in which you are discussing the source and the context in which you find the source will help you determine what counts as a container in each case. If you watch a movie in a theater, you won't identify a separate container after the film title. But if you watch the same movie on a streaming service such as *Netflix*, the container title is the name of the website or application on which you watched the movie. If you read an article in a print journal, the first container will be the journal that the article appears in. If you read it online, the journal may also be part of a second, larger container, such as a database. Thinking about sources as nested in larger containers may help you visualize how a citation works.

The elements you may include in the "container" part of your citation include the following, in this order: the title of the larger container, if it's different from the title of the work; the names of any contributors such as editors or translators; the version or edition; the volume and issue numbers or other numbers such as season and episode; the publisher or sponsor; the date of publication; and a location such as the page numbers, DOI, permalink, or URL. These elements are separated by commas, and the end of the container is marked with a period.

> **Author. Title. Container title, contributor names, version or edition,**
> **number(s), publisher, date, location.**

Most sources won't include all these pieces of information, so include only the elements that are available and relevant to create an acceptable citation. If you need a second container—for instance, if you are citing an article from a journal you found in a database—you simply add it after the first one, beginning with the container title and including as many of the same container elements as you can find. The rest of this chapter offers many examples of how elements and containers are combined to create citations.

Example from student writing One student researching messaging technologies found a potentially useful journal article by searching a library database, Academic Search Premier, through his library's website. The journal is the first container of the article, and the database is the second container.

A complete citation for this article would look like this:

Counts, Scott, and Karen E. Fisher. "Mobile Social Networking as
    Information Ground: A Case Study." *Library and Information Science*
    Research, vol. 32, no. 2, Apr. 2010, pp. 98–115. *Academic Search*
    Premier, https://doi.org/10.1016/j.lisr.2009.10.003.

Notice that the first container includes just four relevant elements—the journal title, number (here, that means the volume and issue numbers), date, and page numbers; and the second container includes just two—the database title and location.

Types of sources Refer to the lists of examples for MLA style in sections 16d and 16e to locate guidelines on citing various types of sources, including print books, print periodicals (journals, magazines, and newspapers), digital written-word sources, and other sources (films, artwork) that consist mainly of material other than written words. A digital version of a source may include updates or corrections that the print version of the same work lacks, so MLA guidelines ask you to indicate where you found the source. If you can't find a model exactly like the source you've selected, see the checklist in 16e.

Parts of citations MLA citations appear in two parts—a brief in-text citation in the body of your written text, and a full citation in the list of works cited, to which the in-text citation directs readers. A basic in-text citation includes the author's name and the page number (for a print source), but many variations on this format are discussed in 16d.

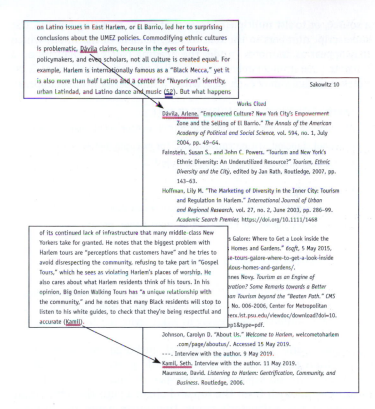

on Latino issues in East Harlem, or El Barrio, led her to surprising conclusions about the UMEZ policies. Commodifying ethnic cultures is problematic, Dávila claims, because in the eyes of tourists, policymakers, and even scholars, not all culture is created equal. For example, Harlem is internationally famous as a "Black Mecca," yet it is also more than half Latino and a center for "Nuyorican" identity, urban Latindad, and Latino dance and music (52). But what happens

Sakowitz 10

Works Cited

Dávila, Arlene. "Empowered Culture? New York City's Empowerment Zone and the Selling of El Barrio." *The Annals of the American Academy of Political and Social Science,* vol. 594, no. 1, July 2004, pp. 49–64.

Fainstein, Susan S., and John C. Powers. "Tourism and New York's Ethnic Diversity: An Underutilized Resource?" *Tourism, Ethnic Diversity and the City,* edited by Jan Rath, Routledge, 2007, pp. 143–63.

Hoffman, Lily M. "The Marketing of Diversity in the Inner City: Tourism and Regulation in Harlem." *International Journal of Urban and Regional Research,* vol. 27, no. 2, June 2003, pp. 286–99. *Academic Search Premier,* https://doi.org/10.1111/1468

of its continued lack of infrastructure that many middle-class New Yorkers take for granted. He notes that the biggest problem with Harlem tours are "perceptions that customers have" and he tries to avoid disrespecting the community, refusing to take part in "Gospel Tours," which he sees as violating Harlem's places of worship. He also cares about what Harlem residents think of his tours. In his opinion, Big Onion Walking Tours has "a unique relationship with the community," and he notes that many Black residents will stop to listen to his white guides, to check that they're being respectful and accurate (Kamil).

s Galore: Where to Get a Look inside the Homes and Gardens." *6sqft,* 5 May 2015, se-tours-galore-where-to-get-a-look-inside ulous-homes-and-gardens/.

nnes Novy. *Tourism as an Engine of eration? Some Remarks towards a Better an Tourism beyond the "Beaten Path."* CMS No. 006-2006, Center for Metropolitan eerx.ist.psu.edu/viewdoc/download?doi=10. ep1&type=pdf.

Johnson, Carolyn D. "About Us." *Welcome to Harlem,* welcometoharlem .com/page/aboutus/. Accessed 15 May 2019.

---. Interview with the author. 9 May 2019.

Kamil, Seth. Interview with the author. 11 May 2019.

Maurrasse, David. *Listening to Harlem: Gentrification, Community, and Business.* Routledge, 2006.

In the text of her research essay (see 16f), Julia Sakowitz paraphrases material from a journal article by anthropologist Arlene Dávila. As shown, she cites the article page on which the original information appears in a parenthetical reference that points readers to the entry for "Dávila, Arlene" in her list of works cited. She also cites portions of a personal interview she has conducted with Seth Kamil, which has no page numbers. These examples show just two of the many ways to cite sources using in-text citations and a list of works cited. You'll need to make case-by-case decisions based on the types of sources you include.

Explanatory notes MLA citation style asks you to include explanatory notes for information that doesn't readily fit into your text but is needed for clarification or further explanation. In addition, MLA permits bibliographic notes for information about or evaluation of a source, or to list multiple sources that relate to a single point. Use superscript numbers in the text to refer readers to the notes, which may appear as endnotes (under the heading *Notes* or *Endnotes* on a separate page immediately before the list of works cited) or as footnotes at the bottom of each page where a superscript number appears.

EXAMPLE OF SUPERSCRIPT NUMBER IN TEXT

Although such communication relies on the written word, many messagers disregard standard writing conventions. For example, below is a snippet from a DM conversation between two girls:[1]

EXAMPLE OF EXPLANATORY NOTE

[1] This transcript of a DM conversation was collected on 20 Nov. 2020. The teenagers' names are concealed to protect their privacy.

16c Following MLA format

The MLA recommends the following format for a research paper. However, check with your instructor before preparing your final draft. For a sample student essay in MLA style, see 16f.

First page and title For a project authored by an individual writer, MLA style does not require a title page. Type each of the following items on separate double-spaced lines on the first page, beginning one inch from the top and aligned with the left margin: your name, the instructor's name, the course name and number, and the date. On the next line, place the title, centered, with no additional spacing above or below the title.

For a group project, create a title page with all members' names, the instructor's name, the course, and the date, all aligned left on separate double-spaced lines. Center the title on a new line a few spaces down.

Margins and spacing Leave one-inch margins at the top and bottom and on both sides of each page. Double-space the entire text, including set-off quotations, notes, tables, and the list of works cited. Indent the first line of a paragraph one-half inch. Indent set-off quotations one-half inch.

Page numbers Include your last name and the page number on each page, one-half inch below the top and aligned with the right margin. For a group project, include all members' last names and the page number; if the names will not all fit on a single line, include only the page number on each page.

Long quotations   When quoting a long passage (more than four typed lines), set the quotation off by starting it on a new line and indenting each line one-half inch from the left margin. Do not enclose the passage in quotation marks (44a).

Headings   While headings are generally not needed for brief essays, readers may find them helpful for long or complex essays. Place each heading in the same style and size. Place headings, boldfaced, at the left margin without any indent. If you need subheadings (level 2, level 3), be consistent in styling them. Capitalize headings as you would titles.

Visuals   Visuals (such as photographs, charts, and tables) should be placed as near as possible to the relevant text. (See 14c for guidelines on incorporating visuals into your text.) Tables should have a label and number (*Table 1*) and a clear title, each on its own line above the table and aligned with the left margin. Give the source information below the table. All other visuals should be labeled *Figure* (usually abbreviated *Fig.*), numbered, and captioned below the visual. The label and caption should appear on the same line. If your caption includes full source information and you do not cite the source anywhere else in your text, it is not necessary to include an entry in your list of works cited. Remember to refer to each visual before it appears in your text, indicating how it contributes to the point(s) that you are making.

16d   Creating MLA in-text citations

MLA style requires a citation in the text of a writing project for every quotation, paraphrase, summary, or other material requiring documentation (see 14d). In-text citations document material from other sources with both signal phrases and parenthetical references. Parenthetical references should include the information your readers need to locate the full citations in the list of works cited at the end of the text. An in-text citation in MLA style gives the reader two kinds of information: (1) it indicates which source on the works-cited page the writer is referring to, and (2) it explains where in the source the material quoted, paraphrased, or summarized can be found, if the source has page numbers or other numbered sections.

The basic MLA in-text citation includes the author's last name—or both a first and last name if the source is being mentioned for the first time in the essay—either in a signal phrase introducing the source material (see 14b) or in parentheses at the end of the sentence. For sources with stable page numbers, it also includes the page number in parentheses at the end of the sentence.

SAMPLE CITATION USING A SIGNAL PHRASE

In his discussion of Monty Python routines, David Crystal notes that the group relished "breaking the normal rules" of language (107).

SAMPLE PARENTHETICAL CITATION

A noted linguist explains that Monty Python humor often relied on "bizarre linguistic interactions" (Crystal 108).

(For digital sources without stable page numbers, see model 2.)

Note in the examples on the following pages where punctuation is placed in relation to the parentheses. We have used underlining in some examples only to draw your attention to important elements. Do not underline anything in your own citations.

LIST OF EXAMPLES

In-text citations in MLA style

1. Basic format for a quotation, 131
2. Digital or nonprint source, 131
3. Two authors, 131
4. Three or more authors, 132
5. Organization as author, 132
6. Unknown author, 132
7. Two or more works by the same author, 132
8. Two or more authors with the same last name, 132
9. Multivolume work, 132
10. Literary work, 133
11. Work in an anthology or collection, 133
12. Sacred text, 133
13. Encyclopedia or dictionary entry, 134
14. Government source, 134
15. Entire work, 134
16. Indirect source (source quoted in another source), 134
17. Two or more sources in one citation, 134
18. Visual, 135

1. Basic format for a quotation The MLA recommends using the author's name in a signal phrase to introduce the material and citing the page number(s) in parentheses.

> Stan Lee claims that his comic-book character, Thor, was "the first regularly published superhero to speak in a consistently archaic manner" (199).

When you do not mention the author in a signal phrase, include the author's last name before the page number(s), if any, in the parentheses. Use no punctuation between the author's name and the page number(s).

> The word *Bollywood* can be considered an insult because it implies that Indian movies are merely "a derivative of the American film industry" (Chopra 9).

2. Digital or nonprint source Give enough information in a signal phrase or in parentheses for readers to locate the source in your list of works cited. If the source lacks numbered pages but has numbered paragraphs, sections, or divisions, use those numbers with the appropriate abbreviation in your parenthetical citation. Do not add such numbers if the source itself does not use them.

> As a *Slate* analysis explains, "Prominent sports psychologists get praised for their successes and don't get grief for their failures" (Engber).

> The author's son points out that his father and Ralph Waldo Emerson, in their lives and their writing, "together . . . met the needs of nearly all that is worthy in human nature" (Hawthorne, ch. 4).

When quoting, paraphrasing, or summarizing from an audio or a video source, include a time stamp for the material you are citing.

> Kalika Bali explains that as the "digital divide between languages" with and without technological resources grows, "the divide between the communities that speak these languages is expanding" (00:04:40–51).

3. Two authors Name both authors in a signal phrase or in parentheses.

> Gilbert and Gubar point out that in the Grimm version of "Snow White," the king "never actually appears in this story at all" (37).

4. Three or more authors Give the first author's name followed by a phrase such as *and others* in a signal phrase. Use the first author's name and *et al.* ("and others") in parentheses.

> Similarly, as Belenky and colleagues assert, examining the lives of women expands our understanding of human development (7).

5. Organization as author Give the group's full name in a signal phrase (for example *Girl Scouts of the United States of America*); in parentheses, shorten the name to the first noun and any preceding adjectives, removing any articles (*A, An, The*).

> One survey reports that seventy-five percent of young people want to elect more women to Congress (Girl Scouts).

6. Unknown author Use the full title, if it is brief, in your text—or a shortened version of the title in parentheses.

> Coca-Cola and similar companies avoid public politics to uphold their images as "emblems of American harmony" ("CEO Activism").

7. Two or more works by the same author Mention the title of the work in a signal phrase, or include a short version of the title in parentheses.

> Old Man Warner complains that the younger people calling for change will next "be wanting to go back to living in caves" (Jackson, "Lottery" 295).

8. Two or more authors with the same last name Include the author's first *and* last names in a signal phrase or first initial and last name in a parenthetical reference.

> One approach to the problem is to introduce nutrition literacy at the elementary level in public schools (E. Chen 15).

9. Multivolume work In parentheses, note the volume number first and then the page number(s), with a colon and one space between them. No volume number is needed if you cite only one volume of the work in your text.

> Modernist writers prized experimentation and gradually even sought to blur the line between poetry and prose, according to Forster (3: 150).

10. Literary work Because literary works are usually available in many different editions, cite the page number(s) from the edition you used followed by a semicolon, and then give other identifying information that will lead readers to the passage in any edition. For a novel, indicate the part or chapter (*175; ch. 4*).

> In utter despair, Dostoyevsky's character Mitya wonders aloud about the "terrible tragedies realism inflicts on people" (376; bk. 8, ch. 2).

For a play, indicate the page number, then the act and/or scene: (*37; sc. 1*). For a verse play, give only the act, scene, and line numbers, separated by periods.

> The witches greet Banquo as "lesser than Macbeth, and greater" (1.3.65).

For a poem, cite the part (if there is one) and line(s), separated by a period. If you are citing only line numbers, use the word *line(s)* in the first citation (*lines 33–34*) and the line number(s) alone in subsequent citations (*34–36*).

> Whitman speculates, "All goes onward and outward, nothing collapses, / And to die is different from what anyone supposed, and luckier" (6.129–30).

11. Work in an anthology or collection Use the name of the author of the work, not the editor of the anthology. Use the page number(s) from the anthology.

> In "How to Write Iranian-America, or The Last Essay," Porochista Khakpour details degrading experiences with English language instructors "who look to you with the shine of love but the stench of pity" (3).

12. Sacred text The first time you cite the work, give the title of the work as in the works cited entry, followed by the book, chapter, and verse (or their equivalent) separated by a period. In your text, spell out the names of books. In parenthetical references, use common abbreviations for books. Omit the source's title from the parentheses in all citations after the first.

> He ignored the warning: "Pride goes before destruction, and a haughty spirit before a fall" (*New Oxford Annotated Bible*, Prov. 16.18).

13. Encyclopedia or dictionary entry An entry from a reference work—such as an encyclopedia or a dictionary—without an author will appear on the works cited list under the entry's title. Enclose the <u>entry title</u> in quotation marks, and place it in parentheses. Omit the page number for sources that are only one page long.

> The word *crocodile* has a complex etymology (<u>"Crocodile"</u> 139–40).

14. Government source In a signal phrase, include the <u>full name</u> of the agency or governing body as given in the works cited list. In a parenthetical citation, <u>shorten the name</u>.

> <u>The National Endowment for the Arts</u> notes that social media and online events play a significant role in "showcasing the importance of the arts to the vitality of the nation" (15).

> Social media and online events play a significant role in "showcasing the importance of the arts to the vitality of the nation" (<u>National Endowment</u> 15).

If you cite more than one agency or department from the same government in your essay, you may choose to standardize the names by beginning with the name of the government (see model 66 in 16e). In that case, when shortening the names, give enough of each one to differentiate the authors: *(United States, National Endowment)*; *(United States, Environmental Protection)*.

15. Entire work Use the author's name in a signal phrase or a parenthetical citation, without any page numbers.

> Michael Pollan explores the issues surrounding food production and consumption from a political angle.

16. Indirect source (source quoted in another source) Use the abbreviation *qtd. in* to indicate that you are using a source that is quoted in another source.

> Jordan "silently marveled" at her Black students' dismissal of Black language in the novel (<u>qtd. in</u> Baker-Bell 24).

17. Two or more sources in one citation List the authors (or titles) in alphabetical order and separate them with semicolons.

> Economists recommend that *employment* be redefined to include unpaid domestic labor (Clark 148; Nevins 39).

18. Visual When you include an image in your text, number it and include a reference to it in your text: *see table 1*; *(see fig. 2)*. Number figures (photos, drawings, cartoons, maps, graphs, and charts) and tables separately. Each visual should include a caption with information about the source—either a complete citation or enough information to direct readers to the works cited entry.

> This trend is illustrated in a chart that includes data distributed by the
> ACT as part of its 2018 analysis (see fig. 1).

If you cite information from a numbered visual in a source and do not present the visual in your essay, use the abbreviation "fig." and the original figure number in place of a page number in your parenthetical citation: *(Manning, fig. 4)*. If you refer to the figure in your text, spell out the word *figure*. If the visual does not have a figure number in the source, use the visual's title or a description in your text and cite the author and page number as for any other source.

    If you are citing a work of art or other stand-alone visual, follow the advice in model 2.

16e Creating an MLA list of works cited

A list of works cited is an alphabetical list of the sources you have referred to in your essay. (If your instructor asks you to list everything you have read as background, call the list *Works Consulted*.)

Formatting a list of works cited

- Start your list on a separate page after the text of your document and any notes.

- Center the heading *Works Cited* (not italicized or in quotation marks) one inch from the top of the page.

- Begin each entry at the left margin, but indent subsequent lines of each entry one-half inch. Double-space the entire list.

- List sources alphabetically by the first word of the works cited entry. Start with the author's name, if available, or the editor's name. If no author or editor is given, start with the title.

List continues on p. 137

LIST OF EXAMPLES

Works cited in MLA style

GUIDELINES FOR AUTHOR LISTINGS

1. One author, 139
2. Multiple authors, 139
3. Organization or group author, 139
4. Unknown author, 139
5. Two or more works by the same author, 139
6. Pseudonym or pen name, 140
7. Screen name or social media account, 140

PRINT BOOKS

8. Basic format for a book, 140
   SOURCE MAP, 141
9. Author and editor both named, 142
10. Editor, no author named, 142
11. Selection in an anthology or chapter in a book with an editor, 142
12. Two or more items from the same anthology, 142
13. Translation, 142
14. Book in a language other than English, 143
15. Graphic narrative or comic, 143
16. Edition other than the first, 143
17. Multivolume work, 143
18. Preface, foreword, introduction, or afterword, 144
19. Entry in a reference book, 144
20. Book that is part of a series, 144
21. Republication (modern edition of an older book), 144
22. More than one publisher's name, 144
23. Book with a title within the title, 145
24. Sacred text, 145

PRINT PERIODICALS

25. Article in a print journal, 147
    SOURCE MAP, 146
26. Article in a print magazine, 147
27. Article in a print newspaper, 147
28. Article that skips pages, 147
29. Editorial or letter to the editor, 147
30. Review, 148

DIGITAL WRITTEN-WORD SOURCES

31. Work from a database, 148
    SOURCE MAP, 149
32. Online article from a journal, 150
33. Online article in a magazine, 150
34. Online article in a newspaper, 150
35. E-book or audiobook, 150
36. Online poem, 151
37. Online editorial or letter to the editor, 152
38. Online review, 152
39. Entry in an online reference work or wiki, 152
40. Short work from a website, 152
    SOURCE MAP, 154
41. Entire website, 153
42. Blog, 155
43. Blog post, 155
44. Comment on a blog post or online article, 155
45. Tweet, 155
46. Other posts on social media, 155
47. E-mail or text message, 156
48. Online interview, 156

LIST OF EXAMPLES

Works cited in MLA style, continued

VISUAL, AUDIO, MULTIMEDIA, AND LIVE SOURCES

49. Film or movie, 156
50. Online video, 157
51. Television (broadcast or online), 157
52. Radio (broadcast or online), 157
53. Television or radio interview, 157
54. Personal interview, 158
55. Music recording, 158
56. Musical composition, 158
57. Video game, 158
58. Lecture or speech, 158
59. Live performance, 159
60. Podcast, 159
61. Work of art or photograph, 159

62. Map or chart, 160
63. Cartoon or comic strip, 160
64. Advertisement, 160

OTHER SOURCES (INCLUDING DIGITAL VERSIONS)

65. Pamphlet or brochure, 160
66. Government publication, 160
67. Published proceedings of a conference, 161
68. Dissertation, 161
69. Classroom materials, 161
70. Letter, 162
71. Manuscript or other unpublished work, 162
72. Legal source, 162

Continued from p. 135

- List the author's last name first, followed by a comma and the first name. If a source has two authors, the second author's name appears first name first (see model 2).

- Capitalize every important word in titles and subtitles. Italicize titles of books and long works, but put titles of shorter works in quotation marks.

Guidelines for author listings

The list of works cited is always arranged alphabetically. The in-text citations in your writing point readers toward particular sources on the list.

NAME CITED IN SIGNAL PHRASE IN TEXT

Robert Zaretsky notes . . .

NAME IN PARENTHETICAL CITATION IN TEXT

. . . (Zaretsky 17).

BEGINNING OF ENTRY IN LIST OF WORKS CITED

Zaretsky, Robert.

Models 1–7 explain how to arrange author names. The information that follows the name depends on the type of work you are citing.

✔ Checklist

Citing Sources That Don't Match Any Model Exactly

What should you do if your source doesn't match any of the models exactly? Suppose, for instance, your source is a translated essay appearing in the fifth edition of an anthology.

✔ Identify a basic model to follow. For example, if you decide that your source looks most like an essay in an anthology, you would start with a citation that looks like model 11.

✔ After listing author and title information (if given), enter as many of the elements of the container as you can find (see 16b): title of the larger container, if any; other contributors, such as editor or translator; version or edition; number(s); publisher; date; and page numbers or other location information such as a DOI, permalink, or URL. End the container with a period. If the container is nested in a larger container, collect the information from the second container as well.

✔ If you aren't sure which model to follow or how to create a combination model with multiple containers, ask your instructor or a consultant in the writing center.

Consult the list of examples at the beginning of this section and choose the model that most closely resembles the source you are using.

1. One author Put the last name first, followed by a comma, the first name (and middle name or initial, if any), and a period.

Cronin, David.

2. Multiple authors For two authors, list the first author with the last name first (see model 1). Follow this with a comma, the word *and*, and the name of the second author with the first name first.

Stiglitz, Joseph E., and Bruce C. Greenwald.

For three or more authors, list the first author followed by a comma and *et al.* ("and others") or list all authors.

Lupton, Ellen, et al.

Lupton, Ellen, Farah Kafei, Jennifer Tobias, Josh A. Halstead, Kaleena
  Sales, Leslie Xia, and Valentina Vergara.

3. Organization or group author When the author is a corporation, an organization, or some other group, start the entry with the name of the group. Omit an article (*A, An,* or *The*) that begins the name. (For a source with a government agency listed as the author, see model 66.)

Human Rights Watch.

Jackson 5.

4. Unknown author When the author is not identified, begin the entry with the title, and alphabetize by the first important word. Italicize titles of books and long works, but put titles of articles and other short works in quotation marks.

*Women of Protest: Photographs from the Records of the National Woman's
  Party*.

"California Sues EPA over Emissions."

5. Two or more works by the same author Arrange the entries alphabetically by title. Include the author's name in the first entry, but in subsequent entries, use three hyphens followed by a period.

Coates, Ta-Nehisi. *Between the World and Me*. Spiegel and Grau, 2015.

---. *We Were Eight Years in Power: An American Tragedy*. One World, 2018.

Note: Use three hyphens only when the work is by *exactly* the same author(s) as the previous entry.

6. Pseudonym or pen name The MLA offers two options.

Saunders, Richard [Benjamin Franklin].

Franklin, Benjamin [*published as* Richard Saunders].

7. Screen name or social media account Start with the account display name, followed by the screen name or handle (if available) in brackets. If the account name is a first and last name, invert it.

Ng, Celeste [@pronounced_ing].

Pat and Stewart [@grammarphobia].

If the account name and handle are very similar, omit the handle. See models 45 and 46 for more on citing social media.

Print books

8. Basic format for a book Take information from the book's title page and copyright page, not from the book's cover. The source map on p. 141 shows where to find information in a typical book.

❶ **Author.** List the last name first. End with a period. For variations, see models 2–6.

❷ **Title.** Italicize the title and any subtitle; capitalize all major words. End with a period.

❸ **Publisher.** Identify the publisher's name as given on the book's title page or copyright page. If there is more than one publisher, separate the names with a slash, leaving a space before and after the slash. Abbreviate *University* and *Press* as *U* and *P*, but do not abbreviate *Press* if *University* is not also in the publisher's name. Omit terms such as *Company* and *Incorporated*. End with a comma.

❹ **Year of publication.** If more than one copyright date is given, use the most recent one. End with a period.

Cabral, Amber. *Allies and Advocates: Creating an Inclusive and Equitable Culture*. Wiley, 2021.

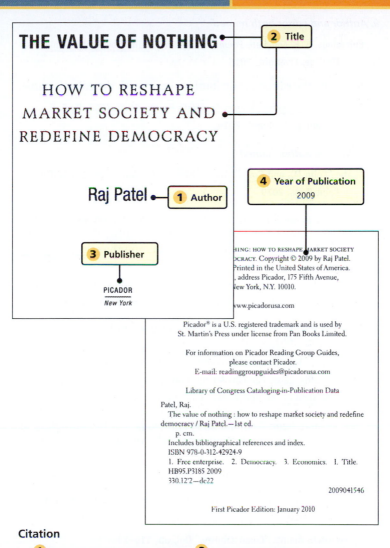

THE VALUE OF NOTHING

2 Title

HOW TO RESHAPE
MARKET SOCIETY AND
REDEFINE DEMOCRACY

Raj Patel

1 Author

4 Year of Publication
2009

3 Publisher

PICADOR
New York

...HING: HOW TO RESHAPE MARKET SOCIETY
...OCRACY. Copyright © 2009 by Raj Patel.
...Printed in the United States of America.
..., address Picador, 175 Fifth Avenue,
...New York, N.Y. 10010.

...www.picadorusa.com

Picador® is a U.S. registered trademark and is used by
St. Martin's Press under license from Pan Books Limited.

For information on Picador Reading Group Guides,
please contact Picador.
E-mail: readinggroupguides@picadorusa.com

Library of Congress Cataloging-in-Publication Data

Patel, Raj.
    The value of nothing : how to reshape market society and redefine
democracy / Raj Patel.—1st ed.
        p. cm.
    Includes bibliographical references and index.
    ISBN 978-0-312-42924-9
    1. Free enterprise. 2. Democracy. 3. Economics. I. Title.
HB95.P3185 2009
330.12'2—dc22
                                                        2009041546

First Picador Edition: January 2010

Citation

1 **2**
Patel, Raj. *The Value of Nothing: How to Reshape Market Society and*

3 **4**
Redefine Democracy. Picador, 2009.

9. Author and editor both named

Cummings, E. E. *Complete Poems, 1904–1962*. Edited by George James
Firmage, Liveright, 2016.

Note: To cite the editor's contribution, begin with the editor's name.

Firmage, George James, editor. *Complete Poems, 1904–1962*. By E. E.
Cummings, Liveright, 2016.

10. Editor, no author named

Coates, Colin M., and Graeme Wynn, editors. *The Nature of Canada*. On
Point Press, 2019.

11. Selection in an anthology or chapter in a book with an editor List
the author(s) of the selection; the selection title; the title of the
book; the editor(s); the publisher; the year; and the selection's page
numbers.

Symanovich, Alaina. "Compatibility." *Ab Terra 2020: A Science Fiction
Anthology*, edited by Yen Ooi, Brain Mill Press, 2020, pp. 116–23.

Note: You may provide original publication information as a second
container (see 16b):

Byatt, A. S. "The Thing in the Forest." *The O. Henry Prize Stories 2003*,
edited by Laura Furman, Anchor Books, 2003, pp. 3–22. Originally
published in *The New Yorker*, 3 June 2002, pp. 80–89.

12. Two or more items from the same anthology List the anthology as
one entry and list each selection separately with a cross-reference to
the anthology.

Challinor, Nels. "Porch Light." Ooi, pp. 107–15.

Ooi, Yen, editor. *Ab Terra 2020: A Science Fiction Anthology*. Brain Mill
Press, 2020.

Symanovich, Alaina. "Compatibility." Ooi, pp. 116–23.

13. Translation

Ullmann, Regina. *The Country Road: Stories*. Translated by Kurt Beals, New
Directions Publishing, 2015.

If the book has an editor and a translator, list both names after the title, in the order they appear on the title page.

> Kant, Immanuel. *"Toward Perpetual Peace" and Other Writings on Politics,*
> *Peace, and History.* Edited by Pauline Kleingeld, translated by David
> L. Colclasure, Yale UP, 2006.

14. Book in a language other than English Capitalize the title according to the conventions of the book's language. Include a translation of the title in brackets, if necessary.

> Vargas Llosa, Mario. *El sueño del celta [The Dream of the Celt].* Alfaguara
> Ediciones, 2010.

15. Graphic narrative or comic If the words and images are created by the same person, cite a graphic narrative just as you would a book (model 8).

> Nguyen, Trung Le. *The Magic Fish.* Random House Graphic, 2020.

If the work is a collaboration, indicate the author or illustrator who is most important to your research before the title of the work. List other contributors after the title, in the order of their appearance on the title page. Label each person's contribution to the work.

> Martínez, Hugo, illustrator. *Wake: The Hidden History of Women-Led Slave*
> *Revolts.* By Rebecca Hall, Simon and Schuster, 2021.

If there are multiple contributors but you are not discussing a specific contributor's work, begin with the title. Treat issue numbers of a comic series like issue numbers of journals, as below.

> *Stealth.* By Mike Costa, illustrated by Nate Bellegarde, colored by Tamra
> Bonvillain, lettered by Sal Cipriano, no. 1, Image Comics, 2020.

16. Edition other than the first

> Spivey, Chris. *Harlem Unbound.* 2nd ed., Chaosium, 2020.

17. Multivolume work Include the total number of volumes after the publication date. If you cite only one volume, give the number of the volume before the publication information.

> Brunetti, Ivan, editor. *An Anthology of Graphic Fiction, Cartoons, and True*
> *Stories.* Yale UP, 2006–08. 2 vols.

Brunetti, Ivan, editor. *An Anthology of Graphic Fiction, Cartoons, and True Stories*. Vol. 2, Yale UP, 2008.

If you cite one volume that is individually titled, include both the title of the volume and the title of the complete set.

Cather, Willa. *Willa Cather: Later Novels*. Edited by Sharon O'Brien, Library of America, 1990. Vol. 2 of *Willa Cather: The Complete Fiction and Other Writings*.

18. Preface, foreword, introduction, or afterword After the writer's name, include the part title, if any, and label for the part. After the book title, indicate the book's author (with *by*) or editor (with *edited by*).

Coates, Ta-Nehisi. Foreword. *The Origin of Others*, by Toni Morrison, Harvard UP, 2017, pp. vii–xvii.

19. Entry in a reference book

Robinson, Lisa Clayton. "Harlem Writers Guild." *Africana: The Encyclopedia of the African and African American Experience*, edited by Kwame Anthony Appiah and Henry Louis Gates Jr., 2nd ed., Oxford UP, 2005, p. 163.

20. Book that is part of a series After the publication information, list the series name (and number, if any) from the title page.

Denham, A. E., editor. *Plato on Art and Beauty*. Palgrave Macmillan, 2012. Philosophers in Depth.

21. Republication (modern edition of an older book) Give the original publication date after the title.

de Mille, Agnes. *Dance to the Piper*. 1951. New York Review Books, 2015.

22. More than one publisher's name If a book's title page gives two publishers' names, separate them with a slash and spaces.

Acevedo, Elizabeth. *With the Fire on High*. HarperTeen / Quill Tree Books, 2019.

23. Book with a title within the title If the book title contains the <u>title of a long work</u> normally italicized, do not italicize the title within the book title. If the book title contains the <u>title of a short work</u> normally placed in quotation marks, retain the quotation marks and italicize the entire title.

Masur, Louis P. *Runaway Dream:* <u>Born to Run</u> *and Bruce Springsteen's American Vision*. Bloomsbury, 2009.

Lethem, Jonathan. <u>"*Lucky Alan*"</u> *and Other Stories*. Doubleday, 2015.

24. Sacred text Give the title of the edition of the sacred text. Add the name of the version, if there is one, before the publisher.

Quran: The Final Testament. Translated by Rashad Khalifa, Authorized English Version with Arabic Text, Universal Unity, 2000.

Print periodicals

The source map on p. 146 shows where to find information in a typical periodical.

1 **Author.** List the last name first. End with a period. For variations, see models 2–6.

2 **Article title.** Put the title and any subtitle in quotation marks; capitalize all major words. Place a period inside the closing quotation mark.

3 **Periodical title.** Italicize the title; capitalize all major words. End with a comma.

4 **Volume and issue.** Give the abbreviation *vol.* and the volume number, and the abbreviation *no.* and the issue number, if the periodical provides them. Put commas after the volume and issue.

5 **Date of publication.** List day (if given), month (abbreviated except for May, June, and July), and year, or season and year, of publication. Do not capitalize seasons. Put a comma after the date.

6 **Page numbers.** Give the abbreviation *p.* (for "page") or *pp.* (for "pages") and the inclusive page numbers. If the article skips pages, put the first page number and a plus sign. End with a period.

Altschuler, Sari. "The Gothic Origins of Global Health." *American Literature,* vol. 89, no. 3, Sept. 2017, pp. 557–90.

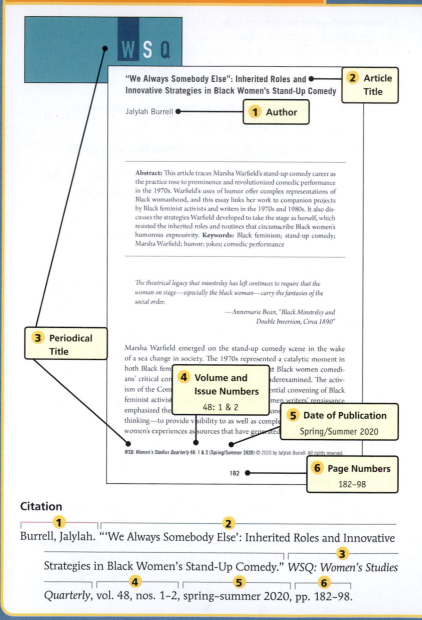

W S Q

"We Always Somebody Else": Inherited Roles and Innovative Strategies in Black Women's Stand-Up Comedy

2 Article Title

Jalylah Burrell

1 Author

Abstract: This article traces Marsha Warfield's stand-up comedy career as the practice rose to prominence and revolutionized comedic performance in the 1970s. Warfield's uses of humor offer complex representations of Black womanhood, and this essay links her work to companion projects by Black feminist activists and writers in the 1970s and 1980s. It also discusses the strategies Warfield developed to take the stage as herself, which resisted the inherited roles and routines that circumscribe Black women's humorous expressivity. **Keywords:** Black feminism; stand-up comedy; Marsha Warfield; humor; jokes; comedic performance

The theatrical legacy that minstrelsy has left continues to require that the woman on stage—especially the black woman—carry the fantasies of the social order.

—Annemarie Bean, "Black Minstrelsy and Double Inversion, Circa 1890"

3 Periodical Title

Marsha Warfield emerged on the stand-up comedy scene in the wake of a sea change in society. The 1970s represented a catalytic moment in both Black fem[...] [...]t Black women comedians' critical con[...] [...]derexamined. The activism of the Com[...] [...]ential convening of Black feminist activist[...] [...]men writers' renaissance emphasized the [...] [...]ons thinking—to provide v[s]ibility to as well as comple[...] women's experiences as sources that have gene[rated...]

4 Volume and Issue Numbers

48: 1 & 2

5 Date of Publication

Spring/Summer 2020

182

6 Page Numbers

182–98

Citation

1 **2**

Burrell, Jalylah. ""We Always Somebody Else': Inherited Roles and Innovative

3

Strategies in Black Women's Stand-Up Comedy." *WSQ: Women's Studies*

4 **5** **6**

Quarterly, vol. 48, nos. 1–2, spring–summer 2020, pp. 182–98.

25. Article in a print journal Include the volume number, the issue number, and the date.

> Beckwith, Sarah. "Reading for Our Lives." *PMLA*, vol. 132, no. 2, Mar.
>
> 2017, pp. 331–36.

26. Article in a print magazine Provide the date and the volume or issue numbers, if any.

> Armstrong, Rich. "Innovative Social-Distancing Volunteer Program
>
> Launched." *Boat U.S.,* 5 Nov. 2020, p. 20.

> Misner, Rebecca. "How I Became a Joiner." *Condé Nast Traveler,* vol. 5,
>
> 2018, pp. 55–56.

27. Article in a print newspaper Include the edition (if listed) and the section number, letter, or name (if listed).

> Fackler, Martin. "Japan's Foreign Minister Says Apologies to Wartime
>
> Victims Will Be Upheld." *The New York Times,* 9 Apr. 2014, late ed.,
>
> p. A6.

Note: For locally published newspapers, add the city in brackets after the name if it is not part of the name: *The Globe and Mail [Toronto]*.

28. Article that skips pages When an article skips pages, give only the first page number and a plus sign.

> Corasaniti, Nick, and Jim Rutenberg. "Record Turnout Hints at Future of
>
> Vote in U.S." *The New York Times,* 6 Dec. 2020, pp. A1+.

29. Editorial or letter to the editor Include the writer's name, if given, and the title, if any. If there is no title or if the source is not clear from the author or title, use the label *Editorial* or *Letter*.

> Editorial Board. "A Misstep by Organizers of Pride." *The New York Times,* 19
>
> May 2021, p. A18.

> MacEwan, Valerie. Letter. *The Believer,* vol. 12, no. 1, Jan. 2014, p. 4.

30. Review

Nussbaum, Emily. "Change Agents: Review of *The Americans* and *Silicon Valley*." *The New Yorker,* 31 Mar. 2014, p. 68.

Jopanda, Wayne Silao. <u>Review of</u> *America Is Not the Heart,* by Elaine Castillo. *Alon: Journal for Filipinx American and Diasporic Studies,* vol. 1, no. 1, Mar. 2021, pp. 106–08.

Digital written-word sources

31. Work from a database Library subscriptions provide access to huge databases of articles, such as Academic Search Premier, ProQuest, and JSTOR. The source map on p. 149 shows where to find information for a work from a database.

1 Author. List the last name first. End with a period. For variations, see models 2–7.

2 Article title. Enclose the title and any subtitle in quotation marks. End with a period.

3 Periodical title. Italicize it. Follow it with a comma.

4 Volume and issue. List the volume and issue number, if any, separated by commas. Use the abbreviations *vol.* and *no.*

5 Date of publication. Include the day (if given), month or season, and year, in that order. Do not capitalize seasons. Add a comma.

6 Page numbers. Give the inclusive page numbers from the print version, using the abbreviations *p.* or *pp.* End with a period.

7 Database name. Italicize the name of the database. End with a comma.

8 Location. Give the DOI or other permalink. If neither is available, give the URL. If a URL is longer than three lines in the list of works cited, you may shorten it. End with a period.

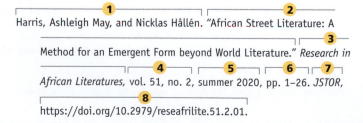

Harris, Ashleigh May, and Nicklas Hållén. "African Street Literature: A Method for an Emergent Form beyond World Literature." *Research in African Literatures,* vol. 51, no. 2, summer 2020, pp. 1–26. *JSTOR,* https://doi.org/10.2979/reseafrilite.51.2.01.

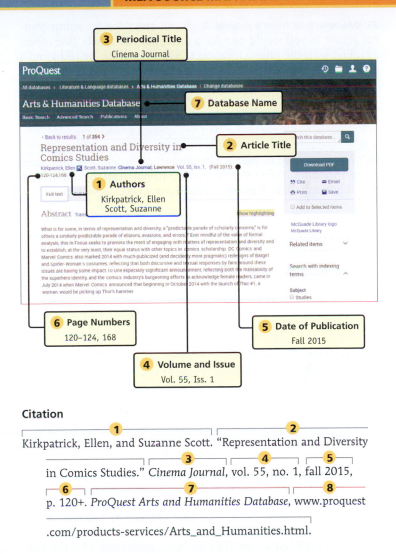

3 Periodical Title
Cinema Journal

7 Database Name

2 Article Title

1 Authors
Kirkpatrick, Ellen
Scott, Suzanne

6 Page Numbers
120–124, 168

5 Date of Publication
Fall 2015

4 Volume and Issue
Vol. 55, Iss. 1

Citation

Kirkpatrick, Ellen, and Suzanne Scott. "Representation and Diversity
in Comics Studies." *Cinema Journal*, vol. 55, no. 1, fall 2015,
p. 120+. *ProQuest Arts and Humanities Database*, www.proquest
.com/products-services/Arts_and_Humanities.html.

32. Online article from a journal Begin an entry for an online journal article as you would one for a print journal article (see model 25). End with the online location (DOI, permalink, or URL) and a period.

> McGuire, Meg. "Women, Healing, and Social Community: Cyberfeminist
> Activities on Reddit." *Kairos,* vol. 25, no. 2, spring 2021,
> kairos.technorhetoric.net/25.2/topoi/mcguire/index.html.

33. Online article in a magazine List the author, article title, and name of the magazine. Then identify the date of publication, and provide a DOI or permalink, if one is available, or a URL.

> Stuart, Tessa. "New Study Suggests Burning Fossil Fuels Contributed to 1
> in 5 Deaths in 2018." *Rolling Stone*, 17 Feb. 2021, www.rollingstone
> .com/politics/politics-news/fossil-fuels-air-pollution-premature
> -deaths-statistics-1127586/.

34. Online article in a newspaper After the name of the newspaper, give the publication date and the DOI or permalink (if you can find one) or URL.

> Jones, Ayana. "Chamber of Commerce Program to Boost Black-Owned
> Businesses." *The Philadelphia Tribune*, 21 Apr. 2021, www.phillytrib.com
> /news/business/chamber-of-commerce-program-to-boost-black-owned
> -businesses/article_6b14ae2f-5db2-5a59-8a67-8bbf974da451.html.

35. E-book or audiobook Provide information as for a print book (see models 8–24). For an e-book, include "E-book ed." before the publisher name.

> Doerr, Anthony. *All the Light We Cannot See*. E-book ed., Scribner, 2014.

For an audiobook, include the phrase *Narrated by* followed by the narrator's full name. If the author and narrator are the same, include only the last name. Then include "audiobook ed.," the publisher, and the year of release.

> de Hart, Jane Sherron. *Ruth Bader Ginsburg: A Life*. Narrated by Suzanne
> Toren, audiobook ed., Random House Audio, 2018.

✔ **Checklist**

Citing Works from Websites

When citing online sources, give as many of the following elements as you can find:

1. **Author.** Provide the author of the work, if you can find one. End with a period.

2. **Title.** Give the title of the work you are citing, ending with a period. If the work is part of a larger container (such as a video on *YouTube*), put the title in quotation marks.

3. **Website title.** If the title you identified is not the name of the website itself, list the website title, in italics, followed by a comma.

4. **Publisher or sponsor.** If the site's publisher or sponsor is different from the title of the site, identify the publisher or sponsor, followed by a comma. If the name is very similar to the site title, omit the publisher.

5. **Date of publication.** Give the date of publication, copyright, or latest update, followed by a comma.

6. **DOI, permalink, or URL.** Give a DOI or permalink (if you can find one) or URL. End with a period. If you do not need to provide live links for your readers, you may remove the protocol (*http://* or *https://*) from a URL. If a URL is longer than three lines in the list of works cited, you may shorten it, leaving at least the website host (for example, *cnn.com* or *www.usda.gov*) in the entry.

7. **Date of access.** If the work does not include any date, add "Accessed" and the day, month (abbreviated, except for May, June, and July), and year you accessed the source. End with a period. If you provided a date before the URL, omit the access date.

36. *Online poem* Include the poet's name, the title of the poem, and the print publication information (if any) for the first container. For the second container, give the website title and the DOI, permalink, or URL.

> Giovanni, Nikki. "Dreams." *Black Feeling, Black Talk, Black Judgment,*
> HarperCollins, 1970. *Poetry Foundation,* www.poetryfoundation.org
> /poems/48224/dreams-56d229494e255.

37. Online editorial or letter to the editor Cite as you would a print editorial or letter to the editor (see model 29). End with the DOI, permalink, or URL.

Kansas City Star Editorial Board. "Kansas Considers Lowering Concealed Carry Age to 18. Why It's Wrong for Many Reasons." *The Kansas City Star*, 9 Mar. 2021, www.kansascity.com/opinion/editorials /article249793143.html.

Rushlow, Lee. "My Recent Postal Ballot Was the Best I've Ever Cast." *The Wall Street Journal*, Dow Jones, 8 Oct. 2020, www.wsj.com /articles/my-recent-postal-ballot-was-the-best-ive-ever-cast -11602183549?reflink=desktopwebshare_permalink.

38. Online review Cite an online review as you would a print review (see model 30). End with the DOI, permalink, or URL.

Bramesco, Charles. "*Honeyland* Couches an Apocalyptic Warning in a Beekeeping Documentary." *The A.V. Club*, G/O Media, 23 July 2019, film.avclub.com/honeyland-couches-an-apocalyptic-warning-in-a -beekeepin-1836624795.

39. Entry in an online reference work or wiki Begin with the title unless the author is named. (A wiki, which is collectively edited, will not include an author.) Include the title of the entry; the name of the work, italicized; the sponsor or publisher; the date of the latest update; and the location (DOI, permalink, or URL). Before using a wiki as a source, check with your instructor.

"Oligarchy, *N*." *Merriam-Webster*, 2021, www.merriam-webster.com /dictionary/oligarchy.

"House Music." *Wikipedia: The Free Encyclopedia*, Wikimedia Foundation, 8 Apr. 2021, en.wikipedia.org/wiki/House_music.

40. Short work from a website To cite a work on a website that is not part of a regularly published journal, magazine, or newspaper, include all of the following elements that are available. You may need to browse other parts of a site to find some of these elements, and some sites may omit elements. Uncover as much information as you can. See the source map on p. 154 for an example.

1. **Author.** List the last name first. End with a period. If no author is given, begin with the title. For variations, see models 2–7.

2. **Title of work.** Enclose the title and any subtitle of the work in quotation marks.

3. **Title of website.** Give the title of the entire website, italicized. Follow it with a comma.

4. **Publisher or sponsor.** Look for the sponsor's name at the bottom of the home page. If the sponsor's name is roughly the same as the site title, omit the sponsor. Follow it with a comma.

5. **Date of publication or latest update.** Give the most recent date, followed by a comma.

6. **Location.** Give the DOI or permalink, if you can find one, or the site's URL, followed by a period.

7. **Date of access.** If the site is undated, end with *Accessed* and the date you accessed the site.

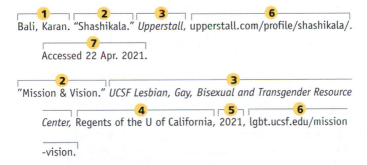

Bali, Karan. "Shashikala." *Upperstall,* upperstall.com/profile/shashikala/.
Accessed 22 Apr. 2021.

"Mission & Vision." *UCSF Lesbian, Gay, Bisexual and Transgender Resource Center,* Regents of the U of California, 2021, lgbt.ucsf.edu/mission -vision.

41. Entire website Follow the guidelines for a work from a website, beginning with the name of the author or editor (if any), followed by the title of the website, italicized; the name of the sponsor or publisher (if different from the name of the site); the date of publication or last update; and the location.

Lift Every Voice. Library of America / Schomburg Center for Research in Black Culture, 2020, africanamericanpoetry.org/.

The Newton Project. 2021, www.newtonproject.ox.ac.uk/.

MLA SOURCE MAP: Works from Websites

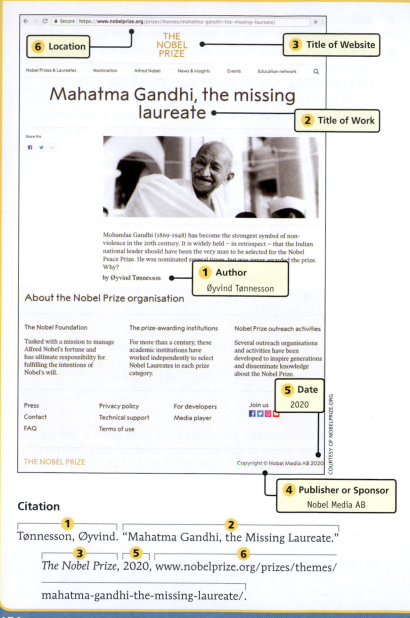

6 Location

3 Title of Website

2 Title of Work

1 Author
Øyvind Tønnesson

5 Date
2020

4 Publisher or Sponsor
Nobel Media AB

COURTESY OF NOBELPRIZE.ORG

Citation

Tønnesson, Øyvind. "Mahatma Gandhi, the Missing Laureate."
The Nobel Prize, 2020, www.nobelprize.org/prizes/themes/
mahatma-gandhi-the-missing-laureate/.

42. *Blog* For an entire blog, give the author's name; the title of the blog, italicized; the publisher (if different from the title of the blog); the date; and the URL. If the site is undated, end with your access date.

> Horgan, John. *Cross-Check*. Scientific American, 2020, blogs
> .scientificamerican.com/cross-check/.

> Ng, Amy. *Pikaland*. 2020, www.pikaland.com.

43. *Blog post* Give the author's name; the title of the post, in quotation marks; the title of the site, italicized; the date of the post; and the URL.

> Edroso, Roy. "No Compassion." *Alicublog,* 18 Mar. 2021, alicublog
> .blogspot.com/2021/03/no-compassion.html.

44. *Comment on a blog post or online article* List the screen name of the commenter and use the label *Comment on* before the title of the post or article. Include the URL to the comment when possible; otherwise, use the URL for the post or article.

> satch. Comment on "No Compassion," by Roy Edroso. *Alicublog,* 20 Mar.
> 2021, 9:50 a.m., disq.us/p/2fu0ulk.

45. *Tweet* Give either the text of the entire tweet in quotation marks, using the writer's capitalization and punctuation, or a brief description if you are focusing on a visual element of the tweet rather than the text in your work. Follow with *Twitter*, then provide the date and end with the URL. (See model 7 for how to style screen names.)

> Abdurraqib, Hanif [@NifMuhammad]. "Tracy Chapman really one of
> the greatest Ohio writers." *Twitter*, 30 Mar. 2021, twitter.com
> /NifMuhammad/status/1377086355667320836.

46. *Other posts on social media* Cite as a short work from a website (see model 40). If the post does not have a title, use the text accompanying the post, if it is brief, as the title; if the post is long, use the first few words followed by an ellipsis. If the post has no title or text, or if you are focusing on a visual element rather than the text in your work, provide a description of the post. (See model 7 for how to style screen names.)

ACLU. "Public officials have . . ." *Facebook,* 10 May 2021, www.facebook
.com/aclu/photos/a.74134381812/10157852911711813.

Rosa, Camila [camixvx]. Illustration of nurses in masks with fists raised.
Instagram, 28 Apr. 2020, www.instagram.com/p/B_h62W9pJaQ/.

Jones, James [@notoriouscree]. "Some traditional hoop teachings
#indigenous #culture #native #powwow." *TikTok,* 6 Apr. 2021,
www.tiktok.com/@notoriouscree/video/6948207430610226438.

47. E-mail or text message

Primak, Shoshana. Text message to the author. 6 May 2021.

Lewis-Truth, Antoine. E-mail to the Office of Student Financial Assistance.
30 Aug. 2020.

48. Online interview Start with the name of the person interviewed. Give the title, if there is one. Then give a descriptive label such as *Interview*, neither italicized nor in quotation marks, and the interviewer, followed by publication information.

Harjo, Joy. "The First Native American U.S. Poet Laureate on How Poetry
Can Counter Hate." Interview by Olivia B. Waxman. *Time,* 22 Aug.
2019, time.com/5658443/joy-harjo-poet-interview/.

Visual, audio, multimedia, and live sources

49. Film or movie If you cite a particular person's work, start with that name. If not, start with the title of the film; then name the director, distributor or production company, and year of release. Other contributors, such as writers or performers, may follow the director. If you viewed the film on a streaming service, include the app or the website name and URL at the end of the entry.

Judas and the Black Messiah. Directed by Shaka King, Warner Bros.
Pictures, 2021.

Youn, Yuh-Jung, performer. *Minari.* Directed by Lee Isaac Chung, Plan B
Entertainment / A24, 2020. *Amazon Prime Video* app.

50. Online video If the video is viewed on a video-sharing site such as *YouTube* or *Vimeo*, put the name of the uploader after the name of the website. If the video emphasizes a single speaker or presenter, list that person as the author. (See model 58 for an example of how to cite a TED Talk.)

> "The Art of Single Stroke Painting in Japan." *YouTube*, uploaded
> by National Geographic, 13 July 2018, www.youtube.com/
> watch?v=g7H8IhGZnpM.

51. Television (broadcast or online) If you are citing a particular episode, begin with the title in quotation marks. Then give the program title in italics. List important contributors (creator, writer, director, narrator, actors), if relevant to your writing; the season and episode numbers; the network, distributor, or production company; and the date of broadcast or publication. Unless you viewed or listened to the program on a live broadcast, end with the site or service on which you accessed it.

> "Shock and Delight." *Bridgerton*, season 1, episode 2, Shondaland / Netflix,
> 2020. *Netflix*, www.netflix.com.

> *Hillary*. Directed by Nanette Burstein, Propagate Content / Hulu, 2020.
> *Hulu* app.

If you are focusing on the work of an episode-specific contributor, you may include that person's name after the episode title.

52. Radio (broadcast or online) If you are citing a particular episode or segment, cite a radio broadcast as you would a television episode (see model 51).

> "Umbrellas Down." *This American Life,* hosted by Ira Glass, WBEZ,
> 10 July 2020.

For a show or segment accessed online, follow the date of posting with the website title, a comma, the URL, and a period.

53. Television or radio interview List the person interviewed and then the title, if any. Then use the label *Interview* and the name of the interviewer. End with information about the program.

> Kendi, Ibram X. Interview by Eric Deggans. *Life Kit*, NPR, 24 Oct. 2020.

54. Personal interview Begin with the <u>name of the person inter-viewed</u>. Then describe the <u>type of interview</u>, followed by the date of the interview.

> Freedman, Sasha. <u>Video interview</u> with the author. 10 Apr. 2021.

55. Music recording List the name of the <u>person or group you wish to emphasize</u> (such as the composer, conductor, or band); the title of the recording or composition; additional contributors, if appropri-ate; the record label; and the year of issue. If you are citing a <u>par-ticular song or selection</u>, include its title, in quotation marks. If you listen to the recording online, include the URL for the recording or the name of the app.

> Bach, Johann Sebastian. *Bach: Violin Concertos.* Performances by Itzhak
> Perlman, Pinchas Zukerman, and English Chamber Orchestra, EMI,
> 2002.

> Bad Bunny. <u>"Vete."</u> *YHLQMDLG*, Rimas, 2020. *Apple Music* app.

56. Musical composition Cite a published score as you would a book. If you include the date that the composition was written, do so immediately after the title.

> Schoenberg, Arnold. *Chamber Symphony No. 1 for 15 Solo Instruments,*
> *Opus 9*. 1906. Dover, 2002.

57. Video game Start with the <u>developer or author</u> (if any). After the title, give the <u>distributor and the date of publication</u>.

> Mojang. *Minecraft Dungeons.* <u>Xbox Game Studios</u>, 2020.

58. Lecture or speech For a live lecture or speech, list the <u>speaker</u>; the title (if any), in quotation marks; the <u>sponsoring institution or group</u>; the date; and the location. Add the label *Lecture* or *Speech* if there is no title or if readers will not otherwise be able to identify the work.

> Gay, Roxane. "Difficult Women, Bad Feminists and Unruly Bodies." <u>Beatty</u>
> <u>Lecture Series</u>, 18 Oct. 2018, McGill University.

For an online lecture or speech, such as a TED Talk, cite as you would an online video (see model 50).

> Kundu, Anindya. "The 'Opportunity Gap' in US Public Education — and How to Close It." *TED*, May 2019, www.ted.com/talks/anindya
> _kundu_the_opportunity_gap_in_us_public_education_and_how
> _to_close_it.

59. Live performance List the title, the appropriate names (such as the writer or performer), the date, and the location.

> Schreck, Heidi. *What the Constitution Means to Me.* Directed by Oliver Butler, 16 June 2019, Helen Hayes Theater, New York City.

60. Podcast Cite a podcast as you would a television or radio episode or series (see models 51 and 52).

> "Childish Gambino: *Because the Internet.*" *Dissect*, hosted by Cole Cuchna, season 7, episode 1, Spotify, Sep. 2020. *Spotify* app.

> *Dolly Parton's America.* Hosted by Jad Abumrad, produced and reported by Shima Oliaee, WNYC Studios, 2019, www.wnycstudios.org/podcasts /dolly-partons-america.

61. Work of art or photograph List the artist's or photographer's name; the work's title, italicized; and the date of composition. Then cite the name of the museum or other location and the city. To cite a reproduction in a book, add the publication information. To cite online artwork, instead give the title of the database or website, italicized, and the DOI, permalink, or URL.

> Bronzino, Agnolo. *Lodovico Capponi.* 1550–55, Frick Collection, New York.

> *General William Palmer in Old Age.* 1810, National Army Museum, London. *White Mughals: Love and Betrayal in Eighteenth-Century India,* by William Dalrymple, Penguin Books, 2002, p. 270.

> Lange, Dorothea. *Migrant Mother, Nipomo, California.* Mar. 1936. *MOMA*, www.moma.org/collection/works/50989.

62. *Map or chart* Cite a map or chart as you would a short work within a longer work. End with the <u>label</u> *Map* or *Chart* if needed for clarity.

> "Australia." *Perry-Castañeda Library Map Collection,* U of Texas Libraries, 2016, legacy.lib.utexas.edu/maps/cia16/australia_sm_2016.gif.

> "New COVID-19 Cases Worldwide." *Coronavirus Resource Center*, Johns Hopkins U and Medicine, 3 May 2021, coronavirus.jhu.edu/data/new-cases. <u>Chart</u>.

63. *Cartoon or comic strip* List the artist's name; the title of the cartoon or comic strip, in quotation marks; and the publication information. If there is no title, use a <u>label</u> (*Cartoon* or *Comic strip*).

> Shiell, Mike. <u>Cartoon</u>. *The Saturday Evening Post*, Jan.–Feb. 2021, p. 8.

> Munroe, Randall. "Heartbleed Explanation." *xkcd,* xkcd.com/1354/. Accessed 10 Oct. 2020.

64. *Advertisement* Include the <u>label</u> *Advertisement* if there is no title.

> <u>Advertisement</u> for Better World Club. *Mother Jones*, Mar.–Apr. 2021, p. 2.

> "The Whole Working-from-Home Thing — Apple." *YouTube*, uploaded by Apple, 13 July 2020, www.youtube.com/watch?v=6_pru8U2RmM.

Other sources (including digital versions)

If an online version is not shown in this section, use the appropriate model for the source and then end with a DOI, permalink, or URL.

65. *Pamphlet or brochure*

> Sierra County Public Health. *Benefits of the COVID-19 Vaccine*. 2021, sierracounty.ca.gov/DocumentCenter/View/5522/Benefits-of-the -COVID-19-Vaccine-Brochure. Brochure.

66. *Government publication* Give the name of the author as presented by the source.

> U.S. Bureau of Labor Statistics. "Consumer Expenditures Report 2019." *BLS Reports*, Dec. 2020, www.bls.gov/opub/reports/consumer -expenditures/2019/home.htm.

If you are using several government sources, you may want to standardize your list of works cited by listing the name of the government, spelled out, followed by the name of any agencies and subagencies.

United States, Department of Labor, Bureau of Labor Statistics. "Consumer
Expenditures Report 2019." *BLS Reports*, Dec. 2020, www.bls.gov
/opub/reports/consumer-expenditures/2019/home.htm.

67. Published proceedings of a conference Cite the proceedings as you would a book.

Zhang, Baosheng, et al., editors. *A Dialogue between Law and History:
Proceedings of the Second International Conference on Facts and
Evidence*. Springer, 2021.

68. Dissertation Italicize the title and add the year the work was accepted, the institution, and a description of the type of degree.

Kabugi, Magana J. *The Souls of Black Colleges: Cultural Production,
Ideology, and Identity at Historically Black Colleges and Universities*.
2020. Vanderbilt U, PhD dissertation. *Vanderbilt University
Institutional Repository*, hdl.handle.net/1803/16103.

69. Classroom materials For materials posted to an online learning management system, include as much information as is available about the source (author, title or description, and any publication information); then give the course, instructor, platform, institution name, date of posting, and URL. For materials delivered in a print or PDF course pack, include the author and title of the work; the words *Course pack for* with the course number and name; *compiled by* with the instructor's name; the term; and the institution name.

Rose, Mike. "Blue-Collar Brilliance." Introduction to College Writing,
taught by Melanie Li. *Blackboard*, Merrimack College, 9 Sept.
2020, blackboard.merrimack.edu/ultra/courses/_25745_1/cl
/readings.

70. Letter Cite a published letter as a work in an anthology (see model 11). If the letter is unpublished, follow this form:

Nadir, Abdul. Letter to the author. 12 Feb. 2021. Typescript.

71. Manuscript or other unpublished work List the author's name; the title (if any) or a description of the material; the date of creation; the name of the library or research institution housing the material, if applicable; and other identifying information.

Woolf, Virginia. "The Searchlight." 1902–1956. Papers of Virginia Woolf,
Smith College, Northampton, MA, series III, box 4, item 184.

72. Legal source For a legislative act (law), give the government body, the Public Law number, and the publication information.

United States, Congress. Public Law 116-136. *United States Statutes at
Large*, vol. 134, 2019, pp. 281–615. *U.S. Government Publishing
Office*, www.govinfo.gov/content/pkg/PLAW-116publ136/uslm
/PLAW-116publ136.xml.

For a court case, name the court and then name the case. Give the date of the decision and the publication information.

United States, Supreme Court. *Miller v. Alabama*. 25 June 2012. *Legal
Information Institute*, Cornell Law School, www.law.cornell.edu
/supremecourt/text/10-9646.

16f Research-based argument, MLA style

STUDENT WRITER

Julia Sakowitz

A research-based argument by Julia Sakowitz appears on the following pages. Julia followed the MLA guidelines described in this chapter.

Sakowitz 1

Julia Sakowitz
Professor Yamboliev
PWR 1
21 May 2019

"We're a Lot More Than Gospel Singing":

Tourism in Harlem

As a New York City resident of the new millennium, I grew up
barely aware that Harlem had ever been a *no-go* zone and couldn't
understand why people of the older generation, my parents included,
were afraid to venture uptown. I knew nothing about the heroin
and crack epidemics of the 1960s, 70s, and 80s and in general was
accustomed to a New York City that was safer than it had been in
years.

Harlem has changed rapidly over the past several decades.
As problems with crime and drug abuse in the storied New York
neighborhood decreased in the 1980s and 1990s, new government-
sponsored and privately funded economic initiatives like the
Upper Manhattan Empowerment Zone (UMEZ) pushed for outside
investment and economic development (Hoffman 288; Zukin et al.
50). In a recent interview, Carolyn Johnson, owner of "Welcome to
Harlem," a boutique tour company, recalled that "[Harlem] went
from 0 to 100 in a short period of time," to the point that even
Harlem residents themselves weren't aware of new businesses in
their neighborhood. Tourism in Harlem clearly played a central
role in this process, both responding to and creating social and
economic change. By 2000, more than 800,000 people were visiting
Harlem each year (Hoffman 288).

It's clear that Harlem's surge in tourism is good for the
city. But an equally important and more complex question is
whether tourism benefits Harlem residents or sells them short.
Close examination of current policy and tour business in Harlem

Sakowitz 2

reveals problems that come with tourism, such as cultural commodification and commercial gentrification, which are made worse by an Empowerment Zone program that favors only the most socioeconomically advantaged residents and outsiders. Although there is no simple solution for tourism in Harlem, small locally owned tour businesses have the potential to more directly and widely benefit the community while causing fewer social and economic problems.

> Presents explicit thesis statement at the end of introductory paragraphs

Economic development policy, particularly the UMEZ, has played a major role in shaping tourism's growth. Founded in 1994, the organization operates programs targeting business investment, loans to small businesses, grants for arts and culture, and employment and business training for residents ("Upper Manhattan"). But promoting tourism is one of its most important aims.

> Includes a shortened title in parentheses for a source with no named author

> Discusses the UMEZ organization and its effects in Harlem

The UMEZ especially focuses on cultural initiatives as a means of drawing tourism, sponsoring a "Catalyst Fund" specifically to "build cultural tourism," funding marketing and publicity for "UMEZ-eligible cultural organizations" ("Upper Manhattan"). This cultural marketing approach to Harlem tourism is not unique to the UMEZ. Recent scholarship on tourism in Harlem concludes that marketing Black and Latino culture is Harlem's golden ticket to escape economic marginalization. Scholar Lily Hoffman identifies Black culture as the driving force that increased tourism to Harlem, claiming that for visitors, Harlem is the embodiment of "Black America and its music and entertainment traditions" (288). In Hoffman's eyes, "capitalizing on ethnic culture" for tourism not only generates revenue but also promotes cultural flourishing and instills community pride (297). Other scholars echo these sentiments, emphasizing that "diversity" culture is Harlem's major and perhaps only asset and that "cultural tourism" has the additional benefit of promoting tolerance and de-stigmatization (Fainstein and Powers; Huning and Novy). But

> When the author is mentioned in a signal phrase, only a page number is needed in parentheses

Sakowitz 3

although it seems reasonable to assume that most tourists come to Harlem expecting to experience black culture, significant cultural complications still stand.

Cultural tourism comes with problems. The power dynamic between a tourist with means and mobility, and Harlem residents, who might lack both, is skewed. One of the most obvious dangers is that visitors will disrespect Harlem and the people who live there, participating in "negative sightseeing" or treating locals as if they're "put on exhibit" (Fainstein and Powers 14). In the popular Lonely Planet guide to New York City, there are hints of a clash between tourists and locals over cultural tourism: "Many locals are upset by visitors [to Harlem churches] who chat during sermons, leave in the middle of services or show up in skimpy attire," Lonely Planet warns. "Plus, for some, there's the uncomfortable sense that African American spirituality is something to be consumed like a Broadway show" (St Louis and Bonnetto 254).

Another, equally important issue stemming from tourism is commercial gentrification, the phenomenon of large chain stores and boutiques replacing stores that serve the poor (Zukin et al. 48). Such changes have long been viewed as positive. A low-income neighborhood often lacks necessary retail infrastructure, instead featuring businesses like used merchandise outlets, check cashing operations, liquor stores, or job training and family services (Hoffman 288). Tourism can encourage middle-class economic activity like supermarkets, commercial banks, and legal and accounting services, which are as much needed by low-income residents as wealthier ones (Hoffman 288). But boutique stores and chain stores, seen in figure 1, can replace services that might still be needed, leaving low-income residents feeling unwelcome (Zukin et al. 48). Economic gain from new businesses also bypasses most Harlem residents: fewer than half of new retail entrepreneurs are residents, according to Zukin and others,

Defines a key term ("gentrification") and shows how it relates to tourism and affects the community

Refers to visual in the text of the essay

Sakowitz 4

COURTESY OF GRAY LINE CITYSIGHTSEEING NEW YORK

Provides figure number and caption; MLA doesn't require visuals in the list of works cited if full publication information is given in a caption

Fig. 1. A typical tour bus passes Harlem's historic Apollo Theater, which now sits amid chain stores. *Uptown Tour*. 2016. *City Sightseeing New York*, www.citysightseeingnewyork.com /nyc-bus-tours/uptown-treasures-harlem-tour-plus.html.

and even those entrepreneurs who are residents overwhelmingly come from the newly arrived middle class (59).

Writer's last name and page number appear on every page

Commercial gentrification can feed into residential gentrification as the neighborhood becomes attractive to new middle-class residents. These might be any of a variety of races and nationalities, including African and African American, but tend to be better educated, have more money, and come from outside New York City (Zukin et al. 59). In fact, tourism itself can facilitate residential gentrification, sometimes overtly through real estate tours much like the Harlem "brownstone tours" that first occurred in the 1980s (Schulz; Sandford 103). Today, this kind of "neighborhood-shopping" continues. Non-Harlemite New Yorkers, visitors, and even real estate moguls will often visit Harlem with Big Onion Walking Tours to ask

Uses a semicolon to separate information about two sources in one citation

Sakowitz 5

pointed questions about whether Harlem is a friendly and safe place
to live (Kamil).

Both commercial and residential gentrification favor outsiders
and newcomers. While it is possible for tourism to economically
empower Harlem and its residents, in reality the greatest economic
gains bypass low-income residents completely.

In this context, Carolyn Johnson, Harlem resident and founder
of "Welcome to Harlem," a self-described Black and "women-owned
visitor center and boutique-tour company," is a unique player ("About
Us"). In the early 2000s, Johnson realized her neighborhood was
changing rapidly and started the website "Welcome to Harlem" in
2004 as an informational tool for the community, so residents could
learn about Harlem's new businesses and venues. In 2008, Johnson
decided to branch out into tourism. Seeing outsiders coming to
Harlem to give bus and walking tours, she decided to complete a
short tour guide training program and start leading tours herself
(Interview). "Welcome to Harlem" now features six different tours,
including jazz tours, food-tasting tours, and historic tours, as well as
"music programs and workshops" ("About Us").

For Johnson, running her own business can be an economic
challenge, but another, equally serious problem is developing a
trustworthy reputation to attract clients. She says she struggled to
get recognition outside the community, noting it was more common
for hotels and tour agencies to recommend large non-Harlem-based
tour companies, which might be able to pay a sizeable commission.
Visibility is a common problem for Harlem-based tour companies.
Almost half of the listed businesses resulting from a Google search
for "Harlem tour" are not Harlem-based businesses, but larger outside
companies, like "New York Visions," "Free Tours by Foot," and "Big
Onion Walking Tours."

In the tour business, which aims to represent a neighborhood
for outsiders, issues of cultural representation are important. For

**Includes
two
personal
interviews
as field
research**

Promotes the benefits of having a Harlem resident represent the community in all its richness

Harlem-based entrepreneurs, offering tours can be a means of self-representation. Johnson's own identity as a Harlem resident motivates her to create tours that disprove negative stereotypes. "Most people think that Harlem is just Sylvia's, the Apollo, and gospel on Sunday," Johnson says. She wants to show that Harlem is a self-contained community, "a lot more than just gospel singing" (Interview).

This point of "authenticity" is so important that Harlem-based companies compete with even more exclusive definitions. The "Welcome to Harlem" website states, "Our tours are led by true Harlemites (those who grew up here or live here) which allows for an authentic and personal experience." According to Seth Kamil, owner of "Big Onion Walking Tours," "authenticity" is not an asset at all. Kamil, who founded his business twenty-five years ago as a graduate student at Columbia University, believes that living in a certain place is no qualification for leading tours, and that the best tours are strongly academic, offering historical fact. Kamil employs mainly graduate students as guides, and his Harlem guides are neither Black nor necessarily Harlem locals. In a recent interview, Kamil questioned the motives of tourists seeking an authentic Harlemite guide and suggested that there is a "subtle racism" that drives tourists to request a Black or Hispanic guide in Harlem, but not in other economically challenged neighborhoods like Chinatown. He stated simply, "We don't play that game" (Kamil).

Presents an opposing point of view

But at the same time, much like "Welcome to Harlem" or Harlem Heritage Tours, Kamil is concerned about representing Harlem fairly and dispelling stereotypes. In addition to focusing on history, his tours aim to express the struggles of living in Harlem because of its continued lack of infrastructure that many middle-class New Yorkers take for granted. He notes that the biggest problem with Harlem tours are "perceptions that customers have" and he tries to avoid disrespecting the community, refusing to take part in "Gospel

STUDENT
WRITING

Sakowitz 7

Tours," which he sees as violating Harlem's places of worship. He
also cares about what Harlem residents think of his tours. In his
opinion, Big Onion Walking Tours has "a unique relationship with
the community," and he notes that many Black residents will stop to
listen to his white guides, to check that they're being respectful and
accurate (Kamil).

Kamil seemed to view "cultural" tours as, at worst, empty and
unethical, and, at best, self-commodifying. Could he be partially
right? Is Harlem-based tour companies' heavy-handed advertising
of "authenticity" based on ethnic status and Harlem residence
demeaning for Harlem residents?

Coming at this same question of cultural commodification
from a different perspective is Arlene Dávila, a scholar whose focus
on Latino issues in East Harlem, or El Barrio, led her to surprising
conclusions about the UMEZ policies. Commodifying ethnic cultures
is problematic, Dávila claims, because in the eyes of tourists,
policymakers, and even scholars, not all culture is created equal. For
example, Harlem is internationally famous as a "Black Mecca," yet it
is also more than half Latino and a center for "Nuyorican" identity,
urban Latinidad, and Latino dance and music (52). But what happens
when visitors' needs and residents' reality just don't align? Dávila
writes:

> By limiting East Harlem's funding eligibility to certain sections
> and imposing requirements that only institutionalized cultural
> industries could meet, EZ virtually guaranteed that cultural
> institutions in Central and West Harlem, which are the most
> established cultural institutions in Upper Manhattan, would be
> most prominently featured in EZ-sponsored tourist promotional
> materials and the ones eligible for the largest amounts of
> funding. (51)

When Latino cultural initiatives have applied for UMEZ
funding, the UMEZ board has questioned the appeal of Latino

Introduces a third important voice in the debate

Block format for a quotation of more than four lines; quotation marks are not needed

The parenthetical citation comes after the period

Sakowitz 8

culture, in one instance rejecting a salsa museum's application because it doubted the international popularity of salsa and the museum's ability to create at least five jobs (Dávila 59). The results of such policy for El Barrio are dramatic: Dávila estimates that as little as six percent of the UMEZ cultural funding was given to Latino initiatives (51).

Transition to final point

But Latino Harlemites aren't the only ones who suffer from the UMEZ policies. Even though the UMEZ funding of tourism and cultural initiatives is supposed to be an equalizing force that elevates those with few resources, its economic prerequisites favor those with money and education (Dávila 58). Harlem residents echo these sentiments. Deborah Faison, a Harlem resident, commented that the technical training the UMEZ provides is "by itself . . . not enough" and that it's necessary to be "in a strong position already to participate" in the program (qtd. in Maurrasse 164). Carolyn Johnson, who receives funding for "Welcome to Harlem" through the UMEZ, believes that UMEZ doesn't do enough for small business and the "people who have been here" (Interview). The ultimate result of the UMEZ's supposedly equal-access programs of economic empowerment through culture is that the "largest beneficiaries under the EZ were developers and outside visitors" (Dávila 61).

Includes "qtd. in" to indicate a source quoted in another source

Writer proposes a policy change and gives examples

If tourism is going to be a means of economic empowerment for Harlem, there's an urgent need to revise UMEZ policy. For example, when allocating funding, the UMEZ should focus less on the revenue and jobs a cultural initiative will create and more on its cultural value to the community. Harlem's cultural life is as important as its economic life, *especially* from the perspective of tourism, because cultivating genuine culture that comes from and serves the community keeps Harlem authentically itself, which is what draws tourists in the first place. Doing otherwise sells the soul of the neighborhood, turning it into a hollow Disneyland version of itself. The UMEZ also needs to take civic participation

Sakowitz 9

and empowerment more seriously. Instead of providing sparse job training and business skills classes, it should take steps to organize community meetings and start more comprehensive programs that would create a genuine sense of resident involvement and power.

Finally, the UMEZ can't remain socioeconomically blind. Doing so benefits those who have economic or social advantage, enabling commercial gentrification rather than uplifting the community. The organization should develop a policy of need-based preference, giving special consideration to long-term residents, minorities, and economically disadvantaged entrepreneurs. Instead of selecting businesses based on how accomplished they seem already, the UMEZ should award grants based on their potential to grow.

With these changes to the UMEZ, Harlem entrepreneurs will be able to receive funding and compete on an even playing field with outside companies like Big Onion Walking Tours without having to sell their identity. Small business will be able to flourish, and Harlem will remain resilient and diverse, a wonderful place to live and a wonderful place to visit.

Conclusion sums up writer's argument and reiterates thesis

Sakowitz 10

Heading centered

Works Cited

Print journal article

Dávila, Arlene. "Empowered Culture? New York City's Empowerment Zone and the Selling of El Barrio." *The Annals of the American Academy of Political and Social Science,* vol. 594, no. 1, July 2004, pp. 49–64.

Chapter in a book with an editor

Fainstein, Susan S., and John C. Powers. "Tourism and New York's Ethnic Diversity: An Underutilized Resource?" *Tourism, Ethnic Diversity and the City*, edited by Jan Rath, Routledge, 2007, pp. 143–63.

Article found in a database

Hoffman, Lily M. "The Marketing of Diversity in the Inner City: Tourism and Regulation in Harlem." *International Journal of Urban and Regional Research,* vol. 27, no. 2, June 2003, pp. 286–99. *Academic Search Premier,* https://doi.org/10.1111/1468 -2427.00448.

Online report

Huning, Sandra, and Johannes Novy. *Tourism as an Engine of Neighborhood Regeneration? Some Remarks towards a Better Understanding of Urban Tourism beyond the "Beaten Path." CMS Working Paper Series*, No. 006-2006, Center for Metropolitan Studies, 2006, citeseerx.ist.psu.edu/viewdoc/download?doi=10 .1.1.544.6506&rep=rep1&type=pdf.

Johnson, Carolyn D. "About Us." *Welcome to Harlem*, welcometoharlem .com/page/aboutus/. Accessed 15 May 2019.

Personal interview

---. Interview with the author. 9 May 2019.

Kamil, Seth. Interview with the author. 11 May 2019.

Print book

Maurrasse, David. *Listening to Harlem: Gentrification, Community, and Business*. Routledge, 2006.

Second and subsequent lines of each entry are indented

Sandford, Mariellen R. "Tourism in Harlem: Between Negative Sightseeing and Gentrification." *The Journal of American Culture,* vol. 10, no. 2, summer 1987, pp. 99–105. *Wiley Online Library,* https://doi.org/10.1111/j.1542-734X.1987.1002_99.x.

Sakowitz 11

Schulz, Dana. "House Tours Galore: Where to Get a Look inside the Area's Most Fabulous Homes and Gardens." *6sqft*, 5 May 2015, www.6sqft.com/house-tours-galore-where-to-get-a-look-inside -the-areas-most-fabulous-homes-and-gardens/.

St Louis, Regis, and Cristian Bonetto. "Harlem and Upper Manhattan." *Lonely Planet New York City,* Lonely Planet, 2014.

"Upper Manhattan Empowerment Zone: Who We Are." *Upper Manhattan Empowerment Zone Development Corporation*, umez.org. Accessed 12 May 2019.

Zukin, Sharon, et al. "New Retail Capital and Neighborhood Change: Boutiques and Gentrification in New York City." *City & Community,* vol. 8, no. 1, Mar. 2009, pp. 47–64. *Wiley Online Library*, https://doi.org/10.1111/j.1540-6040.2009.01269.x.

Short work from a website

Entry for source with no named author begins with title

Source with three or more authors uses *et al.*

17 APA Style

Chapter 17 discusses the basic formats prescribed by the American Psychological Association (APA), guidelines that are widely used for research in the social sciences. For further reference, consult the *Publication Manual of the American Psychological Association,* Seventh Edition (2020).

17a Understanding APA citation style

Why does academic work call for very careful citation practices when writing for the general public may not? The answer is that readers of academic work expect source citations for several reasons:

- Source citations demonstrate that you've done your homework on your topic and that you are a part of the conversation surrounding it.

- Source citations show that you understand the need to give credit when you make use of someone else's intellectual property. (See Chapter 14.)

- Source citations give explicit directions to guide readers who want to look for themselves at the works you're using.

The guidelines for APA style tell you exactly what information to include in your citation and how to format that information.

Types of sources   Refer to the list of examples on pp. 182–83 for guidelines on citing various types of sources—print books (or parts of print books), print periodicals (journals, magazines, and newspapers), and digital written-word sources (an online article or book). A digital version of a source may include updates or corrections that the print version lacks, so it's important to provide the correct information for readers. For sources that consist mainly of material other than written words—such as a film, song, or podcast—consult the "other sources" section of the directory. And if you can't find a model exactly like the source you've selected, see the checklist in 17d.

Articles from web and database sources You need a subscription to look through most databases, so individual researchers almost always gain access to articles in databases through a library that pays to subscribe. The easiest way to tell whether a source comes from a database, then, is that its information is *not* generally available for free. Many databases are digital collections of articles that originally appeared in edited print periodicals, ensuring that an authority has vouched for the accuracy of the information. Such sources often have more credibility than free material available on the web.

Parts of citations APA citations appear in two parts of your text—a brief in-text citation in the body of your written text and a full citation in the list of references, to which the in-text citation directs readers. The most straightforward in-text citations include the author's name, the publication year, and the page number, but many variations on this basic format are discussed in 17c.

In the text of her causal analysis, student Tawnya Redding includes a paraphrase of material from an online journal that she accessed through the publisher's website. She cites the authors' names and the year of publication in a parenthetical reference, pointing readers to the entry for "Baker, F., & Bor, W. (2008)" in her references list.

9

References

Baker, F., & Bor, W. (2008). Can music preference indicate mental health status in young people? *Australasian Psychiatry, 16*(4), 284–288. https://doi.org/10.1080/10398560701879589

George, D., Stickle, K., Rachid, F., & Wopnford, A. (2007). The

alter the mood of at-risk youth in a negative way. This view of the correlation between music and suicide risk is supported by a meta-analysis done by Baker and Bor (2008), in which the authors assert that most studies reject the notion that music is a causal factor and suggest that music preference is more indicative of emotional vulnerability. However, it is still unknown whether these genres can

al music

lescence,

en in

Taiwan. *Issues in Mental Health Nursing, 20*(3), 229–246. https://doi.org/10.1080/016128499248637

Content notes APA style allows you to use content notes, either at the bottom of the page (footnotes) or on a separate page at the end of the text (endnotes), to expand or supplement your text. Indicate such notes in the text by superscript numerals (^{1}), using the footnote function in your word processor. Single-space all footnotes. Indent the first line of each note one-half inch, but begin subsequent lines at the left margin.

SUPERSCRIPT NUMBER IN TEXT

The age of the children involved in the study was an important factor in the selection of items for the questionnaire.[1]

FOOTNOTE

[1]Marjorie Youngston Forman and William Cole of the Child Study Team provided great assistance in identifying appropriate items for the questionnaire.

17b Following APA format

The following formatting guidelines are consistent with APA recommendations for undergraduate student texts. However, check with your instructor before preparing the final draft of a print text.

Title page Double-space the entire title page. Center the title in boldface type three or four lines from the top margin. After one blank double-spaced line, include the following details on separate lines: your name, the department and school in which the course is offered, the course number and name, your instructor's name, and the assignment due date. Insert the page number "1" in the upper right margin.

Margins and spacing Leave margins of one inch on all sides of the page. Do not justify the right margin. Double-space the entire text (except for footnotes), including any headings, set-off quotations (44a), and the list of references. Indent one-half inch from the left margin for the first line of a paragraph and all lines of a set-off quotation.

Page numbers Place the page number in the upper-right corner of each page, in the same position as on the title page.

Long quotations   For a quotation of forty or more words, indent it one-half inch from the left margin, and do not use quotation marks. Place the page reference in parentheses one space after the final punctuation.

Headings   Headings are frequently used within the text of APA-style projects. Center first-level headings and put them in boldface type. Left-align any second-level headings and make them boldface. Third-level headings should be left-aligned, boldface, and italicized. Capitalize all major words and any words of four or more letters.

Visuals   All visuals should include a label, number, and title above the visual. Label tables "Table" and label any other visuals (such as charts, graphs, photographs, and drawings) "Figure" in boldface type. Both tables and figures should have a title in italics on the line below the label. Provide any source information in a note below the table or figure. Begin with the word "Note," italicized and followed by a period. Remember to refer to each visual in your text, stating how it contributes to the point(s) you are making. Tables and figures should generally appear after the paragraph in which they are called out.

17c   Creating APA in-text citations

An in-text citation in APA style always indicates which source on the references page the writer is referring to, and it explains in what year the material was published; for quoted material, the in-text citation also indicates where in the source the quotation can be found.

Note that APA style generally calls for using the past tense or present perfect tense for signal verbs: "Baker (2019) showed" or "Baker (2019) has shown." Use the present tense only to discuss results ("the experiment demonstrates") or widely accepted information ("researchers agree").

We have used underlining in some examples only to draw your attention to important elements. Do not underline anything in your own citations.

1. Basic format for a quotation   Generally, use the author's last name in a signal phrase to introduce the cited material, and place the date, in parentheses, immediately after the author's name. The page number, preceded by "p.," appears in parentheses after the quotation.

> Gitlin (2001) pointed out that "political critics, convinced that the media are rigged against them, are often blind to other substantial reasons why their causes are unpersuasive" (p. 141).

If the author is not named in a signal phrase, place the author's last name, the year, and the page number in parentheses after the quotation: (Gitlin, 2001, p. 141). For a long, set-off quotation (more than forty words), place the page reference in parentheses one space after the final quotation.

For quotations from works without page numbers, include other information such as a paragraph number, a section heading, or a figure number to help readers find the quoted passage.

> Driver (2007) has noticed "an increasing focus on the role of land" in policy debates over the past decade (para. 1).

2. Basic format for a paraphrase or summary Include the author's last name and the year as in model 1. A page number is not required for a summary or a paraphrase, but include one if it would help readers find the material in a long work.

> Gitlin (2001) has argued that critics sometimes overestimate the influence of the media on modern life.

LIST OF EXAMPLES

In-text citations in APA style

1. Basic format for a quotation, 177
2. Basic format for a paraphrase or summary, 178
3. Two authors, 179
4. Three or more authors, 179
5. Corporate or group author, 179
6. Unknown author, 179
7. Two or more authors with the same last name, 180
8. Two or more works by an author in a single year, 180
9. Two or more sources in one parenthetical reference, 180
10. Source reported in another source, 180
11. Personal communication, 180
12. Electronic source, 180
13. Table or figure reproduced in the text, 181

3. Two authors Use both names in all citations. Use "and" in a signal phrase, but use an ampersand (&) in parentheses.

Babcock and Laschever (2003) have suggested that many women do not negotiate their salaries and pay raises as vigorously as their male counterparts do.

A recent study has suggested that many women do not negotiate their salaries and pay raises as vigorously as their male counterparts do (Babcock & Laschever, 2003).

4. Three or more authors List the first author's name followed by "et al." (a Latin abbreviation for "and others").

Another group of researchers reached somewhat different conclusions by designing a study that was less dependent on subjective judgment than were previous studies (Safer et al., 2017).

Based on the results, Safer et al. (2017) determined that the apes took significant steps toward self-expression.

5. Corporate or group author If the name of the organization or corporation is long, spell it out the first time you use it, followed by an abbreviation in brackets. In later references, use the abbreviation only.

FIRST CITATION (Centers for Disease Control and Prevention [CDC], 2018)

LATER CITATIONS (CDC, 2018)

If a government or corporate source lists multiple nested departments or agencies, use the most specific department or agency as the author.

6. Unknown author Use the title or its first few words in a signal phrase or in parentheses. A book's title is italicized, as in the following example; an article's title is placed in quotation marks.

The employment profiles for this time period substantiated this trend (*Federal Employment*, 2001).

7. Two or more authors with the same last name Include the <u>authors' initials</u> in each citation.

<u>S. Bartolomeo</u> (2000) conducted the groundbreaking study on teenage childbearing.

8. Two or more works by an author in a single year Assign <u>lowercase letters</u> ("a," "b," and so on) alphabetically by title, and include the letters after the year.

Gordon (<u>2017b</u>) examined this trend in more detail.

9. Two or more sources in one parenthetical reference List any sources by different authors in alphabetical order by the authors' last names, separated by semicolons: (Cardone, 2020; Lai, 2014). List works by the same author in chronological order, separated by commas: (Lai, 2014, 2017).

10. Source reported in another source Use the phrase "as cited in" to indicate that you are reporting information from a secondary source. Name the <u>original source</u> in your text, but list the <u>secondary source</u> in your list of references.

One reviewer commended the author's "sure understanding of the thoughts of young people" (<u>Brailsford, 1990</u>, as cited in <u>Chow, 2019, para. 9</u>).

11. Personal communication Cite any personal letters, email messages, private electronic postings, telephone conversations, or interviews as shown. Do not include personal communications in the reference list.

R. Nuñez (personal communication, November 4, 2020) supported his claims about service animals with new evidence.

12. Electronic source Cite a web or electronic source as you would a print source, using the author's <u>name</u> and <u>date</u>.

<u>Link and Phelan</u> (<u>2005</u>) argued for broader interventions in public health that would be accessible to anyone, regardless of individual wealth.

The APA recommends the following for electronic sources without names, dates, or page numbers:

AUTHOR UNKNOWN
Use a shortened form of the title in a signal phrase or in parentheses (see model 6). If an organization is the author, see model 5.

DATE UNKNOWN
Use the abbreviation "n.d." (for "no date") in place of the year: (Hopkins, n.d.).

NO PAGE NUMBERS
Use the page numbers for an electronic work in a format, such as PDF, that has stable pagination. If the work does not have stable page numbers, include other information to help your readers find the cited material. For example, you may include a section heading, a paragraph number, a figure or table number, or a time stamp.

> Jacobs and Johnson (2007) have argued that "the South African media is still highly concentrated and not very diverse in terms of race and class" (South African Media after Apartheid section).

13. Table or figure reproduced in the text Number figures (graphs, charts, illustrations, and photographs) and tables separately.

Place a label ("Table 1") and an informative heading ("Hartman's Key Personality Traits") above the table or figure; below, provide information about its source. Begin with the word "Note," italicized and followed by a period.

Table 1

Hartman's Key Personality Traits

Trait category	Color			
	Red	Blue	White	Yellow
Motive	Power	Intimacy	Peace	Fun
Strengths	Loyal to tasks	Loyal to people	Tolerant	Positive
Limitations	Arrogant	Self-righteous	Timid	Uncommitted

Note. Adapted from *The Hartman Personality Profile,* by N. Hayden (http://students.cs.byu.edu/~nhayden/Code/index.php).

If you do not cite the source of the table or figure elsewhere in your text, you do not need to include the source in your list of references.

17d Creating an APA list of references

The alphabetical list of the sources cited in your document is called "References." If your instructor asks that you list everything you have read—not just the sources you cite—call the list "Bibliography."

LIST OF EXAMPLES

References in APA style

GUIDELINES FOR AUTHOR LISTINGS
1. One author, 185
2. Multiple authors, 185
3. Corporate or group author, 185
4. Unknown author, 185
5. Two or more works by the same author, 185

PRINT BOOKS
6. Basic format for a book, 186
   SOURCE MAP, 187
7. Editor, 186
8. Selection in a book with an editor, 188
9. Translation, 188
10. Edition other than the first, 188
11. Multivolume work with an editor, 188
12. Article in a reference work, 188
13. Republished book, 189
14. Book with a title within the title, 189

PRINT PERIODICALS
15. Article in a journal, 191
    SOURCE MAP, 190

16. Article in a magazine, 191
17. Article in a newspaper, 191
18. Editorial or letter to the editor, 191
19. Unsigned article, 191
20. Review, 191
21. Published interview, 191

DIGITAL WRITTEN-WORD SOURCES
22. Article from an online periodical, 192
23. Article from a database, 193
    SOURCE MAP, 194
24. Abstract for an online article, 195
25. Comment on an online article, 195
26. Report or document from a website, 195
    SOURCE MAP, 196
27. Online book, 197
28. Email or private message, 197
29. Posting on social media, 197
30. Blog post, 197
31. Online reference work or wiki entry, 197

➔

LIST OF EXAMPLES

References in APA style, continued

OTHER SOURCES (INCLUDING ONLINE VERSIONS)

32. Government publication, 198
33. Data set or graphic representation of data (chart, graph), 198
34. Dissertation, 198
35. Technical or research report, 199
36. Conference proceedings, 199
37. Paper presented at a meeting or symposium, 199
38. Poster session, 199

39. Presentation slides, 200
40. Film, 200
41. Online video or audio, 200
42. Television episode, 200
43. Television series, 201
44. Podcast episode, 201
45. Podcast series, 201
46. Recording, 201
47. Photograph, 201
48. Advertisement, 201

All the entries in this section of the book use hanging indent format, in which the first line aligns on the left and the subsequent lines indent one-half inch. This is the customary APA format.

Guidelines for author listings

List authors' last names first, and use only initials for first and middle names. The in-text citations in your text point readers toward particular sources in your list of references (see 17c).

NAME CITED IN SIGNAL PHRASE IN TEXT

Lapowsky (2021) has noted . . .

NAME IN PARENTHETICAL CITATION IN TEXT

. . . (Lapowsky, 2021).

BEGINNING OF ENTRY IN LIST OF REFERENCES

Lapowsky, I. (2021).

Checklist

Formatting a List of References

✔ Start your list on a new page after the text of your document but before appendices or notes. Continue consecutive page numbers.

✔ Center the heading "References" in boldface one inch from the top of the page.

✔ Begin each entry at the left margin, but indent subsequent lines one-half inch. Double-space the entire list.

✔ List sources alphabetically by author's last name. If no author is given, alphabetize the source by the first word of the title other than "A," "An," or "The." If the list includes two or more works by the same author, list them in chronological order.

✔ Italicize titles and subtitles of books and periodicals. Do not italicize titles of articles or websites, and do not enclose them in quotation marks.

✔ For titles of books and articles, capitalize only the first word of the title and the subtitle and any proper nouns or proper adjectives.

✔ For titles of periodicals and websites, capitalize all major words.

 Checklist

Combining Parts of Models

What should you do if your source doesn't match the model exactly? Suppose, for instance, that your source is a translation of a republished book with an editor.

✔ Identify a basic model to follow. If you decide that your source looks most like a republished book, for example, start with a citation that looks like model 13.

✔ Look for models that show additional elements in your source. For this example, you would need elements of model 9 (for the translation) and model 7 (for the editor).

✔ Add new elements from other models to your basic model in the order that makes the most sense to you.

✔ If you still aren't sure how to arrange the pieces to create a combination model, ask your instructor.

Models 1–5 below explain how to arrange author names. The information that follows the name of the author depends on the type of work you are citing—a book (models 6–14), a print periodical (models 15–21), a digital written-word source (models 22–31), or another kind of source (models 32–47).

1. One author Give the last name, a comma, the initial(s), and the date in parentheses.

Zimbardo, P. G. (2019).

2. Multiple authors List up to twenty authors, last name first, with commas separating authors' names and an ampersand (&) before the last author's name.

Nwadike, M. E., & Murphy, J. A. (2020).

Note: For a work with more than twenty authors, list the first nineteen, then an ellipsis (. . .), and then the final author's name.

3. Corporate or group author

Resources for Rehabilitation. (2016).

4. Unknown author Begin with the work's title. Italicize the titles of works that are a stand-alone item, such as a book, a movie, a one-time TV special (such as the 2020 Grammy Awards), or a podcast series. Do not italicize titles of works that are part of a larger whole, such as an article in a journal, a chapter in a book, or an episode of a TV or podcast series. Capitalize only the first word of the title and subtitle (if any) and proper nouns and proper adjectives.

Safe youth, safe schools. (2009).

5. Two or more works by the same author List works by the same author in chronological order. Repeat the author's name in each entry.

Goodall, J. (2009).

Goodall, J. (2013).

If the works appeared in the same year, list them alphabetically by <u>title</u>, and assign lowercase <u>letters</u> ("a," "b," etc.) after the dates.

Shermer, M. (2002a). <u>On estimating the lifetime of civilizations</u>. *Scientific American, 287*(2), 33.

Shermer, M. (2002b). <u>Readers who question evolution</u>. *Scientific American, 287*(1), 37.

If the works appeared in the same year but use a more specific date that includes the month or month and day, list the works in chronological order.

Print books

6. Basic format for a book The source map on p. 187 shows where to find information in a typical book. Take information from the book's title page and copyright page, not from the book's cover or a library catalog.

❶ Author. List all authors' last names first, and use only initials for first and middle names. For more about citing authors, see models 1–5.

❷ Publication year. Enclose the year of publication in parentheses.

❸ Title. Italicize the title and any subtitle. Capitalize only the first word of the title and the subtitle and any proper nouns or proper adjectives.

❹ Publisher. List the publisher's name, dropping any corporate abbreviations such as "Inc." or "Co."

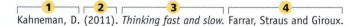
Kahneman, D. (2011). *Thinking fast and slow.* Farrar, Straus and Giroux.

7. Editor For a book with an editor but no author, list the source under the <u>editor's name</u>, followed by the abbreviation "Ed." in parentheses. A second model appears on p. 188.

<u>Schwartz, R. G. (Ed.).</u> (2009). *Handbook of child language disorders.* Psychology Press.

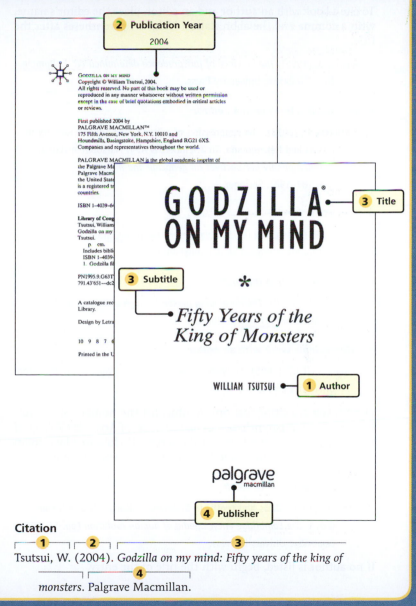

2 Publication Year

2004

GODZILLA ON MY MIND
Copyright © William Tsutsui, 2004.
All rights reserved. No part of this book may be used or
reproduced in any manner whatsoever without written permission
except in the case of brief quotations embodied in critical articles
or reviews.

First published 2004 by
PALGRAVE MACMILLAN™
175 Fifth Avenue, New York, N.Y. 10010 and
Houndmills, Basingstoke, Hampshire, England RG21 6XS.
Companies and representatives throughout the world.

PALGRAVE MACMILLAN is the global academic imprint of
the Palgrave Ma
Palgrave Macmi
the United State
is a registered tr
countries.

ISBN 1–4039–6

Library of Cong
Tsutsui, William
Godzilla on my
Tsutsui.
    p cm.
  Includes bibli
  ISBN 1–4039–
  1. Godzilla fi

PN1995.9.G63T
791.43'651––dc2

A catalogue rec
Library.

Design by Letra

10 9 8 7 6

Printed in the U

3 Title

GODZILLA®
ON MY MIND

*

3 Subtitle

*Fifty Years of the
King of Monsters*

WILLIAM TSUTSUI **1** Author

palgrave
macmillan

4 Publisher

Citation

1 **2** **3**

Tsutsui, W. (2004). *Godzilla on my mind: Fifty years of the king of*

4

monsters. Palgrave Macmillan.

To cite a book with an author and an editor, place the editor's name, with a comma and the abbreviation "Ed.," in parentheses after the title.

> Austin, J. (1995). *The province of jurisprudence determined* (W. E. Rumble, Ed.). Cambridge University Press.

8. Selection in a book with an editor

> Pettigrew, D. (2018). The suppression of cultural memory and identity in Bosnia and Herzegovina. In J. Lindert & A. T. Marsoobian (Eds.), *Multidisciplinary perspectives on genocide and memory* (pp. 187–198). Springer.

9. Translation

> Calasso, R. (2019). *The unnamable present* (R. Dixon, Trans.). Farrar, Straus and Giroux. (Original work published 2017)

10. Edition other than the first

> Berger, K. S. (2018). *The developing person through childhood and adolescence* (11th ed.). Worth.

11. Multivolume work with an editor

> Barnes, J. (Ed.). (1995). *Complete works of Aristotle* (Vols. 1–2). Princeton University Press.

Note: If you are citing just one volume, list the number of the volume you used in parentheses: *Complete works of Aristotle* (Vol. 1). If the volume has its own title, list the series title followed by a colon and the volume number in italics. Then list the volume title.

12. Article in a reference work

> Dean, C. (1994). Jaws and teeth. In S. Jones, R. Martin, & D. Pilbeam (Eds.), *The Cambridge encyclopedia of human evolution* (pp. 56–59). Cambridge University Press.

If no author is listed, begin with the title of the entry.

13. Republished book

Fremlin, C. (2017). *The hours before dawn*. Dover Publications. (Original
work published 1958)

14. Book with a title within the title Do not italicize or enclose in
quotation marks a title within a book title.

Klarman, M. J. (2007). Brown v. Board of Education *and the civil rights
movement*. Oxford University Press.

Print periodicals

The source map on p. 190 shows where to find information in a
sample periodical.

① **Author.** List all authors' last names first, and use only initials for
first and middle names. For more about citing authors, see models
1–5.

② **Publication date.** Enclose the date in parentheses. For journals,
use only the year. For magazines and newspapers, use the year, a
comma, the month (spelled out), and the day, if given.

③ **Article title.** Do not italicize or enclose article titles in quotation
marks. Capitalize only the first word of the article title and subtitle
and any proper nouns or proper adjectives.

④ **Periodical title.** Italicize the periodical title (and subtitle, if any),
and capitalize all major words. Follow the periodical title with a
comma.

⑤ **Volume and issue numbers.** Give the volume number (italicized)
and, without a space in between, the issue number (if given) in
parentheses. Follow with a comma.

⑥ **Page numbers.** Give the inclusive page numbers of the article.
End the citation with a period.

4 Periodical Title

The A M E R I C A N SCHOLAR

5 Volume and Issue Numbers
Vol. 75, No. 2

Spring 2006 | Vol. 75, No. 2

2 Publication Date
Spring 2006

The A M E R I C A N SCHOLAR

3 Article Title

Leaving Race Behind

Our growing Hispanic population creates a golden opportunity

AMITAI ETZIONI ● **1** Author

Some years ago the United States government asked me what my race was. I was reluctant to respond because my 50 years of practicing sociology—and some powerful personal experiences—have underscored for me what we all know to one degree or another, that racial divisions bedevil America, just as they do many other societies across the world. Not wanting to encourage these divisions, I refused to check off one of the specific racial options on the U.S. Census form and instead marked a box labeled "Other." I later found out that the federal government did not accept such an attempt to de-emphasize race, by me or by some 6.75 million other Americans who tried it. Instead the government assigned me to a racial category, one it chose for me. Learning this made me conjure up what I admit is a far-fetched association. I was in this place once before. When I was a Jewish child in Nazi Germany in the early 1930s, many Jews who saw themselves as good Germans wanted to "pass" as Aryans. But the Nazi regime would have none of it. Never mind, they told these Jews, *we determine* who is Jewish and who is not. A similar practice prevailed in the Old South, where if you had one drop of African blood you were a Negro, disregarding all other facts and considerations, including how you saw yourself.

You might suppose that in the years since my little Census-form protest

Amitai Etzioni is University Professor at George Washington University and the author of *The Monochrome Society*.

2 0 ● **6** Page Numbers

Citation

1 **2** **3**

Etzioni, A. (2006). Leaving race behind: Our growing Hispanic population

4 **5** **6**

creates a golden opportunity. *The American Scholar, 75*(2), 20–30.

15. Article in a journal Include the issue number (in parentheses and not italicized) after the volume number (italicized).

Ganegoda, D. B., & Bordia, P. (2019). I can be happy for you, but not all the time: A contingency model of envy and positive empathy in the workplace. *Journal of Applied Psychology, 104*(6), 776–795.

16. Article in a magazine Include the month (and day, if given).

Vlahos, J. (2019, March). Alexa, I want answers. *Wired*, 58–65.

If the magazine uses volume and issue numbers, include them.

Koch, C. (2019, October). Is death reversible? *Scientific American, 321*(4), 34–37.

17. Article in a newspaper

Finucane, M. (2019, September 25). Americans still eating too many low-quality carbs. *The Boston Globe*, B2.

18. Editorial or letter to the editor Add an identifying label.

Doran, K. (2019, October 12). Homeless who look like grandma or grandpa [Letter to the editor]. *The New York Times*, A22.

19. Unsigned article

Annual meeting announcement. (2003, March). *Cognitive Psychology, 46*(2), 227.

20. Review Identify the work reviewed.

Hall, W. (2019). [Review of the book *How to change your mind: The new science of psychedelics,* by M. Pollan]. *Addiction, 114*(10), 1892–1893.

21. Published interview For an interview published in print, begin with the interviewer. If the interviewee is not named in the title of the work, as in this example, include the interviewee's name in a signal phrase.

Tracy, A. (2019, December). The super Speaker. *Vanity Fair,* (712), 96–103.

Checklist

Citing Digital Sources

When citing sources accessed online or from an electronic database, include as many of the following elements as you can find:

✔ **Author.** Give the author's name, if available.

✔ **Publication date.** Include the date of electronic publication, if available. When no publication date is available, use "n.d." ("no date").

✔ **Title.** If the source is not from a larger work, italicize the title.

✔ **Print publication information.** For articles from online journals, magazines, or reference databases, give the publication title and other publishing information as you would for a print periodical (see models 15–21).

✔ **Retrieval information.** If a DOI (digital object identifier) is available, include it after the publication information with no period at the end. If there is no DOI, include a URL for the article except if the article is from a database (see model 23). If a DOI or URL is long, you can include a shortened form by using a site like shortdoi.org or bitly.com. If the work is intended to be updated frequently, include the retrieval date.

 Checklist

Citing Sources without Models in APA Style

You may need to cite a source for which you cannot find a model in APA style. If so, collect as much information as you can find about the author, title, date, and so on, with the goal of helping readers find the source for themselves. Then look at the models in this chapter to see which one most closely matches the type of source you are using.

Some digital sources can be especially tricky. If that's the case, ask your instructor's advice.

Digital written-word sources

22. Article from an online periodical Give the author, date, title, and publication information as you would for a print document.

Include both the volume and issue numbers for all journal articles. If the article has a digital object identifier (DOI), include it. If there is no DOI, include a stable, direct-link URL, if available. If the URL is lengthy, you can include a shortened form.

> Daly, J. (2019, August 2). Duquesne's med school plan part of national trend to train more doctors. *Pittsburgh Post-Gazette*. https://bit.ly/2Vzrm2l

> Bruns, A. (2017). Consequences of partner incarceration for women's employment. *Journal of Marriage and Family, 79*(5), 1331–1352. https://doi.org/10.1111/jomf.12412

23. Article from a database The source map on p. 194 shows where to find information for a typical article from a database.

1 **Author.** Include the author's name as you would for a print source. List all authors' last names first, and use initials for first and middle names. For more about citing authors, see models 1–5.

2 **Publication date.** Enclose the date in parentheses. For journals, use only the year. For magazines and newspapers, use the year, a comma, the month, and the day if given.

3 **Article title.** Capitalize only the first word of the article title and the subtitle and any proper nouns or proper adjectives.

4 **Periodical title.** Italicize the periodical title.

5 **Volume and issue number.** For journals and magazines, give the volume number (italicized) and the issue number (in parentheses).

6 **Page numbers.** Give inclusive page numbers.

7 **Retrieval information.** If the article has a DOI (digital object identifier), include it after the publication information; do not include the name of the database. If there is no DOI, do not include a URL. Do not add a period after the DOI.

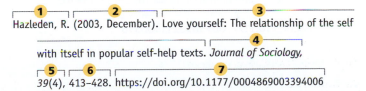

Hazleden, R. (2003, December). Love yourself: The relationship of the self with itself in popular self-help texts. *Journal of Sociology, 39*(4), 413–428. https://doi.org/10.1177/0004869003394006

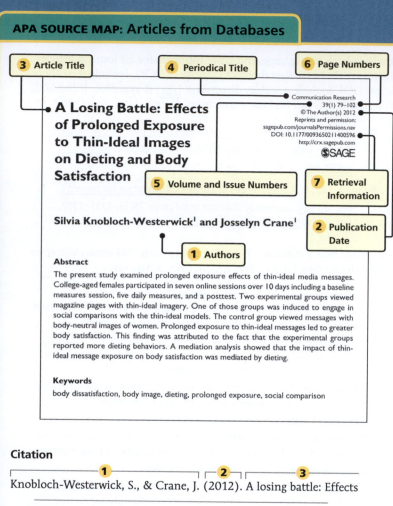

3 Article Title

4 Periodical Title

6 Page Numbers

Communication Research
39(1) 79–102
© The Author(s) 2012
Reprints and permission:
sagepub.com/journalsPermissions.nav
DOI: 10.1177/0093650211400596
http://crx.sagepub.com

A Losing Battle: Effects of Prolonged Exposure to Thin-Ideal Images on Dieting and Body Satisfaction

5 Volume and Issue Numbers

7 Retrieval Information

2 Publication Date

Silvia Knobloch-Westerwick[1] and Josselyn Crane[1]

1 Authors

Abstract

The present study examined prolonged exposure effects of thin-ideal media messages. College-aged females participated in seven online sessions over 10 days including a baseline measures session, five daily measures, and a posttest. Two experimental groups viewed magazine pages with thin-ideal imagery. One of those groups was induced to engage in social comparisons with the thin-ideal models. The control group viewed messages with body-neutral images of women. Prolonged exposure to thin-ideal messages led to greater body satisfaction. This finding was attributed to the fact that the experimental groups reported more dieting behaviors. A mediation analysis showed that the impact of thin-ideal message exposure on body satisfaction was mediated by dieting.

Keywords

body dissatisfaction, body image, dieting, prolonged exposure, social comparison

Citation

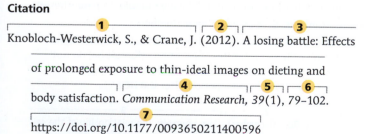

1 **2** **3**

Knobloch-Westerwick, S., & Crane, J. (2012). A losing battle: Effects

of prolonged exposure to thin-ideal images on dieting and

4 **5** **6**

body satisfaction. *Communication Research, 39*(1), 79–102.

7

https://doi.org/10.1177/0093650211400596

24. Abstract for an online article Include a label.

Gudjonsson, G. H., & Young, S. (2010). Does confabulation in memory predict suggestibility beyond IQ and memory? [Abstract]. *Personality & Individual Differences, 49*(1), 65–67. https://doi.org/10.1016/j. paid.2010.03.014

25. Comment on an online article Give the writer's real name (if known) or screen name. If the comment has no title, use up to the first twenty words as the title. Then, in square brackets, include the words "Comment on the article" and the article title in quotation marks. Provide a URL to the comment (if available) or to the article.

lollyl2. (2019, September 25). My husband works in IT in a major city down South. He is a permanent employee now, but for years [Comment on the article "The Google workers who voted to unionize in Pittsburgh are part of tech's huge contractor workforce"]. *Slate*. https://fyre.it/0RT8HmeL.4

26. Report or document from a website The source map on p. 196 shows where to find information for a report from a website. Include all of the following information that you can find.

1 **Author.** If one is given, include the author's name (see models 1–5). List last names first, and use only initials for first names. The site's sponsor may be the author. If no author is identified, begin the citation with the title of the document.

2 **Publication date.** Enclose the date of publication in parentheses. Use "n.d." ("no date") when no publication date is available.

3 **Title of work.** Italicize the title. Capitalize only the first word of the title and subtitle and any proper nouns or proper adjectives.

4 **Retrieval information.** Include the name of the website (with no italics), if different from the author. End with the URL, and do not add a period at the end of the URL.

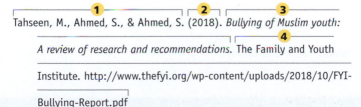

Tahseen, M., Ahmed, S., & Ahmed, S. (2018). *Bullying of Muslim youth: A review of research and recommendations.* The Family and Youth Institute. http://www.thefyi.org/wp-content/uploads/2018/10/FYI-Bullying-Report.pdf

APA SOURCE MAP: Reports and Works from Websites

2 Publication Date
March 14, 2013

4 Retrieval Information

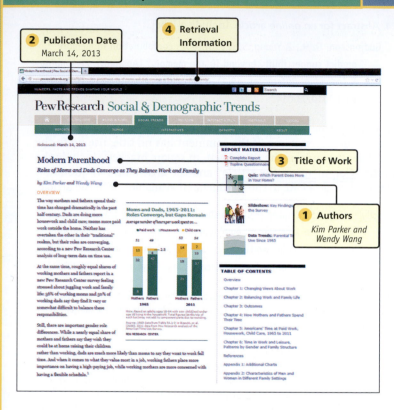

3 Title of Work

1 Authors
Kim Parker and Wendy Wang

Citation

1 **2** **3**
Parker, K., & Wang, W. (2013, March 14). *Modern parenthood: Roles of*

moms and dads converge as they balance work and family.

4
Pew Research Center. http://www.pewsocialtrends.org/2013/03/14/

modern-parenthood-roles-of-moms-and-dads-converge-as-they-

balance-work-and-family/

27. *Online book* Give the original print publication date, if different, in parentheses at the end of the entry.

> Russell, B. (2008). *The analysis of mind*. Project Gutenberg. https://
>   www.gutenberg.org/files/2529/2529-h/2529-h.htm (Original work
>   published 1921)

28. *Email or private message* Do not include entries for email messages or any postings that are private and cannot be retrieved by your readers. Instead, cite these sources in your text as forms of personal communication (see item 11 in 17c).

29. *Posting on social media* List an online posting in the references list only if it is retrievable by readers. Provide the author's name, if given, followed by the screen name in brackets. If only the screen name is known, provide it without brackets. Include the date of posting and up to the first twenty words of the post. List any attachments, such as images, videos, or links, and include a descriptive label, such as "[Tweet]" or "[Status update]," in separate brackets. Provide the website or app name and the URL for the post.

> National Science Foundation [@NSF]. (2019, October 13). *Understanding
>   how forest structure drives carbon sequestration is important for
>   ecologists, climate modelers and forest managers, who are working on*
>   [Thumbnail with link attached] [Tweet]. Twitter. https://twitter.com/
>   NSF/status/1183388649263652864

30. *Blog post* Include the title of the blog post and the name of the blog.

> Fister, B. (2019, February 14). Information literacy's third wave. *Library
>   Babel Fish*. https://www.insidehighered.com/blogs/library-babel-fish/
>   information-literacy%E2%80%99s-third-wave

31. *Online reference work or wiki entry* Use the date of posting, or "n.d." ("no date") if there is none. Include the retrieval date and URL. If the wiki has archived versions, like Wikipedia, instead use the date of posting and URL of the archived version you read.

> Merriam-Webster. (n.d.). Adscititious. In *Merriam-Webster.com dictionary*.
>   Retrieved November 5, 2019, from https://www.merriam-webster.
>   com/dictionary/adscititious

Behaviorism. (2019, October 11). In *Wikipedia*. https://en.wikipedia.
org/w/index.php?title=Behaviorism&oldid=915544724

Other sources (including online versions)

32. Government publication

Berchick, E. R., Barnett, J. C., & Upton, R. D. (2019, September 10).
Health insurance coverage in the United States: 2018 (Report No.
P60-267). U.S. Census Bureau. https://www.census.gov/library/
publications/2019/demo/p60-267.html

If no author is listed, begin with the department that produced the
document. Any broader organization the department belongs to can
be included as the publisher.

National Park Service. (2019, April 11). *Travel where women made
history: Ordinary and extraordinary places of American women.*
U.S. Department of the Interior. https://www.nps.gov/subjects/
travelwomenshistory/index.htm

33. Data set or graphic representation of data (chart, graph)

Reid, L. (2019). *Smarter homes: Experiences of living in low carbon homes
2013–2018* [Data set]. UK Data Service. https://doi.org/10.5255/
UKDA-SN-853485

Centers for Disease Control and Prevention. (2020, May 9). *New cases by
day* [Chart]. U.S. Department of Health & Human Services. https://
www.cdc.gov/coronavirus/2019-ncov/cases-updates/cases-in-us.html

34. Dissertation
Include the granting university in brackets after the
title. If you retrieved the dissertation from a database, give the publication number and database name. If you retrieved it from the
granting university's website, provide the URL.

Bacaksizlar, N. G. (2019). *Understanding social movements through
simulations of anger contagion in social media* (Publication No.
13805848) [Doctoral dissertation, University of North Carolina at
Charlotte]. ProQuest Dissertations & Theses.

Degli-Esposti, M. (2019). *Child maltreatment and antisocial behaviour in the United Kingdom: Changing risks over time* [Doctoral dissertation, University of Oxford]. Oxford University Research Archive. https://ora.ox.ac.uk/objects/uuid:6d5a8e55-bd19-41a1-8ef5-ef485642af89

35. *Technical or research report* Give the report number, if available, in parentheses after the title.

McCool, R., Fikes, R., & McGuinness, D. (2003). *Semantic web tools for enhanced authoring* (Report No. KSL-03-07). Knowledge Systems Laboratory, Stanford University. www.ksl.stanford.edu/KSL_Abstracts/KSL-03-07.html

36. *Conference proceedings*

Robertson, S. P., Vatrapu, R. K., & Medina, R. (2009). YouTube and Facebook: Online video "friends" social networking. In *Conference proceedings: YouTube and the 2008 election cycle* (pp. 159–176). ScholarWorks@UMass Amherst. http://scholarworks.umass.edu/jitpc2009

37. *Paper presented at a meeting or symposium* Include the location and the dates of the entire meeting or symposium, even if the paper presentation occurred on a specific day.

Vasylets, O. (2019, April 10–13). *Memory accuracy in bilinguals depends on the valence of the emotional event* [Paper presentation]. XIV International Symposium of Psycholinguistics, Tarragona, Spain.

38. *Poster session*

Wood, M. (2019, January 3–6). *The effects of an adult development course on students' perceptions of aging* [Poster session]. Forty-First Annual National Institute on the Teaching of Psychology, St. Pete Beach, FL, United States. https://nitop.org/resources/Documents/2019%20Poster%20Session%20II.pdf

39. Presentation slides

Centers for Disease Control and Prevention. (2019, April 16). *Building local
    response capacity to protect families from emerging health threats*
    [Presentation slides]. CDC Stacks. https://stacks.cdc.gov/view/cdc/77687

40. Film Include the director's name and the <u>original release year</u>.
You do not need to specify the format unless it is a <u>special version</u>
such as an extended cut. Include the label "[Film]" and the production company (or companies) after the title.

Peele, J. (Director). (<u>2017</u>). *Get out* [Film]. Universal Pictures.

Hitchcock, A. (Director). (<u>1959</u>). *The essentials collection: North by
    northwest* [Film; <u>five-disc special ed. on DVD</u>]. Metro-Goldwyn-Mayer;
    Universal Pictures Home Entertainment.

41. Online video or audio Think of the author of an online video or
audio file as the person or organization that posted it. For a TED
Talk, for example, the presenter is the author if the video was
accessed on the TED website. However, if the TED Talk was accessed
on YouTube, then TED becomes the author because the TED organization posted the video.

Wray, B. (2019, May). *How climate change affects your mental health*
    [Video]. TED Conferences. https://www.ted.com/talks/britt_wray_
    how_climate_change_affects_your_mental_health

TED. (2019, September 20). *Britt Wray: How climate change affects
    your mental health* [Video]. YouTube. https://www.youtube.com/
    watch?v=IlDkCEvsYw

When deciding whether to italicize the title of the video or audio
file, consider whether it is part of a series (regular font) or a stand-
alone item (italics).

42. Television episode

Waller-Bridge, P. (Writer), & Bradbeer, H. (Director). (2019, March 18).
    The provocative request (Season 2, Episode 3) [TV series episode].
    In P. Waller-Bridge, H. Williams, & J. Williams (Executive Producers),
    Fleabag. Two Brothers Pictures; BBC.

43. Television series

Waller-Bridge, P., Williams, H., & Williams, J. (Executive Producers). (2016–2019). *Fleabag* [TV series]. Two Brothers Pictures; BBC.

44. Podcast episode

West, S. (Host). (2018, July 27). Logical positivism (No. 120) [Audio podcast episode]. In *Philosophize this!* https://philosophizethis.org/logical-positivists/

45. Podcast series

Abumrad, J., & Krulwich, R. (Hosts). (2002–present). *Radiolab* [Audio podcast]. WNYC Studios. https://www.wnycstudios.org/podcasts/radiolab/podcasts

46. Recording

Carlile, B. (2018). The mother [Song]. On *By the way, I forgive you*. Low Country Sound; Elektra.

47. Photograph

McHardy, Amanda. (2018). *Art of the self portrait* [Photograph]. https://amandamchardyphotos.wordpress.com/portfolio/#jp-carousel-148

48. Advertisement

Centers for Disease Control and Prevention. (2021). *Mask up America* [Advertisement]. Ad Council. https://www.adcouncil.org/asset/mask-up-america-favorite-things/203568618.

17e   **Research-based essay, APA style**

STUDENT WRITER

Martha Bell

On the following pages is a paper by Martha Bell that conforms to the APA guidelines described in this chapter.

Page number in upper right-hand corner of every page

The Mystery of Post-Lyme Disease Syndrome

Title (boldface), writer's name, department and school, course number and title, professor, and date centered and double-spaced

Martha Bell

Department of Language and Literature,

Eastern Mennonite University

WRIT 130C: College Writing

Professor Eads

October 28, 2016

2

The Mystery of Post-Lyme Disease Syndrome

The Centers for Disease Control and Prevention (CDC) estimates a total of 300,000 cases of Lyme disease annually. Many medical professionals believe Lyme disease can be cured in a matter of weeks with a simple antibiotic treatment. In some cases, however, patients develop post-Lyme disease syndrome, sometimes called "chronic Lyme disease," exhibiting persistent symptoms of Lyme after initial treatment is completed. The scientific community, divided over the causes of post-Lyme disease syndrome, cannot agree on the best treatment for the syndrome. Although Lyme disease is preventable, people are still vulnerable to infection; consequently, there is a need for more research and collaboration with a focus on developing the technology to perform replicable studies, which may subsequently lead to an effective treatment algorithm for post-Lyme disease syndrome.

Prevention

Ixodes ticks, also known as blacklegged and deer ticks, are infected with the bacterium *Borrelia burgdorferi*, responsible for Lyme disease (Hawker et al., 2012). Since being bitten by an infected tick is the only known way of contracting Lyme disease, evading Ixodes ticks is an effective measure. According to M'ikanatha et al. (2013), "Lyme disease is acquired peridomestically and the risk is highest in residential settings abutting areas with forests, meadows, and high prevalence of deer" (p. 168). While adult ticks are more active in the cooler months, developing Ixodes ticks, called nymphs, feed the most during the spring and summer months (Centers for Disease Control and Prevention [CDC], 2016d). Therefore, avoiding areas such as meadows and grasslands in the spring and summer seasons aids in preventing Lyme disease.

Using permethrin repellent on clothes and 20 to 30 percent DEET insect repellent on the skin also keeps ticks away (Brody, 2013). Other measures include wearing light-colored clothing to make ticks

Full title boldface and centered

Introduction provides background information

Boldface centered headings help organize review

Reference to work with more than two authors uses "et al."

First reference to organization gives abbreviation in brackets for later references

3

more visible, wearing long sleeves and long pants, tucking shirts into pants and pants into socks, and taping closed open areas of clothing when spending time outdoors in areas where ticks are prevalent (Hawker et al., 2012). Additionally, individuals should keep yards and houses clean to avert mammals, such as deer and rodents, that carry Ixodes ticks, and should check pets for ticks.

Transition sentence moves readers from one idea to the next

Though all of these measures greatly reduce the chance of receiving a tick bite, they are not foolproof. The bacterium *B. burgdorferi* takes approximately 36 to 48 hours to become infectious after the tick has bitten an individual (Hawker et al., 2012). A bull's-eye rash called erythema migrans is the only unique symptom of Lyme disease. It appears 3 to 32 days after infection (Hawker et al., 2012). According to one study, only 70 to 80 percent of Lyme disease victims develop erythema migrans; therefore, other symptoms must be assessed (Steere & Sikand, 2003, p. 2472). Other characteristics of Lyme disease include fevers, headaches, stiff neck, swollen lymph nodes, body aches, fatigue, facial palsy, polyarthritis, aseptic meningitis, peripheral root lesions, radiculopathy, and

Multiple citations in parentheses listed alphabetically and separated by semicolon

myocarditis (CDC, 2016c; Hawker et al., 2012).

On average, it takes a few weeks for infected individuals to produce antibodies against *B. burgdorferi* (CDC, 2016a). Consequently, most cases of Lyme disease have better outcomes and recovery rates when antibiotics are administered quickly (CDC, 2016e). Administered in the beginning stages of Lyme disease, antibiotics help speed recovery and prevent more serious symptoms, such as heart and nervous system problems, from developing (Lantos, 2011, Introduction section).

Erythema migrans is not always present, and other symptoms of Lyme disease are similar to those of other illnesses. Therefore, Lyme disease may be misdiagnosed and untreated. Stricker (2007) explained that "in the absence of typical features of Lyme disease, patients may go on to develop a syndrome with multiple nonspecific

4

symptoms that affect various organ systems, including the joints, muscles, nerves, brain, and heart" (p. 149). Conversely, even when patients receive proper antibiotic treatment for two to four weeks, they can continue to experience symptoms.

Paren-
thetical
citation for
quotation
includes
page
number

Post-Lyme Disease Syndrome

The majority of Lyme disease patients are cured after multiple weeks of antibiotics; however, 10 to 15 percent of patients acquire relapsing nonspecific symptoms such as fatigue, arthritis, and short-term memory problems that can persist for months or even years (Brody, 2013). When there is no other possible origin of the nonspecific symptoms, and the individual has had proper treatment for Lyme disease, the patient is classified as having post-Lyme disease syndrome (Lantos, 2011). Marques (2008) explained, "The appearance of post-Lyme disease symptoms seems to correlate with disseminated diseases, a greater severity of illness at presentation, and delayed antibiotic therapy, but not with the duration of the initial antibiotic therapy" (p. 343). The medical community is unsure of how to treat the nonspecific symptoms or what causes them (Lantos, 2011, "A Clinical Approach" section).

Possible Sources of Post-Lyme Disease Syndrome

Scientists are unable to identify the exact source of post-Lyme disease syndrome for several reasons. Identifying patients is difficult because of the general nature of the symptoms. Several surveys demonstrate that a relatively high percentage of the overall population reports nonspecific symptoms, such as fatigue, chronic pain, or cognitive dysfunction after a tick bite (Lantos, 2011, Post-Lyme Disease Syndromes section). In addition, researchers struggle to find participants for their studies (Marques, 2008, p. 342). Study participants must have previous documentation of contracting Lyme disease, which significantly diminishes the testing population (Lantos, 2011).

Scientists and physicians suspect the source of post-Lyme disease syndrome to be multifactorial. Plausible causes of reoccurring

5

nonspecific symptoms include "persistent infection of *B. burgdorferi*, other tick-borne infections, part of the expected resolution of symptoms after treatment, postinfective fatigue syndrome, autoimmune mechanisms, and intercurrent conditions" (Marques, 2008, p. 343). Nevertheless, only a few ideas have been thoroughly explored thus far by the scientific community. The majority of scientists believe remaining damage to tissue and the immune system from the infection causes post-Lyme disease syndrome; however, some believe persistent infection of the bacteria is the source (CDC, 2016b).

Despite complications, a majority of the medical community considers persistent symptoms to be a result of residual damage to the tissues and the immune system that occurred during the infection. These "autoimmune" reactions, which the body uses against foreign elements, occur in infections similar to Lyme disease such as campylobacter, chlamydia, and strep throat (CDC, 2016b). Patients report their nonspecific symptoms improving over time after the typical antibiotic treatment (Marques, 2008, p. 342). Physicians who followed their patients with post-Lyme disease syndrome for extended times also see nonspecific symptoms resolve without further antibiotic treatment (Marques, 2008, p. 347). Consequently, post-Lyme disease syndrome may be a natural evolution of the body healing after an intense infection.

A smaller portion of the medical community considers persistent infection of the microorganism *B. burgdorferi* as the cause of post-Lyme disease syndrome. Recently published studies performed on animals show signs of ongoing infection of the bacterium. One scientific study infected mice with *B. burgdorferi* and gave them intense treatment of antibiotics that should have wiped out the bacterium (Bockenstedt et al., 2012). Bockenstedt et al. (2012) observed the mice over a period of time and found "that infectious spirochetes are rapidly eliminated after institution of antibiotics, but inflammatory *B. burgdorferi* antigens persist adjacent to cartilage and

6

in the enthuses" (p. 2652). This is one of the first studies to show continuous effects of the harmful microorganism in post-Lyme disease syndrome (Embers et al., 2012, Discussion section). Another scientific study was conducted on nonhuman primates, rhesus macaques. Once again the scientists infected the animals with *B. burgdorferi* and then four to six months later administered an antibiotic treatment to half of the monkeys (Embers et al., 2012). Their results also confirmed that *B. burgdorferi* could withstand antibiotic treatment in rhesus macaques and proceed to cause post-Lyme disease syndrome (Embers et al., 2012, Discussion section). Nonetheless, these results showing perpetual infection as the cause of post-Lyme disease syndrome have yet to be replicated in humans.

In contrast, many studies over the years contradict the theory of ongoing infection, though these studies have not been confirmed true in humans. Lantos (2011) clarified that "no adequately controlled, hypothesis-driven study using a repeatable method has demonstrated that viable *B. burgdorferi* is found in patients with persistent post-Lyme symptoms any more frequently than in those with favorable outcomes" (Biological Plausibility section). Most scientific studies trying to prove persistent infection of *B. burgdorferi* have not been replicated because their procedures and techniques are at fault. The problem derives from the technology that detects the microorganism (Lantos, 2011, Biological Plausibility section).

PCR and *B. burgdorferi* culture are commonly used to find evidence of the bacteria in the body; however, both have "low sensitivity in most body fluids from patients with Lyme disease" (Marques, 2008, p. 353). Even though other methods, such as finding antibodies in immune complexes, changes in C6 antibody levels, and PCR in urine samples, have been tried, none prove helpful (Marques, 2008, p. 353). Therefore, the persistent infection of *B. burgdorferi* has not yet successfully been proven as the cause of post-Lyme disease syndrome.

Presents opposing studies and points of view

7

Post-Lyme Disease Syndrome Treatment

Since the cause of post-Lyme disease syndrome is controversial, treatment for the infection varies from patient to patient and physician to physician. Treatment is still in the experimental stages, meaning no set treatment algorithm currently exists. Numerous patients rely on long-term antibiotic medication, despite the overwhelming defying scientific evidence against this treatment (CDC, 2016b). The research studies that focus on prolonged antibiotic treatment observe no dramatic difference in benefits or recoveries of those who had the treatment and those who did not (Marques, 2008, p. 353). On the contrary, many long-term antibiotic research studies found that post-Lyme disease syndrome patients develop harmful side effects. These adverse health effects include "catheter-associated venous thromboembolism, catheter-associated septicemia, allergic reactions and ceftriaxone-induced gallbladder toxicity" (Lantos, 2011, "Extended Antibiotics" section). Therefore, most of the scientific community considers long-term antibiotic treatment for chronic Lyme disease a harmful, risky, and unbeneficial plan.

Most of the scientific community advises against the use of long-term antibiotics because of potential adverse effects. Nevertheless, a small minority of physicians have observed improvements with long-term antibiotics. Because numerous studies show a lack of benefit to long-term antibiotics, these hopeful patients may be experiencing a placebo effect, which occurs when patients improve because they believe they are receiving an effective treatment (Marques, 2008, p. 356).

Solving the Mystery

Individuals can take various simple preventive measures to avoid contracting Lyme disease. If the infection is contracted, those who seek prompt treatment increase the chance of full recovery and decrease the chance of developing post-Lyme disease syndrome. However, these steps do not guarantee complete avoidance of post-

Shortened section heading in quotation marks

Lyme disease syndrome. Finding the source of post-Lyme disease syndrome will lead to a specific treatment plan that effectively heals patients. Many scientists deem the source of post-Lyme disease syndrome to be a natural autoimmune reaction; conversely, a few other scientists consider persistent infection as the cause. Both theories, however, need better technology to prove their accuracy. Since scientists disagree about the source of post-Lyme disease syndrome, a variety of experimental treatments have arisen. Replicable studies are needed so that an effective treatment for post-Lyme disease syndrome can be found.

Conclusion indicates need for further research

9

References

References
begin on a
new page;
heading is
centered
and
boldface

Bockenstedt, L., Gonzalez, D., Haberman, A., & Belperron, A. (2012).
Spirochete antigens persist near cartilage after murine Lyme
borreliosis therapy. *The Journal of Clinical Investigation, 122*(7),
2652–2660. https://doi.org/10.1172/JCI58813

Article from
an online
newspaper

Brody, J. (2013, July 8). When Lyme disease lasts and lasts. *The New
York Times*. https://well.blogs.nytimes.com/2013/07/08/when-
lyme-disease-lasts-and-lasts

Centers for Disease Control and Prevention. (2016a). *Diagnosis and
testing*. https://www.cdc.gov/lyme/diagnosistesting/index.html

Two or
more works
by the same
author
in the
same year
arranged
alpha-
betically by
title; letters
added after
year

Centers for Disease Control and Prevention. (2016b). *Post-treatment Lyme
disease syndrome*. https://www.cdc.gov/lyme/postlds/index.html

Centers for Disease Control and Prevention. (2016c). *Signs and
symptoms of untreated Lyme disease*. https://www.cdc.gov/
lyme/signs_symptoms/index.html

Centers for Disease Control and Prevention. (2016d). *Transmission*.
https://www.cdc.gov/lyme/transmission/index.html

Centers for Disease Control and Prevention. (2016e). *Treatment*.
https://www.cdc.gov/lyme/treatment/index.html

All authors
up to
twenty
listed

Embers, M. E., Barthold, S. W., Borda, J. T., Bowers, L., Doyle, L.,
Hodzic, E., Jacobs, M. B., Hasenkampf, N. R., Martin, D. S.,
Narasimhan, S., Phillippi-Falkenstein, K. M., Purcell, J. E.,
Ratterree, M. S., & Philipp, M. T. (2012). Persistence of *Borrelia
burgdorferi* in rhesus macaques following antibiotic treatment
of disseminated infection. *PLoS ONE*, *7*(1). https://doi.org/
10.1371/journal.pone.0029914

Print book

Hawker, J., Begg, N., Blair, L., Reintjes, R., Weinberg, J., & Ekdahl,
K. (2012). *Communicable disease control and health protection
handbook* (3rd ed.). John Wiley & Sons.

Journal
article with
DOI

Lantos, P. (2011). Chronic Lyme disease: The controversies and the
science. *Expert Review of Anti-Infective Therapy, 9*(7), 787–797.
https://doi.org/10.1586/eri.11.63

10

Marques, A. (2008). Chronic Lyme disease: A review. *Infectious Disease Clinics of North America, 22*(2), 341–360. https://doi.org/10.1016/j.idc.2007.12.011

M'ikanatha, N. M., Lynfield, R., Van Beneden, C. A., & de Valk, H. (2013). *Infectious disease surveillance* (2nd ed.). John Wiley & Sons.

Steere, A., & Sikand, V. (2003). The presenting manifestations of Lyme disease and the outcomes of treatment [Letter to the editor]. *The New England Journal of Medicine, 348*(24), 2472–2474. https://doi.org/10.1056/NEJM200306123482423

Stricker, R. (2007). Counterpoint: Long-term antibiotic therapy improves persistent symptoms associated with Lyme disease. *Clinical Infectious Diseases, 45*(2), 147–157. https://doi.org/10.1086/518853

Letter to the editor

18 *Chicago* Style

The style guide of the University of Chicago Press has long been used in history as well as in other areas of the arts and humanities. The Seventeenth Edition of *The Chicago Manual of Style* (2017) provides a complete guide to *Chicago* style, including two systems for citing sources. This chapter presents the notes and bibliography system.

18a Understanding *Chicago* citation style

Why does academic work call for very careful citation practices when writing for the general public may not? The answer is that readers of academic work expect source citations for several reasons:

- Source citations demonstrate that you've done your homework on your topic and that you are a part of the conversation surrounding it.

- Source citations show that you understand the need to give credit when you make use of someone else's intellectual property. (See Chapter 14.)

- Source citations give explicit directions to guide readers who want to look for themselves at the works you're using.

Guidelines from *The Chicago Manual of Style* will tell you exactly what information to include in your citation and how to format that information.

Types of sources   Refer to the list of examples in *Chicago* style on pp. 216–17. You will need to be careful to tell your readers whether you read a print version or a digital version of a source. Digital magazine and newspaper articles may include updates or corrections that the print version lacks; digital books may not number pages or screens the same way the print book does. If you are citing a source with media elements—such as a film, song, or artwork—consult the "Other sources" section of the examples. And if you can't find a model exactly like the source you've selected, see the box on p. 217.

Articles from web and database sources You need a subscription to look through most databases, so individual researchers almost always gain access to articles in databases through a school or public library that pays to subscribe. The easiest way to tell whether a source comes from a database, then, is that its information is *not* generally available free to anyone with an Internet connection. Many databases are digital collections of articles that originally appeared in edited print periodicals, ensuring that an authority has vouched for the accuracy of the information. Such sources may have more credibility than free material available on the web.

Parts of citations   Citations in *Chicago* style will appear in three places in your text—a note number in the text marks the material from the source, a footnote or an endnote includes information to identify the source (or information about supplemental material), and the bibliography provides the full citation.

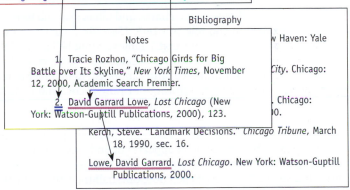

Chicago is a city for the working man. Nowhere is this more evident than in its architecture. David Garrard Lowe, author of *Lost Chicago*, notes that early Chicagoans "sought reality, not fantasy, and the reality of America as seen from the heartland did not include the pavilion of princes or the castles of kings."2 The inclination toward unadorned, sturdy buildings began in the late nineteenth century.

Bibliography

Notes

1. Tracie Rozhon, "Chicago Girds for Big Battle over Its Skyline," *New York Times*, November 12, 2000, Academic Search Premier.

2. David Garrard Lowe, *Lost Chicago* (New York: Watson-Guptill Publications, 2000), 123.

w Haven: Yale

City. Chicago:

Chicago:
0.

Kerch, Steve. "Landmark Decisions." *Chicago Tribune*, March 18, 1990, sec. 16.

Lowe, David Garrard. *Lost Chicago*. New York: Watson-Guptill Publications, 2000.

18b   Following *Chicago* format

Title page   About halfway down the title page, center the full title of your project and your name. Unless otherwise instructed, at the bottom of the page also list the course name, the instructor's name, and the date submitted. Do not type a number on this page.

Margins and spacing　Leave one-inch margins at the top, bottom, and sides of your pages. Double-space the entire text, including block quotations and between entries in the notes and bibliography.

Page numbers　Number all pages (except the title page) in the upper right-hand corner. Also use a short title or your name before page numbers. Check to see if your instructor has a preference on whether to count the title page as part of the text (if so, the first text page will be page 2) or as part of the front matter (if so, the first text page will be page 1).

Long quotations　For a long quotation, indent one-half inch (or five spaces) from the left margin and do not use quotation marks. *Chicago* defines a long quotation as one hundred words or eight lines, though you may set off shorter quotations for emphasis (44a).

Headings　*Chicago* style allows, but does not require, headings. Many students and instructors find them helpful.

Visuals　Visuals (photographs, charts, and tables) should be placed as near as possible to the relevant text. (See 14c for guidelines on incorporating visuals into your text.) Tables should be labeled *Table,* numbered, and captioned. All other visuals should be labeled *Figure* (abbreviated *Fig.*), numbered, and captioned. Remember to refer to each visual in your text, pointing out how it contributes to the point(s) you are making.

Notes　Notes can be footnotes (each one appearing at the bottom of the page on which its citation appears) or endnotes (in a list on a separate page at the end of the text). (Check your instructor's preference.) Indent the first line of each note one-half inch and begin with a number, a period, and one space before the first word. All remaining lines of the entry are aligned with the left margin. Single-space footnotes and endnotes, with a double space between each entry.

Use superscript numbers ([1]) to mark citations in the text. Place the superscript number for each note just after the relevant quotation, sentence, clause, or phrase. Type the number after any punctuation mark except the dash, and do not leave a space before the superscript. Number citations sequentially throughout the text. When you use signal phrases to introduce source material, note that *Chicago* style requires you to use the present tense (*citing Bebout's studies, Meier argues . . .*).

IN THE TEXT

Thompson points out that African American and Puerto Rican prisoners at Attica were more likely than white prisoners to have their mail censored and family visits restricted.[19]

IN THE FIRST NOTE REFERRING TO THE SOURCE

19. Heather Ann Thompson, *Blood in the Water: The Attica Prison Uprising of 1971 and Its Legacy* (New York: Pantheon Books, 2016), 13.

After giving complete information the first time you cite a work, shorten additional references to that work: list only the author's last name, a shortened version of the title, and the page number. If the second reference to the work immediately follows the first reference, list only the author's name and the page number.

IN FIRST AND SUBSEQUENT NOTES

19. Heather Ann Thompson, *Blood in the Water: The Attica Prison Uprising of 1971 and Its Legacy* (New York: Pantheon Books, 2016), 13.

20. Thompson, 82.

21. Julia Sweig, *Inside the Cuban Revolution* (Cambridge, MA: Harvard University Press, 2002), 21.

22. Thompson, *Blood in the Water,* 304.

Bibliography   Begin the list of sources on a separate page after the main text and any endnotes. Continue numbering the pages consecutively. Center the title *Bibliography* (without underlining, italics, or quotation marks) one inch below the top of the page. Double-space, and then begin each entry at the left margin. Indent the second and subsequent lines of each entry one-half inch, or five spaces.

List sources alphabetically by authors' last names or by the first major word in the title if the author is unknown. See 18d for an example of a *Chicago*-style bibliography.

In the bibliographic entry, include the same information as in the first note for that source, but omit the page reference. Give the first author's last name first, followed by a comma and the first name; separate the main elements of the entry with periods rather than commas; and do not enclose the publication information for books in parentheses.

IN THE BIBLIOGRAPHY

Thompson, Heather Ann. *Blood in the Water: The Attica Prison Uprising of 1971 and Its Legacy*. New York: Pantheon Books, 2016.

LIST OF EXAMPLES

Notes and bibliographic entries in *Chicago* style

PRINT AND DIGITAL BOOKS

1. One author, 218
2. Multiple authors, 218
3. Organization as author, 218
4. Unknown author, 219
5. Online book, 219
6. Electronic book (e-book), 219
7. Book with an editor, 219
8. Selection in an anthology or chapter in a book with an editor, 220
9. Introduction, preface, foreword, or afterword, 220
10. Translation, 220
11. Edition other than the first, 220
12. Multivolume work, 220
13. Work with a title within the title, 221
14. Sacred text, 221
15. Source quoted in another source, 221

PRINT AND DIGITAL PERIODICALS

16. Article in a print journal, 221
17. Article in an online journal, 222
18. Journal article from a database, 222
    SOURCE MAP, 224
19. Article in a print magazine, 223
20. Article in an online magazine, 223
21. Magazine article from a database, 223
22. Article in a newspaper, 225
23. Article in an online newspaper, 225
24. Newspaper article from a database, 225
25. Book review, 225

ONLINE SOURCES

26. Work from a website, 226
    SOURCE MAP, 228
27. Entire website, 227
28. Online reference work, 227
29. Blog post, 227
30. Email, social media messages, and other personal communications, 229
31. Social media post, 229
32. Podcast, 229
33. Online audio or video, 229

LIST OF EXAMPLES

Notes and bibliographic entries in *Chicago* style, continued

OTHER SOURCES

34. Published or broadcast interview, 230

35. DVD or Blu-ray, 230

36. Sound recording, 230

37. Work of art, 230

38. Pamphlet, report, or brochure, 231

39. Government document, 231

18c Creating *Chicago* notes and bibliographic entries

The following examples demonstrate how to format both notes and bibliographic entries according to *Chicago* style. The note, which is numbered, appears first; the bibliographic entry, which is not numbered, appears below the note. We have used underlining in some examples only to draw your attention to important elements. Do not underline anything in your own citations.

> **Checklist**
>
> **Citing Sources without Models in *Chicago* Style**
>
> To cite a source for which you cannot find a model, collect as much information as you can find—about the creator, title, date of creation or update, and location of the source—with the goal of helping your readers find the source for themselves, if possible. Then look at the models in this section to see which one most closely matches the type of source you are using.
>
> Some digital sources can be especially tricky. If that's the case, ask your instructor's advice.

Print and digital books

The note for a book typically includes five elements: author's name, title and subtitle, city of publication and publisher, year, and page number(s) or electronic locator information for the information in the note. The bibliographic entry usually includes all these elements but the page number (and does include a URL or other locator if the book is digitally published), but it is styled differently: commas separate major elements of a note, but a bibliographic entry uses periods.

1. One author

1. Ibram X. Kendi, *How to Be an Antiracist* (New York: One World, 2019), 73.

Kendi, Ibram X. *How to Be an Antiracist*. New York: One World, 2019.

2. Multiple authors

2. Mark Littman and Fred Espenak, *Totality: The Great American Eclipses of 2017 and 2024* (New York: Oxford University Press, 2017), 35.

Littman, Mark, and Fred Espenak. *Totality: The Great American Eclipses of 2017 and 2024*. New York: Oxford University Press, 2017.

With four or more authors, you may give the first-listed author followed by et al. in the note. In the bibliography, list all the authors' names.

2. Stephen J. Blank et al., *Conflict, Culture, and History: Regional Dimensions* (Miami: University Press of the Pacific, 2002), 276.

Blank, Stephen J., Lawrence E. Grinter, Karl P. Magyar, Lewis B. Ware, and Bynum E. Weathers. *Conflict, Culture, and History: Regional Dimensions*. Miami: University Press of the Pacific, 2002.

3. Organization as author

3. World Intellectual Property Organization, *Intellectual Property Profile of the Least Developed Countries* (Geneva: World Intellectual Property Organization, 2002), 43.

World Intellectual Property Organization. *Intellectual Property Profile of the Least Developed Countries*. Geneva: World Intellectual Property Organization, 2002.

4. Unknown author

4. *Broad Stripes and Bright Stars* (Kansas City, MO: Andrews McMeel, 2002), 10.

Broad Stripes and Bright Stars. Kansas City, MO: Andrews McMeel, 2002.

5. Online book

5. Dorothy Richardson, *Long Day: The Story of a New York Working Girl, as Told by Herself* (New York: Century, 1906; UMDL Texts, 2010), 159, http://quod.lib.umich.edu/cgi/t/text/text-idx?c=moa;idno =AFS7156.0001.001.

Richardson, Dorothy. *Long Day: The Story of a New York Working Girl, as Told by Herself.* New York: Century, 1906. UMDL Texts, 2010. http://quod.lib.umich.edu/cgi/t/text/text-idx?c=moa;idno =AFS7156.0001.001.

6. Electronic book (e-book)

6. Atul Gawande, *Being Mortal: Medicine and What Matters in the End* (New York: Metropolitan, 2014), chap. 3, Nook.

Gawande, Atul. *Being Mortal: Medicine and What Matters in the End.* New York: Metropolitan, 2014. Nook.

7. Book with an editor

7. Leopold von Ranke, *The Theory and Practice of History,* ed. Georg G. Iggers (New York: Routledge, 2010), 135.

von Ranke, Leopold. *The Theory and Practice of History.* Edited by Georg G. Iggers. New York: Routledge, 2010.

If an edited book has no author, put the editor's name first.

7. James H. Fetzer, ed., *The Great Zapruder Film Hoax: Deceit and Deception in the Death of JFK* (Chicago: Open Court, 2003), 56.

Fetzer, James H., ed. *The Great Zapruder Film Hoax: Deceit and Deception in the Death of JFK.* Chicago: Open Court, 2003.

8. Selection in an anthology or chapter in a book with an editor

8. Denise Little, "Born in Blood," in *Alternate Gettysburgs,* ed. Brian Thomsen and Martin H. Greenberg (New York: Berkley Publishing Group, 2002), 245.

Give the inclusive page numbers of the selection or chapter in the bibliographic entry.

Little, Denise. "Born in Blood." In *Alternate Gettysburgs.* Edited by Brian Thomsen and Martin H. Greenberg, 242–55. New York: Berkley Publishing Group, 2002.

9. Introduction, preface, foreword, or afterword

9. Ta-Nehisi Coates, foreword to *The Origin of Others,* by Toni Morrison (Cambridge, MA: Harvard University Press, 2017), xi.

Give the inclusive page numbers of the section cited in the bibliographic entry.

Coates, Ta-Nehisi. Foreword to *The Origin of Others,* by Toni Morrison, vii–xvii. Cambridge, MA: Harvard University Press, 2017.

10. Translation

10. Suetonius, *The Twelve Caesars,* trans. Robert Graves (London: Penguin Classics, 1989), 202.

Suetonius. *The Twelve Caesars.* Translated by Robert Graves. London: Penguin Classics, 1989.

11. Edition other than the first

11. Dee Brown, *Bury My Heart at Wounded Knee: An Indian History of the American West,* 4th ed. (New York: Owl Books, 2007), 12.

Brown, Dee. *Bury My Heart at Wounded Knee: An Indian History of the American West,* 4th ed. New York: Owl Books, 2007.

12. Multivolume work

12. John Watson, *Annals of Philadelphia and Pennsylvania in the Olden Time,* vol. 2 (Washington, DC: Ross & Perry, 2003), 514.

Watson, John. *Annals of Philadelphia and Pennsylvania in the Olden Time.* Vol. 2. Washington, DC: Ross & Perry, 2003.

13. Work with a title within the title Use quotation marks around any title within a book title.

13. John A. Alford, *A Companion to "Piers Plowman"* (Berkeley: University of California Press, 1988), 195.

Alford, John A. *A Companion to "Piers Plowman."* Berkeley: University of California Press, 1988.

14. Sacred text Do not include sacred texts in the bibliography.

14. Luke 18:24–25 (New International Version).

14. Qur'an 7:40–41.

15. Source quoted in another source Identify both the original and the secondary source.

15. Frank D. Millet, "The Filipino Leaders," *Harper's Weekly,* March 11, 1899, quoted in Richard Slotkin, *Gunfighter Nation: The Myth of the Frontier in Twentieth-Century America* (New York: HarperCollins, 1992), 110.

Millet, Frank D. "The Filipino Leaders." *Harper's Weekly,* March 11, 1899. Quoted in Richard Slotkin, *Gunfighter Nation: The Myth of the Frontier in Twentieth-Century America* (New York: HarperCollins, 1992), 110.

Print and digital periodicals

The note for an article in a periodical typically includes the author's name, the article title, and the periodical title. The format for other information, including the volume and issue numbers (if any) and the date of publication, as well as the page number(s) to which the note refers, varies according to the type of periodical and whether you consulted it in print, on the web, or in a database. In a bibliographic entry for a journal or magazine article from a database or a print periodical, also give the inclusive page numbers.

16. Article in a print journal

16. Catherine Bishop and Angela Woollacott, "Business and Politics as Women's Work: The Australian Colonies and the Mid-Nineteenth-Century Women's Movement," *Journal of Women's History* 28, no. 1 (2016): 87.

Bishop, Catherine, and Angela Woollacott. "Business and Politics as Women's Work: The Australian Colonies and the Mid-Nineteenth-Century Women's Movement." *Journal of Women's History* 28, no. 1 (2016): 84–106.

17. Article in an online journal Give the DOI, preceded by *https://doi .org/*. If there is no DOI, include the article URL. If page numbers are provided, include them as well.

17. Jeffrey J. Schott, "America, Europe, and the New Trade Order," *Business and Politics* 11, no. 3 (2009), https://doi.org/10.2202/1469 -3569.1263.

Schott, Jeffrey J. "America, Europe, and the New Trade Order." *Business and Politics* 11, no. 3 (2009). https://doi.org/10.2202/1469 -3569.1263.

18. Journal article from a database The source map on p. 224 shows where to find information for a typical article.

1 **Author.** In a note, list the author(s) first name first. In the bibliographic entry, list the first author last name first, comma, first name; list other authors first name first.

2 **Article title.** Enclose the title and subtitle (if any) in quotation marks, and capitalize major words. In the notes section, put a comma before and after the title. In the bibliography, put a period before and after.

3 **Periodical title.** Italicize the title and subtitle, and capitalize all major words. For a magazine or newspaper, follow with a comma.

4 **Volume and issue numbers (for journals) and date.** For journals, follow the title with the volume number, a comma, the abbreviation *no.,* and the issue number; enclose the publication year in parentheses and follow with a colon. (For other periodicals, give the month and year or month, day, and year, not in parentheses, followed by a colon.)

5 **Page numbers.** In a note, give the page where the information is found. In the bibliographic entry, give the page range.

6 **Retrieval information.** Provide the article's DOI, if one is given, the name of the database, or a stable URL for the article. Because you provide stable retrieval information, you do not need to identify the electronic format of the work (i.e., PDF). End with a period.

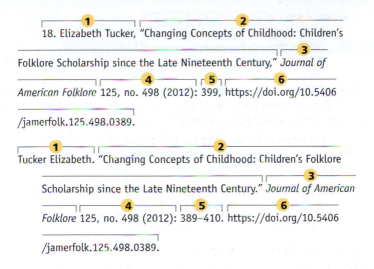

18. Elizabeth Tucker, "Changing Concepts of Childhood: Children's Folklore Scholarship since the Late Nineteenth Century," *Journal of American Folklore* 125, no. 498 (2012): 399, https://doi.org/10.5406 /jamerfolk.125.498.0389.

Tucker Elizabeth. "Changing Concepts of Childhood: Children's Folklore Scholarship since the Late Nineteenth Century." *Journal of American Folklore* 125, no. 498 (2012): 389–410. https://doi.org/10.5406 /jamerfolk.125.498.0389.

19. Article in a print magazine

19. Terry McDermott, "The Mastermind: Khalid Sheikh Mohammed and the Making of 9/11," *New Yorker,* September 13, 2010, 42.

McDermott, Terry. "The Mastermind: Khalid Sheikh Mohammed and the Making of 9/11." *New Yorker,* September 13, 2010, 38–51.

20. Article in an online magazine

20. Tracy Clark-Flory, "Educating Women Saves Kids' Lives," *Salon,* September 17, 2010, http://www.salon.com/life/broadsheet/2010/09/17 /education_women/index.html.

Clark-Flory, Tracy. "Educating Women Saves Kids' Lives." *Salon,* September 17, 2010. http://www.salon.com/life/broadsheet/2010/09/17 /education_women/index.html.

21. Magazine article from a database

21. Sami Yousafzai and Ron Moreau, "Twisting Arms in Afghanistan," *Newsweek,* November 9, 2009, 8, Academic Search Premier.

Yousafzai, Sami, and Ron Moreau. "Twisting Arms in Afghanistan." *Newsweek,* November 9, 2009. 8. Academic Search Premier.

CHICAGO SOURCE MAP: Articles from Databases

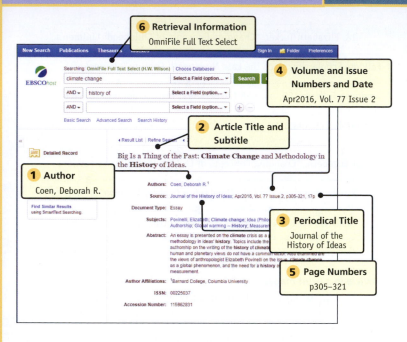

6 Retrieval Information — OmniFile Full Text Select

4 Volume and Issue Numbers and Date — Apr2016, Vol. 77 Issue 2

2 Article Title and Subtitle

1 Author — Coen, Deborah R.

3 Periodical Title — Journal of the History of Ideas

5 Page Numbers — p305–321

Citation

ENDNOTE

1. Deborah R. Coen, "Big Is a Thing of the Past: Climate Change and Methodology in the History of Ideas," *Journal of the History of Ideas* 77, no. 2, April 2016: 310, OmniFile Full Text Select.

BIBLIOGRAPHIC ENTRY

Coen, Deborah R. "Big Is a Thing of the Past: Climate Change and Methodology in the History of Ideas." *Journal of the History of Ideas* 77, no. 2, April 2016: 305–21. OmniFile Full Text Select.

22. Article in a newspaper Do not include page numbers for a newspaper article, but you may include the section, if any.

22. Caroline E. Mayer, "Wireless Industry to Adopt Voluntary Standards," *Washington Post,* September 9, 2003, sec. E.

Chicago recommends that newspaper articles appear in the notes section only, not in the bibliography. Check your instructor's preference. A bibliography entry would look like this:

Mayer, Caroline E. "Wireless Industry to Adopt Voluntary Standards." *Washington Post,* September 9, 2003, sec. E.

23. Article in an online newspaper

23. Somini Sengupta, "How a Seed Bank, Almost Lost in Syria's War, Could Help Feed a Warming Planet," *New York Times,* October 13, 2017, https://www.nytimes.com/2017/10/13/climate/syria-seed-bank.html.

Sengupta, Somini. "How a Seed Bank, Almost Lost in Syria's War, Could Help Feed a Warming Planet." *New York Times,* October 13, 2017. https://www.nytimes.com/2017/10/13/climate/syria-seed-bank .html.

24. Newspaper article from a database

24. Demetria Irwin, "A Hatchet, Not a Scalpel, for NYC Budget Cuts," *New York Amsterdam News,* November 13, 2008, Academic Search Premier.

Irwin, Demetria. "A Hatchet, Not a Scalpel, for NYC Budget Cuts." *New York Amsterdam News,* November 13, 2008. Academic Search Premier.

25. Book review After the information about the book under review, give publication information for the appropriate kind of source (see models 16–24).

25. Roderick MacFarquhar, "China's Astounding Religious Revival," review of *The Souls of China: The Return of Religion after Mao,* by Ian Johnson, *New York Review of Books*, June 8, 2017, http://www.nybooks .com/articles/2017/06/08/chinas-astounding-religious-revival/.

MacFarquhar, Roderick. "China's Astounding Religious Revival." Review of *The Souls of China: The Return of Religion after Mao,* by Ian Johnson. *New York Review of Books,* June 8, 2017. http://www.nybooks.com /articles/2017/06/08/chinas-astounding-religious-revival/.

Online sources

Notes and bibliographic entries for online sources typically include the author; the title of the work; the name of the site; the sponsor of the site, if different from the name of the site or name of the author; the date of publication or most recent update; and a URL. If the online source does not indicate when it was published or last modified, include your date of access.

26. Work from a website See the source map on p. 228.

1 **Author.** In a note, list the author(s) first name first. In a bibliographic entry, list the first author last name first, comma, first name; list additional authors first name first. Note that the sponsor may serve as the author.

2 **Document title.** Enclose the title in quotation marks, and capitalize all major words. In a note, put a comma before and after the title. In the bibliography, put a period before and after the title.

3 **Title of website.** Capitalize all major words. If the site's title is analogous to a book or periodical title, italicize it. In the notes section, put a comma after the title. In the bibliography, put a period after the title.

4 **Sponsor of site.** If the sponsor is the same as the author or site title, you may omit it. End with a comma (in the note) or a period (in the bibliographic entry).

5 **Date of publication or last modification.** If a time stamp is given, include it. If no date is available, include your date of access (with the word *accessed*). End with a comma (in the note) or a period (in the bibliographic entry).

6 **Retrieval information.** Give the URL for the work and end with a period.

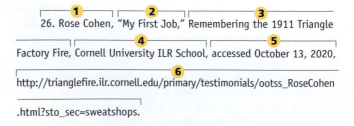

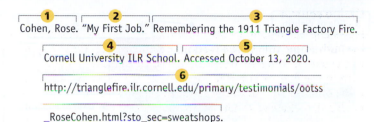

Cohen, Rose. "My First Job." Remembering the 1911 Triangle Factory Fire.
Cornell University ILR School. Accessed October 13, 2020.
http://trianglefire.ilr.cornell.edu/primary/testimonials/ootss
_RoseCohen.html?sto_sec=sweatshops.

27. Entire website For clarity, you may add the word *website* in parentheses after the title.

27. Rutgers School of Arts and Sciences, Rutgers Oral History Archive (website), 2017, http://oralhistory.rutgers.edu/.

Rutgers School of Arts and Sciences. Rutgers Oral History Archive (website). 2017. http://oralhistory.rutgers.edu/.

28. Online reference work In a note, use *s.v.*, the abbreviation for the Latin *sub verbo* ("under the word") to help your reader find the entry. Include the date the entry was posted, last modified, or accessed. Do not list reference works such as encyclopedias or dictionaries in your bibliography.

28. *Encyclopedia Britannica,* s.v. "Monroe Doctrine," accessed October 12, 2017, https://www.britannica.com/event/Monroe-Doctrine.

29. Blog post Treat a blog post as a short work from a website (see model 26).

29. Jai Arjun Singh, "On the Road in the USSR," *Jabberwock* (blog), November 29, 2007, http://jaiarjun.blogspot.com/2007/11/on-road-in -ussr.html.

Chicago recommends that blog posts appear in the notes section only, not in the bibliography. Check your instructor's preference. A bibliography reference would look like this:

Singh, Jai Arjun. "On the Road in the USSR." *Jabberwock* (blog), November 29, 2007. http://jaiarjun.blogspot.com/.

CHICAGO SOURCE MAP: Works from Websites

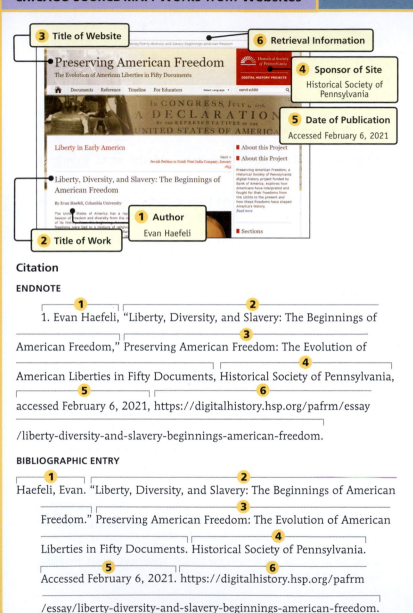

3 Title of Website

6 Retrieval Information

Preserving American Freedom
The Evolution of American Liberties in Fifty Documents

4 Sponsor of Site
Historical Society of Pennsylvania

5 Date of Publication
Accessed February 6, 2021

Liberty in Early America

Liberty, Diversity, and Slavery: The Beginnings of American Freedom

By Evan Haefeli, Columbia University

1 Author
Evan Haefeli

2 Title of Work

Citation

ENDNOTE

1. Evan Haefeli, "Liberty, Diversity, and Slavery: The Beginnings of American Freedom," Preserving American Freedom: The Evolution of American Liberties in Fifty Documents, Historical Society of Pennsylvania, accessed February 6, 2021, https://digitalhistory.hsp.org/pafrm/essay /liberty-diversity-and-slavery-beginnings-american-freedom.

BIBLIOGRAPHIC ENTRY

Haefeli, Evan. "Liberty, Diversity, and Slavery: The Beginnings of American Freedom." Preserving American Freedom: The Evolution of American Liberties in Fifty Documents. Historical Society of Pennsylvania. Accessed February 6, 2021. https://digitalhistory.hsp.org/pafrm /essay/liberty-diversity-and-slavery-beginnings-american-freedom.

30. Email, social media messages, and other personal communications
Cite email messages, social media messages, personal interviews, and other personal communications, such as letters and telephone calls, in the text or in a note only; do not cite them in the bibliography.

30. Kareem Adas, Facebook private message to author, February 11, 2020.

31. Social media post In place of a title, include the text of the post, up to the first 160 characters.

31. NASA (@nasa), "This galaxy is a whirl of color," Instagram photo, September 23, 2017, https://www.instagram.com/p /BZY8adnnZQJ/.

NASA. "This galaxy is a whirl of color." Instagram photo, September 23, 2017. https://www.instagram.com/p/BZY8adnnZQJ/.

32. Podcast Treat a podcast as a short work from a website (see model 26). Include the type of podcast or file format (if downloadable), the time stamp, and the URL.

32. Toyin Falola, "Creativity and Decolonization: Nigerian Cultures and African Epistemologies," Episode 96, November 17, 2015, in *Africa Past and Present,* African Online Digital Library, podcast, MP3 audio, 43:44, http://afripod.aodl.org/2015/11/afripod-96/.

Falola, Toyin. "Creativity and Decolonization: Nigerian Cultures and African Epistemologies." Episode 96, November 17, 2015. *Africa Past and Present*. African Online Digital Library. Podcast, MP3 audio, 43:44. http://afripod.aodl.org/2015/11/afripod-96/.

33. Online audio or video Treat an online audio or video source as a short work from a website (see model 26). If the source is downloadable, give the medium or file format and a time stamp before the URL.

33. Alyssa Katz, "Did the Mortgage Crisis Kill the American Dream?" YouTube video, 4:32, posted by NYCRadio, June 24, 2009, http://www .youtube.com/watch?v=uivtwjwd_Qw.

Katz, Alyssa. "Did the Mortgage Crisis Kill the American Dream?" YouTube video, 4:32. Posted by NYCRadio. June 24, 2009. http://www .youtube.com/watch?v=uivtwjwd_Qw.

Other sources

34. Published or broadcast interview

34. David O. Russell, interview by Terry Gross, *Fresh Air*, WNYC, February 20, 2014.

Russell, David O. Interview by Terry Gross. *Fresh Air*. WNYC, February 20, 2014.

Interviews you conduct are considered personal communications (see model 30).

35. DVD or Blu-ray Include both the date of the original release and the date of release for the format you are citing.

35. *American History X,* directed by Tony Kaye (1998; Los Angeles: New Line Studios, 2002), DVD.

Kaye, Tony, dir. *American History X.* 1998; Los Angeles: New Line Studios, 2002. DVD.

36. Sound recording

36. "Work," MP3 audio, track 4 on Rihanna, *Anti*, Roc Nation, 2016.

Rihanna. "Work." *Anti*. Roc Nation, 2016, MP3 audio.

37. Work of art   Works of art usually can be mentioned in the text rather than cited in a note or bibliography entry. Check your instructor's preference.

37. Hope Gangloff, *Vera*, 2015, acrylic on canvas, Kemper Museum of Contemporary Art, Kansas City, MO.

Gangloff, Hope. *Vera*. 2015. Acrylic on canvas. Kemper Museum of Contemporary Art, Kansas City, MO.

If you refer to a reproduction, give the publication information.

37. Mary Cassatt, *The Child's Bath,* 1893, oil on canvas, *Art Access*, The Art Institute of Chicago, accessed October 13, 2017, http://www .artic.edu/aic/collections/exhibitions/Impressionism/Cassatt.

Cassatt, Mary. *The Child's Bath*. 1893. Oil on canvas. *Art Access*. The Art Institute of Chicago. Accessed October 13, 2017. http://www.artic .edu/aic/collections/exhibitions/Impressionism/Cassatt.

38. Pamphlet, report, or brochure   Information about the author or publisher may not be readily available, but give enough information to identify your source.

38. International Monetary Fund, *Western Hemisphere: Tale of Two Adjustments,* World Economic and Financial Surveys (Washington, DC: International Monetary Fund, 2017), 29.

International Monetary Fund. *Western Hemisphere: Tale of Two Adjustments*. World Economic and Financial Surveys. Washington, DC: International Monetary Fund, 2017.

39. Government document

39. U.S. House Committee on Ways and Means, *Economic Mobility Act of 2019*, 116th Cong., 1st sess. (Washington, DC: Government Printing Office, 2020), 23.

U.S. House Committee on Ways and Means. *Economic Mobility Act of 2019*. 116th Cong., 1st sess. Washington, DC: Government Printing Office, 2020.

18d Excerpts from a research-based history essay, *Chicago* style

STUDENT WRITER

Amanda Rinder

On the following pages are excerpts from an essay by Amanda Rinder that conforms to the *Chicago* guidelines described in this chapter.

Rinder 2

First page of body text is p. 2

Essay refers to each figure by number

Thesis introduced

Double-spaced text

Source cited using superscript numeral

Only one city has the "Big Shoulders" described by Carl Sandburg: Chicago (fig. 1). So renowned are its skyscrapers and celebrated building style that an entire school of architecture is named for Chicago. Presently, however, the place that Frank Sinatra called "my kind of town" is beginning to lose sight of exactly what kind of town it is. Many of the buildings that give Chicago its distinctive character are being torn down in order to make room for new growth. Both preserving the classics and encouraging new creation are important; the combination of these elements gives Chicago architecture its unique flavor. Witold Rybczynski, a professor of urbanism, told Tracie Rozhon of the *New York Times,* "Of all the cities we can think of . . . we associate Chicago with new things, with building new. Combining that with preservation is a difficult task, a tricky thing. It's hard to find the middle ground in Chicago."[1] Yet finding a middle ground is essential if the city is to retain the original character that sets it apart from the rest. In order to maintain Chicago's

Figure caption includes number, short title, and source

Fig. 1. Chicago skyline, circa 1940s. (Postcard courtesy of Minnie Dangburg.)

Rinder 9

Notes

1. Tracie Rozhon, "Chicago Girds for Big Battle over Its Skyline," *New York Times,* November 12, 2000, Academic Search Premier.

2. David Garrard Lowe, *Lost Chicago* (New York: Watson-Guptill Publications, 2000), 123.

3. *Columbia Encyclopedia*, 6th ed. (2000), s.v. "Louis Sullivan."

4. Daniel Bluestone, *Constructing Chicago* (New Haven: Yale University Press, 1991), 105.

5. Alan J. Shannon, "When Will It End?" *Chicago Tribune,* September 11, 1987, quoted in Karen J. Dilibert, *From Landmark to Landfill* (Chicago: Chicago Architectural Foundation, 2000), 11.

6. Steve Kerch, "Landmark Decisions," *Chicago Tribune*, March 18, 1990, sec. 16.

7. John W. Stamper, *Chicago's North Michigan Avenue* (Chicago: University of Chicago Press, 1991), 215.

8. Alf Siewers, "Success Spoiling the Magnificent Mile?" *Chicago Sun-Times*, April 9, 1995.

9. Paul Gapp, "McCarthy Building Puts *Landmark Law on a Collision Course with Developers,*" Chicago Tribune, April 20, 1986, quoted in Karen J. Dilibert, *From Landmark to Landfill* (Chicago: Chicago Architectural Foundation, 2000), 4.

10. Paul Gapp, quoted in Karen J. Dilibert, 4.

11. Rozhon, "Chicago Girds for Big Battle."

12. Kerch, "Landmark Decisions."

13. Robert Bruegmann, *The Architects and the City* (Chicago: University of Chicago Press, 1997), 443.

Article in database (note 1)

Print book (note 2)

Indirect source (note 5)

Reference to previous source (note 10)

Second reference to source (note 11)

Rinder 10

Bibliography

Print book　　Bluestone, Daniel. *Constructing Chicago*. New Haven: Yale University
　　　　　　　　Press, 1991.

　　　　　　　　Bruegmann, Robert. *The Architects and the City*. Chicago: University of
　　　　　　　　Chicago Press, 1997.

Pamphlet　　Dilibert, Karen J. *From Landmark to Landfill*. Chicago: Chicago
　　　　　　　　Architectural Foundation, 2000.

Newspaper　　Kerch, Steve. "Landmark Decisions." *Chicago Tribune*, March 18, 1990,
article　　　　sec. 16.

　　　　　　　　Lowe, David Garrard. *Lost Chicago*. New York: Watson-Guptill
　　　　　　　　Publications, 2000.

Article from　　Rozhon, Tracie. "Chicago Girds for Big Battle over Its Skyline." *New
database　　　*York Times*, November 12, 2000. Academic Search Premier.

　　　　　　　　Siewers, Alf. "Success Spoiling the Magnificent Mile?" *Chicago Sun-
Bibliography　　*Times*, April 9, 1995.
entries use
hanging　　　Stamper, John W. *Chicago's North Michigan Avenue*. Chicago: University
indent and　　　of Chicago Press, 1991.
are not
numbered

19 CSE Style

Writers in the physical sciences, the life sciences, and mathematics often use the documentation style set forth by the Council of Science Editors (CSE). Guidelines for citing print sources can be found in *Scientific Style and Format: The CSE Manual for Authors, Editors, and Publishers,* Eighth Edition (2014).

19a Following CSE format

Title page   Center the title of your paper. Beneath it, center your name. Include other relevant information, such as the course name and number, the instructor's name, and the date submitted.

Margins and spacing   Leave standard one-inch margins at the top and bottom and on both sides of each page. Double-space the text and the references list.

Page numbers   Type a short version of the paper's title and the page number in the upper right-hand corner of each page. Omit the page number on the title page and number the first page of text as page 2.

Abstract   CSE style frequently calls for a one-paragraph abstract. The abstract should be on a separate page, right after the title page, with the title *Abstract* centered one inch from the top of the page.

Headings   Use headings when possible to help readers quickly find the contents of a section of the paper.

Tables and figures   Tables and figures must be labeled *Table* or *Figure* and numbered separately, one sequence for tables and one for figures. Give each table and figure a short, informative title. Be sure to introduce each table and figure in your text, and comment on its significance.

List of references   Start the list of references on a new page at the end of the paper, and continue to number the pages consecutively. Center the title *References* one inch from the top of the page, and double-space before beginning the first entry.

19b Creating CSE in-text citations

In CSE style, citations within the text follow one of three formats.

- The *citation-sequence format* calls for a <u>superscript number</u> or a number in parentheses after any mention of a <u>source</u>. The sources are numbered in the order they appear. Each number refers to the same source every time it is used. The first source mentioned in the paper is numbered 1, the second source is numbered 2, and so on.

- The *citation-name format* also calls for a <u>superscript number</u> or a number in parentheses after any mention of a <u>source</u>. The numbers are added *after* the list of references is completed and alphabetized, so that the source numbered 1 is alphabetically first in the list of references, 2 is alphabetically second, and so on.

- The *name-year format* calls for the <u>last name</u> of the author and the <u>year of publication</u> in parentheses after any mention of a source. If the last name appears in a signal phrase, the name-year format allows for giving only the year of publication in parentheses.

Before deciding which system to use, ask your instructor's preference.

1. In-text citation using citation-sequence or citation-name format

<u>VonBergen</u>[12] provides the most complete discussion of this phenomenon.

For the citation-sequence and citation-name formats, you would use the same superscript ([12]) for each subsequent citation of this work by VonBergen.

2. In-text citation using name-year format

<u>VonBergen</u> (<u>2003</u>) provides the most complete discussion of this phenomenon.

<u>Hussar</u>'s two earlier studies of juvenile obesity (<u>1995, 1999</u>) examined only children with diabetes.

The classic examples of such investigations (<u>Morrow</u> <u>1968</u>; <u>Bridger et al.</u> <u>1971</u>; <u>Franklin and Wayson</u> <u>1972</u>) still shape the assumptions of current studies.

If a work has three or more authors, use the first author's name and *et al.* in the in-text citation.

19c Creating a CSE list of references

The citations in the text of a paper correspond to items on a list titled *References*, which starts on a new page at the end of the paper. Continue to number the pages consecutively, center the title *References* one inch from the top of the page, and double-space before beginning the first entry. Start each entry aligned left and indent subsequent lines one-quarter inch.

The order of the entries depends on which format you follow:

- **Citation-sequence format:** number and list the references in the order they are first cited in the text.
- **Citation-name format:** list and number the references in alphabetical order.
- **Name-year format:** list the references, unnumbered, in alphabetical order.

In the following examples, you will see that both the citation-sequence and citation-name formats call for listing the date after the publisher's name in references for books and after the periodical name in references for articles. The name-year format calls for listing the date immediately after the author's name in any kind of reference.

CSE style also specifies the treatment and placement of the following basic elements in the list of references:

- **Author.** List all authors last name first, and use only initials for first and middle names. Do not place a comma after the author's last name, and do not place periods after or spaces between the initials. Use a period after the last initial of the last author listed.
- **Title.** Do not italicize titles and subtitles of books and titles of periodicals. Do not enclose titles of articles in quotation marks. For books and articles, capitalize only the first word of the title and any proper nouns or proper adjectives. Abbreviate and capitalize all major words in a periodical title.

As you refer to these examples, pay attention to how publication information (publishers for books, details about periodicals for articles) and other specific elements are styled and punctuated. We have used underlining in some examples only to draw your attention to important elements. Do not underline anything in your own citations.

LIST OF EXAMPLES

References in CSE style

BOOKS

1. One author, 238
2. Two or more authors, 238
3. Organization as author, 239
4. Book prepared by editor(s), 239
5. Section of a book with an editor, 239
6. Chapter of a book, 240
7. Paper or abstract in conference proceedings, 240

PERIODICALS

8. Article in a journal, 240

9. Article in a magazine, 241
10. Article in a newspaper, 241

DIGITAL SOURCES

11. Material from an online database, 242
12. Article in an online journal, 242
13. Article in an online newspaper, 243
14. Online book, 243
15. Website, 243
16. Government website, 243

Books

1. One author

CITATION-SEQUENCE AND CITATION-NAME

1. Tyson ND. Astrophysics for people in a hurry. New York (NY): Norton; 2017.

NAME-YEAR

Tyson ND. 2017. Astrophysics for people in a hurry. New York (NY): Norton.

2. Two or more authors List all authors up to ten. If there are more than ten authors, follow the tenth with the abbreviation *et al.*

CITATION-SEQUENCE AND CITATION-NAME

2. Wojciechowski BW, Rice NM. Experimental methods in kinetic studies. 2nd ed. St. Louis (MO): Elsevier Science; 2003.

NAME-YEAR

Wojciechowski BW, Rice NM. 2003. Experimental methods in kinetic studies. 2nd ed. St. Louis (MO): Elsevier Science.

3. Organization as author

CITATION-SEQUENCE AND CITATION-NAME

3. World Health Organization. The world health report 2002: reducing risks, promoting healthy life. Geneva (Switzerland): The Organization; 2002.

Place the organization's <u>abbreviation</u> at the beginning of the name-year entry, and use the abbreviation in the corresponding in-text citation. Alphabetize the entry by the <u>first word</u> of the full name, not by the abbreviation.

NAME-YEAR

[<u>WHO</u>] <u>World</u> Health Organization. 2002. The world health report 2002: reducing risks, promoting healthy life. Geneva (Switzerland): The Organization.

4. Book prepared by editor(s)

CITATION-SEQUENCE AND CITATION-NAME

4. Torrence ME, Isaacson RE, <u>editors</u>. Microbial food safety in animal agriculture: current topics. Ames (IA): Iowa State University Press; 2003.

NAME-YEAR

Torrence ME, Isaacson RE, <u>editors</u>. 2003. Microbial safety in animal agriculture: current topics. Ames (IA): Iowa State University Press.

5. Section of a book with an editor

CITATION-SEQUENCE AND CITATION-NAME

5. Kawamura A. Plankton. <u>In</u>: Perrin MF, Wursig B, Thewissen JGM, <u>editors</u>. Encyclopedia of marine mammals. San Diego (CA): Academic Press; 2002. <u>p. 939–942</u>.

NAME-YEAR

Kawamura A. 2002. Plankton. <u>In</u>: Perrin MF, Wursig B, Thewissen JGM, <u>editors</u>. Encyclopedia of marine mammals. San Diego (CA): Academic Press. <u>p. 939–942</u>.

6. Chapter of a book

CITATION-SEQUENCE AND CITATION-NAME

6. Honigsbaum M. The fever trail: in search of the cure for malaria. New
   York (NY): Picador; 2003. Chapter 2, The cure; p. 19–38.

NAME-YEAR

Honigsbaum M. 2003. The fever trail: in search of the cure for malaria.
   New York (NY): Picador. Chapter 2, The cure; p. 19–38.

7. Paper or abstract in conference proceedings

CITATION-SEQUENCE AND CITATION-NAME

7. Gutierrez AP. Integrating biological and environmental factors in crop
   system models [abstract]. In: Integrated Biological Systems Conference;
   2003 Apr 14–16; San Antonio, TX. Beaumont (TX): Agroeconomics
   Research Group; 2003. p. 14–15.

NAME-YEAR

Gutierrez AP. 2003. Integrating biological and environmental factors
   in crop system models [abstract]. In: Integrated Biological Systems
   Conference; 2003 Apr 14–16; San Antonio, TX. Beaumont (TX):
   Agroeconomics Research Group. p. 14–15.

Periodicals

Provide volume and issue numbers for journals. For magazines,
include the month and year or the month, day, and year. For newspaper articles, include the section designation and column number,
if any, and the date. For all periodicals, give inclusive page numbers.
For rules on abbreviating journal titles, consult the CSE manual or
ask an instructor.

8. Article in a journal

CITATION-SEQUENCE AND CITATION-NAME

8. Citrin DE. Recent developments in radiotherapy. New Engl J Med.
   2017;377(11):1065–1075.

NAME-YEAR

Citrin DE. 2017. Recent developments in radiotherapy. <u>New Engl J Med</u>. 377(11):1065–1075.

9. Article in a magazine

CITATION-SEQUENCE AND CITATION-NAME

9. Livio M. Moving right along: the accelerating universe holds secrets to dark energy, the Big Bang, and the ultimate beauty of nature. Astronomy. 2002 Jul:34–39.

NAME-YEAR

Livio M. 2002 Jul. Moving right along: the accelerating universe holds secrets to dark energy, the Big Bang, and the ultimate beauty of nature. Astronomy. 34–39.

10. Article in a newspaper

CITATION-SEQUENCE AND CITATION-NAME

10. Kolata G. Bone diagnosis gives new data but no answers. New York Times (National Ed.). 2003 Sep 28;Sect. 1:1 (col. 1).

NAME-YEAR

Kolata G. 2003 Sep 28. Bone diagnosis gives new data but no answers. New York Times (National Ed.). Sect. 1:1 (col. 1).

Digital sources

These examples use the citation-sequence or citation-name system. To adapt them to the name-year system, delete the note number and place the update date immediately after the author's name.

The basic entry for most sources accessed through the Internet should include the following elements:

- **Author.** Give the author's name, if available, last name first, followed by the initial(s) and a period.
- **Title.** For book, journal, and article titles, follow the style for print materials. For all other types of electronic material, reproduce the title that appears on the screen.

- **Description.** Identify sources such as images, infographics, podcasts, videos, blogs, and social media posts with descriptive words in brackets: [infographic], [video], [podcast, episode 12].
- **Place of publication.** For online books and websites, include the place of publication as you would for print sources.
- **Publisher.** For material other than journal articles from websites and online databases, include the individual or organization that produces or sponsors the site. If no publisher can be determined, use the words *publisher unknown* in brackets.
- **Dates.** Cite three important dates if possible: the date that the publication was placed on the Internet or the copyright date; the latest date of any update or revision; and the date you accessed the publication.
- **Page, document, volume, and issue numbers.** When citing a portion of a larger work or site, list the inclusive page numbers or document numbers of the specific item being cited. For journals or journal articles, include volume and issue numbers. If exact page numbers are not available, include in brackets the approximate length in computer screens, paragraphs, or bytes: [2 screens], [10 paragraphs], [332K bytes].
- **Address.** Include the URL or other electronic address, followed by a period.

11. Material from an online database

11. Shilts E. Water wanderers. Can Geographic. 2002 [accessed 2010 Jan 27];122(3):72–77. Academic Search Premier. http://www.ebscohost .com/. Document No.: 6626534.

12. Article in an online journal

12. Perez P, Calonge TM. Yeast protein kinase C. J Biochem. 2002 Oct [accessed 2016 Nov 3];132(4):513–517. http://edpex104.bcasj.or.jp /jb-pdf/132-4/jb132-4-513.pdf

13. Article in an online newspaper

13. Gorman J. Trillions of flies can't all be bad. New York Times. 2017 Nov 13 [accessed 2017 Dec 1]. https://nyti.ms/2hwjhw0

14. Online book

14. Patrick TS, Allison JR, Krakow GA. Protected plants of Georgia. Social Circle (GA): Georgia Department of Natural Resources; c1995 [accessed 2013 Dec 3]. http://www.georgiawildlife.com/content/displaycontent .asp?txtDocument=89&txtPage=9

To cite a portion of an online book, give the name of the part after the publication information: *Chapter 6, Encouraging germination*. See model 6.

15. Website

15. Geology and public policy. Boulder (CO): Geological Society of America; c2010 [updated 2010 Jun 3; accessed 2015 Sep 19]. http://www.geosociety.org/geopolicy.htm

16. Government website

16. Health disparities in cancer: reducing health disparities in cancer. Atlanta (GA): Centers for Disease Control and Prevention (US); 2012 Nov 14 [updated 2014 Jul 21; accessed 2017 Nov 13]. http://www.cdc.gov /cancer/healthdisparities/basic_info/disparities.htm

19d STUDENT WRITING **Excerpts from a literature review for biology, CSE style**

The following excerpts from a literature review by Joanna Hays for a biology class conforms to the name-year format in the CSE guidelines described in this chapter.

Running head has short title, page number

Overview

Niemann-Pick Disease (NP) occurs in patients with deficient acid sphingomyelinase (ASM) activity as well as with the lysosomal accumulation of sphingomyelin. It is an autosomal recessive disorder (Levran et al. 1991). As recently as 1991, researchers had classified two major phenotypes: Type A and Type B (Levran et al. 1991). In more recent studies several more phenotypes have been identified, including Types C and D. Each type of NP has distinct characteristics and effects on the patient. NP is distributed worldwide, but is closely associated with Ashkenazi Jewish descendants. Niemann-Pick Disease is relevant to the molecular world today because of advances being made in the ability to identify mutations, to trace ancestry where the mutation may have originated, and to counsel patients with a high potential of carrying the disease. Genetic counseling primarily consists of confirmation of the particular disease and calculation of the possible future reappearance in the same gene line (Brock 1974). The following discussion will summarize the identification of mutations causing the various forms of NP, the distribution of NP, as well as new genotypes and phenotypes that are correlated with NP.

Headings organize project

Mutations Causing NP

Levran et al. (1991) inform readers of the frequent identification of missense mutations in the gene associated with Ashkenazi Jewish persons afflicted by Type A and Type B NP. This paper identifies the mutations associated with NP and the beginning of many molecular techniques to develop diagnoses. Greer et al. (1998) identify a new mutation that is specifically identified to be the cause of Type D. NP in various forms is closely associated with the founder effect caused by a couple married in the early 1700s in what is now Nova Scotia. Simonaro et al. (2002) discusses the distribution of Type B NP as well as new phenotypes and genotypes. All three of these papers identify

Niemann-Pick Disease 9

References

Brock DJH. 1974. Prenatal diagnosis and genetic counseling. J Clin Pathol Suppl. (R Coll Path.) 8:150–155.

Greer WL, Ridell DC, Gillan TL, Girouard GS, Sparrow SM, Byers DM, Dobson MJ, Neumann PE. 1998. The Nova Scotia (type D) form of Niemann-Pick disease is caused by a G3097 $\rightarrow$ T transversion in NPC1. Am J Hum Genet 63:52–54.

Levran O, Desnick RJ, Schuchman EH. 1991. Niemann-Pick disease: a frequent missense mutation in the acid sphingomyelinase gene of Ashkenazi Jewish type A and B patients. P Natl Acad Sci USA 88:3748–3752.

Simonaro CM, Desnick RJ, McGovern MM, Wasserstein MP, Schuchman EH. 2002. The demographics and distribution of type B Niemann-Pick disease: novel mutations lead to new genotype/phenotype correlations. Am J Hum Genet 71:1413–1419.

Alphabetical by name

Style: Effective Language

20   **Language and Identity**   248

21   **Writing across Cultures, Communities, and Identities**   250

22   **Language That Builds Common Ground**   254

23   **Language Varieties**   260

24   **Word Choice**   268

20 Language and Identity

Draw a circle in the middle of a piece of paper or screen and put your name in it. Then add spokes pointing out from all around that circle and take some time to list words that identify you: your relationship to family and others (sister, brother, mentor, friend); your major interests (musician, sports fan, runner, reader, gamer); your background (nationality, hometown, race, religion, sexual orientation); personal attributes you claim or that others use to label you (good student, friendly, shy). Some of the words you've written are bits of language that help you to construct your identity. Others may be words that other people have used to identify you, words you may or may not agree with or accept.

Identity is a familiar word, but it's worth pausing to think a bit about what it means. Most scholars would define identity as a web of relationships built up through language—it's how you understand your relationship to the world around you and use that understanding to imagine possibilities for your future. In more everyday terms, identity is the way you think about yourself and the characteristics that define you. And language is the tool you have for naming these characteristics.

Parts of your identity are stable—your age, for example, or your birthplace. But much of identity is constructed through social interactions with other people and with institutions and is thus flexible, subject to change and evolution. So identities can be multiple and shifting. They can also be imposed on you by other people or institutions that use language to label you in a way that is inappropriate, unfair, or unacceptable to you. In these ways, language works to construct who you are and who you can be.

20a Recognizing how the language of others can shape identity

Look back at the circle and spokes you drew and the words you attached to the spokes. Underline the ones that you think may be labels others would put on you. If you've found any words like "gifted athlete" or "bad at math" or "outsider" or "immigrant" or "top of the class," are these descriptors ones that *you have chosen* as part of your identity? Research has shown that children who are put into groups labeled according to ability levels tend to simply adapt to that label. Mike Rose, now a professor at UCLA, has written about being placed in a vocational (non-college-bound) track: "I lived down to expectations." In Rose's case, he was eventually able to resist and reject that label, with the help of a teacher. But until he did so, that label—non-college-bound—was a part of his identity. In the same way, author and linguist Geneva Smitherman recalls being put in "special education" courses because of the way she spoke—using African American English. She learned that if she just *stayed silent*, she advanced rapidly in school. She learned to circumvent a broken system that labeled her one way in order to assert her own sense of identity.

It's worth taking time to ask how you use language (especially labels) to "identify" other people, both those you know and those you don't know. While all people tend to categorize others as a way to understand them (she's a *sorority girl*; he's a *baller*), those labels may not be accurate or important to the other person's own understanding of themselves—and may indeed be oversimplifications or stereotypes. Open-minded, ethical college writers take care not to impose identities on others, just as they resist letting others impose identities on them.

20b Using language to shape your own identity

One of your main goals as a college writer is not only to be aware of how the language of other people and groups can shape your identity but to resist such efforts by making sure that you are the person doing that shaping as much as possible. Professor Mike Rose (see 20a) had a chance to reject the label of lower-track student, but what's even more important is that he seized the opportunity to begin defining himself as a high-performing honors student who would eventually earn a PhD. Poet and artist Gloria Anzaldúa often asked her students "who is the *you* you want to be in ten years?" In her own case, Anzaldúa remembers being discouraged from writing and reading—and being criticized and even punished for her unique writing style. But these criticisms did not stop her from thinking of herself as a writer and pursuing her own idea of just what that meant. She literally wrote herself into being the writer and person she envisioned. Her message to students: you can do the same thing!

In addition, college writers need to think about whose voices are heard and whose may be ignored in certain situations. Smitherman (see 20a) was disrespected for the way she spoke and wrote, but once she learned and used the "power language" of standardized English, she used her linguistic expertise to gain respect and then *challenge* that "power language." She mixes dialects in different ways, and this style and voice is part of her identity. As another example, a student speaking or writing from the identity of a beginner or novice may not get the respect that one writing from an identity of expertise does. A student writing about mental health issues among college students, for example, might draw on her experience and expertise as an activist for mental health resources on campus, or as a double major in biology and psychology, or as a suicide attempt survivor. Or perhaps all of these aspects of her identity may help to establish her *ethos,* or her credibility (see also 9e). As a college writer, aim to be confident in your own identity, to communicate from an identity of your own choosing, and to imagine and pursue other identities you want to embrace.

 EXERCISE 20.1 Take a few minutes to jot down notes in response to these questions: How do I shape my own identity through language? How do other people and groups or institutions shape my identity through language? How do I use language that may be shaping the identities of others? Then write a paragraph describing how you would like to make changes to these identities or this use of language.

21 Writing across Cultures, Communities, and Identities

People today often communicate instantaneously across vast distances and cultures and across a wide range of professional and personal identities. Businesspeople complete multinational transactions, students take online classes at distant universities, and conversations circle the globe via social media. No surprise, then, that during the COVID-19 pandemic, U.S. governmental and health organizations found themselves striving to provide useful information to people from a range of cultures and language backgrounds, and to provide it in ways that could be understood across all those differences.

You will surely find yourself writing to (or with) people from other communities, cultures, language groups, and countries. In this era of rapid global communication, you must know how to write effectively across these cultures and communities. As always, remember that people from any community or culture have complex, intersecting identities informed by many factors, including class, ethnicity, race, religion, sexual orientation, gender, physical ability, age, and others. As a writer, your goals are to think very carefully about those you are addressing, to understand as much as possible about where they are coming from, and to acknowledge and respect the range of differences you will encounter.

21a Thinking about what seems "normal"

More than likely, your judgments about what is "normal" are based on assumptions that you are not aware of. Most of us tend to see our own way as the "normal" or right way to do things. If your ways seem inherently right, then perhaps you assume that other ways are somehow less than right. To communicate effectively with people across cultures and communities, recognize the norms that guide your own behavior and how those norms differ from those of other people.

- Know that most ways of communicating are influenced by cultural contexts and differ from one culture or community to the next as well as within cultures.
- Observe the ways that people from cultures or communities other than your own communicate, and be flexible and respectful.
- Respect the differences among individuals within a culture or community. Don't assume that all members of a community behave in the same way or value the same things.

21b Clarifying meaning

All writers face challenges in trying to communicate across space, languages, and cultures. You can address these challenges by working to be sure that you understand what others say—and that they understand you. In such situations, take care to be explicit about the meanings of the words you use. In addition, don't hesitate to ask people to explain a point if you're not absolutely sure you understand, and invite responses by asking whether you're making yourself clear or what you could do to be *more* clear.

21c Meeting audience expectations

When you do your best to meet an audience's expectations about how a text should work, your writing is more likely to have the desired effect. In practice, figuring out what audiences want, need, or expect can be difficult—especially when you are writing in public spaces online and your audience can be composed of anyone, anywhere. If you know little about your potential audience, carefully examine your assumptions about your readers.

Expectations about your authority as a writer   Writers communicating across cultures often encounter audiences who have differing attitudes about authority and about the relationship between the writer and the people being addressed. In the United States, students are frequently asked to establish authority in their writing—by drawing on personal experience, by reporting on research, or by taking a position for which they can offer strong evidence and support. But some cultures position student writers as novices, whose job is to learn from others who have greater authority. When you write, think carefully about your audience's expectations and attitudes toward authority.

- What is your relationship to those you are addressing?
- What knowledge are you expected to have? Is it appropriate for you to demonstrate that knowledge—and if so, how?
- What is your goal—to answer a question? to make a point? to agree? something else?
- What tone is appropriate? If in doubt, show respect: politeness is rarely if ever inappropriate.

Expectations about persuasive evidence   You should think carefully about how to use evidence in writing, and pay attention to what counts as evidence to members of groups you are trying to persuade.

Are facts, concrete examples, or statistical data most convincing to the intended audience? Does the testimony of experts count heavily as evidence? What people are considered trustworthy experts, and why? Do firsthand personal experiences or narratives offer particularly persuasive evidence? Will the audience value citations from religious or philosophical texts, proverbs, or everyday wisdom? Are there other sources that would be considered strong evidence? If analogies are used as support, which kinds are most powerful?

Once you determine what counts as evidence in your own thinking and writing, consider where you learned to use and value this kind of evidence. You can ask these same questions about how members of other cultures use evidence.

Expectations about organization   The organizational patterns that you find pleasing are likely to be deeply embedded in your own culture. Many U.S. readers expect a well-organized piece of writing to use the following structure: introduction and thesis, necessary background, overview of the parts, systematic presentation of evidence, consideration of other viewpoints, and conclusion.

However, in cultures that value indirection, subtlety, or repetition, writers tend to prefer different organizational patterns. When writing for global audiences, think about how you can organize material to get your message across effectively. Consider where to state your thesis or main point (at the beginning, at the end, somewhere else, or not at all) and whether to use a straightforward organization or to employ digressions or repetitions to good effect.

Expectations about style   Effective style varies broadly across communities and cultures and depends on the rhetorical situation—your purpose, audience, and so on. Even so, there is one important style question to consider when writing across cultures: what level of formality is most appropriate? In most writing to a general audience in the United States, a fairly informal style is often acceptable, even appreciated. Many cultures, however, tend to value a more formal approach. When in doubt, err on the side of formality in writing to people from other cultures, especially to your elders or to those in authority. Use appropriate titles (*Dr. Moss, Professor Mejía*); avoid slang or jargon that may be unfamiliar to those in your audience; use complete words and sentences (even in email); and use first names only if invited to do so.

INSTEAD OF	TRY USING
anchorman, anchorwoman	anchor
businessman	businessperson, business executive
congressman	member of Congress, representative
fireman	firefighter
male nurse	nurse
man, mankind	person, the people, humanity, the human race
policeman, policewoman	police officer
woman engineer	engineer

Considering pronoun choices Take special care with personal pronouns, since the use of *she* and *he* leaves out many people who do not identify with either of those terms, including some people with non-binary or gender-nonconforming identities. For this reason, many now use singular *they/them/theirs*, as in "Fallon asked to borrow my book, so I gave it to *them*." (See 36b.) Others use alternative gender-neutral pronouns such as *ve/ver/vis*, *ze/hir/hirs*, or *ze/zir/zirs*, as in "Ze called me, so I called zir back." Still others are just fine with *he* or *she*.

Today, linguists seem to agree that singular *they* has won out over alternatives and writers are increasingly embracing this usage. You may have noticed that it's become standard to declare your pronouns on personal and professional email, on personal websites, and on other forms of communication. For example, here's the signature line from an email message:

Taylor Johanneson
Director of the Initiative for Social Justice
Pronouns: *they, their, theirs*
tjohanneson@isj.org

Perhaps you have been asked to declare your pronouns in an academic or professional scenario.

Using *they/their* instead of *he/she* may take some getting used to, but then we have assimilated many changes to our language;

what once seemed awkward now seems absolutely normal. And, of course, there are other ways of avoiding *he/she* usage.

- Just cut out the pronoun: instead of "Before anyone can safely board an airplane, he or she must fill out a COVID-19 questionnaire," why not say "Before safely boarding an airplane, a passenger must fill out a COVID-19 questionnaire."

- Drop the third-person singular pronoun: instead of "Before every passenger exits the airplane, he or she must fill out a form providing contact information," why not say "Before passengers exit the airplane, they must fill out a form providing contact information."

Choosing gender-neutral, nonsexist language is one very important way to try to include—and to respect—all members of your potential audience.

EXERCISE 22.2 Take a look at the following advertisement for a social media internship, noting any language in the ad that might today be considered sexist or noninclusive. Revise the passage, substituting nonsexist and/or inclusive language as necessary.

Social Media Intern

Join our team of men and women who love music and love promoting entertainment events. Come help us boost brand engagement and create buzz! This is a remote position, so the ideal candidate will work with our digital marketing team but set his or her own schedule. The social media intern will contribute his or her ideas daily for blog posts, tweets, videos, and press releases and can expect to research audience needs and competing content. The ideal candidate will demonstrate his or her analytical skills by tracking customer engagement and suggesting follow-up campaigns. He or she will also have the opportunity to attend live and online concert events. Come work with our 9-man marketing team—a friendly, open-minded group!

22c Examining assumptions about race and ethnicity

Generalizations about racial and ethnic groups can result in especially harmful stereotyping. To build common ground, then, avoid language that ignores differences not only among individual members of a race or ethnic group but also among subgroups. Be aware, for instance, of the diverse places from which Americans of Spanish-speaking ancestry have come.

When writing about an ethnic or racial group, how can you refer to that group in terms that its members actually desire? Doing so is sometimes not an easy task, for terms can change often and vary widely.

The word *colored*, for example, was once widely used in the United States to refer to Americans of African ancestry. By the 1950s, the preferred term had become *Negro*. This changed in the 1960s, however, as *Black* came to be preferred by most, though certainly not all, members of the community. Since the late 1980s, both *Black* and *African American* have been widely used.

Once widely used, the term *American Indian* has been challenged as inaccurate. According to author Benny Wayne Sully, a Sicangu Lakota Native, it's best to refer to *Indigenous Peoples*, *First Nations*, or *Native Americans*—or, if possible, to use the specific name of the nation or pueblo, such as *Chippewa* or *Zuni*, or the specific clan, such as the *Navajo Towering House Clan*. Many people once referred to as *Eskimo* are more appropriately referred to as *Inuit* or a more specific term such as *Tsimshian*, *Yupik*, *Haida*, or *Tlingit*.

Latino and *Latina* (or the gender-neutral *Latinx*) are geographic references; these words describe people who trace their ancestry to any country in Latin America—Mexico, Central America, South America, or the Caribbean. *Hispanic*, on the other hand, describes people who trace their ancestry to a Spanish-speaking county. For example, Native Brazilians, who speak Portuguese as their first language, are Latinx but not Hispanic.

You may have seen or heard the word *Caucasian* used to refer to white people. The term is both outdated as well as geographically inaccurate (white people aren't all descendants of people from the Caucasus region that lies between Europe and Asia). For decades, the U.S. census listed the single term *white* as a racial category to be selected. But for the 2020 census, the term is first defined as "all individuals who identify with one or more nationalities or ethnic groups originating in Europe, the Middle East, or North Africa. Examples of these groups include, but are not limited to, German, Irish, English, Italian, Lebanese, Egyptian, Polish, French, Iranian, Slavic, Cajun, and Chaldean." The census form then provides boxes for those filling out the census to be specific about their ethnic background. In the United States, white people seem increasingly inclined to identify with a more specific ethnic group.

Ethnic terminology changes often enough to challenge the most careful writers—including writers who belong to the groups they are writing about. Consider your words carefully and seek information about ways members of groups refer to themselves, but don't expect one person to speak for all members of a group or expect unanimity on such terms.

22d Considering abilities and disabilities

According to the most recent U.S. census, one in five Americans is a person with a disability of some kind; millions more will have a disability sometime in their lives. Think of everyone you know who wears glasses, hearing aids, or other prosthetic devices, of those who have limited mobility, vision, or hearing (or none), of those who are color-blind, of those who have cognitive processing differences. In fact, you yourself may be a person with a disability. It's a mistake, then, to ignore such differences, since doing so makes it more difficult to reach all audience members and build common ground with them. A few tips may be helpful here:

- When you are using color, remember that everyone won't see it as you may. When putting colors next to one another, then, use those on opposite sides of the color spectrum, such as purple and gold, in order to achieve the highest contrast.

- Make sure all your readers can access the content in a digital text— by providing alternative text (called "alt text") for all visuals so they will make sense when read by a screen reader and by providing captions for sound files and longer audio content.

- Check the website for the Americans with Disabilities Act for guidelines on designing accessible web texts (www.ada.gov).

- In peer groups or in class, think about whether members would rather receive documents in very large type or as audio files. Try to accommodate the needs of all peers.

- In presentations, make sure to face any audience members who are lip reading, or check to see if a sign language interpreter may be needed.

If you have trouble processing letters and sounds in sequence, try "talking pens" that can scan words and read them aloud, or voice-recognition programs that can transcribe dictated text. If you have difficulty taking notes on a computer or in a notebook, try dictating them into a word processor with voice-recognition capability. Or check out other assistive technologies such as reading and writing software that offers help with everything from audio and visual options to mechanics, punctuation, and formatting.

EXERCISE 22.3 Review the following sentences for offensive or inappropriate references or terms. If a sentence contains unacceptable terms, rewrite it. Example:

> Passengers
> ~~Elderly passengers~~ on the cruise ship *Romance Afloat* will enjoy
> ^
> swimming, shuffleboard, and nightly movies.

1. The doctor and the male nurse had different bedside manners when tending to the patients in their care.
2. Barack Obama was the first ~~colored~~ president of the United States. *black*
3. The Oriental girl who works at the bank is always pleasant and efficient.
4. My family recently moved into an area full of ~~rednecks.~~ *southerners*
5. Our skylight was installed last week by a ~~woman~~ carpenter.

---

23   Language Varieties

When Pulitzer Prize–winning author Junot Díaz spoke to a group of college students in California, he used colloquial English and Spanish—plus more than a little profanity—and the students loved every minute of it, cheering throughout the talk. Later, when he was interviewed on National Public Radio, however, Díaz addressed his nationwide, maybe even worldwide, audience using more formal—though also less colorful—English. As a college student, you will often need to think about how to make language choices that will fit the occasion and audience you are addressing while also reflecting your unique identity as a language user with access to a large and rich language repertoire.

23a Practicing language awareness

Recognizing the crucial role language plays in shaping identity has led some writers to conclude that "I am my language." Author and artist Gloria Anzaldúa certainly makes that case when she says that she wants *all* of her languages to be recognized *and respected* as part of her identity: the standardized English and Spanish she has learned, working class/slang English, the northern Mexican Spanish dialect, and Tex-Mex, the regional Spanish of Texas and New Mexico. Anzaldúa's recognition of the inextricable relationship between language and identity is echoed by Nobel Prize–winning novelist Toni Morrison:

> The language, only the language . . . is the thing that Black people love so much. . . . It's a love, a passion, its function is like a preacher's to make you stand up out of your seat, make you lose yourself and hear yourself. The worst of all possible things that could happen would be to lose that language. There are certain things I cannot say without recourse to my language.
>
> —Toni Morrison

Think for a moment about the languages and varieties of languages or dialects that are part of your background and who you are. Today 25 percent of people in the United States speak a language other than English at home. But even if you think of yourself as speaking only English, you probably know and use a number of dialects. If you come from Boston or Birmingham, from Minnesota or the mountains of Eastern Tennessee, or from another region of the country, you probably speak the regional dialect common to that area. In addition, you may be learning a professional dialect (like the specialized language of computer programmers) or using one associated with groups you belong to (surfers or political activists). The dialects and languages you have at your disposal are what allow you to communicate effectively and powerfully with a wide range of audiences.

Language, Culture, and Context

Respecting Black Language

The Africans who were brought to America in chains by white captors some 400 years ago spoke many languages. Expected by slaveholders to communicate in English, they used their ingenuity to develop a *creole*, or mix of different languages, that eventually became what we now know as African American or Black language, along the way enriching English with many words of African origin, including foods (*banana, okra, yam*), musical instruments (*banjo, marimba*), animals (*zebra, mamba*), and musical terms (*jazz, juke, jive*). In spite of widespread anti-literacy laws, many enslaved people persevered in learning to read and write—and then taught others to do so. As they learned, they developed the rich rhythms and rhetorical practices rooted in the African verbal tradition associated with the expressive power of Black language today, language that is used—and celebrated—locally and globally through the spread of African American culture. Remember, though, that Black language is by no means uniform or static but rather broadly and deeply diverse.

This broad and inclusive view respects the validity and power of all languages and dialects available to writers and speakers today. It also recognizes that languages are never fixed but rather flexible and changing across time and place and genre.

23b   What is standardized English?

One variety of English, often referred to as "standard" or "standardized," has been taught prescriptively in schools and used in much of the national media, as well as in business and government, by those having social, cultural, and economic power. The story of how this dialect came to such power—came to be "standard"—is long and complex, but there's no doubt that it has worked to privilege some and to erase, oppress, and silence others. If you've been made fun of for "talking country," been refused housing on the basis of how you spoke, or been punished in school for the language you use, you have experienced the linguistic discrimination—sometimes referred to as *linguicism*—that has characterized much of this country's history. (For a provocative analysis of linguicism, check out scholar and spoken word artist Jamila Lyiscott's TED talk, "Three Ways to Speak English.")

Understanding discrimination based on race and class is one important step in practicing language awareness and in recognizing that no one language or dialect is inherently superior to another. Rather, the hierarchy that places one above another is socially constructed as part of a power structure that ripples throughout our society. In fact, standardized English is only one of many varieties of English, and even it varies widely according to purpose and audience. And while standardized English is still widely taught and used in schools, writers and speakers are changing it, making it more conversational and more informal—and bringing in other dialects and other languages to challenge its dominant role.

All languages and all varieties or dialects of English are legitimate forms we should recognize and value: if "variety is the spice of life," then language variety in the United States makes us a particularly flavorful culture. Research shows that the ability to communicate in multiple languages and varieties of English is a valuable asset to writers, an ability that you can certainly use to your advantage, both in academic and nonacademic writing. In fact, many writers and speakers of English move seamlessly among languages and varieties of English, creating unique special effects and helping to connect to their audiences. Here are just a few of the ways writers today are pushing beyond the boundaries of standardized English to use other languages and dialects to communicate powerfully and effectively.

Evoking a place or community Weaving together regional varieties and standardized English can be very effective in creating a sense of place in your writing. Here, an anthropologist writing about one Carolina community takes care to let the residents speak their minds—and in their own words:

> For Roadville, schooling is something most folks have not gotten enough of, but everybody believes will do something toward helping an individual "get on." In the words of one oldtime resident, "Folks that ain't got no schooling don't get to be nobody nowadays."
> —Shirley Brice Heath, *Ways with Words*

Varieties of language, including slang and colloquial expressions, can also help writers evoke other kinds of communities. (See also 24a.)

Connecting with a community Whether you are indigenous or trace your ancestry to Europe, Asia, Latin America, Africa, or elsewhere, your heritage lives on in the rich diversity of the English language. See how one writer uses Hawaiian Pidgin, now an official language of Hawaii, to paint a picture of young teens hearing a "chicken skin" story from their grandmother.

> "—So, rather dan being rid of da shark, da people were stuck with many little ones, for dere mistake."
>
> Then Grandma Wong wen' pause, for dramatic effect, I guess, and she wen' add, "Dis is one of dose times. . . . Da time of da sharks."
>
> Those words ended another of Grandma's chicken skin stories. The stories she told us had been passed on to her by her grandmother, who had heard them from her grandmother. Always skipping a generation.
>
> —Rodney Morales, *When the Shark Bites*

Notice how the narrator of the story presents information necessary to the story line mostly in standardized English, though with a decided Hawaiian Pidgin rhythm, and Hawaiian Pidgin to represent spoken language. This use demonstrates that the writer is a member of the community whose language he is representing and thus builds credibility with others in the community. Writers must take care, however, in using the language of communities other than their own. When used inappropriately, such language can have an opposite effect, perhaps destroying credibility and alienating your audience.

Illustrating a point See how distinguished linguist Geneva Smitherman mixes varieties of English as she discusses the ability of Black language not only to survive but to thrive:

> Black or African American Language (BL or AAL) is a style of speaking English words with Black flava—with Africanized semantic, grammatical, pronunciation, and rhetorical patterns. . . . Despite elitist language pronouncements, despite language eradication efforts in the schools, despite White America's ambivalence toward the language, "speaking Black" has persisted over generations and decades. The language is bound up with and symbolic of identity, camaraderie, culture, and home. And it ain gon nowhere.
>
> —Geneva Smitherman, *Word from the Mother:*
> *Language and African Americans*

Here, Smitherman underscores the point she is making by using BL pronunciation ("flava") to punctuate a sentence that is otherwise written in standardized English. And she ends the passage with a short, powerful BL sentence that embodies and illustrates her larger point.

These examples—and so many others like them—demonstrate a point made by historian of African American women's literacies Jacqueline Jones Royster following her delivery of a keynote address. A member of the audience approached Royster after her speech, which was entitled "When the First Voice You Hear Is Not Your Own," to say she was "so glad" to hear Royster speaking in her "authentic voice." Royster's response: "I have many voices, and they are all authentic." In fact, we all have many voices, many languages and language varieties that constitute our full repertoire, and they too are all authentic.

23c   Bringing in other languages

You might use a language other than English for the same reasons you might use different dialects of English: to represent the actual words of a speaker, to make a point, to connect with your audience, or to get their attention. See how Gerald Haslam uses Spanish to capture his great-grandmother's words and to make a point about his relationship to her.

> "*Expectoran su sangre!*" exclaimed Great-grandma when I showed her the small horned toad I had removed from my breast pocket. I turned toward my mother, who translated: "They spit blood."
> "*De los ojos,*" Grandma added. "From their eyes," mother explained, herself uncomfortable in the presence of the small beast.
> —Gerald Haslam, *California Childhood*

And here, a student writer uses her native Spanish as she writes a literacy narrative about her experience growing up in Puerto Rico and learning English.

> "Todo se ve bien . . ." my father would start and look at me with his right eyebrow raised. The same gesture I forced myself to learn, staring at a mirror for a month, just so I could prove to him that it didn't intimidate me. "¿Qué pasó con Inglés?" I would simply look away and shrug my shoulders, desperately avoiding the gaze of disappointment that his eyes would try to burn on me. After all, I was his first born, and there were a lot

of expectations to meet. "¿Voy a ver un cambio para el próximo semestre, verdad?" And without glancing back at him, I would answer a soft, "Sí."

In elementary school, I got A's and B's in every course except one: English. Young and naive, born and raised on a Spanish-speaking island, I never understood why I needed another language.

—Paola García-Muñiz

Note that García-Muñiz includes Spanish in her narrative without translating it. In this case, the student deliberately chose to include the phrases in Spanish because she wanted to represent her two worlds (two languages) in the essay so that "the audience would better understand what I was talking about: it wasn't about making it simpler or harder for readers to read, but allowing them to visualize the story exactly as it happened."

Another student describes how he combines multiple languages as part of his learning process. Taking notes in multiple languages, he says, "helps [him] save time."

I think that note-taking activities play a significant role in the retention of ideas. Using multiple languages such as Hindi, Sanskrit, and English increases the speed of this activity and helps me retain knowledge of

 ## Language, Culture, and Context

Recognizing Global Varieties of English

Like other world languages, English is used in many countries, so it has many global varieties. For example, British English differs somewhat from U.S. English in certain vocabulary (*bonnet* for *hood* of a car), syntax (*to hospital* rather than *to the hospital*), spelling (*centre* rather than *center*), and pronunciation. In your travels, you may have encountered Canadian English, Australian English, or New Zealand English. Or in Singapore, where English introduced by colonizers was later chosen to serve as a "bridge" among many ethnic groups, Singaporean Colloquial English developed—and became so popular that the government mounted the Speak Good English Movement, an attempt to mandate Standard Singapore English in all schools. The more you visit other countries and cultures, the more global varieties of English you will find.

these languages for a long time. I mainly use Hindi to present my ideas briefly and Sanskrit to describe the actions of the subject. I use multiple languages because it helps me save time during note-taking, as well as retain knowledge about Hindi and Sanskrit languages.

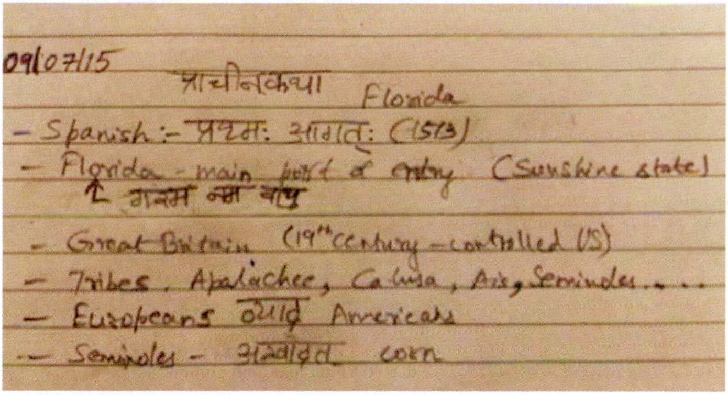

Fig. 1. Photo of my notes. By the author, 7 Sept. 2015.

—Shravan Yandra

Like these students, you may want to bring other languages into your writing to help you communicate more efficiently and effectively with your audiences.

EXERCISE 23.1 Spend a few minutes thinking about the following questions, adapted from materials available through Teaching for Tolerance, and then jot down answers to them:

What does a really smart, brainy person sound like?

What does a really not-smart person sound like?

What does a really bad person sound like?

What does a hero sound like?

What do authority figures sound like?

What does someone you admire the most sound like?

Bring your notes to class for discussion. What do your answers suggest about what kind of language or varieties of language you value most, respect most? Where do these ideas come from? In what ways, if any, do your answers represent linguistic discrimination, or *linguicism*?

EXERCISE 23.2
Working with a partner, brainstorm what you know about the way languages change and what causes those changes. Then do some online investigating. What can you find out about how the English language has changed in the last several hundred years? Take notes on what you find—and on what you may know from your own experience. What strikes you as surprising in what you have learned? What patterns do you see in the changes? What are the most recent changes you can find out about, and how do you see yourself and your own experiences in these changes? (This exercise is shared courtesy of Kristin vanEyk at the University of Michigan.)

24 Word Choice

Deciding which word is the right word can be a challenge. It's not unusual to find many words that have similar but subtly different meanings, and each makes a different impression on your audience. For instance, the "pasta with marinara sauce" presented in a restaurant may look and taste much like the "macaroni and gravy" served at an Italian family dinner, but the choice of one label rather than the other tells us not only about the food but also about the people serving it and the people to whom they expect to serve it.

24a Using levels of formality

In an email or letter to a friend or close associate, informal everyday language is often a good choice. For a lot of academic and professional writing, however, which addresses people you may not know well, you may want to choose the more formal conventions of standardized English.

EMAIL TO SOMEONE YOU KNOW WELL

▶ Myisha is great, super energetic—hire her if you can!

LETTER OF RECOMMENDATION TO SOMEONE YOU DO NOT KNOW

▶ I am pleased to recommend Myisha Fisher. She will bring good ideas and extraordinary energy to your organization.

Slang and colloquial language   Slang, context-specific language used more often in speech than in writing, is often confined to a relatively small group and changes very quickly, though some slang gains wide use (*ripoff*, *zine*). Colloquial language, such as *a lot*, *in a bind*, or *snooze*, is less informal, more widely used, and longer lasting than most slang. Vernacular refers to everyday speech or dialect and may include colloquialisms and slang.

Slang and colloquial language are important parts of any language, but they can risk not being understood by those who don't know the slang terms. If you are writing for a general audience about how digital currency is challenging traditional money and you use a term like *bread* or *benjamins*, some readers may not know what you mean, and others may be irritated by what they see as a frivolous reference to a serious subject.

EXERCISE 24.1   Revise each of the following sentences to use appropriate formality consistently. Example:

> Although   feel excited   as soon as
> I can ~~get all enthused~~ about writing, ~~but~~ I sit down to write my
> ^   ^ blank.   ^
> mind goes ~~right to sleep.~~
>   ^

1. At the conclusion of Jane Austen's classic novel *Pride and Prejudice*, the two eldest Bennet sisters both get ~~hitched.~~ *marry*

2. I agree with many of his environmental policies, but that proposal is totally ~~nuts.~~ *illogical*

3. The celebrated Shakespearean actor gave *an exceptional* the performance of a lifetime, despite the ~~lame~~ *lackluster* supporting cast.

4. Moby Dick's ~~humongous~~ size was matched only by Ahab's obsessive desire to ~~wipe him out.~~ *poach him*

5. The refugees had suffered great hardships, but now they were able to see ~~the light at the end of the tunnel.~~ *more positive outcomes*

Jargon   Jargon is the special vocabulary of a particular trade or profession, enabling members to speak and write concisely to one another. Reserve jargon for an audience that will understand your terms. The example that follows, from a web page about digital cameras, uses jargon appropriately for an interested and knowledgeable audience.

> Image quality for mirrorless models is similar to that of a dSLR with an equivalent lens. Performance of midrange models has gotten

appeal to an audience by showing that you are considerate of people's feelings, they can also sound insincere or evasive.

Doublespeak is language used to hide or distort the truth. During massive layoffs in the business world, companies may describe a job-cutting policy as *employee repositioning, deverticalization,* or *rightsizing.* The public—and particularly those who lose their jobs—recognize such terms as doublespeak.

EXERCISE 24.2 For each of the scenarios that follow, note who the audience would be for the piece of writing. Then indicate the level of formality—formal or informal—that would be appropriate. Be prepared to explain your answer. Example:

> **An online forum for people who are interested in Harley-Davidson motorcycles**
> Audience is others who share your passion; informal

1. A text to a childhood friend across the country
2. An email requesting an interview in response to an online job posting
3. A brochure explaining the recycling policies of your community to local residents
4. A letter to the editor of the *Washington Post* explaining that a recent editorial failed to consider all the facts about health insurance
5. A cover letter asking a professor to accept the late paper you are sending after the end of the semester

24b Considering denotation and connotation

The words *enthusiasm, passion,* and *obsession* all carry roughly the same denotation, or dictionary meaning. But the connotations, or associations, are quite different: an *enthusiasm* is a pleasurable and absorbing interest; a *passion* has a strong emotional component and may affect someone positively or negatively; an *obsession* is an unhealthy attachment that excludes other interests.

Note the differences in connotation among the following three statements:

▶ Students Against Racism (SAR) erected a temporary barrier on the campus oval, saying the structure symbolized "the many barriers to those discriminated against by university policies."

1. The Democrats are conspiring on a new education bill. *developing*
2. CEOs always waltz away with millions in salary, stock options, and pensions while the little people who keep the company running get peanuts. *obtain* *work for the company* *minimum wage*
3. The United States is turning into a nation of fatsos. *facing increasing obesity*
4. Tree-huggers ranted about the Explorer's gas mileage outside the Ford dealership. *enviormentalists* *spoke*
5. Naïve voters often stumble to the polls and blindly pick whatever names they see first. *First time* *are* *unsure who to pick*

24c Using general and specific language effectively

Effective writers balance general words (those that name groups or classes) with specific words (those that identify individual and particular things). Abstractions, which are types of general words, refer to things we cannot perceive through our five senses. Specific words are often concrete, naming things we can see, hear, touch, taste, or smell. If your aim is to bring a scene to life in your reader's mind, using specific, concrete words along with action verbs will help you do so.

GENERAL	LESS GENERAL	SPECIFIC	MORE SPECIFIC
website	dating website	LGBTQ dating website	BiCupid

ABSTRACT	LESS ABSTRACT	CONCRETE	MORE CONCRETE
culture	visual art	painting	Lawrence's *The Migration Series*

EXERCISE 24.5 Rewrite each of the following sentences to be more specific and more concrete. Example:

The truck entered the roadway.
The red Ford F150 entered Interstate 95.

1. That book was interesting.
2. They couldn't decide what to eat.
3. I pulled over and waited for the tow truck.
4. The castle is very old.
5. Jorge sat at the bus stop.

EXERCISE 24.6 Identify the similes and metaphors in each of the following numbered items, and decide how each contributes to your understanding of the passage or sentence in which it appears. Example:

> Her strong arms, her kisses, the clean soap smell of her face, her voice calming me—all of this was gone. She was like a statue in a church.
> —Louise Erdrich, "Shamengwa"

like a statue in a church (simile): vividly emphasizes the woman's cold, stone-like persona

1. Smell is a potent wizard that transports us across thousands of miles and all the years we have lived.
   —Helen Keller, *The World I Live In*

2. He sometimes thinks marriage is like a football game and he's quarter-backing the underdog team.
   —Stephen King, "Premium Harmony"

3. The senses feed shards of information to the brain like microscopic pieces of a jigsaw puzzle.
   —Diane Ackerman, *A Natural History of the Senses*

4. I like cemeteries too because they are huge, densely populated cities.
   —Guy de Maupassant, "The Graveyard Sisterhood"

5. The sun was a wide crescent, like a segment of tangerine.
   —Annie Dillard, "Total Eclipse"

EXERCISE 24.7 Choose the appropriate word in each set of parentheses. Example:

Antifreeze can have a toxic (affect/__effect__) on pets.

People need antifreeze in (their/there/they're) cars in cold (weather/whether). Unfortunately, antifreeze also tastes (grate/great) to cats and dogs, who drink it from the greenish puddles commonly (scene/seen) on asphalt. Antifreeze made of ethylene glycol causes kidney failure and has (lead/led) to the deaths of many pets. (Its/It's) not (to/too/two) hard to protect (your/you're) animals from antifreeze poisoning, however. First, (buy/by) antifreeze that does not contain ethylene glycol, in spite of (its/it's) higher cost. Second, do not let pets wander out of (cite/sight/site) when they are outdoors. Third, if a pet acts sick, get help even if the animal (seams/seems) to improve—animals with antifreeze poisoning appear to feel better shortly before they (die/dye).

Style: Effective Sentences

25 **Varying Sentences** 278

26 **Consistency and Completeness** 280

27 **Coordination and Subordination** 283

28 **Conciseness** 287

29 **Parallelism** 290

30 **Shifts** 293

25 Varying Sentences

Why should writers pay special attention to style today? Because more than ever before, information is coming at us in fire-hose quantities, so much information that we can't possibly attend to even a fraction of it. In such a time, researchers and media theorists point out, what most attracts and holds our attention is the style in which the information is presented. It's worth spending some time, then, on making sure the sentences you write are stylistically appropriate and powerful. Variety in sentence structures will help you get and keep your readers' attention.

25a Varying sentence length

Is there a "just right" length for a sentence? Not a chance. Rather, like most of the choices writers make, sentence length depends on your purpose, audience, and topic: a children's story, for instance, may call for mostly short sentences, whereas an article on nuclear disarmament may call for considerably longer ones. While a series of short or long sentences can sometimes be effective, varying sentence length can work well in college writing, where the punch of a short sentence after a longer one is powerful:

> To become a doctor, you spend so much time in the tunnels of preparation—head down, trying not to screw up, just going from one day to the next—that it is a shock to find yourself at the other end, with someone offering you a job. But the day comes.
>
> —Atul Gawande

25b Varying sentence openings

If sentence after sentence begins with a subject, the passage will usually seem "choppy" and monotonous. Take a look at the revisions to the following passage, which help to vary the sentence openings and make the passage more effective and easy to read:

278

▶ The way football and basketball are played is as interesting as the
          Because football   *each*
players. ~~Football~~ is a game of precision/, ~~Each~~ play is diagrammed
         ^   ^
                                     however,
to accomplish a certain goal. Basketball, is a game of endurance.
 In fact, a   ^
A basketball game looks like a track meet; the team that drops
^
of exhaustion first, loses. Basketball players are often compared
              their
to artists/; ~~The players'~~ graceful moves and slam dunks are their
         ^

masterpieces.

The editing adds variety by using a subordinating word (*Because*) and a prepositional phrase (*In fact*) in linking sentences. Varying sentence openings prevents the passage from seeming to jerk or lurch along.

You can vary sentence openings by using transitions, phrases, and dependent clauses:

TRANSITIONS

▶ *In contrast*, our approach will save time and money.

▶ *Nevertheless*, the show must go on.

PHRASES

▶ *Before dawn*, the tired commuters drink their first cups of coffee.

▶ *Frustrated by the delays*, the drivers started honking their horns.

DEPENDENT CLAUSES

▶ *What they want* is a place to call home.

▶ *Because the hills were dry*, the fire spread rapidly.

EXERCISE 25.1 The following paragraph can be improved by varying sentence length. Revise it, creating some short, emphatic sentences and combining other sentences to create more effective long sentences. Add words or change punctuation as you need to.

Before planting a tree, a gardener needs to choose a good location and dig a deep enough hole. The location should have the right kind of soil, sufficient drainage, and enough light for the type of tree chosen. The hole should be slightly deeper than the root-ball and about twice as wide. The gardener must unwrap the root-ball, for even burlap, which is biodegradable, may be treated with chemicals that will eventually damage the roots. The roots may have grown into a compact ball if the tree has been in a pot for some time, and they should be separated or cut apart in this case. The gardener should set the root-ball into the hole and then begin to fill the hole with loose dirt. After filling the hole completely, the gardener should make sure to water the tree thoroughly. New plantings require extra water and extra care for about three years before they are well rooted.

26 Consistency and Completeness

If you listen carefully to the conversations around you, you will hear speakers use different styles to get their points across. The words, tone, and structure they choose have a big impact on your impression of them—their personality and credibility, for example—and their ideas. Often, you will hear inconsistent and incomplete structures. For instance, during an interview with Kelly Ripa and Ryan Seacrest, Oprah Winfrey described a recent trip to New Zealand, part of her "year of adventure":

> It should be on your bucket list. Put it on your bucket list. And look at that water [on the slide] behind me—it is like crystal blue, I mean, no kind of Instagram fixin' up stuff. No filter. Nothing. It just is like . . . because the water's coming off of the glaciers and it enters . . . and it's just like, from the minerals, it's like pure turquoise.

Because Winfrey is talking casually, some of her sentences begin one way but then move in another direction. The **mixed structures** pose no problem for listeners—they sound like everyday conversations—but sentences such as these can be confusing in writing. For this reason, using consistent and complete sentence structure will help get and hold your readers' attention.

26a   Revising confusing sentence structure

Beginning a sentence with one grammatical pattern and then switching to another one can confuse readers.

MIXED   The fact that I get up at 5:00 AM, a wake-up time
            that explains why I'm always tired in the evening.

This sentence starts out with a **subject** (*The fact*) followed by a **dependent clause** (*that I get up at 5:00 AM*). The sentence needs a predicate to complete the **independent clause**, but instead it moves to another **phrase** followed by a dependent clause (*a wake-up time that explains why I'm always tired in the evening*), and a **fragment** results.

REVISED   The fact that I get up at 5:00 AM explains why
            I'm always tired in the evening.

Deleting *a wake-up time that* changes the rest of the sentence into a **predicate**.

FAULTY   In some car ads sell a lifestyle more than a
            product.

REVISED   Some car ads sell a lifestyle more than a product.

The revised sentence begins with a proper subject rather than a prepositional phrase.

26b   Matching subjects and predicates

Another kind of mixed structure, called *faulty predication*, occurs when a subject and predicate do not fit together grammatically or simply do not make sense together.

▶   A characteristic that I admire is ~~a person who is generous.~~ generosity.

    A person is not a characteristic.

▶   The rules of the corporation ~~expect~~ require that employees ~~to~~ be on time.

    Rules cannot expect anything.

Is when, is where, the reason . . . is because　Although you will often hear these expressions in everyday use, such constructions are inappropriate in academic or professional writing.

▶ A stereotype is ~~when someone characterizes~~ a group. ~~unfairly.~~
　　^an unfair characterization of^

▶ Spamming is ~~where companies send~~ electronic junk mail.
　　^the practice of sending^

▶ ~~The reason~~ I like to play soccer ~~is~~ because it provides aerobic exercise.

26c　Making complete comparisons

When you compare two or more things, make the comparison complete and clear.

▶ I was often embarrassed because my parents were so different/
　　^from my friends' parents.^

Adding *from my friends' parents* completes the comparison.

UNCLEAR	Aneil always felt more affection for his brother than his sister.
CLEAR	Aneil always felt more affection for his brother <u>than his sister did</u>. OR Aneil always felt more affection for his brother <u>than he did for his sister</u>.

EXERCISE 26.1　Revise this passage so that all sentences are grammatically and logically consistent and complete.

　　A concentrated animal feeding operation, or CAFO, is when a factory farm raises thousands of animals in a confined space. Vast amounts of factory-farm livestock waste, dumped into giant lagoons, which are an increasingly common sight in rural areas of this country. Are factory-farm operations healthy for neighbors, for people in other parts of the country, and the environment?

　　One problem with factory farming is the toxic waste that has contaminated groundwater in the Midwest. In addition, air quality produces bad-smelling and sometimes dangerous gases that people nearby have to breathe. When a factory farm's neighbors complain may not be able to close the operation. The reason is because most factory farms have powerful corporate backers.

Not everyone is angry about the CAFO situation; consumers get a short-term benefit from a large supply of pork, beef, and chicken that is cheaper than family farms can raise. However, many people think that these operations damage our air and water more than small family farms.

27 Coordination and Subordination

You may notice a difference between your spoken and your written language. In speech, most people tend to use *and* and *so* as all-purpose connectors.

> He enjoys psychology, and he has to study hard.

The meaning of this sentence may be perfectly clear in speech, which provides clues with voice, facial expressions, and gestures. In writing, however, the same sentence could have more than one meaning.

> Although he enjoys psychology, he has to study hard.

> He enjoys psychology although he has to study hard.

The first sentence links two ideas with a **coordinating conjunction**, *and*; the other two sentences link ideas with a **subordinating conjunction**, *although*. A coordinating conjunction gives the ideas equal emphasis, and a subordinating conjunction emphasizes one idea more than another.

27a Relating equal ideas

When you want to give equal emphasis to different ideas in a sentence, link them with a coordinating conjunction (*and*, *but*, *for*, *nor*, *or*, *so*, *yet*) or a semicolon.

▶ They acquired horses, **and** their ancient nomadic spirit was suddenly free of the ground.

▶ There is perfect freedom in the mountains, <u>but</u> it belongs to the eagle and the elk, the badger and the bear.

—N. Scott Momaday, *The Way to Rainy Mountain*

Coordination can help make explicit the relationship between two separate ideas.

▶ My son watches *The Simpsons* religiously/;̶ ̶F̶o̶r̶c̶e̶d̶ ^{forced} to choose, he would probably take Homer Simpson over ^his sister.

Connecting these two sentences with a semicolon strengthens the connection between two closely related ideas.

When you connect ideas in a sentence, make sure that the relationship between the ideas is clear.

▶ Surfing the internet is a common way to spend leisure time, a̶n̶d̶ ^{but} it should not replace human contact. ^

What does being a common form of leisure have to do with replacing human contact? Changing *and* to *but* better relates the two ideas.

EXERCISE 27.1 Using the principles of coordination to signal equal importance, combine and revise the following group of short sentences into several longer and more effective ones. Add or delete words as necessary.

The room was crowded. I wondered if no one had heard of COVID-19. People stood close together. No one had a mask on. They were laughing and shouting, even singing. I stood outside and watched. Maybe I should take a chance. I came to my senses. I adjusted my mask. I turned and walked away. I would stay safe at least for tonight.

27b Distinguishing main ideas

Subordination allows you to distinguish major points from minor points or to bring supporting details into a sentence. If, for instance, you put your main idea in an **independent clause**, you might then put any less significant ideas in **dependent clauses**, **phrases**, or even single words. The following sentence underlines the subordinated point:

▶ Mrs. Viola Cullinan was a plump woman <u>who lived in a three-bedroom house somewhere behind the post office.</u>

—Maya Angelou, "My Name Is Margaret"

The dependent clause adds some important information about Mrs. Cullinan, but it is subordinate to the independent clause.

Notice that the choice of what to subordinate rests with the writer and depends on the intended meaning. Angelou might have given the same basic information differently:

▶ Mrs. Viola Cullinan, <u>a plump woman</u>, lived in a three-bedroom house somewhere behind the post office.

Subordinating the information about Mrs. Cullinan's size to that about her house would suggest a slightly different meaning. As a writer, you must think carefully about what you want to emphasize and subordinate information accordingly.

Subordination also establishes logical relationships among different ideas. These relationships are often specified by subordinating conjunctions.

SOME COMMON SUBORDINATING CONJUNCTIONS

after	if	until
although, even though	once	when
as, as if	since	where
because	that, so that	while
before	though	

The following sentence underlines the subordinate clause and italicizes the subordinating word:

▶ She usually rested her smile until late afternoon <u>*when* her women friends dropped in and Miss Glory, the cook, served them cold drinks on the closed-in porch.</u>

—Maya Angelou, "My Name Is Margaret"

Using too many coordinate structures can be monotonous and can make it hard for readers to recognize the most important ideas. Subordinating lesser ideas can help highlight the main ideas.

▶ Many people check email in the evening, and so they turn on the
computer. ~~They~~ *Though they* may intend to respond only to urgent messages,
a friend sends a link to a blog post, ~~and~~ *which* they decide to read ~~it~~ for

Eventually,

just a short while~~/. and~~ they get engrossed in Facebook, and they
end up spending the whole evening in front of the screen.

Determining what to subordinate

▶ *Although our*

~~Our~~ new boss can be difficult, ~~although~~ she has revived and
maybe even saved the division.

The editing puts the more important information—that the new boss
has saved part of the company—in an independent clause and subor-
dinates the rest.

Avoiding too much subordination

When too many subordi-
nate clauses are strung together, readers may not be able to keep
track of the main idea in the independent clause.

TOO MUCH SUBORDINATION

▶ Philip II sent the Spanish Armada to conquer England, which
was ruled by Elizabeth, who had executed Mary because she was
plotting to overthrow Elizabeth, who was a Protestant, whereas
Mary and Philip were Roman Catholics.

REVISED

▶ Philip II sent the Spanish Armada to conquer England, which was
ruled by Elizabeth, a Protestant. She had executed Mary, a Roman
Catholic like Philip, because Mary was plotting to overthrow her.

Putting the facts about Elizabeth executing Mary into an independent
clause makes key information easier to recognize.

EXERCISE 27.2 Revise the following paragraph, using coordination and
subordination where appropriate to clarify the relationships
among ideas.

Reggae is a style of music. It originated in Jamaica in the late 1960s.
Reggae evolved out of earlier types of Jamaican music. Ska was one of reggae's main influences. It has a fast-paced rhythm. It accents the second and
fourth beats of each measure. Ska developed in Jamaica in the late 1950s.
It combined elements of calypso music and American jazz and rhythm and
blues. Reggae emerged in the late 1960s. Reggae songs focus on politics and

racial equality. They resonated with the youths of the time. Youths of the time were rising up in protest movements around the world. Musicians Bob Marley and Jimmy Cliff became internationally famous in the 1970s. Reggae gained a permanent place in popular music around the world.

28 Conciseness

If you have a Twitter account, you probably know a lot about being concise—that is, about getting messages across in no more than 280 characters. When *New York Times* editor Bill Keller tweeted, "Twitter makes you stupid. Discuss," his comment drew a large number of responses, including a very concise message from his wife: "I don't know if Twitter makes you stupid, but it's making you late for dinner. Come home." **Conciseness** is often a feature of good writing.

28a Eliminating redundant words

Sometimes writers add words for emphasis, saying that something is large *in size* or red *in color* or that two ingredients should be combined *together*. The italicized words are redundant (unnecessary for meaning), as are the deleted words in the following examples:

▶ ~~Compulsory~~ A attendance at assemblies is required.

▶ The auction featured ~~contemporary~~ "antiques" made recently.

▶ Many different forms of hazing occur, such as physical ~~abuse~~ and mental abuse.

28b Eliminating empty words

Words that contribute little or no meaning to a sentence include vague **nouns** like *area*, *kind*, *situation*, and *thing* as well as vague **modifiers** like *definitely*, *major*, *really*, and *very*. Delete such words, or find a more specific way to say what you mean.

H   strongly influence
▶ ~~The~~ housing ~~situation~~ can ~~have a really significant impact on~~
           ^   ^   social
~~the social aspect of~~ a student's life.
                  ^

28c Replacing wordy phrases

Many common **phrases** can be reduced to a word or two with no loss in meaning.

WORDY	CONCISE
at that point in time	then
at the present time	now/today
due to the fact that	because
for the purpose of	for
in order to	to
in spite of the fact that	although

EXERCISE 28.1 Make each of the following sentences clear and concise by eliminating unnecessary words and phrases and by making additions or revisions as needed. Example:

The ~~incredible, unbelievable~~ feats that Houdini performed amazed ~~and astounded all of~~ his audiences ~~who came to see him~~.

1. Harry Houdini, whose real birth name was Ehrich Weiss, made the claim that he had been born in Appleton, Wisconsin, but in actual fact he was born into the world in Budapest, Hungary.

2. Shortly after Houdini's birth, his family moved to Appleton, where his father served as the one and only rabbi in Appleton at that point in time.

3. Houdini gained fame as a really great master escape artist.

4. His many numerous escapes included getting out of a giant sealed envelope without tearing it and walking out of jail cells that were said to be supposedly escape-proof.

5. Before his untimely early death, Houdini told his brother to burn and destroy all papers describing how Houdini's illusions worked.

28d Simplifying sentence structure

Using simple grammatical structures can tighten and strengthen your sentences considerably.

▶ Hurricane Katrina, ~~which was certainly~~ one of the most
  widespread
  powerful storms ever to hit the Gulf Coast, caused damage.
                                                    ^   ^
  ~~to a very wide area.~~

Strong verbs *Be* **verbs** (*is, are, was, were, been*) often result in wordiness. (See also 33j.)

            harms
▶ A high-fat, high-cholesterol diet ~~is bad for~~ your heart.
                                      ^

Expletives Sometimes expletive constructions such as *there is, there are,* and *it is* introduce a topic effectively; often, however, your writing will be better without them.

     M
▶ ~~There are m~~any people ~~who~~ fear success because they believe
           ^
  they do not deserve it.

          P   need
▶ ~~It is necessary for p~~residential candidates to perform well on
        ^   ^
  television.

Active voice Some writing situations call for the passive **voice**, but it is always wordier than the active—and often makes for dull or even difficult reading (see 31f).

  Gower
▶ ~~In Gower's research, it was~~ found that pythons often dwell
  ^
  in trees.

| **EXERCISE 28.2** | Revise the following paragraph so that each sentence is as concise as possible. Combine or divide sentences if necessary. |

In this day and age, many people obsess over fitness or the way they look or their appearance. As a result of this very widespread obsession, people quite frequently flock to gyms and other places that offer great opportunities for all kinds of really strenuous exercise. They are absolutely positively sure that spending hours and hours on Peloton machines will improve their health but also make them definitely more attractive. In addition, they make use of lots of diet or health supplements and expensive creams and other potions that are supposedly going to improve the tone or resilience of their skin. All in all, they are willing to spend quite remarkable sums of money chasing after a way to look and feel and perform better. I for one have to wonder whether they are getting what they hope and believe they are paying for.

29 Parallelism

If you look and listen, you will see parallel grammatical structures in everyday use. Bumper stickers often use parallelism to make their messages memorable (*Minds are like parachutes; both work best when open*), as do rap lyrics and jump-rope rhymes. In addition to creating pleasing rhythmic effects, parallelism can help clarify meaning.

29a Making items in a series or list parallel

All items in a series should be in parallel form—all **nouns**, all **verbs**, all prepositional **phrases**, and so on. Parallelism makes a series both graceful and easy to follow.

▶ In the eighteenth century, armed forces could fight <u>in open fields</u> and <u>on the high seas</u>. Today, they can clash <u>on the ground anywhere</u>, <u>on the sea</u>, <u>under the sea</u>, and <u>in the air</u>.
—Donald Snow and Eugene Brown, *International Relations*

The parallel structure of the phrases, and of the sentences themselves, highlights the contrast between the eighteenth century and today.

▶ The children ran down the hill, skipped over the lawn, and
jumped
~~were jumping~~ into the swimming pool.
^

▶ The duties of the job include babysitting, housecleaning, and
  preparing
  ~~preparation of~~ meals.
  ^

Items that are in a list, in a formal outline, and in headings should
be parallel.

▶ Kitchen rules: (1) Coffee to be made only by library staff.

  (2) Coffee service to be closed at 4:00 PM. (3) Doughnuts to be
  Coffee materials not to be handled by
  kept in cabinet. (4) ~~No faculty members should handle coffee~~
  faculty.   ^
  ~~materials.~~

29b Making paired ideas parallel

Parallel structures can help you pair two ideas effectively. The more
nearly parallel the two structures are, the stronger the connection
between the ideas will be.

▶ I type in one place, but I write all over the house.

—Toni Morrison

▶ Writers are often more interesting on the page than they are in
  the flesh.
  ~~person.~~
  ^
  In these examples, the parallel structures help readers see an important contrast between two ideas or acts.

With conjunctions   When you link ideas with *and, but, or, nor,
for, so,* or *yet,* try to make the ideas parallel by using the same structure after: *either . . . or, both . . . and, neither . . . nor, not . . . but, not
only . . . but also, just as . . . so,* and *whether . . . or.*

           who is
▶ Consult a friend in your class or who is good at math.
           ^

                           accepts
▶ The wise politician promises the possible and ~~should accept~~ the
  inevitable.   ^

                           live in
▶ I wanted not only to go away to school but also to New England.
                                                     ^

30b Revising shifts in voice

Do not shift between the **active voice** (she *sold* it) and the **passive voice** (it *was sold*) without a reason. Sometimes a shift in voice is justified, but often it only confuses readers.

▶ Two youths approached ~~me,~~ and ~~I was~~ asked for my opinion in a survey.
me
^

The original sentence shifts from active to passive voice, so it is unclear who asked for the opinion.

30c Revising shifts in point of view

Unnecessary shifts in point of view between first person (*I* or *we*), second person (*you*), and third person (*he*, *she*, *it*, *one*, or *they*), or between singular and plural subjects, can be very confusing to readers.

You
▶ ~~One~~ can do well on this job if you budget your time.
^

Is the writer making a general statement or giving advice to someone? Revising the shift eliminates this confusion.

EXERCISE 30.2 Revise each of the following sentences to eliminate an unnecessary shift in voice or point of view. Example:

I
When I remember to take deep breaths and count to ten, ~~you~~ really
^
my
can control ~~your~~ anger.
^

1. "Notorious RBG" was a nickname used by fans of Supreme Court justice Ruth Bader Ginsburg because her fiery dissents inspired admiration and action.

2. I had planned to walk home after the movie, but you shouldn't be on campus alone after dark.

3. When largely peaceful protests against police brutality spread across the country, scenes of vandalism were focused on by the media.

4. Instructors at the studio cooperative offer a wide variety of dance lessons, and art and voice training are also given there.

5. We knew that emails promising free gifts were usually scams, but you couldn't resist clicking on the link just to see.

30d Revising shifts between direct and indirect discourse

When you quote someone's exact words, you are using direct discourse: *She said, "I'm an editor."* When you report what someone says without repeating the exact words, you are using indirect discourse: *She said she was an editor.* Shifting between direct and indirect discourse in the same sentence can cause problems, especially with questions.

▶ Bob asked what could ~~he~~ do to helpᵗ.
     he

The editing eliminates an awkward shift by reporting Bob's question indirectly. It could also be edited to quote Bob directly: *Bob asked, "What can I do to help?"*

EXERCISE 30.3 Eliminate the shifts between direct and indirect discourse in the following sentences by putting the direct discourse into indirect form. Example:

Steven Pinker ~~stated~~ that ~~my~~ book is meant for people who use
   states   *his*
language and respect it.

1. Richard Rodriguez acknowledges that intimacy was not created by a language; "it is created by intimates."

2. Chris said that during a semester abroad, "I really missed all my friends."

3. The bewildered neighbor asked Ricardo, "What the heck he thought he was doing on the roof?"

4. Loren Eiseley feels an urge to join the birds in their soundless flight, but in the end he knows that he cannot, and "I was, after all, only a man."

5. The instructor told us, "Please submit your assignments to the course website" and that she might give us a quiz.

Grammar

31 **Verbs and Verb Phrases** 298

32 **Nouns and Noun Phrases** 313

33 **Subject-Verb Agreement** 319

34 **Adjectives and Adverbs** 325

35 **Modifier Placement** 329

36 **Pronouns** 333

37 **Prepositions and Prepositional Phrases** 342

38 **Comma Splices and Fused Sentences** 345

39 **Sentence Fragments** 349

31 Verbs and Verb Phrases

One famous restaurant in New Orleans offers to bake, broil, pan-fry, BBQ, deep-fry, poach, sauté, fricassée, blacken, or scallop any of the fish entrées on its menu. To someone ordering—or cooking—at this restaurant, the important distinctions lie entirely in the **verbs**.

31a Using regular and irregular verb forms

You can create all verb tenses from four verb forms: the **base form**, the past **tense**, the past **participle**, and the present participle. For **regular verbs**, the past tense and past participles are formed by adding -*d* or -*ed*. Present participles are formed by adding -*ing*.

BASE FORM	PAST TENSE	PAST PARTICIPLE	PRESENT PARTICIPLE
love	loved	loved	loving
honor	honored	honored	honoring
obey	obeyed	obeyed	obeying

An **irregular verb** does not follow the -*ed* or -*d* pattern. If you are unsure about whether a verb is regular or irregular, or what the correct form is, consult the following list or a dictionary. Dictionaries list any irregular forms under the entry for the base form.

Some common irregular verbs

BASE FORM	PAST TENSE	PAST PARTICIPLE	PRESENT PARTICIPLE
be	was/were	been	being
begin	began	begun	beginning
break	broke	broken	breaking
bring	brought	brought	bringing
choose	chose	chosen	choosing
come	came	come	coming
do	did	done	doing

draw	drew	drawn	drawing
drink	drank	drunk	drinking
eat	ate	eaten	eating
fall	fell	fallen	falling
feel	felt	felt	feeling
fly	flew	flown	flying
get	got	gotten, got	getting
give	gave	given	giving
go	went	gone	going
hang (suspend)[1]	hung	hung	hanging
have	had	had	having
keep	kept	kept	keeping
lead	led	led	leading
lie (recline)[2]	lay	lain	lying
prove	proved	proved, proven	proving
ring	rang	rung	ringing
run	ran	run	running
speak	spoke	spoken	speaking
swim	swam	swum	swimming
swing	swung	swung	swinging
take	took	taken	taking
wake	woke, waked	waked, woken	waking
write	wrote	written	writing

[1] *Hang* meaning "execute by hanging" is regular: *hang, hanged, hanged.*

[2] *Lie* meaning "tell a falsehood" is regular: *lie, lied, lied.*

EXERCISE 31.1   Underline each verb or verb phrase in the following sentences. Example:

Many people throughout the United States <u>commemorate</u> the end of slavery on Juneteenth.

1. On June 19, 1865, Union soldiers brought news that all enslaved people were free to Galveston, Texas.

2. But this event occurred two and a half years after President Lincoln signed the Emancipation Proclamation.

3. According to one legend, an earlier messenger was murdered on his way to deliver the news to Texas.

4. Others said that the troops withheld the news in order for slaves to keep harvesting cotton.

5. Whatever the reasons for the delay, the formerly enslaved people of Texas took in their first breaths of freedom.

EXERCISE 31.2   Complete each of the following sentences by filling in each blank with the past tense or past participle of the verb listed in parentheses. Example:

Frida Kahlo ___*became*___ (become) one of Mexico's foremost painters.

1. Frida Kahlo _____ (grow) up in Mexico City, where she _____ (spend) most of her life.

2. She _____ (be) born in 1907, but she often _____ (say) that her birth year _____ (be) 1910.

3. In 1925 a bus accident _____ (leave) Kahlo horribly injured.

4. The accident _____ (break) her spinal column and many other bones, so Kahlo _____ (lie) in bed in a body cast for months.

5. She had always _____ (be) a spirited young woman, and she _____ (take) up painting to avoid boredom while convalescing.

31b Building verb phrases

Verb phrases can be built up out of a main **verb** and one or more **helping** (auxiliary) **verbs**.

▶ Immigration figures <u>are rising</u> every year.

▶ Immigration figures <u>have risen</u> every year.

Language, Culture, and Context

Seeing Grammar as Flexible

Teachers of writing often dread telling new acquaintances what they do for a living because too often they hear: "Oh, I better watch my grammar." While speakers of any language acquire its grammar as they learn, learning a second language or a dialect like standardized English (which no one grows up speaking) takes effort. While there are some "rules" of grammar that almost always apply—such as word order in English—much of what counts as rules are just conventions—widely accepted uses that develop and change over time. In addition, English and its many dialects are flexible, allowing writers to follow—or resist—conventions depending on purpose, audience, and stance.

Verb phrases have strict rules of order. If you try to rearrange the words in either of these sentences, you will find that most alternatives are impossible. You cannot say *Immigration figures rising are every year.*

Putting auxiliary verbs in order

In the sentence *Immigration figures may have been rising,* the main verb *rising* follows three auxiliaries: *may, have,* and *been.* Together these auxiliaries and the main verb make up a verb phrase.

- *May* is a **modal** that indicates possibility; it is followed by the base form of a verb.
- *Have* is an auxiliary verb that in this case indicates the perfect tense; it must be followed by a past participle (*been*).
- Any form of *be,* when it is followed by a present participle ending in *-ing* (such as *rising*), indicates the **progressive** tense.
- *Be* followed by a past participle, as in *New immigration policies have been passed in recent years*, indicates the passive voice (31f).

As the following chart shows, when two or more auxiliaries appear in a verb phrase, they follow a particular order based on the type of auxiliary: (1) modal, (2) a form of *have* that indicates a perfect tense, (3) a form of *be* that indicates a progressive tense, and (4) a form of *be* that indicates the passive voice. (Few sentences include all four kinds of auxiliaries.)

	Modal	Perfect *Have*	Progressive *Be*	Passive *Be*	Main Verb	
Sonia	—	has	—	been	invited	to visit a family in Prague.
She	should	—	—	be	finished	with school soon.
The invitation	must	have	—	been	sent	in the spring.
She	—	has	been	—	studying	Czech.
She	may	—	be	—	feeling	nervous.
She	might	have	been	—	expecting	to travel elsewhere.
The trip	will	have	been	being	planned	for a month by the time she leaves.

Only one modal is permitted in a verb phrase.

▶ She will ~~can~~ speak Czech much better soon.

be able to

✔ Checklist

Editing the Verbs in Your Writing

✔ Check verb endings that cause you trouble. (31a)

✔ Double-check forms of *lie* and *lay*, *sit* and *set*, *rise* and *raise*. (31d)

✔ Refer to action in a literary work (such as a novel, poem, or story) in the present tense. (31e)

✔ Check that verb tenses in your writing express meaning accurately. (31e)

✔ Use passive voice appropriately. (31f)

Forming auxiliary verbs Whenever you use an auxiliary, check the form of the word that follows.

Modal + base form Use the base form of a verb after *can, could, will, would, shall, should, may, might,* and *must: Alice can read Latin.* In many other languages, modals like *can* or *must* are followed by the **infinitive** (*to* + base form). Do not substitute an infinitive for the base form in English.

▶ Alice can ~~to~~ read Latin.

Perfect **have,** *has,* or **had** *+ past participle* To form the perfect tenses, use *have, has,* or *had* with a past participle: *Everyone has gone home. They have been working all day.*

Progressive **be** *+ present participle* A progressive form of the verb is signaled by two elements, a form of the auxiliary *be* (*am, is, are, was, were, be,* or *been*) and the *-ing* form of the next word: *The children are studying.* Be sure to include both elements.

▶ The children _∧ studying science. [*are*]

▶ The children are ~~study~~ science. [*studying*]

Some verbs are rarely used in progressive forms. These are verbs that express unchanging conditions or mental states rather than deliberate actions: *believe, belong, hate, know, like, love, need, own, resemble, understand.*

Passive **be** *+ past participle* Use *am, is, are, was, were, being, be,* or *been* with a past participle to form the passive voice.

▶ Tagalog is spoken in the Philippines.

Notice that the word following the progressive *be* (the present participle) ends in *-ing,* but the word following the passive *be* (the past participle) never ends in *-ing.*

PROGRESSIVE JaVale is studying music.

PASSIVE Natasha was taught by a famous violinist.

If the first auxiliary in a verb phrase is a form of *be* or *have,* it must show either present or past tense and must agree with the subject: *JaVale has played in an orchestra.*

EXERCISE 31.3	Rewrite the following passage by adding appropriate forms

of *have* and main-verb endings or forms for the verbs in parentheses. Example:

I _like_ (like) to try new foods, so I _have eaten_ (eat) in many different kinds of restaurants in my life.

Several times, I _____ (hear) people musing about the bravery of the first person who ever _____ (eat) a lobster. It _____ (be) an interesting question: what do you _____ (think) _____ (make) anyone do such a thing? But personally, I _____ (wonder) all my life about how ancient people _____ (discover) the art of baking bread. After all, preparing a lobster _____ (be) pretty simple in comparison to baking. Bread _____ (feed) vast numbers of people for centuries, so it certainly _____ (be) a more important food source than lobster, too. Those of us who _____ (love) either lobster or bread, or both, _____ (be) grateful to those who _____ (give) us such a wonderful culinary legacy.

31c Using infinitives and gerunds

Knowing whether to use an **infinitive** (*to read*) or a **gerund** (*reading*) in a sentence may be a challenge.

INFINITIVE

▶ My adviser urged me <u>to apply</u> to several colleges.

GERUND

▶ <u>Applying</u> took a great deal of time.

In general, infinitives tend to represent intentions, desires, or expectations, while gerunds tend to represent facts. The infinitive in the first sentence tells us that applying is desired but not yet accomplished, while the gerund in the second sentence tells us that the application process was actually carried out.

The association of intention with infinitives and facts with gerunds can often help you decide which one to use when another verb immediately precedes it.

INFINITIVES

▶ Kumar expected <u>to get</u> a good job after graduation.

▶ Last year, Jorge decided <u>to become</u> a math major.

▶ The strikers have agreed <u>to go</u> back to work.

GERUNDS

▶ Jerzy enjoys <u>going</u> to the theater.

▶ We resumed <u>working</u> after our coffee break.

▶ Alycia appreciated <u>getting</u> candy from Sean.

A few verbs can be followed by either an infinitive or a gerund. With some, such as *begin* and *continue,* the choice makes little difference in meaning. With others, however, the difference in meaning is striking.

▶ Carlos was working as a medical technician, but he stopped <u>to study</u> English.

The infinitive indicates that Carlos left his job because he intended to study English.

▶ Carlos stopped <u>studying</u> English when he left the United States.

The gerund indicates that Carlos actually studied English but then stopped.

 Language, Culture, and Context

Checking Usage with Search Engines

Search engines can help you check sentence structure and word usage. For example, if you are not sure whether to use an infinitive form (*to* verb) or a gerund (*-ing*) for the verb *confirm* after the main verb *expect,* you can search for both *"expected confirming"* and *"expected to confirm"* to see which phrase yields more results. The results will indicate that *expected to confirm* is the more commonly used expression. Be sure to click through a few pages of the search results to make sure that most results come from ordinary sentences rather than from headlines or phrases that may be constructed differently from standardized English.

The distinction between fact and intention is a tendency, not a rule, and other rules may override it. Always use a gerund—not an infinitive—directly following a **preposition**.

▶ This fruit is safe for ~~to eat.~~ *eating.*

You can also remove the preposition and keep the infinitive.

▶ This fruit is safe ~~for~~ to eat.

31d   Using *lie* and *lay*, *sit* and *set*, *rise* and *raise*

These pairs of verbs cause confusion because both verbs in each pair have similar-sounding forms and somewhat related meanings. In each pair, one verb is **transitive**, meaning that it is followed by a direct **object** (*I lay the package on the counter*). The other is intransitive, meaning that it does not have an object (*He lies on the floor, unable to move*). The best way to avoid confusing these verbs is to memorize their forms and meanings.

BASE FORM	PAST TENSE	PAST PARTICIPLE	PRESENT PARTICIPLE	-S FORM
lie (recline)	lay	lain	lying	lies
lay (put)	laid	laid	laying	lays
sit (be seated)	sat	sat	sitting	sits
set (put)	set	set	setting	sets
rise (get up)	rose	risen	rising	rises
raise (lift)	raised	raised	raising	raises

▶ The doctor asked the patient to ~~lay~~ *lie* on his side.

▶ Tamika ~~sat~~ *set* the vase on the table.

▶ Jaime ~~rose~~ *raised* himself to a sitting position.

EXERCISE 31.4   Choose the appropriate verb form in each of the following sentences. Example:

The boys laid/<u>lay</u> on the couch, hoping for something good on TV.

1. My grandparents rose/raised from poverty to own their own farm.
2. Finished at last, the weary student laid/lay the book down and went to bed.
3. The students sat/set their digital devices down and stared grimly at the new teacher.
4. Lie/lay your packages down and stay for supper.
5. Don't just lie/lay there; do something!

31e Using verb tenses

Tenses show when the verb's action takes place. The three **simple tenses** are the **present tense**, the **past tense**, and the **future tense**.

PRESENT TENSE	I <u>ask</u>, <u>write</u>
PAST TENSE	I <u>asked</u>, <u>wrote</u>
FUTURE TENSE	I <u>will ask</u>, <u>will write</u>

More complex aspects of time are expressed through **progressive**, **perfect**, and **perfect progressive** forms of the simple tenses.

PRESENT PROGRESSIVE	Liz <u>is asking</u>, <u>is writing</u>
PAST PROGRESSIVE	Liz <u>was asking</u>, <u>was writing</u>
FUTURE PROGRESSIVE	Liz <u>will be asking</u>, <u>will be writing</u>
PRESENT PERFECT	Liz <u>has asked</u>, <u>has written</u>
PAST PERFECT	Liz <u>had asked</u>, <u>had written</u>
FUTURE PERFECT	Liz <u>will have asked</u>, <u>will have written</u>
PRESENT PERFECT PROGRESSIVE	Liz <u>has been asking</u>, <u>has been writing</u>
PAST PERFECT PROGRESSIVE	Liz <u>had been asking</u>, <u>had been writing</u>
FUTURE PERFECT PROGRESSIVE	Liz <u>will have been asking</u>, <u>will have been writing</u>

The simple tenses locate an action only within the three basic time frames of present, past, and future. Progressive forms express continuing actions; perfect forms express completed actions; perfect progressive forms express actions that continue up to some point in the present, past, or future.

Special purposes of the present tense   When writing about action in literary works, use the present tense.

> realizes   is
> ▶ Ishmael slowly ~~realized~~ all that ~~was~~ at stake in the search for the white whale.

General truths or scientific facts should also be in the present tense, even when the **predicate** in the main **clause** is in the past tense.

> makes
> ▶ Pasteur demonstrated that his boiling process ~~made~~ milk safe to drink.

In general, when you are quoting, summarizing, or paraphrasing a work, use the present tense.

> writes
> ▶ Adam Banks ~~wrote~~ that we should "fly on, reaching for the stars we cannot yet map, see, or scan."

But when using APA (American Psychological Association) style, report the results of your experiments or another researcher's work in the past tense (*wrote*, *noted*) or the present perfect tense (*has discovered*). (For more on APA style, see Chapter 17.)

> noted
> ▶ Comer (1995) ~~notes~~ that protesters who deprive themselves of food are seen not as dysfunctional but rather as "caring, sacrificing, even heroic" (p. 5).

EXERCISE 31.5   From the following list, identify the form of each verb or verb phrase in each of the numbered sentences.

simple present	past perfect
simple past	present progressive
present perfect	past progressive

Example:

> Residents are preparing for wildfires.   *present progressive*

1. Sasha was getting ready for bed when the wildfire warning sounded.

2. At first, she thought firefighters were controlling the fire.

3. But within an hour, Sasha saw the fire come over the hill and roar down to the houses below.

4. The family had rehearsed their evacuation plan; they left everything behind and raced to the car.

5. They escaped with their lives and now hope the fire has spared their home.

EXERCISE 31.6   Complete each of the following sentences by filling in the blank with an appropriate form of the verb given in parentheses. Because more than one form will sometimes be possible, choose one form and then be prepared to explain the reasons for your choice. Example:

People _have been practicing/have practiced_ (practice) the art of yoga for thousands of years.

1. The word *yoga* _____ (come) from Sanskrit.

2. Although many people today _____ (begin) a yoga practice purely for physical exercise, it is actually a path to spirituality that _____ (date) back thousands and thousands of years.

3. Yoga's popularity in America _____ (explode) over the last decade.

4. As a result of this surge in popularity, many yoga studios _____ (open) throughout the city.

5. When you _____ (begin) a yoga practice, it is important to find a reputable teacher who _____ (receive) proper certification.

Sequencing verb tenses   When you use the appropriate tense for each action, readers can follow time changes easily.

had
▶ **By the time he lent her the money, she declared bankruptcy.**
The revision makes clear that the bankruptcy occurred before the loan.

31f **Using active and passive voice**

Voice tells whether a **subject** is acting (*He questions us*) or being acted upon (*He is questioned*). When the subject is acting, the verb is in the **active voice**; when the subject is being acted upon, however, the verb is in the **passive voice**. Most contemporary writers use the active voice as much as possible because it makes their prose stronger and livelier. To shift a sentence from passive to active voice, make the performer of the action the subject of the sentence.

▶ ~~The~~ My sister took the prizewinning photograph. ~~was taken by my sister.~~

Use the passive voice when you want to emphasize the recipient of an action rather than the performer of the action.

▶ John Lewis <u>was eulogized</u> by three former Presidents of the United States.

In scientific and technical writing, use the passive voice to focus attention on what is being studied.

▶ The volunteers' food intake <u>was</u> closely <u>monitored</u>.

EXERCISE 31.7 Convert each sentence from active to passive voice or from passive to active, and note the differences in emphasis these changes make. Example:

The largest fish was caught by me.
I caught the largest fish.

1. Online retailers were swamped by customers on Black Friday.
2. Police used tear gas and pepper bullets on the protesting students.
3. Fans of BTS were thrilled with the release of *Map of the Soul: 7*.
4. My favorite dinner was cooked by my mother on my birthday.
5. The lead part in the school play was gotten by Ivan.

31g Using mood appropriately

The **mood** of a verb indicates the writer's attitude toward what he or she is saying. The indicative mood states facts or opinions and asks questions: *I did the right thing. Did I do the right thing?* The imperative mood gives commands and instructions: *Do the right thing.* The **subjunctive mood** (used primarily in **dependent clauses** beginning with *that* or *if*) expresses wishes and conditions that are contrary to fact: *If I were doing the right thing, I'd know it.*

The present subjunctive uses the base form of the verb with all subjects.

▶ It is important that children <u>be</u> ready for a new sibling.

The past subjunctive is the same as the simple past except for the verb *be*, which uses *were* for all subjects.

▶ He spent money as if he <u>had</u> infinite credit.

▶ If the store <u>were</u> better located, it would attract more customers.

Because the subjunctive creates a rather formal tone, many people today substitute the indicative mood in informal conversation.

INFORMAL

▶ If the store <u>was</u> better located, it would attract more customers.

For academic or professional writing, use the subjunctive in the following contexts:

CLAUSES EXPRESSING A WISH

▶ He wished that his brother ~~was~~ _{were} still living nearby.

***THAT* CLAUSES EXPRESSING A REQUEST OR DEMAND**

▶ The plant inspector insists that a supervisor ~~is~~ _{be} on site at all times.

***IF* CLAUSES EXPRESSING A CONDITION THAT DOES NOT EXIST**

▶ If public transportation ~~was~~ _{were} widely available in the U.S., fewer Americans would commute by car.

One common error is to use *would* in both clauses. Use the subjunctive in the *if* clause and *would* in the other clause.

▶ If I ~~would have~~ _{had} played harder, I would have won.

> **EXERCISE 31.8** Revise the following sentences that do not use the appropriate subjunctive verb forms required in formal or academic writing. Example:

> *were*
> If money ~~was~~ no object, I would have one house in the mountains,
> ^
> one on the beach, and one in the city.

1. The only requirement is that all applicants are over eighteen years of age.

2. Malcolm is acting as if he was the only one who worked on the project.

3. Even if PPE was widely available, the hospital is still running low on ventilators.

4. If she would have gone to the doctor sooner, the symptoms would not be so severe.

5. I wish I was a more diligent student.

31h Using conditional sentences appropriately

English distinguishes among many different types of conditional sentences: sentences that focus on questions and that are introduced by *if* or its equivalent. Each of the following examples makes different assumptions about the likelihood that what is stated in the *if* **clause** is true:

▶ If you *practice* (or *have practiced*) writing often, you *learn* (or *have learned*) what your main problems are.

This sentence assumes that what is stated in the *if* clause may be true; any verb tense that is appropriate in a simple sentence may be used in both the *if* clause and the main clause.

▶ If you *practice* writing for the rest of this term, you *will* (or *may*) *understand* the process better.

This sentence makes a prediction and again assumes that what is stated may turn out to be true. Only the main clause uses the future tense (*will understand*) or a modal that can indicate future time (*may understand*). The *if* clause must use the present tense.

▶ If you *practiced* (or *were to practice*) writing every day, it *would* eventually *seem* easier.

This sentence indicates doubt that what is stated will happen. In the *if* clause, the verb is either past—actually, past subjunctive (31g)—or *were to* + the base form, though it refers to future time. The main clause contains *would* + the base form of the main verb.

▶ **If you *practiced* writing on Mars, *you would find* no one to read your work.**

This sentence imagines an impossible situation. Again, the past subjunctive is used in the *if* clause, although here past time is not being referred to, and *would* + the base form is used in the main clause.

▶ **If you *had practiced* writing in ancient Egypt, you *would have used* hieroglyphics.**

This sentence shifts the impossibility back to the past; obviously you won't find yourself in ancient Egypt. But a past impossibility demands a form that is "more past": the past perfect in the *if* clause and *would* + the present perfect form of the main verb in the main clause.

EXERCISE 31.9 Revise each of the following sentences so that both the *if* clause and the main, or independent, clause contain appropriate verb forms. If any sentence does not contain an error, write *Correct*. Example:

> If you want to determine your own work schedule, you ~~would~~
>   *are*
> probably ~~be~~ considering being an Uber driver.
>   ^

1. Until recently, many people thought that the gig economy will continue to expand unless workers will be allowed to earn benefits.

2. If market growth had continued, that prediction might come true.

3. Instead, many in the gig economy will have a hard time if the coronavirus continues unabated.

4. If consumers are forced to rely on takeout food services, however, thousands of potential Uber drivers applied.

5. If ride-share companies were to pay well, applicants would flood their hiring site.

32 **Nouns and Noun Phrases**

Everyday life is filled with **nouns**: orange *juice*, *hip-hop*, the morning *news*, a *bus* to *work*, *meetings*, *pizza*, *tweets*, *Diet Coke*, *errands*, *dinner* with *friends*, a *chapter* in a good *book*. Every language includes nouns. In English, words called articles (*a* book, *an* email, *the* news) often accompany nouns.

32a　Understanding count and noncount nouns

Nouns in English can be either **count nouns** or **noncount nouns**. Count nouns refer to distinct individuals or things that can be directly counted: *a doctor, an egg, a child; doctors, eggs, children*. Noncount nouns refer to masses, collections, or ideas without distinct parts: *milk, rice, courage*. You cannot count noncount nouns except with a preceding **phrase**: <u>*a glass of*</u> *milk,* <u>*three grains of*</u> *rice,* <u>*a little*</u> *courage*.

Count nouns usually have singular and plural forms: *tree, trees*. Noncount nouns usually have only a singular form: *grass*.

COUNT	NONCOUNT
people (plural of *person*)	humanity
tables, chairs, beds	furniture
letters	mail
pebbles	gravel
suggestions	advice

Some nouns can be either <u>count</u> or <u>noncount</u>, depending on their meaning.

COUNT	Before video games, children played with <u>marbles</u>.
NONCOUNT	The palace floor was made of <u>marble</u>.

When you learn a noun in English, you will therefore need to learn whether it is count, noncount, or both. Many dictionaries provide this information.

EXERCISE 32.1　Identify each of the common nouns in the following short paragraph as either a count or a noncount noun. The first one, from a review of Chippewa author Louise Erdrich's work, has been done for you.

> *count noun*
> Erdrich's <u>career</u> has been an act of resistance against racism—the hateful and the sentimental varieties—and the implacable force of white America's ignorance. In one powerful book after another, she has carved [American] Indians' lives, histories, and stories back into our national literature, a canon once determined to wipe them away.
>
> —Ron Charles

32b Using determiners

Determiners are words that identify or quantify a noun, such as <u>this</u> study, <u>all</u> people, <u>his</u> suggestions.

COMMON DETERMINERS

- the articles *a, an, the*
- *this, these, that, those*
- *my, our, your, his, her, its, their*
- possessive nouns and noun phrases (<u>Sheila's</u> paper, <u>my friend's</u> book)
- *whose, which, what*
- *all, both, each, every, some, any, either, no, neither, many, much, (a) few, (a) little, several, enough*
- the numerals *one, two,* etc.

These determiners . . .	. . . can precede these noun types	Examples
a, an, each, every	singular count nouns	<u>a</u> book <u>an</u> American <u>each</u> word <u>every</u> Buddhist
this, that	singular count nouns noncount nouns	<u>this</u> book <u>that</u> milk
(a) *little, much*	noncount nouns	<u>a little</u> milk <u>much</u> affection
some, enough	noncount nouns plural count nouns	<u>some</u> milk <u>enough</u> trouble <u>some</u> books <u>enough</u> problems
the	singular count nouns plural count nouns noncount nouns	<u>the</u> doctor <u>the</u> doctors <u>the</u> information
these, those, (a) *few, many, both, several*	plural count nouns	<u>these</u> books <u>those</u> plans <u>a few</u> ideas <u>many</u> students <u>both</u> hands <u>several</u> trees

Determiners with singular count nouns Every singular count noun must be preceded by a determiner. Place any adjectives between the determiner and the noun.

▶   my
  sister
  ^

▶   the
  growing population
  ^

▶   that
  old neighborhood
  ^

Determiners with plural nouns or noncount nouns Noncount and plural nouns sometimes have determiners and sometimes do not. For example, *This research is important* and *Research is important* are both acceptable but have different meanings.

32c   Using articles

Articles (*a, an,* and *the*) are a type of determiner. In English, choosing which article to use—or whether to use an article at all—can be challenging. Although there are exceptions, the following general guidelines can help.

Using *a* or *an* Use indefinite articles *a* and *an* with singular count nouns. Use *a* before a consonant sound (*a car*) and *an* before a vowel sound (*an uncle*). Consider sound rather than spelling: *a house, an hour.*

    A or *an* tells readers they do not have enough information to identify specifically what the noun refers to. Compare the following sentences:

▶   I need <u>a</u> new coat for the winter.

▶   I saw <u>a</u> coat that I liked at Dayton's, but it wasn't heavy enough.

The coat in the first sentence is hypothetical rather than actual. Since it is indefinite to the writer and the reader, it is used with *a,* not *the.* The second sentence refers to an actual coat, but since the writer cannot expect the reader to know which one, it is used with *a* rather than *the.*

If you want to speak of an indefinite quantity rather than just one indefinite thing, use *some* or *any* with a noncount noun or a plural count noun. Use *any* in either negative sentences or questions.

▶ This stew needs <u>some</u> more salt.

▶ I saw <u>some</u> plates that I liked at Gump's.

▶ This stew doesn't need <u>any</u> more salt.

Using *the* Use the definite article *the* with both count and noncount nouns whose identity is known or is about to be made known to readers. The necessary information for identification can come from the noun phrase itself, from elsewhere in the text, from context, from general knowledge, or from a **superlative**.

▶ Let's meet at <u>the</u> fountain in front of Dwinelle Hall.

The phrase *in front of Dwinelle Hall* identifies the specific fountain.

▶ Last Saturday, a fire that started in a restaurant spread to a nearby clothing store. ~~Store~~ <u>The store</u> was saved, although it suffered water damage.

The word *store* is preceded by *the,* which directs our attention to the information in the previous sentence, where the store is first identified.

▶ She asked him to shut <u>the</u> door when he left her office.

The context shows that she is referring to her office door.

▶ She is now one of <u>the</u> best hip-hop artists in the neighborhood.

The superlative *best* identifies the noun *hip-hop artists.*

No article Noncount and plural count nouns can be used without an article to make generalizations:

▶ In this world nothing is certain but death and taxes.

—Benjamin Franklin

Franklin refers not to a particular death or specific taxes but to death and taxes in general, so no article is used with *death* or with *taxes*.

English differs from many other languages that use the definite article to make generalizations. In English, a sentence like *The ants live in colonies* can refer only to particular, identifiable ants, not to ants in general.

EXERCISE 32.2   Each of the following sentences contains an error with a noun phrase. Revise each sentence. Example:

a

Many people use small sponge to clean their kitchen counters.
                    ^

1. Bacteria are invisible organisms that can sometimes make the people sick.

2. Dangerous germs such as salmonella are commonly found in a some foods.

3. When a cook prepares chicken on cutting board, salmonella germs may be left on the board.

4. Much people regularly clean their kitchen counters and cutting boards to remove bacteria.

5. Unfortunately, a warm, wet kitchen sponge is a ideal home for bacteria.

EXERCISE 32.3   Insert articles as necessary in the following passage. If no article is needed, leave the space blank. Example:

One of __*the*__ things that makes _____ English unique
is __*the*__ number of _____ English words.

_____ English language has _____ very large vocabulary. About _____ 200,000 words are in _____ everyday use, and if _____ less common words are included, _____ total reaches more than _____ million. This makes _____ English _____ rich language, but also _____ difficult one to learn well. In addition, _____ rules of English grammar are sometimes confusing. They were modeled on _____ Latin rules, even though _____ two languages are very different. Finally, _____ fact that _____ English has _____ large number of _____ words imported from _____ other languages makes _____ English spelling very hard to master.

33 Subject-Verb Agreement

The everyday word *agreement* refers to an accord of some sort: you reach an agreement with your boss; friends agree to go to a movie. This meaning covers grammatical **agreement** as well. <u>**Verbs**</u> must agree with their <u>**subjects**</u> in number (singular or plural) and in **person** (first, second, or third).

To make a verb in the **present tense** agree with a third-person singular subject, add *-s* or *-es* to the **base form**.

▶ A vegetarian <u>diet</u> <u>lowers</u> the risk of heart disease.

To make a verb in the present tense agree with any other subject, use the base form of the verb.

▶ <u>I</u> <u>miss</u> my family.
▶ <u>They</u> <u>live</u> in another state.

Have and *be* do not follow the *-s* or *-es* pattern with third-person singular subjects. *Have* changes to *has*; *be* has irregular forms in both the present tense and the **past tense**.

▶ <u>War</u> <u>is</u> hell.
▶ The <u>soldier</u> <u>was</u> brave beyond the call of duty.

33a Checking for words between subject and verb

Make sure the verb agrees with the simple subject and not with another **noun** that falls between them.

▶ Many books on the best-seller list ~~has~~ ^{have} little literary value.

The simple subject is *books*, not *list*.

Be careful when you use *as well as*, *along with*, *in addition to*, *together with*, and similar phrases. They do not make a singular subject plural.

▶ A passenger, as well as the driver, ~~were~~ ^{was} injured in the accident.

Though this sentence has a grammatically singular subject, it would be clearer with a compound subject: *The driver and a passenger were injured in the accident.*

33b Checking agreement with compound subjects

Compound subjects joined by *and* are generally plural.

▶ A backpack, a canteen, and a rifle ~~was~~ *were* issued to each recruit.

When subjects joined by *and* are considered a single unit or refer to the same person or thing, they take a singular verb form.

▶ The lead singer and chief songwriter *wants* to make the new songs available online.

    The singer and songwriter are the same person.

▶ Drinking and driving ~~remain~~ *remains* a major cause of highway accidents and fatalities.

    In this sentence, *drinking and driving* is considered a single activity, and a singular verb is used.

With subjects joined by *or* or *nor*, the verb agrees with the part closer to the verb.

▶ Neither my roommate nor my neighbors *like* my loud music.

▶ Either the witnesses or the defendant *is* lying.

    If you find this sentence awkward, put the plural noun closer to the verb: *Either the defendant or the witnesses are lying.*

EXERCISE 33.1 Underline the appropriate verb form in each of the following sentences. Example:

Bankers, politicians, and philanthropists alike is/<u>are</u> becoming increasingly interested in microfinance.

1. Many microlending institutions, such as the Grameen Bank, has/have been in existence for decades.

2. In microlending, credit or small loans is/are provided to poor entrepreneurs in developing nations.

3. These borrowers and their families usually do/does not possess the collateral required for more traditional loans.

4. A person running a small business or farm is/are often the primary recipient of a loan.

5. A list of the benefits of microlending includes/include economic mobility and support for entrepreneurs.

33c Making verbs agree with collective nouns

Collective nouns—such as *family*, *team*, *audience*, *group*, *jury*, *crowd*, *band*, *class*, and *committee*—and fractions can take either singular or plural verbs, depending on whether they refer to the group as a single unit or to the multiple members of the group. The meaning of a sentence as a whole is your guide.

▶ After deliberating, the jury *reports* its verdict.

   The jury acts as a single unit.

▶ The jury still *disagree* on a number of counts.

   The members of the jury act as multiple individuals.

▶ Two-thirds of the park ~~have~~ has burned.

   Two-thirds refers to the single portion of the park that burned.

▶ One-third of the student body ~~was~~ were commuters.

   One-third here refers to the students who commuted as individuals.

Treat phrases starting with *the number of* as singular and with *a number of* as plural.

SINGULAR	The number of applicants for the internship *was* unbelievable.
PLURAL	A number of applicants *were* put on the waiting list.

> ✔ **Checklist**

Editing for Subject-Verb Agreement

✔ Identify the subject that goes with each verb to check for agreement problems. (33a)

✔ Check compound subjects joined by *and, or,* and *nor.* (33b)

✔ Check any collective-noun subjects to determine whether they refer to a group as a single unit or as multiple members. (33c)

✔ Check indefinite-pronoun subjects. Most take a plural verb. (33d)

33d Making verbs agree with indefinite pronouns

Indefinite pronouns do not refer to specific persons or things. Most take singular verb forms.

SOME COMMON INDEFINITE PRONOUNS

another	each	much	one
any	either	neither	other
anybody	everybody	nobody	somebody
anyone	everyone	no one	someone
anything	everything	nothing	something

▶ Of the two jobs, <u>neither holds</u> much appeal.

         depicts
▶ Each of the plays ~~depict~~ a hero undone by a tragic flaw.

Both, few, many, others, and *several* are plural.

▶ Though <u>many apply</u>, <u>few are</u> chosen.

All, any, enough, more, most, none, and *some* can be singular or plural, depending on the noun they refer to.

▶ All of the cake *was* eaten.

▶ All of the candidates *promise* to improve the schools.

33e Making verbs agree with *who, which,* and *that*

When the relative **pronouns** *who, which,* and *that* are used as subjects, the verb agrees with the **antecedent** of the pronoun (36b).

▶ Fear is an <u>ingredient</u> that goes into creating stereotypes.

▶ Guilt and fear are <u>ingredients</u> that go into creating stereotypes.

Problems often occur with the words *one of the.* In general, *one of the* takes a plural verb, while *the only one of the* takes a singular verb.

▶ Carla is one of the employees who always ~~works~~ *work* overtime.

Some employees always work overtime. Carla is among them. Thus *who* refers to *employees,* and the verb is plural.

▶ Nina is the only one of the employees who always ~~work~~ *works* overtime.

Only one employee, Nina, always works overtime. Thus *one* is the antecedent of *who,* and the verb form must be singular.

33f Making linking verbs agree with subjects

A **linking verb** should agree with its subject, which usually precedes the verb, not with the subject complement, which follows it.

▶ These three key treaties ~~is~~ *are* the topic of my talk.

The subject is *treaties,* not *topic.*

▶ Nero Wolfe's passion ~~were~~ *was* orchids.

The subject is *passion,* not *orchids.*

33g Making verbs agree with subjects that end in -s

Some words that end in -s seem to be plural but are singular in meaning and thus take singular verb forms.

▶ Measles still ~~strike~~ *strikes* many people in North America.

Some nouns of this kind (such as *statistics* and *politics*) may be either singular or plural, depending on context.

> **SINGULAR**   Statistics *is* a course I really dread.
>
> **PLURAL**   The statistics in that study *are* questionable.

33h Checking for subjects that follow the verb

In English, verbs usually follow subjects. When this order is reversed, make the verb agree with the subject, not with a noun that happens to precede it.

>   stand
> ▶ Beside the barn ~~stands~~ silos filled with grain.
>
> The subject, *silos*, is plural, so the verb must be *stand*.

In sentences beginning with *there is* or *there are* (or *there was* or *there were*), *there* is just an introductory word; the <u>subject</u> follows the <u>verb</u>.

> ▶ There <u>are</u> five basic <u>positions</u> in classical ballet.

33i Making verbs agree with titles and words used as words

Titles and words used as words always take singular verb forms, even if their own forms are plural.

>   describes
> ▶ *One Writer's Beginnings* ~~describe~~ Eudora Welty's childhood.
>
>   is
> ▶ *Steroids* ~~are~~ a little word that packs a big punch in the world of sports.

> **EXERCISE 33.2**   Revise each of the following sentences as necessary to establish subject-verb agreement. Example:
>
>   has
> A museum displaying O. Winston Link's photographs ~~have~~ opened in Roanoke, Virginia.
>
> 1. Anyone interested in steam locomotives have probably already heard of the photographer O. Winston Link.

2. Imagine that it are the 1950s, and Link is creating his famous photographs.

3. The steam locomotives—the "iron horses" of the nineteenth century—has begun to give way to diesel engines.

4. Only the Norfolk & Western rail line's Appalachian route still use steam engines.

5. Link and his assistant Thomas Garver sets up nighttime shots of steam locomotives.

33j Considering forms of *be* in varieties of English

Conventions for subject-verb agreement with *be* in both spoken and vernacular varieties of English may differ from those of academic English. For instance, an Appalachian speaker might say "I been down" rather than "I have been down"; a speaker of African American vernacular might say "He at work" or "He working" rather than "He is at work." These usages are legitimate and often very effective forms, and you may want to use such phrases in your writing, especially to create special effects or to connect with your audience. (For more on using varieties of English, see Chapter 23.)

34 Adjectives and Adverbs

Adjectives and **adverbs** can add indispensable differences in meaning to the words they describe or modify. In basketball, for example, there is an important difference between a *flagrant* foul and a *technical* foul, a layup and a *reverse* layup, and an *angry* coach and an *abusively angry* coach. In each instance, the **modifiers** are crucial to accurate communication.

Adjectives modify **nouns** and **pronouns**; they answer the questions *which? how many?* and *what kind?* Adverbs modify **verbs**, adjectives, and other adverbs; they answer the questions *how? when? where?* and *to what extent?* Many adverbs are formed by adding *-ly* to adjectives (*slight, slightly*), but some are formed in other ways (*outdoors*) or have forms of their own (*very*).

34a Using adjectives after linking verbs

When adjectives come after **linking verbs** (such as *is*), they usually describe the **subject**: *I am patient*. Note that in specific sentences, certain verbs may or may not be linking verbs—*appear, become, feel, grow, look, make, prove, seem, smell, sound,* and *taste,* for instance. When a word following one of these verbs modifies the <u>subject</u>, use an <u>adjective</u>; when it modifies the <u>verb</u>, use an <u>adverb</u>.

ADJECTIVE	<u>Fluffy</u> looked <u>angry</u>.
ADVERB	Fluffy <u>looked</u> <u>angrily</u> at the poodle.

Linking verbs suggest a state of being, not an action. In the preceding examples, *looked angry* suggests the state of being angry; *looked angrily* suggests an angry action.

In everyday conversation, you will often hear (and perhaps use) adjectives in place of adverbs. For example, people often say *go quick* instead of *go quickly*. When you write in academic and professional English, however, use adverbs to modify verbs, adjectives, and other adverbs.

▶ You can feel the song's meter if you listen ~~careful.~~ *carefully.*

▶ The audience was ~~real~~ *really* disappointed by the show.

Good, well, bad,* and *badly The modifiers *good, well, bad,* and *badly* cause problems for many writers because the distinctions between *good* and *well* and between *bad* and *badly* are often not observed in conversation. Problems also arise because *well* can function as either an adjective or an adverb.

▶ I look ~~well~~ *good* in blue.

▶ Now that the fever has broken, I feel ~~good~~ *well* again.

▶ I play the trumpet ~~good.~~ *well.*

▶ I feel ~~badly~~ *bad* for the Toronto fans.

▶ Their team played ~~bad.~~ *badly.*

Language, Culture, and Context

Using Adjectives with Plural Nouns

In Spanish, Russian, and many other languages, adjectives agree in number with the nouns they modify. In English, adjectives do not change number in this way: *the kittens are cute* (not *cutes*).

EXERCISE 34.1 Identify the adjectives and adverbs in each of the following sentences, underlining the adjectives once and the adverbs twice. Remember that articles and some pronouns can function as adjectives. Example:

> Clubs in Harlem provided a perfectly supportive atmosphere for up-and-coming Black musicians.

1. Minton's famous playhouse, the birthplace of bebop, opened in 1938.
2. Wildly popular nightly jam sessions featured well-known musicians such as Thelonious Monk and Dizzy Gillespie.
3. They founded a brand new style of jazz, full of fast beats and complicated rhythms.
4. Because it was so sophisticated and complex, bebop kept listeners happily coming in for decades.
5. I wonder what popular contemporary musical forms loyally trace their origins to much loved and admired bebop?

EXERCISE 34.2 Expand each of the following sentences by adding appropriate adjectives and adverbs. Delete *the* if need be. Example:

> Three   thoroughly   nervous
> ~~The~~ veterinarians examined the patient.
>   ^   ^   ^

1. I attended the protest march.
2. Many people enjoy video games.
3. Each of her superiors praised her work for the Environmental Protection Agency.
4. A corporation can fire workers.
5. The NASA mission accomplished its goal.

EXERCISE 34.3 Revise each of the following sentences to maintain correct adverb and adjective use. Then, for each adjective and adverb you've revised, point out the word that it modifies. Example:

> *commonly* ↓
> Almost every language ~~common~~ uses nonverbal cues that people
> ^
> can interpret.

1. Most people understand easy that raised eyebrows indicate surprise.
2. You are sure familiar with the idea that bodily motions are a kind of language, but is the same thing true of nonverbal sounds?
3. If you feel sadly, your friends may express sympathy by saying, "Awww."
4. When food tastes well, diners often murmur "Mmmm!"
5. These nonverbal signals are called "paralanguage," and they are quick becoming an important field of linguistic study.

34b   Using comparatives and superlatives

Most adjectives and adverbs have three forms: positive, **comparative**, and **superlative**. You usually form the comparative and superlative of one- or two-syllable adjectives by adding *-er* and *-est*: *short, shorter, shortest*. With some two-syllable adjectives, longer adjectives, and most adverbs, use *more* and *most* (or *less* and *least*): *scientific, more scientific, most scientific; elegantly, more elegantly, most elegantly*. Some short adjectives and adverbs have irregular comparative and superlative forms: *good, better, best; badly, worse, worst*.

Comparatives versus superlatives   In academic writing, use the comparative to compare two things; use the superlative to compare three or more things.

▶ Rome is a much *older* city than New York.

> *oldest*
▶ Damascus is one of the ~~older~~ cities in the world.
> ^

Double comparatives and superlatives   Double comparatives and superlatives are those that unnecessarily use both the *-er* or *-est* ending and *more* or *most*. Occasionally, these forms can add a special emphasis, as in the title of Spike Lee's movie *Mo' Better Blues*.

In academic and professional writing, however, it's safest not to use *more* or *most* before adjectives or adverbs ending in *-er* or *-est*.

▶ Paris is the ~~most~~ loveliest city in the world.

Absolute concepts   Some readers consider modifiers such as *perfect* and *unique* to be absolute concepts; according to this view, a thing is either unique or it isn't, so modified forms of the concept don't make sense. However, many seemingly absolute words have multiple meanings, all of which are widely accepted as correct. For example, *unique* may mean *one of a kind* or *unequaled*, but it can also simply mean *distinctive* or *unusual*.

If you think your readers will object to a construction such as *more perfect* (which appears in the U.S. Constitution), then avoid such uses.

EXERCISE 34.4   Revise the following sentences to use comparatives and superlatives correctly, clearly, and effectively. A variety of acceptable answers is possible for each sentence. Example:

When Macbeth and Lady Macbeth plot to kill the king, she shows

herself to be the ~~most~~ *more* ambitious of the two.

1. Some critics consider *Hamlet* to be Shakespeare's most finest tragedy.
2. Romeo and Juliet are probably the famousest lovers in all of literature.
3. Did you like the movie *Titus* or the play *Titus Andronicus* best?
4. One of my earlier memories is of hearing a song from *As You Like It*.
5. Shakespeare supposedly knew little Latin, but most people today know even littler.

35   **Modifier Placement**

To be effective, **modifiers** should clearly refer to the words they modify and should be positioned close to those words. Consider this command:

DO NOT USE THE ELEVATORS IN CASE OF FIRE.

Should we avoid the elevators altogether, or only in case there is a fire? Repositioning the modifier *in case of fire* eliminates such confusion—and makes clear that we are to avoid the elevators only if there is a fire: IN CASE OF FIRE, DO NOT USE THE ELEVATORS.

35a   Revising misplaced modifiers

Modifiers can cause confusion or ambiguity if they are not close enough to the words they modify or if they seem to modify more than one word in the sentence.

▶ She teaches a seminar this term ~~on voodoo~~ at Skyline College.
   on voodoo

   The voodoo is not at the college; the seminar is.

▶ ~~Billowing from the window, he~~ saw clouds of smoke.
   He ... *billowing from the window.*

   People cannot billow from windows.

▶ *After he lost the 1962 race,* Nixon told reporters that he planned to get out of politics. ~~after he lost the 1962 race.~~

   Nixon did not predict that he would lose the race.

Limiting modifiers   Be especially careful with the placement of limiting modifiers such as *almost*, *even*, *just*, *merely*, and *only*. In general, these modifiers should be placed right before or after the words they modify. Putting them in other positions may produce not just ambiguity but a completely different meaning.

AMBIGUOUS	The court *only* hears civil cases on Tuesdays.
CLEAR	The court hears <u>only</u> civil cases on Tuesdays.
CLEAR	The court hears civil cases on Tuesdays <u>only</u>.

Squinting modifiers   If a modifier can refer either to the word before it or to the word after it, it is a squinting modifier. Put the modifier where it clearly relates to only a single word.

SQUINTING	Students who practice writing *often* will benefit.
REVISED	Students who <u>often</u> practice writing will benefit.
REVISED	Students who practice writing will <u>often</u> benefit.

EXERCISE 35.1 Revise each of the following sentences by moving any misplaced modifiers so that they clearly modify the words they are intended to. You may have to change grammatical structures for some sentences. Example:

> Elderly people and students live in the neighborhood
> full of identical tract houses
> surrounding the university/. ~~which is full of identical tract houses.~~
>   ^   ^

1. Some people continued to have large house parties during COVID-19, which was foolish.

2. The spoken word artist captivated the entire audience rapping with verve.

3. I went through the process of diving off the high board in my mind.

4. The city approximately spent twelve million dollars on the new stadium.

5. Am I the only person who cares about modifiers in sentences that are misplaced?

35b Revising disruptive modifiers

Disruptive modifiers interrupt connections between parts of a sentence, making it hard for readers to follow the progress of a thought.

> If they are cooked too long, vegetables will
> ▶ ~~Vegetables will, if they are cooked too long,~~ lose most of their
>   ^
> nutritional value.

Split infinitives In general, do not place a modifier between the *to* and the **verb** of an **infinitive** (*to often complain*). Doing so makes it hard for readers to recognize that the two go together.

>   surrender
> ▶ Hitler expected the British to fairly quickly. ~~surrender.~~
>   ^   ^

In certain sentences, however, a modifier sounds awkward if it does not split the infinitive. Most language experts consider split infinitives acceptable in such cases. Another option is to reword the sentence to eliminate the infinitive altogether.

SPLIT	I hope *to* almost *equal* my last year's income.
REVISED	I hope that I will earn almost as much as I did last year.

EXERCISE 35.2 Revise each of the following sentences by moving disruptive modifiers and split infinitives as well as by repositioning any squinting modifier so that it unambiguously modifies either the word(s) before it or the word(s) after it. Example:

> The course we hoped would engross us completely bored us.
>
> *The course we hoped would completely engross us bored us.*
>
> or
>
> *The course we hoped would engross us bored us completely.*

1. He remembered vividly enjoying the sound of Camila Cabello's singing.
2. Bookstores sold, in the first week after publication of Michelle Obama's *Becoming*, 1.4 million copies.
3. The mayor promised after her reelection she would not raise taxes.
4. The collector who owned the painting originally planned to leave it to a museum.
5. Doctors can now restore limbs that have been severed partially to a functioning condition.

35c Revising dangling modifiers

Dangling modifiers are words or **phrases** that modify nothing in the rest of a sentence. They often *seem* to modify something that is implied but not actually present in the sentence. Dangling modifiers frequently appear at the beginnings or ends of sentences, as in the following example:

DANGLING Exploding in rapid bursts of red, white, and blue, the picnickers cheered for the Fourth of July celebration.

REVISED With fireworks exploding in rapid bursts of red, white, and blue, the picnickers cheered for the Fourth of July celebration.

To revise a dangling modifier, often you need to add a **subject** that the modifier clearly refers to; sometimes you have to turn the modifier into a phrase or a **clause**.

> ▶ Reluctantly, the hound ~~was given~~ *our family gave* to a neighbor.
>
> In the original sentence, was the dog reluctant, or was someone else who is not mentioned reluctant?

> When he was
> ~~As~~ a young boy, his grandparents told stories of their years as
> ^
> migrant workers.

His grandparents, together, were never a young boy.

> My
> ~~Thumbing through the magazine, my~~ eyes automatically noticed
> ^   as I was thumbing through the magazine.
> the perfume ads/
>   ^

Eyes cannot thumb through a magazine.

EXERCISE 35.3 Revise each of the following sentences to correct the dangling modifiers. Example:

a viewer gets
Watching television news, an impression ~~is given~~ of constant
                                          ^
disaster.

1. High ratings are pursued by emphasizing fires and murders.
2. Interviewing famous chefs, little consideration is shown for their privacy.
3. To provide comic relief, heat waves and blizzards are attributed to the weather forecaster.
4. Featured as a field investigator, the credentials of the reporter also include lead news writer.
5. As a visual medium, complex issues are hard to present in a televised format.

36 Pronouns

As words that stand in for **nouns**, **pronouns** carry a lot of weight in our everyday discourse. The following directions show why it's important for a pronoun to refer clearly to a specific noun or pronoun **antecedent**:

> When you see a dirt road on the left side of Winston Lane, follow it for two more miles.

The word *it* could mean either the dirt road or Winston Lane.

36a Considering a pronoun's role in the sentence

Most speakers of English usually know intuitively when to use *I*, *me*, and *my*. The choices reflect differences in **case**, the form a pronoun takes to indicate its function in a sentence. Pronouns functioning as **subjects** or subject complements are in the subjective case (*I*); those functioning as **objects** are in the objective case (*me*); those functioning as possessives are in the possessive case (*my*).

SUBJECTIVE	OBJECTIVE	POSSESSIVE
I	me	my/mine
we	us	our/ours
you	you	your/yours
he/she/it	him/her/it	his/her/hers/its
they	them	their/theirs
who/whoever	whom/whomever	whose

Problems tend to occur in the following situations.

In subject complements Americans routinely use the objective case for subject complements in conversation: *Who's there? It's <u>me</u>.* If the subjective case for a subject complement sounds stilted or awkward (*It's I*), try rewriting the sentence using the pronoun as the subject (*I'm here*).

▶ <u>I was the</u>
~~The~~ first person to see Kishore after the awards. ~~was I.~~
  ^   ^

Before gerunds Pronouns before a **gerund** should be in the possessive case.

▶ The doctor argued for <u>their</u> ~~them~~ writing a living will.
                         ^

With *who, whoever, whom,* and *whomever* Today's speakers tend not to use *whom* and *whomever*, which can create a very formal tone. But for academic and professional writing in which formality is appropriate, remember that problems distinguishing between *who* and *whom* occur most often in two situations: when they begin a question, and when they introduce a **dependent clause** (39d). You can determine whether to use *who* or *whom* at the beginning of a question by answering the question using a personal pronoun. If the answer is in the subjective case, use *who*; if it is in the objective case, use *whom*.

▶ Whom
~~Who~~ did you visit?
^
I visited *them. Them* is objective, so *whom* is correct.

▶ Who
~~Whom~~ do you think wrote the story?
^
I think *she* wrote the story. *She* is subjective, so *who* is correct.

If the pronoun acts as a subject or subject complement in the clause, use *who* or *whoever*. If the pronoun acts as an object in the clause, use *whom* or *whomever*.

▶ Anyone can hypnotize a person ~~whom~~ wants to be hypnotized.
who
^
The verb of the clause is *wants*, and its subject is *who*.

▶ Whomever
~~Whoever~~ the party suspected of disloyalty was executed.
^
Whomever is the object of *suspected* in the clause *whomever the party suspected of disloyalty*.

In compound structures   When a pronoun is part of a compound subject, complement, or object, put it in the same case you would use if the pronoun were alone.

▶ he
When ~~him~~ and Zelda were first married, they lived in New York.
^

▶ This morning saw yet another conflict between my sister and ~~I.~~
me.
^

In elliptical constructions   Elliptical constructions are sentences in which some words are understood but left out. When an elliptical construction ends in a pronoun, put the pronoun in the case it would be in if the construction were complete.

▶ His sister has always been more athletic than *he* [is].

In some elliptical constructions, the case of the pronoun depends on the meaning intended.

✔ Checklist

Editing Pronouns

✔ Make sure all pronouns in subject complements are in the subjective case. (36a)

✔ Check for correct use of *who*, *whom*, *whoever*, and *whomever*. (36a)

✔ In compound structures, check that pronouns are in the same case they would be in if used alone. (36a)

✔ When a pronoun follows *than* or *as*, complete the sentence mentally to determine whether the pronoun should be in the subjective or objective case. (36a)

✔ Check that pronouns agree with indefinite-pronoun antecedents, and revise sexist and noninclusive pronouns. (36b)

✔ Be sensitive to pronoun choices; do not assume that all individuals identify with either *he* or *she*. (36b)

✔ Identify the antecedent that a pronoun refers to. Supply one if none appears in the sentence. If more than one possible antecedent is present, revise the sentence. (36c)

▶ Nolan likes Lily more than *she* [likes Lily].

She is the subject of the omitted verb *likes*.

▶ Nolan likes Lily more than [he likes] *her*.

Her is the object of the omitted verb *likes*.

With *we* and *us* before a noun   If you are unsure about whether to use *we* or *us* before a noun, use whichever pronoun would be correct if the noun were omitted.

      We
▶ ~~Us~~ fans never give up hope.

Without *fans*, *we* would be the subject.

               us
▶ The Broncos depend on ~~we~~ fans.

Without *fans*, *us* would be the object of the preposition *on*.

EXERCISE 36.1 Some of the following sentences contain underlined pronouns used incorrectly. Revise each of the incorrect sentences so that they contain correct pronouns. Example:

me
Eventually, the headwaiter told Kim, Stanley, and I that we could be
^
seated.

1. Who do you think is the better tennis player, Mac or he?
2. Her and Lena made signs for the rally before they left.
3. When we asked, the seller promised we that the software would work on our computer.
4. Though even the idea of hang gliding made Gretchen and she nervous, they gave it a try.
5. The teacher said us had asked thoughtful questions.

EXERCISE 36.2 Insert *who, whoever, whom,* or *whomever* appropriately in the blank in each of the following sentences. Example:

Marisa is someone __who__ will go far.

1. Professor Quinones asked _____ we wanted to collaborate with.
2. I would appreciate it if _____ made the mess in the kitchen could clean it up.
3. _____ shall I say is calling?
4. True crime podcasts appeal to _____ is interested in intrigue, suspense, storytelling, deviance, and justice.
5. I have no sympathy for _____ was caught driving drunk after the party Friday night.

EXERCISE 36.3 Choose the correct pronoun from the pair in parentheses in each of the following sentences. Example:

Of the group, only (she/her) and I finished the race.

1. All the other job applicants were far more experienced than (I/me).
2. Only (he/him) and the two dressmakers knew what his top-secret fall line would be like.

3. When Jessica and (she/her) first met, they wondered if they would be friends.

4. I know that I will never again meet anyone as impressive as (she/her).

5. To (we/us) New Englanders, hurricanes are a far bigger worry than tornadoes.

36b Making pronouns agree with antecedents

The **antecedent** of a pronoun is the word the pronoun refers to. Pronouns and antecedents are said to agree when they match up in **person**, number, and gender.

SINGULAR   The choirmaster raised his baton.

PLURAL   The boys picked up their music.

The use of the plural pronoun *they* to refer to singular antecedents is also acceptable. (See p. 339 for more on inclusive pronouns.)

SINGULAR   The choirmaster raised their baton.

Compound antecedents   Whenever a compound antecedent is joined by *or* or *nor*, the pronoun agrees with the nearer or nearest antecedent. If the parts of the antecedent are of different genders, this kind of sentence can be awkward and may need to be revised.

AWKWARD   Neither Ann nor Marc got *his* grade.

REVISED   Ann didn't get *her* grade, and neither did Marc.

When a compound antecedent contains both singular and plural parts, the sentence may sound awkward unless the plural part comes last.

▶ Neither the blog nor the newspapers would reveal their sources.

Collective-noun antecedents   A collective noun such as *herd*, *team*, or *audience* may refer to a group as a single unit. If so, use a singular pronoun.

▶ The *committee* presented *its* findings to the board.

When a collective noun refers to the members of the group as individuals, however, use a plural pronoun.

▶ The *herd* stamped *their* hooves and snorted nervously.

Indefinite-pronoun antecedents **Indefinite pronouns** do not refer to specific persons or things. Most indefinite pronouns are always singular; a few are always plural. Some can be singular or plural depending on the context.

▶ *One* of the ballerinas lost *her* balance.

▶ *Many* in the audience jumped to *their* feet.

SINGULAR	*Some* of the furniture was showing *its* age.
PLURAL	*Some* of the farmers abandoned *their* land.

Inclusive pronouns and singular *they* Remember that pronouns often refer to antecedents of unknown gender. Many writers use *he or she*, *his or her*, and so on to refer to such antecedents: *Every citizen should know his or her legal rights*, for example. However, such wording ignores or even excludes people who do not identify as male or female or who do not use *he* or *she* pronouns. Recasting the sentence in the plural is one alternative that is more inclusive: *All citizens should know their legal rights*. But note that "singular *they*" is now widely used and accepted (*Every citizen should know their legal rights*), providing another good alternative. When in doubt, you may also choose to eliminate pronouns altogether: *Every citizen should have some knowledge of basic legal rights*. For more on gender-neutral pronouns and singular *they*, see 22b.

EXERCISE 36.4 Revise the following sentences as needed to create pronoun-antecedent agreement and to eliminate any exclusionary, sexist, or awkward pronoun references. Some sentences can be revised in more than one way. For the sentence that is correct as written, write *Correct*. Example:

Almost everyone will encounter some type of allergy in his lifetime.

Most people will encounter some type of allergy in their lifetime.

1. In general, neither dust mites nor pollen can cause life-threatening reactions, but it is among the most common allergens known.

2. A family that is prone to allergies may have a higher than usual percentage of allergic diseases, but their specific allergies are not necessarily the same for all family members.

3. If a person suspects that he might have an allergy, he can go to the doctor for a skin test or blood test.

4. Because of the severity and frequency of nut allergies in small children, a typical day-care center has rules specifying that they cannot allow any nut products.

5. Every meal and treat that is brought into a center must be screened to make sure their contents are nut-free.

36c　Making pronouns refer to clear antecedents

If a pronoun does not refer clearly to a specific antecedent, readers will have trouble making the connection between the two.

Ambiguous antecedents　In cases where a pronoun could refer to more than one antecedent, revise the sentence to make the meaning clear.

▶ The car went over the bridge just before ~~it~~ *the bridge* fell into the water.

What fell into the water—the car or the bridge? The revision makes the meaning clear.

▶ Kerry told Ellen, *"I* ~~that she~~ should be ready soon*."*

Reporting Kerry's words directly, in quotation marks, eliminates the ambiguity.

Vague use of *it, this, that,* and *which*　The words *it, this, that,* and *which* often function as a shortcut for referring to something mentioned earlier. Like other pronouns, each must refer to a specific antecedent.

▶ When the senators realized the bill would be defeated, they tried to postpone the vote but failed. ~~It~~ *The entire effort* was a fiasco.

and her sudden wealth

▶ Jasmine just found out that she won the lottery, ~~which~~ explains
her resignation.

Indefinite use of *you, it,* and *they*   In conversation, we often
use *you, it,* and *they* in an indefinite sense in such expressions as *you
never know* and *on television, they said.* In academic and professional
writing, however, use *you* only to mean "you, the reader," and *they*
or *it* only to refer to a clear antecedent.

people

▶ Commercials try to make ~~you~~ buy without thinking.

The

▶ ~~On the~~ Weather Channel/~~it~~ reported a powerful earthquake in
China.

Many restaurants in France

▶ ~~In France, they~~ allow dogs. ~~in many restaurants.~~

Implied antecedents   A pronoun may suggest a noun antecedent
that is implied but not present in the sentence.

▶ Detention centers routinely blocked efforts by ~~detainees'~~ families

detainees.

and lawyers to locate ~~them.~~

EXERCISE 36.5   Revise each of the following sentences to clarify pronoun
reference. All the items can be revised in more than one
way. If a pronoun refers ambiguously to more than one possible antecedent,
revise the sentence to reflect each possible meaning. Example:

After Jane left, Miranda found her keys.

Miranda found Jane's keys after Jane left.

or

Miranda found her own keys after Jane left.

1. Quint trusted Smith because she had worked for her before.
2. Not long after the company set up the subsidiary, it went bankrupt.
3. When Deyon was reunited with his father, he wept.
4. Bill smilingly announced to Ed his promotion.
5. On the weather forecast, it said to expect snow in the overnight hours.

37 Prepositions and Prepositional Phrases

Words such as *to* and *from,* which show the relationships between other words, are **prepositions**. They are one of the more challenging elements of English writing.

37a Choosing the right preposition

Even if you usually know where to use prepositions, you may have difficulty knowing which preposition to use. Each of the most common prepositions has a wide range of different applications, and this range never coincides exactly from one language to another. See, for example, how *in* and *on* are used in English.

▶ The peaches are <u>in</u> the refrigerator.

▶ The peaches are <u>on</u> the table.

▶ Is that a diamond ring <u>on</u> your finger?

The Spanish translations of these sentences all use the same preposition (*en*), a fact that might lead you astray in English.

There is no easy solution to the challenge of using English prepositions idiomatically, but a few strategies can make it less troublesome.

Know typical examples The **object** of the preposition *in* is often a container that encloses something; the object of the preposition *on* is often a horizontal surface that supports something touching it.

IN	The peaches are *in* the refrigerator.
	There are still some pickles *in* the jar.
ON	The peaches are *on* the table.

Learn related examples Prepositions that are not used in typical ways may still show some similarities to typical examples.

IN	You shouldn't drive *in* a snowstorm.

Like a container, the falling snow surrounds the driver. The preposition *in* is used for many weather-related expressions.

ON   Is that a diamond ring *on* your finger?

The preposition *on* is used to describe things you wear.

Use your imagination   Mental images can help you remember figurative uses of prepositions.

IN   Michael is *in* love.

Imagine a warm bath—or a raging torrent—in which Michael is immersed.

ON   I've just read a book *on* social media.

Imagine the book sitting on a shelf labeled "Social Media."

Learn prepositions as part of a system   In identifying the location of a place or an event, the three prepositions *in, on,* and *at* can be used. *At* specifies the exact point in space or time; *in* is required for expanses of space or time within which a place is located or an event takes place; and *on* must be used with the names of streets (but not exact addresses) and with days of the week or month.

AT   There will be a meeting tomorrow *at* 9:30 AM *at* 160
            Main Street.

IN   I arrived *in* the United States *in* January.

ON   The airline's office is *on* Fifth Avenue.
            I'll be moving to my new apartment *on* September 30.

EXERCISE 37.1   Insert one or more appropriate prepositions in each of the following sentences. Example:

We will have the answer ___by___ four o'clock this afternoon.

1. Shall we eat _____ the kitchen or just take food _____
   the deck?

2. I hate biking _____ the city _____ rush hour.

3. Have you ever cried _____ a really sad movie?

4. Griffin won the race _____ more than a full meter.

5. Some contemporary string quartets are known _____ their
   experimental styles.

37b Using two-word verbs idiomatically

Some words that look like prepositions do not always function as prepositions. Consider the following sentences:

▶ The balloon rose *off* the ground.

▶ The plane took *off* without difficulty.

In the first sentence, *off* is a preposition that introduces the prepositional phrase *off the ground*. In the second sentence, *off* neither functions as a preposition nor introduces a prepositional phrase. Instead, it combines with *took* to form a two-word **verb** with its own meaning. Such a verb is called a phrasal verb, and the word *off*, when used in this way, is called an adverbial particle. Many prepositions can function as particles to form phrasal verbs.

The verb + particle combination that makes up a phrasal verb is a single entity that cannot usually be torn apart.

▶ The plane took without difficulty. ~~off.~~
         off
         ^

Exceptions include some phrasal verbs that are transitive, meaning that they take a direct **object**. Some of these verbs have particles that may be separated from the verb by the object.

▶ I *picked up my baggage* at the terminal.

▶ I *picked my baggage up* at the terminal.

If a personal **pronoun** is used as the direct object, it *must* separate the verb from its particle.

▶ I picked up ~~it~~ at the terminal.
         it
         ^

In idiomatic two-word verbs where the second word is a preposition, the preposition can never be separated from the verb.

▶ We *ran into* our neighbor on the train. [not *ran our neighbor into*]

The combination *run + into* has a special meaning (find by chance). Therefore, *run into* is a two-word verb.

EXERCISE 37.2   Identify each italicized expression as either a two-word verb or a verb + preposition. Example:

Look up John Brown the next time you're in town. *two-word verb*

1. George was still *looking for* the keys when we left.
2. I always *turn down* the thermostat when I go to bed or leave the house.
3. Marion *gave back* the borrowed scarf.
4. Jimmy *takes after* his father, poor thing.
5. The car *turned into* the driveway.

38 Comma Splices and Fused Sentences

A **comma splice** results from placing only a comma between **independent clauses**—groups of words that can stand alone as a sentence. We often see comma splices used effectively to give slogans a catchy rhythm, for example.

▶ **Dogs have owners, cats have staff.** —Bumper Sticker

A related construction is a **fused sentence**, or run-on, which results from joining two independent clauses with no punctuation or connecting word between them. The bumper sticker as a fused sentence would be "Dogs have owners cats have staff."

In academic and professional English, using comma splices or fused sentences will almost always be identified as an error, so be careful if you are using them for special effect.

38a Separating the clauses into two sentences

The simplest way to revise comma splices or fused sentences is to separate them into two sentences.

COMMA SPLICE   My mother spends long hours every spring

tilling the soil and moving manure**/.**
T
this part of gardening is nauseating.
^

If the clauses are very short, making them two sentences may sound abrupt and terse, so another method of revision may be preferable.

38b Linking the clauses with a comma and a coordinating conjunction

If the two clauses are closely related and equally important, join them with a comma and a **coordinating conjunction** (*and*, *but*, *or*, *nor*, *for*, *so*, or *yet*).

FUSED SENTENCE   Interest rates fell, so people began borrowing more money.

38c Linking the clauses with a semicolon

If the ideas in the two clauses are closely related and you want to give them equal emphasis, link them with a semicolon.

COMMA SPLICE   This photograph is not at all realistic; it uses dreamlike images to convey its message.

Be careful when you link clauses with a **conjunctive adverb** like *however* or *therefore* or with a **transition** like *in fact*. In such sentences, the two clauses must be separated by a semicolon or by a comma and a coordinating conjunction.

COMMA SPLICE   Many low-income countries have high birthrates; therefore, most of their citizens are young.

 Language, Culture, and Context

Judging Sentence Length

In U.S. academic contexts, readers sometimes find a series of short sentences "choppy" and hard to read. If you want to connect two independent clauses into one sentence, join them using one of the methods discussed in this chapter to avoid creating a comma splice or fused sentence. Another useful tip for writing in standardized English is to avoid writing several very long sentences in a row. If you find this pattern in your writing, try breaking it up by including a shorter sentence occasionally. You might also read your writing aloud or have someone read it to you: if you begin to lose the meaning of a sentence, it may be too long.

38d Rewriting the two clauses as one independent clause

Sometimes you can reduce two spliced or fused independent clauses to a single independent clause.

FUSED SENTENCE   Most
~~A large part~~ of my mail is advertisements
ʌ
and
~~most of the rest is~~ bills.
ʌ

38e Rewriting one independent clause as a dependent clause

When one independent clause is more important than the other, try converting the less important one to a **dependent clause** by adding an appropriate **subordinating conjunction**.

COMMA SPLICE   Although
Zora Neale Hurston is now regarded as one of
ʌ
America's major novelists, she died in obscurity.

In the revision, the writer emphasizes the second clause and makes the first one into a dependent clause by adding the subordinating conjunction *although*.

FUSED SENTENCE   , which reacted against mass production,
The arts and crafts movement called for

handmade objects. ~~it reacted against mass~~
ʌ
~~production.~~

In the revision, the writer chooses to emphasize the first clause (the one describing what the movement advocated) and make the second clause into a dependent clause.

38f Linking the two clauses with a dash

In informal writing, you can use a dash to join the two clauses, especially when the second clause elaborates on the first clause.

COMMA SPLICE   —
Exercise trends come and go/ this year yoga
ʌ
is hot.

EXERCISE 38.1   Revise each of the following comma splices or fused sentences by using the method suggested in brackets after the sentence. Example:

> but
>
> Americans think of slavery as a problem of the past, it still exists in some parts of the world. [Join with a comma and a coordinating conjunction.]

1. We tend to think of slavery only in U.S. terms in fact, it began long before the United States existed and still goes on. [Separate into two sentences.]

2. Slavery has existed in Mauritania for centuries it continues today. [Join with a comma and a coordinating conjunction.]

3. Members of Mauritania's ruling group are called the Beydanes, they are an Arab Berber tribe also known as the White Moors. [Recast as one independent clause.]

4. Another group in Mauritania is known as the Haratin or the Black Moors, they are native West Africans. [Separate into two sentences.]

5. In modern-day Mauritania, many of the Haratin are still enslaved, they serve the Beydanes. [Join with a semicolon.]

EXERCISE 38.2   Revise the following paragraph, eliminating comma splices by using a period or a semicolon. Then revise the paragraph again, this time using any of these three methods:

Separate independent clauses into sentences of their own.

Recast two or more clauses as one independent clause.

Recast one independent clause as a dependent clause.

Comment on the two revisions. What differences in rhythm do you detect? Which version do you prefer, and why?

My sister Julie is planning a much-needed vacation, obviously she is very excited. At first, she hoped for a cruise to the Bahamas, in fact, she went so far as to book a flight. When the virus hit and the economic crisis occurred she decided to change plans why not take a road trip instead? Julie decided to drive from Santa Fe to San Francisco, also she wanted at least one friend to go with her why not? She plotted out the trip so that she would not have to drive more than 300 miles a day, that made her feel she could manage without getting too tired. In the end she and her best friend ended the trip in San Diego, what an adventure they had!

39 Sentence Fragments

Sentence fragments are often used to make writing sound conversational, as in this Twitter post:

> Realizing that there are no edible **#bagels** in this part of Oregon. Sigh.

Or they often create a special effect, as in this familiar advertisement:

> "Got milk?"

As these examples show, **fragments**—groups of words that are punctuated as sentences but are not sentences—often appear in intentionally informal writing and in public writing that aims to attract attention or give a phrase special emphasis. But think carefully before using fragments for special effect in academic or professional writing, where some readers might regard them as errors.

39a Identifying sentence fragments

A group of words must meet three criteria to form a complete sentence. If it does not meet all three, it is a fragment. Revise a fragment by combining it with a nearby sentence or by rewriting it as a complete sentence.

1. A sentence must have a subject.

2. A sentence must have a verb, not just a verbal.

   VERB   The terrier is *barking*.

   VERBAL   The terrier *barking*.

3. Unless it is a question, a sentence must have at least one clause that does not begin with a subordinating word. Following are some common subordinating words:

although	how	though	whether
as	if	unless	which
because	since	when	who
before	that	where	

39b Revising phrase fragments

A **phrase** is a group of words that lacks a **subject**, a **verb**, or both. When a phrase is punctuated like a sentence, it becomes a fragment. To revise a phrase fragment, attach it to an independent clause, or make it a separate sentence.

▶ CNN is broadcasting the debates/ ~~With~~ ^{with} discussions afterward.

With discussions afterward is a prepositional phrase, not a sentence. The editing combines the phrase with an independent clause.

▶ The town's growth is controlled by zoning laws/ ^a ~~A~~ strict set of regulations for builders and corporations.

A strict set of regulations for builders and corporations is a phrase renaming *zoning laws.* The editing attaches the fragment to the sentence containing that noun.

▶ Kamika stayed out of law school for three months after Linda was born. ^{She did so to} ~~To~~ recuperate and to take care of her baby.

The revision—adding a subject (*she*) and a verb (*did*)—turns the fragment into a separate sentence.

Fragments beginning with transitions If you introduce an example or explanation with a transitional word or phrase like *also, for example, such as,* or *that,* be certain you write a sentence, not a fragment.

▶ Joan Didion has written on many subjects/ ^{such} ~~Such~~ as the Hoover Dam and migraine headaches.

The second word group is a phrase, not a sentence. The editing combines it with an independent clause.

EXERCISE 39.1 Choose a magazine or web advertisement that contains intentional fragments. Rewrite the advertisement to eliminate all sentence fragments. Be prepared to explain how your version and the original differ in impact and why you think the copywriters for the ad chose to use fragments rather than complete sentences.

39c Revising compound-predicate fragments

A fragment occurs when one part of a compound **predicate** lacks a subject but is punctuated as a separate sentence. Such a fragment usually begins with *and*, *but*, or *or*. You can revise it by attaching it to the independent clause that contains the rest of the predicate.

▶ They sold their house~~/ And~~ ^and^ moved into an apartment.

39d Revising clause fragments

A **dependent clause** contains both a subject and a verb, but it cannot stand alone as a sentence; it depends on an independent clause to complete its meaning. A dependent clause usually begins with a **subordinating conjunction**, such as *after, because, before, if, since, that, though, unless, until, when, where, while, who,* or *which.* You can usually combine dependent-clause fragments with a nearby independent clause.

▶ When I decided to switch to part-time work~~/~~^,^ I gave up a lot of my earning potential.

If you cannot smoothly attach a clause to a nearby independent clause, try deleting the opening subordinating word and turning the dependent clause into a sentence.

▶ Most injuries in automobile accidents occur in two ways. ^An^ ~~When an~~ occupant either is hurt by something inside the car or is thrown from the car.

EXERCISE 39.2 Revise each of the following fragments, either by combining fragments with independent clauses or by rewriting them as separate sentences. Example:

Zoe looked close to tears. Standing with her head bowed.

Standing with her head bowed, Zoe looked close to tears.

or

Zoe looked close to tears. She was standing with her head bowed.

1. The Weeknd is famous for his pop songs. For example, "Starboy" and "Blinding Lights."

2. Attempting to win the science fair. I built a five-foot solar-powered submarine.

3. Diners in Creole restaurants might try shrimp gumbo. Or order turtle soup.

4. My community group saved our local watershed from logging. Working together to improve our environment.

5. In 2020, hundreds of thousands of activists worked toward racial justice. Marches and demonstrations in which they protested police brutality.

EXERCISE 39.3 Underline every fragment you find in the following para-graph. Then revise the paragraph. You may combine or re-arrange sentences as long as you retain the original content.

To study abroad or not. That is a major decision for many college students. Some will consider domestic programs at universities across the country. Traditionally, approaching their junior year. Opportunities for study in major cities and in small villages. Programs to satisfy every interest and major. There's a lot to think about. Applications, courses, airfare, accommodations, and visas. Those who accept the challenge are generally rewarded. With a once-in-a-lifetime opportunity. Students who travel to international destinations can thoroughly immerse themselves in the culture, language, traditions, and foods of their host country. And end up with new friends, an enhanced résumé, and a sense of self-reliance. Why not check with your college today? To see what kinds of global and domestic study programs you might apply to.

Punctuation/ Mechanics

40   **Commas**   354

41   **Semicolons**   365

42   **End Punctuation**   367

43   **Apostrophes**   370

44   **Quotation Marks**   373

45   **Other Punctuation**   377

46   **Capital Letters**   384

47   **Abbreviations and Numbers**   387

48   **Italics and Hyphens**   390

40 Commas

It's hard to go through a day without encountering directions of some kind, and commas often play a crucial role in how you interpret instructions. See how important the comma is in the following directions for making hot cereal:

Add Cream of Wheat slowly, stirring constantly.

That sentence tells the cook to *add the cereal slowly*. If the comma came before the word *slowly*, however, the cook might add all of the cereal at once and *stir slowly*.

40a Setting off introductory elements

In general, use a comma after any word, **phrase**, or **clause** that precedes the **subject** of the sentence.

▶ However, health care costs keep rising.

▶ Wearing new tap shoes, Audrey prepared for the recital.

▶ To win the game, players need both skill and luck.

▶ Fingers on the keyboard, Maya waited for the test to begin.

▶ While her friends watched, Lila practiced her gymnastics routine.

Some writers omit the comma after a short introductory element that does not seem to require a pause after it. However, you will never be wrong if you use a comma.

EXERCISE 40.1 In the following sentences, add any commas that are needed after the introductory element. Example:

As early as 1400 BC, chocolate was used in what is now Latin America.

1. Strangely enough for centuries chocolate was only known as a drink.
2. Even stranger chocolate did not include sugar.
3. By the 1600s chocolate was a favorite though bitter drink of wealthy people in Europe.

4. In the early nineteenth century a Dutch chemist finally figured out how to make chocolate less bitter.

5. Later in the century solid chocolate was created and the rest is history!

40b Separating clauses in compound sentences

A comma usually precedes a **coordinating conjunction** (*and, but, or, nor, for, so,* or *yet*) that joins two **independent clauses** in a compound sentence.

▶ The climbers must reach the summit today, or they will have to turn back.
                                          ^

 Checklist

Editing for Commas

Research for this book shows that five of the most common errors in college writing involve commas.

✔ Check that a comma separates an introductory word, phrase, or clause from the main part of the sentence. (40a)

✔ Look at every sentence that contains a coordinating conjunction (*and, but, or, nor, for, so,* or *yet*). If the groups of words before and after this conjunction both function as complete sentences, use a comma before the conjunction. (40b)

✔ Look at each adjective clause beginning with *which, who, whom, whose, when,* or *where* and at each phrase and appositive. If the rest of the sentence would have a different meaning without the clause, phrase, or appositive, do not set off the element with commas. (40c)

✔ Make sure that adjective clauses beginning with *that* are not set off with commas. Do not use commas between subjects and verbs, verbs and objects or complements, or prepositions and objects; to separate parts of compound constructions other than compound sentences; to set off restrictive clauses; or before the first or after the last item in a series. (40i)

✔ Do not use a comma alone to separate two sentences. (See Chapter 38.)

With very short clauses, you can sometimes omit the comma (*She saw her chance and she took it*). But always use the comma if there is a chance the sentence will be misread without it.

▶ I opened the heavy junk drawer, and the cabinet door jammed.

Use a semicolon rather than a comma when the clauses are long and complex or contain their own commas.

▶ When these early migrations took place, the ice was still confined to the lands in the far north; but eight hundred thousand years ago, when man was already established in the temperate latitudes, the ice moved southward until it covered large parts of Europe and Asia.
—Robert Jastrow, *Until the Sun Dies*

EXERCISE 40.2 Use a comma and a coordinating conjunction (*and, but, or, for, nor, so,* or *yet*) to combine each of the following pairs of sentences into one sentence. Delete or rearrange words if necessary. Example:

> There is a lot of talk these days about computer viruses/, ~~Many~~ **yet many** people do not know what they really are.

1. Computer viruses are software programs. They are created to spread from one computer to another.

2. A biological virus cannot replicate itself. A virus must inject its DNA into a cell to reproduce.

3. Similarly, a computer virus must hitch on to some other computer program. Then it can launch itself.

4. These viruses can be totally destructive or basically benign. When people think of computer viruses, they generally think of the former.

5. Most viruses spread easily via attachments. People should never open an email attachment unless they know the sender.

40c Setting off nonrestrictive elements

Nonrestrictive elements are word groups that do not limit, or restrict, the meaning of the noun or pronoun they modify. Setting nonrestrictive elements off with commas shows your readers that the information is not essential to the meaning of the sentence.

Restrictive elements, on the other hand, *are* essential to meaning and should *not* be set off with commas. The same sentence may mean different things with and without the commas:

▶ The bus drivers rejecting the management offer remained on strike.

▶ The bus drivers, rejecting the management offer, remained on strike.

The first sentence says that only *some* bus drivers, the ones rejecting the offer, remained on strike. The second says that *all* the drivers did.

Since the decision to include or omit commas influences how readers will interpret your sentence, you should think especially carefully about what you mean and use commas (or omit them) accordingly.

RESTRICTIVE   Drivers *who have been convicted of DUI* should lose their licenses.

In the preceding sentence, the clause *who have been convicted of DUI* is essential because it explains that only drivers who have been convicted of drunken driving should lose their licenses. Therefore, it is *not* set off with commas.

NONRESTRICTIVE   The two drivers involved in the accident, *who have been convicted of DUI*, should lose their licenses.

In this sentence, however, the clause *who have been convicted of DUI* is not essential to the meaning because it does not limit what it modifies, *The two drivers involved in the accident*, but merely provides additional information about these drivers. Therefore, the clause *is* set off with commas.

To decide whether an element is restrictive or nonrestrictive, mentally delete the element, and see if the deletion changes the meaning of the rest of the sentence. If the deletion *does* change the meaning, you should probably not set the element off with commas. If it *does not* change the meaning, the element probably requires commas.

Adjective and adverb clauses   An **adjective** clause that begins with *that* is always restrictive; do not set it off with commas. An adjective clause beginning with *which* may be either restrictive or nonrestrictive; however, some writers prefer to use *which* only for nonrestrictive clauses, which they set off with commas.

RESTRICTIVE CLAUSES

▶ The claim *that men like seriously to battle one another to some sort of finish* is a myth.

> —John McMurtry, "Kill 'Em! Crush 'Em! Eat 'Em Raw!"

The adjective clause is necessary to the meaning because it explains which claim is a myth; therefore, the clause is not set off with commas.

▶ The man/ who rescued Jana's puppy/ won her eternal gratitude.

The adjective clause is necessary to the meaning because it identifies the man, so it takes no commas.

NONRESTRICTIVE CLAUSES

▶ I borrowed books from the rental library of Shakespeare and Company, *which was the library and bookstore of Sylvia Beach at 12 rue de l'Odeon.*
> —Ernest Hemingway, *A Moveable Feast*

The adjective clause is not necessary to the meaning of the independent clause and therefore is set off with a comma.

An **adverb** clause that follows a main clause does *not* usually require a comma to set it off unless the adverb clause expresses contrast.

▶ The park became a popular gathering place, although nearby residents complained about the noise.

The adverb clause expresses contrast, so it is set off with a comma.

Phrases Participial **phrases** may be restrictive or nonrestrictive. Prepositional phrases are usually restrictive, but sometimes they are not essential to the meaning of a sentence and thus are set off with commas.

NONRESTRICTIVE PHRASES

▶ The NBA star's little daughter, refusing to be ignored, interrupted the interview.

Using commas around the participial phrase (*refusing to be ignored*) makes it nonrestrictive.

Appositives An **appositive** is a **noun** or noun phrase that renames a nearby noun. When an appositive is not essential to identify what it renames, it is set off with commas.

NONRESTRICTIVE APPOSITIVES

▶ Savion Glover, the award-winning dancer, taps like poetry in motion.

Savion Glover's name identifies him; the appositive *the award-winning dancer* provides extra information.

RESTRICTIVE APPOSITIVES

▶ Mozart's opera/ *The Marriage of Figaro/* was considered revolutionary.

The phrase is restrictive because Mozart wrote more than one opera. Therefore, it is *not* set off with commas.

EXERCISE 40.3 First, underline the restrictive or nonrestrictive elements in the following sentences. Then, use commas to set off the non-restrictive elements in any of the sentences that contain such elements. Example:

A Tale of Two Cities, one of Charles Dickens's most famous works, was first published in 1859.

1. Everyone who runs in the race will get a T-shirt and a small backpack.
2. Mammals that have pouches to protect their young are known as marsupials.
3. Wasabi a root that is related to horseradish originated in Japan.
4. Plagiarism does occur on college campuses even though it is dishonest and illegal.
5. The game will go into overtime if neither team scores within the next two minutes.

40d Separating items in a series

▶ He has plundered our seas, ravaged our coasts, burnt our towns, and destroyed the lives of our people.

—Declaration of Independence

You may see a series with no comma after the next-to-last item, particularly in newspaper writing. Occasionally, however, omitting the comma can cause confusion.

► **All the cafeteria's vegetables—broccoli, green beans, peas, and carrots—were cooked to a gray mush.**

Without the comma after *peas*, you wouldn't know if there were three choices (the third being a *mixture* of peas and carrots) or four.

Coordinate adjectives—two or more adjectives that relate equally to the noun they modify—should be separated by commas.

► **The long, twisting, muddy road led to a shack in the woods.**

In a sentence like *The cracked bathroom mirror reflected his face*, however, *cracked* and *bathroom* are not coordinate because *bathroom mirror* is the equivalent of a single word, which is modified by *cracked*. Hence they are *not* separated by commas.

You can usually determine whether adjectives are coordinate by inserting *and* between them. If the sentence makes sense with the *and* added, the adjectives are coordinate and should be separated by commas.

► **They are sincere *and* talented *and* inquisitive researchers.**

The sentence makes sense with the *and*s, so the adjectives should be separated by commas: *They are sincere, talented, inquisitive researchers*.

► **Byron carried an elegant ~~and~~ pocket watch.**

The sentence does not make sense with *and*, so the adjectives *elegant* and *pocket* should not be separated by a comma: *Byron carried an elegant pocket watch*.

See 41b for separating items in a series with semicolons.

EXERCISE 40.4 In the following sentences, add any commas that are needed to set off words, phrases, or clauses in a series. Example:

The waiter brought water, menus, and an attitude.

1. I am looking forward to visiting Rome Venice and Florence.
2. The moon circles the earth the earth revolves around the sun and the sun is just one star in the galaxy.

3. The pelican landed in my yard climbed up onto the deck and admired its reflection in the sliding glass doors.

4. Lin-Manuel Miranda says the only Broadway shows he saw as a kid were *Les Miz Cats* and *Phantom*.

5. During the pandemic, people avoided public transportation stopped traveling by air and stayed away from even small gatherings.

40e Setting off parenthetical and transitional expressions

Parenthetical expressions add comments or information. Because they often interrupt the flow of a sentence, they are usually set off with commas.

▶ Some studies have shown that chocolate, of all things, helps prevent tooth decay.

Transitions (such as *as a result*), **conjunctive adverbs** (such as *however*), and other expressions used to connect parts of sentences are usually set off with commas.

▶ Ozone is a by-product of dry cleaning, for example.

40f Setting off contrasting elements, interjections, direct address, and tag questions

▶ I asked you, *not your brother,* to sweep the porch.

▶ *Holy cow,* did you see that?

▶ Remember, *sir,* that you are under oath.

▶ The governor did not veto the bill, *did she?*

EXERCISE 40.5 Revise each of the following sentences, using commas to set off parenthetical and transitional expressions, contrasting elements, interjections, words used in direct address, and tag questions. Example:

Passengers, thank you for your attention.

1. Ouch that COVID-19 test actually hurt!
2. Doctor Fauci could you tell us how often we will need vaccine booster shots?
3. And could you in addition tell us what we might do to prevent future pandemics?
4. Some communities as a result of their diligence were able to reopen their economies along with their schools in early 2021.
5. Some communities outside the U.S. I am sorry to say fared worse.

40g Setting off parts of dates and addresses

Dates   Use a comma between the day of the week and the month, between the day of the month and the year, and between the year and the rest of the sentence, if any.

▶ **On Wednesday, November 26, 2008, gunmen arrived in Mumbai by boat.**

Do not use commas with dates in inverted order or with dates consisting of only the month and the year.

▶ **Kerry dated the letter <u>5 August 2016</u>.**

▶ **Thousands of Germans swarmed over the wall in <u>November 1989</u>.**

Addresses and place-names   Use a comma after each part of an address or a place-name, including the state if there is no ZIP code. Do not precede a ZIP code with a comma.

▶ **Forward my mail to the Department of English, The Ohio State University, Columbus, Ohio 43210.**

▶ **Portland, Oregon, is much larger than Portland, Maine.**

40h Setting off quotations

Commas set off a quotation from words used to introduce or identify the source of the quotation. A comma following a quotation goes *inside* the closing quotation mark.

▶ **A German proverb warns, "Go to law for a sheep, and lose your cow."**

▶ "All I know about grammar," said Joan Didion, "is its infinite
power."

Do not use a comma following a question mark or an exclamation
point.

▶ "Out, damned spot!⁄" cries Lady Macbeth.

Do not use a comma to introduce a quotation with *that* or when
you do not quote a speaker's exact words.

▶ The writer of Ecclesiastes concludes that⁄ "all is vanity."
▶ Patrick Henry declared⁄ that he wanted either liberty or death.

EXERCISE 40.6 Revise each of the following sentences, using commas appropriately with dates, addresses and place-names, titles,
numbers, and quotations. Example:

The store's original location was 2373 Broadway, New York City.

1. "Education is not the filling of a pail, but the lighting of a fire" said
   William Butler Yeats.
2. The White House address is 1600 Pennsylvania Avenue Washington
   DC.
3. On July 21 1969 Neil Armstrong became the first person to walk on the
   moon.
4. "Neat people are lazier and meaner than sloppy people" according to
   Suzanne Britt.
5. Atlanta Georgia has a population of more than half a million.

40i Avoiding unnecessary commas

Excessive use of commas can spoil an otherwise fine sentence.

Around restrictive elements Do not use commas to set off
restrictive elements—elements that limit, or define, the meaning of
the words they modify or refer to (40c).

▶ I don't let my children watch movies⁄that are violent.
▶ The actor⁄ Denzel Washington⁄ might win the award.

Between subjects and verbs, verbs and objects or complements, and prepositions and objects Do not use a comma between a subject and its **verb**, a verb and its **object** or complement, or a **preposition** and its object.

▶ Watching movies late at night/ allows me to relax.

▶ Parents must decide/ what time their children should go to bed.

▶ The winner of/ the prize for community service stepped forward.

In compound constructions In compound constructions other than compound sentences, do not use a comma before or after a coordinating conjunction that joins the two parts (38b).

▶ Improved health care/ and more free trade were two of the administration's goals.

> The *and* joins parts of a compound subject, which should not be separated by a comma.

▶ Mark Twain trained as a printer/ and worked as a steamboat pilot.

> The *and* joins parts of a compound predicate, which should not be separated by a comma.

In a series Do not use a comma before the first or after the last item in a series.

▶ The auction included/ furniture, paintings, and china.

▶ The swimmer took slow, elegant, powerful/ strokes.

EXERCISE 40.7 Revise each of the following sentences, deleting unnecessary commas. If a sentence contains no unnecessary commas, write *Correct*. Example:

> Workaholics are people/ who can't seem to make time for anything but work.

1. Contrary to popular belief, workaholics are not, simply born that way.

2. Instead they slowly acquire the habit of working, constantly, and don't even notice it.

3. Why can't workaholics learn to give up some work time, or at least take some breaks?

4. Perhaps, workaholics suffer from an anxiety disorder.

5. If that is the case, they should consider seeking help, from a therapist.

41 Semicolons

The following public-service announcement, posted in New York City subway cars, reminded commuters what to do with a used newspaper at the end of the ride:

> Please put it in a trash can; that's good news for everyone.

The semicolon in the subway announcement separates two clauses that could have been written as separate sentences. Semicolons, which create a pause stronger than that of a comma but not as strong as the full pause of a period, show close connections between related ideas.

41a Linking independent clauses

Although a comma and a **coordinating conjunction** often join **independent clauses** (38b), semicolons provide writers with more subtle ways of signaling closely related clauses. The clause following a semicolon often restates an idea expressed in the first clause; it sometimes expands on or presents a contrast to the first.

▶ Immigration acts were passed; newcomers had to prove, besides moral correctness and financial solvency, their ability to read.
> —Mary Gordon, "More Than Just a Shrine"

The semicolon gives the sentence an abrupt rhythm that suits the topic: laws that imposed strict requirements.

If two independent clauses joined by a coordinating conjunction contain commas, you may use a semicolon instead of a comma before the conjunction to make the sentence easier to read.

▶ Every year, whether the Republican or the Democratic party is in office, more and more power drains away from the individual to feed vast reservoirs in far-off places; and we have less and less say about the shape of events which shape our future. —William F. Buckley Jr., "Why Don't We Complain?"

A semicolon should link independent clauses joined by a **conjunctive adverb** such as *however* or *therefore* or a **transition** such as *as a result* or *for example*.

► The circus comes as close to being the world in microcosm as anything I know; in a way, it puts all the rest of show business in the shade. —E. B. White, "The Ring of Time"

EXERCISE 41.1 Combine each of the following pairs of sentences into one sentence by using a semicolon. Example:

I decided to start my diet this week/; ~~Not~~ *not* surprisingly, a package just arrived from my mother with brownies, cookies, and three different flavors of popcorn.

1. This sofa is much too big. It will never fit inside my Prius.

2. The business could no longer afford to pay its bills or its employees. Therefore, the owners filed for bankruptcy.

3. German shepherds are known for their intelligence. They are also known for their protective behavior.

4. Once students live off-campus, most begin cooking their own meals. Nevertheless, some choose to maintain their school dining plans.

5. Natalia ran a marathon in four hours and two minutes. Unfortunately, this time did not qualify her for the Boston Marathon.

41b Separating items in a series containing other punctuation

Ordinarily, commas separate items in a series (40d). But when the items themselves contain commas or other punctuation, semicolons make the sentence clearer.

► Anthropology encompasses archaeology, the study of ancient civilizations through artifacts/; linguistics, the study of the structure and development of language/; and cultural anthropology, the study of language, customs, and behavior.

41c Avoiding misused semicolons

Use a comma, not a semicolon, to separate an independent clause from a **dependent clause** or **phrase**.

▶ The police found fingerprints/**, which they used to identify the** thief.

▶ The new system would encourage students to register for courses online/**, thus streamlining registration.**

Use a colon, not a semicolon, to introduce a series or list.

▶ The reunion tour includes the following bands/**: Urban Waste, Murphy's Law, Rapid Deployment, and Ism.**

EXERCISE 41.2 Revise each of the following sentences to correct the misuse of semicolons. If the semicolon in a sentence is appropriate as written, write *Correct*. Example:

> The new system would encourage high school students to take more academic courses/**, thus strengthening college preparation.**

1. To make the tacos, I need to buy; ground beef, beans, and tortillas.

2. For four glorious but underpaid weeks; I'll be working in Yosemite this summer.

3. Luis enjoys commuting to work on the train; although it can get crowded at rush hour.

4. Some gardeners want; low-maintenance plants, limited grass to mow, and low water usage.

5. Alicia slept through most of her art history lectures; as a result, she failed the course.

42 End Punctuation

Periods, question marks, and exclamation points often appear in advertising to create special effects:

Just do it.

Got milk?

I'm lovin' it!

End punctuation tells us how to read each sentence—as a matter-of-fact statement, a question for the reader, or an enthusiastic exclamation.

42a Using periods

Use a period to close sentences that make statements or give mild commands.

▶ **All books are either dreams or swords.** —Amy Lowell

▶ **Don't use a fancy word if a simpler word will do.**
—George Orwell, "Politics and the English Language"

A period also closes indirect questions, which report rather than ask questions.

▶ **I asked how old the child was.**

In standardized American English, periods are used with most abbreviations. However, more and more abbreviations are currently appearing without periods.

Mr.	MD	BCE *or* B.C.E.
Ms.	PhD	AD *or* A.D.
Sen.	Jr.	PM *or* p.m.

Some abbreviations rarely if ever appear with periods. These include the postal abbreviations of state names, such as FL and TN, and most groups of initials (NCAA, CIA, AIDS, YMCA, UNICEF). If you are not sure whether an abbreviation should include periods, check a dictionary or follow the style guidelines you are using for a research paper. (For more about abbreviations, see Chapter 47.)

Do not use an additional period when a sentence ends with an abbreviation that has its own period.

▶ **The social worker referred me to John Pintz Jr./**

42b Using question marks

Use question marks to close sentences that ask direct questions.

▶ **How is the human mind like a computer, and how is it different?**
—Kathleen Stassen Berger and Ross A. Thompson,
The Developing Person through Childhood and Adolescence

Question marks do not close indirect questions, which report rather than ask questions.

▶ **She asked whether I opposed his nomination.̷**

42c Using exclamation points

Use an exclamation point to show surprise or strong emotion. Use these marks sparingly because they can distract your readers or suggest that you are exaggerating.

▶ **In those few moments of geologic time will be the story of all that has happened since we became a nation. And what a story it will be!**
—James Rettie, "But a Watch in the Night"

EXERCISE 42.1 Revise each of the following items, inserting end punctuation in the appropriate places and eliminating any inappropriate punctuation. If a sentence is correct as written, write *Correct*. Example:

> Over the centuries, some of history's most interesting characters have been women.̷

1. In China, the brief reign of Empress Wu from 690 to 705 CE saw some changes that benefited women.
2. "Which Harry Potter book did you like best," Maya asked Leah?
3. Do you remember who said, "We are the ones we've been waiting for. We are the change we seek!"
4. The child cried, "Owie Owie" as her mother pulled off the bandage!
5. Stop, thief.

42d Using end punctuation in informal writing

In informal writing, especially on social media, writers today are more likely to omit end punctuation entirely. Research also shows that ellipses (. . .), or "dots," are on the rise; they can be used to signal a trailing off of a thought, to raise questions about what is being left out, to leave open the possibility of further communication, or simply to indicate that the writer doesn't want or need to finish the sentence. Exclamation marks can convey an excited or a chatty tone, so they are used more frequently in informal writing, though they get old pretty quickly—and advertisers call them the "kiss of death." And some writers have argued that using a period at the end of a text or tweet rather than no punctuation at all can suggest that the writer is irritated or angry. The meaning of end punctuation is changing in informal contexts, so pay attention to how others communicate, and use what you learn in your own social writing.

43 Apostrophes

The little apostrophe can make a big difference in meaning. The following sign at a neighborhood swimming pool, for instance, says something different from what the writer probably intended:

> Please deposit your garbage (and your guests) in the trash receptacles before leaving the pool area.

The sign indicates that the guests, not their garbage, should be deposited in trash receptacles. Adding a single apostrophe would offer a more neighborly statement: *Please deposit your garbage (and your guests') in the trash receptacles before leaving the pool area.*

43a Signaling possessive case

The possessive case denotes ownership or possession. Add an apostrophe and -*s* to form the possessive of most singular **nouns**, including those that end in -*s*, and of **indefinite pronouns** (33d). The possessive forms of personal **pronouns** do not take apostrophes: *yours, his, hers, its, ours, theirs.*

▸ The <u>bus's</u> fumes overpowered her.

▸ George <u>Lucas's</u> movies have been wildly popular.

▸ <u>Anyone's</u> guess is as good as mine.

Plural nouns To form the possessive case of plural nouns not ending in -s, add an apostrophe and -s. For plural nouns ending in -s, add only the apostrophe.

▶ The <u>men's</u> department sells suits.

▶ The <u>clowns'</u> costumes were bright green and orange.

Compound nouns For compound nouns, make the last word in the group possessive.

▶ Both her <u>daughters-in-law's</u> birthdays fall in July.

Two or more nouns To signal individual possession by two or more owners, make each noun possessive.

▶ Great differences exist between <u>Jerry Bruckheimer's</u> and <u>Ridley Scott's</u> films.

Bruckheimer and Scott produce different films.

To signal joint possession, make only the last noun possessive.

▶ <u>Wallace and Gromit's</u> creator is Nick Park.

Wallace and Gromit have the same creator.

EXERCISE 43.1 Complete each of the following sentences by inserting 's or an apostrophe alone to form the possessive case of the italicized words. Example:

trolls'
Many conspiracy theories are nothing but Internet ~~trolls~~ invented
stories.

1. Such theories go viral on social media because of *people* gullibility.

2. *Technologys* power to inform is great, but so is its power to misinform.

3. A hoax is easily disseminated because of the *recipients* inability to see through it.

4. Many of these conspiracy theories prey on *consumers* fears.

5. Have you heard the one about how *deodorants* ingredients supposedly cause cancer?

43b Signaling contractions

Contractions are two-word combinations formed by leaving out certain letters, which are replaced by an apostrophe (*it is, it has/ it's; will not/won't*).

Contractions are common in conversation and informal writing. Academic and professional work, however, often calls for greater formality.

Distinguishing *its* and *it's*   *Its* is a possessive **pronoun**—the possessive form of *it*. *It's* is a contraction for *it is* or *it has*.

▶ This disease is unusual; <u>its</u> symptoms vary from person to person.

▶ <u>It's</u> a difficult disease to diagnose.

> **EXERCISE 43.2**   Revise each of the following sentences so that it uses contractions. Remove any misused apostrophes. Example:
>
> I'll
> ~~I will~~ bring sushi to the potluck dinner.
>   ^

1. Genevieve was not even three years old when she moved here from Germany, so she does not have a German accent.

2. You will see plenty of TV advertisements for alcoholic beverages, but you will not see any for tobacco products.

3. Whose dog keeps scratching it's ears?

4. It has been almost ten years, but I cannot forget how I felt on the night we received the terrible news.

5. Let us go to the later movie, after he has had a chance to finish his homework.

43c Understanding apostrophes and plural forms

Many style guides now advise against using apostrophes for plurals.

▶ The gymnasts need marks of <u>8s</u> and <u>9s</u> in order to qualify for the finals.

Other guidelines call for an apostrophe and *-s* to form the plural of numbers, letters, and words referred to as terms.

▶ The five <u>Shakespeare's</u> in the essay were spelled five different ways.

Check your instructor's preference.

44 Quotation Marks

"Hilarious!" "A great family movie!" "A must see!" Quotation marks are a key component of statements like these from movie ads; they make the praise more believable by indicating that it comes from people other than the movie promoter. Quotation marks identify a speaker's exact words or the titles of short works.

44a Signaling direct quotation

▶ The crowd chanted "Celtics, Celtics" as they waited for the game to begin.

▶ Jasmine smiled and said, "Son, this is one incident that I will never forget."

Use quotation marks to enclose the words of each speaker within running dialogue. Mark each shift in speaker with a new paragraph.

> "I want no proof of their affection," said Elinor; "but of their engagement I do."
> "I am perfectly satisfied of both."
> "Yet not a syllable has been said to you on the subject, by either of them." —Jane Austen, *Sense and Sensibility*

Single quotation marks Single quotation marks enclose a quotation within a quotation. Open and close the quoted passage with double quotation marks, and change any quotation marks that appear *within* the quotation to single quotation marks.

▶ Baldwin says, "The title 'The Uses of the Blues' does not refer to music; I don't know anything about music."

Long quotations To quote a passage that is more than four typed lines, set the quotation off by starting it on a new line and indenting it one-half inch from the left margin. This format, known as block quotation, does not require quotation marks.

> In "Suspended," Joy Harjo tells of her first awareness of jazz as a child:
>
> > My rite of passage into the world of humanity occurred then, via jazz.
> > The music made a startling bridge between the familiar and strange
> > lands, an appropriate vehicle, for . . . we were there when jazz was
> > born. I recognized it . . . as a way to speak beyond the confines of
> > ordinary language. (84)

This block quotation, including the ellipsis dots and the page number in parentheses at the end, follows the style of the Modern Language Association, or MLA (see Chapter 16). The American Psychological Association, or APA, has different guidelines for setting off block quotations (see Chapter 17).

Poetry When quoting poetry, if the quotation is brief (fewer than four lines), include it within your text. Separate the lines of the poem with slashes, each preceded and followed by a space, in order to tell the reader where one line of the poem ends and the next begins.

> In one of his best-known poems, Robert Frost remarks, "Two roads
> diverged in a yellow wood, and I— / I took the one less traveled by / And
> that has made all the difference."

To quote more than three lines of poetry, indent the block one-half inch from the left margin. Do not use quotation marks. Take care to follow the spacing, capitalization, punctuation, and other features of the original poem.

> The duke in Robert Browning's poem "My Last Duchess" is clearly a jealous,
> vain person, whose arrogance is illustrated through this statement:
>
> > She thanked men—good! but thanked
> > Somehow—I know not how—as if she ranked
> > My gift of a nine-hundred-years-old name
> > With anybody's gift. (lines 31–34)

EXERCISE 44.1 In the following sentences, add quotation marks each time someone else's exact words are being used. Some sentences may not require quotation marks; mark correct sentences *Correct*. Example:

"Your phone's ringing!" yelled Phil from the end of the hall.

1. My banjo teacher told me that I have to practice at least three hours a day or face the fact that I'll never be a good player.
2. It's not fair, she told him. You always win.
3. They kill the white girl first is the first sentence of Toni Morrison's *Paradise*.
4. I could not believe the total devastation of Beirut, he wrote.
5. Keep your opinions to yourselves, Dad muttered as he served the lumpy oatmeal.

44b Identifying titles of short works and definitions

Use quotation marks to enclose the titles of short poems, short stories, articles, essays, songs, sections of books, and episodes of television and radio programs. Quotation marks also enclose definitions.

▶ The essay "The Art of Stephen Curry" analyzes some reasons for the success of the Warriors' star.

▶ In social science, the term *sample size* means "the number of individuals being studied in a research project."

—Kathleen Stassen Berger and Ross A. Thompson, *The Developing Person through Childhood and Adolescence*

EXERCISE 44.2 Revise each of the following sentences by using quotation marks appropriately to signal both titles and definitions. Example:

One of the best short stories we read last semester was "The Story of an Hour" by Kate Chopin.

1. The term *emoji*, which means a small digital image used to express an emotion, comes from Japanese.
2. Girl by Jamaica Kincaid is a single-sentence short story.

3. Lady Gaga's Stupid Love was a top hit in 2020.
4. My favorite episode of the Netflix series *Unsolved Mysteries* is The Men in Black.
5. The *New York Times* article Dealing with Student Debt helps college graduates understand the best way to handle their student loans.

44c Using quotation marks with other punctuation

Periods and commas go *inside* closing quotation marks.

▶ "Don't compromise yourself," said Janis Joplin. "You are all you've got."

Colons, semicolons, and footnote numbers go *outside* closing quotation marks.

▶ I felt one emotion after finishing "Eveline": sorrow.

▶ Tragedy is defined by Aristotle as "an imitation of an action that is serious and of a certain magnitude."[1]

Question marks, exclamation points, and dashes go *inside* if they are part of the quoted material, *outside* if they are not.

PART OF THE QUOTATION

▶ The cashier asked, "Would you like a receipt?"

NOT PART OF THE QUOTATION

▶ What is the theme of "The Birth-Mark"?

44d Avoiding misused quotation marks

Do not use quotation marks for indirect quotations—those that do not use someone's exact words.

▶ Mother smiled and said that /"she was sure she would never forget the incident."/

Do not use quotation marks merely to add emphasis to particular words or phrases.

▶ The hikers were startled by the appearance of a /"gigantic"/ grizzly bear.

Do not use quotation marks around slang or colloquial language; they create the impression that you are apologizing for using those words. If you have a good reason to use slang or a colloquial term, use it without quotation marks.

▶ After our twenty-mile hike, we were completely exhausted and ready to ʲ̶turn in.ʲ̶

EXERCISE 44.3   Revise each of the following sentences, using quotation marks appropriately.

1. Should America the Beautiful or Lift Every Voice and Sing replace The Star-Spangled Banner as the national anthem?

2. In the chapter called The Last to See Them Alive, Truman Capote shows the utterly ordinary life of the Kansas family.

3. Several popular films have used ABBA hits such as Dancing Queen and Take a Chance on Me.

4. After working a double shift, we were completely "exhausted."

5. My dictionary defines *isolation* as the quality or state of being alone.

45   Other Punctuation

Parentheses, brackets, dashes, colons, slashes, and ellipses are everywhere. Every URL includes colons and slashes, many sites use brackets or parentheses to identify updates and embedded media, and dashes and ellipses are increasingly common in writing that expresses conversational informality.

You can also use these punctuation marks for more formal purposes: to signal relationships among parts of sentences, to create particular rhythms, and to help readers follow your thoughts.

45a   Using parentheses

Use parentheses to enclose material that is of minor or secondary importance in a sentence—material that supplements, clarifies, comments on, or illustrates what precedes or follows it.

▶ Inventors and men of genius have almost always been regarded as fools at the beginning (and very often at the end) of their careers.

—Fyodor Dostoyevsky

▶ *Hamilton* (the musical by Lin-Manuel Miranda) won eleven Tony Awards in 2016.

Parentheses are also used to enclose textual citations and numbers or letters in a list.

▶ Freud and his followers have had a most significant impact on the ways abnormal functioning is understood and treated (Joseph, 1991). —Ronald J. Comer, *Abnormal Psychology*

The in-text citation in this sentence shows the style of the American Psychological Association (APA).

▶ Five distinct styles can be distinguished: (1) Old New England, (2) Deep South, (3) Middle American, (4) Wild West, and (5) Far West or Californian. —Alison Lurie, *The Language of Clothes*

With other punctuation A period may be placed either inside or outside a closing parenthesis, depending on whether the parenthetical text is part of a larger sentence. A comma, if needed, is always placed *outside* a closing parenthesis (and never before an opening one).

▶ Gene Tunney's single defeat in an eleven-year career was to a flamboyant and dangerous fighter named Harry Greb ("The Human Windmill"), who seems to have been, judging from boxing literature, the dirtiest fighter in history.

—Joyce Carol Oates, *On Boxing*

45b Using brackets

Use brackets to enclose any parenthetical elements in material that is itself within parentheses. Brackets should also be used to enclose any explanatory words or comments you are inserting into a quotation.

▶ Eventually, the investigation had to examine the major agencies (including the National Security Agency [NSA]) that were conducting covert operations.

▶ Massing notes that "on average, it [Fox News] attracts more than eight million people daily."

The bracketed words clarify the meaning of *it* in the original quotation.

In the quotation in the following sentence, the artist Gauguin's name is misspelled. The bracketed word *sic*, which means "so," tells readers that the person being quoted—not the writer who has picked up the quotation—made the mistake.

▶ One admirer wrote, "She was the most striking woman I'd ever seen—a sort of wonderful combination of Mia Farrow and one of Gaugin's [*sic*] Polynesian nymphs."

EXERCISE 45.1 Revise the sentences below, using parentheses and brackets correctly. Change any other punctuation as needed.

1. The words *media elite* have been said so often usually by people who are themselves elite members of the media that the phrase has taken on a life of its own.

2. Are the media really elite, and are they really liberal, as talk-show regulars (Ann Coulter, for example argue)?

3. Media critic Eric Alterman has coined the term "so-called liberal media" [SCLM] because he believes that the media have been intimidated by criticism.

4. An article in the *Journal of Communication* discussing the outcomes of recent U.S. elections explained that "claiming the media are liberally biased perhaps has become a core rhetorical strategy" used by conservatives, qtd. in Alterman 14.

5. Some progressive groups (including Fairness and Accuracy in Reporting (FAIR)) keep track of media coverage of political issues.

45c Using dashes

Use dashes to insert a comment or to highlight material in a sentence.

▶ The pleasures of reading itself—who doesn't remember?—were like those of Christmas cake, a sweet devouring.

—Eudora Welty, "A Sweet Devouring"

A single dash can be used to emphasize material at the end of a sentence, to mark a sudden change in tone, to indicate hesitation in speech, or to introduce a summary or an explanation.

▶ Like you, he's black and from Harvard. Other than that, you
  know nothing—just the name, and it's an odd one.
                                        —Michelle Obama, *Becoming*

▶ In walking, the average adult person employs a motor mechanism
  that weighs about eighty pounds—sixty pounds of muscle and
  twenty pounds of bone.   —Edwin Way Teale

Dashes give more emphasis than parentheses to the material they
enclose or set off. Many word-processing programs automatically
convert two typed hyphens with no spaces before or after into a
solid dash.

| **EXERCISE 45.2** | Revise the following sentences so that dashes are used cor-
rectly. Example: |

  In some states California, for example banks are no longer allowed

  to charge ATM users an additional fee for withdrawing money.

1. Many consumers accept that they have to pay additional fees for services like bank machines if they don't want to pay, they don't have to
   use the service.

2. Nevertheless—extra charges seem to be added to more and more services all the time.

3. Some of the charges are ridiculous why should hotels charge guests a
   fee for making a toll-free telephone call?

4. The hidden costs of service fees are irritating people feel that their bank
   accounts are being nibbled to death.

5. But some of the fees consumers are asked to pay—are more than simply
   irritating.

45d   Using colons

Use a colon to introduce an explanation, an example, an **appositive**, a series, a list, or a quotation.

▶ At the baby's one-month birthday party, Ah Po gave him the Four
  Valuable Things: ink, inkslab, paper, and brush.
                              —Maxine Hong Kingston, *China Men*

Use a colon rather than a comma to introduce a quotation when the lead-in is a complete sentence on its own.

▶ In his presentation, Tristan Harris made a stark claim: "Never before in history have the decisions of a handful of designers (mostly men, white, living in San Francisco, aged 25–30) working at three companies had so much impact on how millions of people around the world spend their attention."

Colons are also used after salutations in letters; with numbers indicating hours, minutes, and seconds; with ratios; with biblical chapters and verses; with titles and subtitles; and in bibliographic entries in some styles.

▶ Dear Dr. Goswami:

▶ 4:59 PM

▶ a ratio of 5:1

▶ Ecclesiastes 3:1

▶ *The Mamba Mentality: How I Play*

▶ Boston: Bedford/St. Martin's

Misused colons Do not put a colon between a **verb** and its **object** or complement (unless the object is a quotation), between a **preposition** and its object, or after such expressions as *such as*, *especially*, and *including*.

▶ Some natural fibers are̸ cotton, wool, silk, and linen.

▶ In poetry, additional power may come from devices such as̸ simile, metaphor, and alliteration.

EXERCISE 45.3 Insert a colon in each of the following sentences that needs one. Remove any misused colons. Example:

I love books except̸ sappy romances, horror stories, and westerns.

1. During the eulogy, former President George W. Bush quoted from Matthew 22, 36–40.

2. Looking around at cardboard cutout fans filling the arena, LeBron James laughed "I can't hear you!"

3. All we could do was watch as the other boats reeled in fish after fish, bass, pike, trout, and perch.

4. Rose has trophies for several different sports, including: basketball, lacrosse, softball, and soccer.

5. My roommate's annoying habits include: forgetting to lock the door, leaving dirty dishes in the sink, and playing loud video games late at night.

45e Using slashes

Use a slash to separate alternatives.

▶ **Then there was Daryl, the cabdriver/bartender.**
—John L'Heureux, *The Handmaid of Desire*

Use a slash, preceded and followed by a space, to divide lines of poetry quoted within running text.

▶ **The speaker of Sonnet 130 says of his mistress, "I love to hear her speak, yet well I know / That music hath a far more pleasing sound."**

Slashes also separate parts of fractions and URLs: 1/3, 15/16, https://nytimes.com.

45f Using ellipses

An ellipsis is three equally spaced dots that indicate that something has been omitted from a quoted passage. Just as you should carefully use quotation marks around any material that you are quoting directly from a source, so you should carefully use an ellipsis to indicate that you have left out part of a quotation that otherwise appears to be a complete sentence. Ellipses have been used in the following example to indicate two omissions—one in the middle of the sentence and one at the end:

ORIGINAL TEXT

▶ **The quasi-official division of the population into three economic classes called high-, middle-, and low-income groups rather misses the point, because as a class indicator the amount of money is not as important as the source.**
—Paul Fussell, "Notes on Class"

WITH ELLIPSES

▶ As Paul Fussell argues, "The quasi-official division of the population into three classes . . . rather misses the point. . . ."

When you omit the last part of a quoted sentence, add a period before the ellipsis—for a total of four dots. Be sure a complete sentence comes before the four dots. If your shortened quotation ends with a source citation (such as a page number, a name, or a title), place the documentation source in parentheses after the three ellipsis points and the closing quotation mark but before the period.

▶ Packer argues, "The Administration is right to reconsider its strategy . . ." (34).

You can also use an ellipsis to indicate a pause or a hesitation in speech in the same way that you can use a dash for that purpose. (For more uses of ellipses in informal writing, see 42d.)

▶ Then the voice, husky and familiar, came to wash over us—"The winnah, and still heavyweight champeen of the world . . . Joe Louis." —Maya Angelou, *I Know Why the Caged Bird Sings*

You are probably used to seeing ellipses everywhere on social media. Author Clay Shirkey thinks the "ellipsis explosion" results from people trying to emulate speaking, with ellipses used to indicate a pause in the way that "ah" or "uh" does in speech. But overuse can get out of hand and lead to sloppy writing. When you use ellipses, make sure you use them to good effect.

EXERCISE 45.4 Read the following passage. Then assume that the underlined portions have been left out in a reprinting of the passage. Indicate how you would use ellipses to indicate those deletions. Example:

Saving money is difficult ~~for young people in entry-level positions~~ but it is important.

Should people <u>who are just getting started in their careers</u> think about saving for retirement? Those who begin to save in their twenties <u>are making a wise financial decision. They</u> are putting away money that can earn compound interest for decades. Even if they save only a hundred dollars a month, and even if they stop saving when they hit age thirty-five, the total forty years later will be impressive. On the other hand, people who wait until they are fifty to begin saving will have far less money put aside at the age of sixty-five.

46 **Capital Letters**

Capital letters are a key signal in everyday life. Look around any store to see their importance: you can shop for Levi's or *any* blue jeans, for Pepsi or *any* cola, for Kleenex or *any* tissue. In each of these instances, the capital letter indicates the name of a particular brand.

46a **Capitalizing the first word of a sentence**

With very few exceptions, capitalize the first word of a sentence. If you are quoting a full sentence, capitalize its first word.

▶ **President John F. Kennedy said, "Let us never negotiate out of fear."**

Capitalization of a nonquoted sentence following a colon is optional.

▶ **Gould cites the work of Darwin: The [*or* the] theory of natural selection incorporates the principle of evolutionary ties among all animals.**

Capitalize a sentence within parentheses unless the parenthetical sentence is inserted into another sentence.

▶ **Gould cites the work of Darwin. (Other researchers cite more recent evolutionary theorists.)**

▶ **Gould cites the work of Darwin (see p. 150).**

When citing poetry, follow the capitalization of the original poem. Though most poets capitalize the first word of each line in a poem, some do not.

▶ **Morning sun heats up the young beech tree**
leaves and almost lights them into fireflies

—June Jordan, "Aftermath"

46b Capitalizing proper nouns and proper adjectives

Capitalize proper **nouns** (those naming specific persons, places, and things) and most **adjectives** formed from proper nouns. All other nouns are common nouns and are not capitalized unless they are used as part of a proper noun: *a street*, but *Elm Street*.

Capitalized nouns and adjectives include personal names; nations, nationalities, and languages; months, days of the week, and holidays (but not seasons of the year); geographical names; structures and monuments; ships, trains, aircraft, and spacecraft; organizations, businesses, and government institutions; academic institutions and courses; historical events and eras; and religions, with their deities, followers, and sacred writings. For trade names, follow the capitalization you see in company advertising or on the product itself.

PROPER	COMMON
Ryan Coogler	a director
Brazil, Brazilian	a nation, a language
Pacific Ocean	an ocean
Environmental Protection Agency	a federal agency
Political Science 102	a political science course
the Qur'an	a holy book
Catholicism	a religion
Cheerios, iPhone	cereal, a smartphone
Halloween	a holiday in the fall

46c Capitalizing titles before proper names

When used alone or following a proper name, most titles are not capitalized. One common exception is the word *president*, which many writers capitalize whenever it refers to the President of the United States.

Professor Gordon Chang	my history professor
Dr. Teresa Ramirez	Teresa Ramirez, our doctor

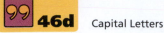

46d Capitalizing titles of works

Capitalize most words in titles of books, articles, speeches, stories, essays, plays, poems, documents, films, paintings, and musical compositions. Do not capitalize articles (*a*, *an*, *the*), **prepositions**, **conjunctions**, and the *to* in an **infinitive** unless they are the first or last words in a title or subtitle.

Walt Whitman: A Life	Declaration of Independence
Black Is King	"Letter from Birmingham Jail"
"I Just Wanna Love U"	*The Living Dead*

46e Revising unnecessary capitalization

Capitalize compass directions only if the word designates a specific geographical region.

► John Muir headed west, motivated by the desire to explore.

► Water rights are an increasingly contentious issue in the West.

Capitalize family relationships only if the word is used as part of a name or as a substitute for the name.

► When she was a child, my mother shared a room with my aunt.

► I could always tell when Mother was annoyed with Aunt Rose.

EXERCISE 46.1 Capitalize words as needed in each of the following sentences. Example:

>   T S E   T W L   F   F
> t. s. eliot, who wrote *the waste land*, was an editor at faber and faber.

1. the late chadwick boseman, star of *marshall* and *black panther*, was born in 1977 in south carolina.

2. the battle of lexington and concord was fought in april 1775.

3. i will cite the novels of julia alvarez, in particular *in the time of butterflies.*

4. i wondered if my new levi's were faded enough.

5. We drove east over the east river on the williamsburg bridge.

47 Abbreviations and Numbers

Anytime you look up an address, you see an abundance of abbreviations and numbers, as in the following listing from a Google map:

Tarrytown Music Hall   13 Main St   Tarrytown, NY

Abbreviations and numbers allow writers to present detailed information in a small amount of space.

47a Using abbreviations

Certain titles are normally abbreviated.

Ms. Lisa Ede   Henry Louis Gates Jr.
Mr. Mark Otuteye   Afsoon Foorohar, MD

Religious, academic, and government titles should be spelled out in academic writing but can be abbreviated in other writing when they appear before a full name.

Rev. Fleming Rutledge   Reverend Rutledge
Prof. Jaime Mejía   Professor Mejía
Sen. Tammy Duckworth   Senator Duckworth

Business, government, and science terms   As long as you can be sure your readers will understand them, use common abbreviations such as *PBS*, *NASA*, and *DNA*. If an abbreviation may be unfamiliar, spell out the full term the first time you use it, and give the abbreviation in parentheses; after that, you can use the abbreviation by itself. Use abbreviations such as *Co.*, *Inc.*, *Corp.*, and *&* only if they are part of a company's official name.

▶ The Comprehensive Test Ban (CTB) Treaty was first proposed in the 1950s. For those nations signing it, the CTB would bring to a halt all nuclear weapons testing.

▶ Years ago, Sears, Roebuck & Co. was the only large ~~corp.~~ in town.
                                                        corporation
                                                        ^

With numbers The following abbreviations are acceptable with specific years and times:

399 BCE ("before the Common Era")

49 CE ("Common Era")

11:15 AM (*or* a.m.)

9:00 PM (*or* p.m.)

Symbols such as % and $ are acceptable with figures (*$11*) in academic writing, but not with words (*eleven dollars*). Units of measurement can be abbreviated in charts and graphs (*4 in.*) but not in the body of a paper (*four inches*).

In notes and source citations Some Latin abbreviations required in notes and in source citations are not appropriate in the body of a paper.

cf.	compare (*confer*)
e.g.	for example (*exempli gratia*)
et al.	and others (*et alii/et aliae*)
etc.	and so forth (*et cetera*)
i.e.	that is (*id est*)
N.B.	note well (*nota bene*)

In addition, except in notes and source citations, do not abbreviate such terms as *chapter*, *page*, and *volume* or the names of months, states, cities, or countries. Two exceptions are *Washington, D.C.*, and *U.S.* The latter abbreviation is acceptable as an **adjective** but not as a **noun**: *U.S. borders* but *in the United States*.

EXERCISE 47.1 Revise each of the following sentences to eliminate any abbreviations that would be inappropriate in academic writing. If a sentence is correct, write *Correct*. Example:

> international
> The ~~intl.~~ sport of belt sander racing began in a hardware store.
> ^

1. Nielson Hardware in Point Roberts, WA, was the site of the world's first belt sander race in 1989.

2. The power tools are placed on a thirty-ft. track and plugged in; the sander to reach the end first wins.

3. Today, the International Belt Sander Drag Race Association (IBSDRA) sponsors tours of winning sanders, an international championship, and a website that sells IBSDRA T-shirts.

4. An average race lasts two seconds, but the world champion modified sander raced the track in 1.52 secs.

5. The fastest sanders run on very coarse sandpaper—a no. sixteen grit is an excellent choice if it's available.

47b Using numbers

If you can write out a number in one or two words, do so. Use figures for longer numbers.

▶ The petition was ignored by ~~38~~ people.
  thirty-eight

▶ A baseball is held together by ~~two hundred sixteen~~ red stitches.
  216

If one of several numbers *of the same kind* in the same sentence requires a figure, you should use figures for all the numbers in that sentence.

▶ A starter audio system can range in cost from ~~one hundred dollars~~ to $2,599.
  $100

When a sentence begins with a number, either spell out the number or rewrite the sentence.

▶ 119 years of CIA labor ~~cost taxpayers sixteen million dollars.~~
  Taxpayers spent sixteen million dollars for

In general, use figures for the following:

ADDRESSES	23 Main Street; 175 Fifth Avenue
DATES	September 11, 2001; 30 August 2007; 4 BCE; the 1860s
DECIMALS AND FRACTIONS	65.34; 8½
EXACT AMOUNTS OF MONEY	$7,348; $1.46 trillion; $2.50; thirty-five (*or* 35) cents
PERCENTAGES	77 percent (*or* 77%)
SCORES AND STATISTICS	an 8–3 Red Sox victory; an average age of 22
TIME OF DAY	6:00 AM (*or* a.m.)

| EXERCISE 47.2 | Revise the numbers in the following sentences as necessary for correctness and consistency. If a sentence is correct, write |

Correct. Example:

>   365
> There are ~~three hundred sixty-five~~ days in a year, except for leap
>   ^   366
> years, which have ~~three hundred sixty-six~~ days.
>   ^

1. *The Simpsons* has been on the air for more than 28 seasons, making it the longest-running prime-time series ever in American television.

2. After 4 years of college, I expect to graduate on May ten, 2024.

3. The hotel is located at three-zero-one Dauphin Street, New Orleans, Louisiana.

4. The last time she checked, Kira had 3,457 followers on Instagram; I have only eighty-two, and I like it that way!

5. 248 new members joined the public radio station during this year's pledge drive, compared with just 92 new members last year.

48   Italics and Hyphens

Italics and hyphens are useful in clarifying meaning. In the sentence "Many people read *People* on the subway every day," the italics (and the capital letter) make it clear to us that *People* is a publication. And in the sentence "Transactions in a web-enabled environment are secure," the hyphen makes it clear that "enabled" is not the verb in the sentence.

48a   Italicizing titles

In general, use italics for titles and subtitles of long works; use quotation marks for shorter works.

| **BOOKS** | *March* |
| **FILMS AND VIDEOS** | *Parasite* |

LONG MUSICAL WORKS	*Metropolis: Suite 1*
LONG POEMS	*Bhagavad Gita*
MAGAZINES AND JOURNALS	*Ebony; Journal of Media Ethics*
NEWSPAPERS	the Cleveland *Plain Dealer*
PAINTINGS AND SCULPTURE	Kehinde Wiley's *Hunger*
PODCASTS	Michael Barbaro's *The Daily*
PLAYS	*West Side Story*
RADIO SERIES	*Marketplace*
ALBUM-LENGTH RECORDINGS	Kendrick Lamar's *Damn*
SOFTWARE	*Quicken*
TELEVISION SERIES	*GLOW*

Do not italicize titles of sacred books, such as the Bible and the Qur'an; public documents, such as the Constitution and the Magna Carta; or your own papers.

48b Italicizing words, letters, and numbers used as terms

▶ On the back of LeBron James's jersey was the famous *23*.

▶ One characteristic of some New York speech is the absence of postvocalic *r*—for example, pronouncing the word *four* as "fouh."

48c Italicizing non-English words

Italicize words from other languages unless they have become part of English—like the Italian "pasta," for example. If a word is in an English dictionary, it does not need italics.

▶ At last one of the phantom sleighs gliding along the street would come to a stop, and with gawky haste Mr. Burness in his fox-furred *shapka* would make for our door.

—Vladimir Nabokov, *Speak, Memory*

48d Using italics for emphasis

Italics can help create emphasis in writing, but it is usually better to do so with sentence structure and word choice.

▶ Great literature and a class of literate readers are nothing new in India. What is new is the emergence of a gifted generation of Indian writers *working in English.* —Salman Rushdie

EXERCISE 48.1 In each of the following sentences, underline any words that should be italicized, and circle any italicized words that should not be. If a title requires quotation marks instead of italicization, add them. Example:

The (United States) still abounds with regional speech—for example, many people in the Appalachians still use local words such as <u>crick</u> and <u>holler</u>.

1. *Regionalism*, a nineteenth-century literary movement, focused on the language and customs of people in areas of the country not yet affected by industrialization.

2. Regional writers produced some American classics, such as Mark Twain's Huckleberry Finn and James Fenimore Cooper's Last of the Mohicans.

3. Twain, not an admirer of Cooper's work, wrote a scathing essay about his predecessor called *The Literary Offenses of James Fenimore Cooper.*

4. Some of the most prolific regional writers were women like Kate Chopin, who wrote her first collection of short stories, Bayou Folk, to help support her family.

5. The stories in *Bayou Folk*, such as the famous *Désirée's Baby*, focus on the natives of rural Louisiana.

48e Using hyphens with compound words

Compound nouns Some are one word (*rowboat*), some are separate words (*hard drive*), and some require hyphens (*sister-in-law*). You should consult a dictionary to be sure.

Compound adjectives Hyphenate most compound **adjectives** that precede a noun, but not those that follow a noun.

a *well-liked* boss   My boss is *well liked.*

Never hyphenate an -ly adverb and an adjective.

▶ They used a widely/distributed mailing list.

Fractions and compound numbers   Use a hyphen to write out fractions and to spell out compound numbers from twenty-one to ninety-nine.

one-seventh   fifty-four thousand

48f   Avoiding unnecessary hyphens

Do not hyphenate the parts of a two-word verb such as *depend on*, *turn off*, or *tune out* (37b).

▶ Each player must pick/up a medical form before tryouts.

The words *pick up* act as a verb and should not be hyphenated.

Be sure that the two words indeed function as a verb in the sentence; if they function as an adjective, a hyphen may be needed.

▶ Let's sign up for the early class.
▶ Where is the sign-up sheet?

The adjective *sign-up*, which modifies the noun *sheet*, needs a hyphen.

Do not hyphenate a subject complement—a word group that follows a **linking verb** and describes the subject.

▶ Audrey is almost seventeen years old.

| EXERCISE 48.2 | Insert hyphens as needed. A dictionary will help you with some of these items. If an item does not require a hyphen, write *Correct*. Example: |

full‑bodied wine
   ^

1. a thirty nine year old woman
2. a long time customer
3. his father in law
4. devil may care attitude
5. widely known poet

Glossary of Usage

Conventions of usage are not carved in stone; rather, they vary from time to time and culture to culture. Like other language choices you must make, matters of usage depend on what your purpose is and on what is appropriate for a particular audience at a particular time.

a, an Use *a* with a word that begins with a consonant (*a book*), a consonant sound such as "y" or "w" (*a euphoric moment, a one-sided match*), or a sounded *h* (*a hemisphere*). Use *an* with a word that begins with a vowel (*an umbrella*), a vowel sound (*an X-ray*), or a silent *h* (*an honor*).

accept, except The verb *accept* means "receive" or "agree to." *Except* is usually a preposition that means "aside from" or "excluding." *All the plaintiffs except Mr. Kim decided to accept the settlement.*

advice, advise The noun *advice* means "opinion" or "suggestion"; the verb *advise* means "offer advice." *Doctors advise everyone to get vaccinated, but some people ignore the advice.*

affect, effect As a verb, *affect* means "influence" or "move the emotions of"; as a noun, it means "emotions" or "feelings." *Effect* is a noun meaning "result"; less commonly, it is a verb meaning "bring about." *The storm affected a large area. Its effects included widespread power failures. The drug effected a major change in the patient's affect.*

all ready, already *All ready* means "fully prepared." *Already* means "previously." *We were all ready for Lucy's party when we learned that she had already left.*

all right, alright Avoid the spelling *alright*.

all together, altogether *All together* means "all in a group" or "gathered in one place." *Altogether* means "completely" or "everything considered." *When the board members were all together, their mutual distrust was altogether obvious.*

allude, elude *Allude* means "refer indirectly." *Elude* means "avoid" or "escape from." *The candidate did not even allude to her opponent. The suspect eluded the police for several days.*

allusion, illusion An *allusion* is an indirect reference. An *illusion* is a false or misleading appearance. *The speaker's allusion to the Bible created an illusion of piety.*

395

a lot Avoid the spelling *alot*.

already See *all ready, already*.

alright See *all right, alright*.

altogether See *all together, altogether*.

among, between In referring to two things or people, use *between*. In referring to three or more, use *among*. *The relationship between the twins is different from that among the other three children.*

amount, number Use *amount* with quantities you cannot count; use *number* for quantities you can count. *A small number of volunteers cleared a large amount of brush.*

an See *a, an*.

and/or Avoid this term except in business or legal writing. Instead of *fat and/or protein*, write *fat, protein, or both*.

any body, anybody, any one, anyone *Anybody* and *anyone* are pronouns meaning "any person." *Anyone* [or *anybody*] *would enjoy this film*. *Any body* is an adjective modifying a noun. *Any body of water has its own ecology*. *Any one* is two adjectives or a pronoun modified by an adjective. *Customers could buy only two sale items at any one time*. *The winner could choose any one of the prizes*.

anyway, anyways In writing, use *anyway*, not *anyways*.

as, as if, like In academic and professional writing, use *as* or *as if* instead of *like* to introduce a clause. *The dog howled as if* [not *like*] *it were in pain*. *She did as* [not *like*] *I suggested*.

assure, ensure, insure *Assure* means "convince" or "promise"; its direct object is usually a person or persons. *She assured voters she would not raise taxes*. *Ensure* and *insure* both mean "make certain," but *insure* usually refers specifically to protection against financial loss. *When the city rationed water to ensure that the supply would last, the Browns could no longer afford to insure their car-wash business*.

as to Do not use *as to* as a substitute for *about*. *Karen was unsure about* [not *as to*] *Bruce's intentions*.

at, where See *where*.

awhile, a while Always use *a while* after a preposition such as *for, in,* or *after*. *We drove awhile and then stopped for a while*.

bad, badly Use *bad* after a linking verb such as *be, feel,* or *seem.* Use *badly* to modify an action verb, an adjective, or another verb. *The server felt <u>bad</u> because the dinner was <u>badly</u> prepared.*

beside, besides *Beside* is a preposition meaning "next to." *Besides* can be a preposition meaning "other than" or an adverb meaning "in addition." *No one <u>besides</u> Francesca would sit <u>beside</u> the barking dog.*

between See *among, between.*

can, may *Can* refers to ability and *may* to possibility or permission. *Since I <u>can</u> sing gospel music, I <u>may</u> be chosen as a soloist.*

compare to, compare with *Compare to* means "regard as similar." *Jamie <u>compared</u> the loss <u>to</u> a heartbreak. Compare with* means "examine to find differences or similarities." *<u>Compare</u> Spike Lee's films <u>with</u> Jordan Peele's.*

complement, compliment *Complement* means "go well with." *Compliment* means "praise." *Guests <u>complimented</u> her on how her earrings <u>complemented</u> her gown.*

comprise, compose *Comprise* means "contain." *Compose* means "make up." *The class <u>comprises</u> twenty students. Twenty students <u>compose</u> the class.*

conscience, conscious *Conscience* means "a sense of right and wrong." *Conscious* means "awake" or "aware." *Lisa was <u>conscious</u> of a guilty <u>conscience</u>.*

consequently, subsequently *Consequently* means "as a result"; *subsequently* means "then." *He quit, and <u>subsequently</u> his wife lost her job; <u>consequently</u>, they had to sell their house.*

continual, continuous *Continual* means "repeated at regular or frequent intervals." *Continuous* means "continuing or connected without a break." *The damage done by <u>continuous</u> erosion was increased by the <u>continual</u> storms.*

could of *Have,* not *of,* should follow *could, would, should,* or *might. We could <u>have</u>* [not *of*] *invited them.*

criteria, criterion *Criterion* means "standard of judgment" or "necessary qualification." *Criteria* is the plural form. *Image is the wrong <u>criterion</u> for choosing a president.*

data *Data* is the plural form of the Latin word *datum,* meaning "fact." Although *data* is used informally as either singular or plural, in academic or professional writing, treat *data* as plural. *These data indicate that fewer people are testing positive for COVID-19.*

different from, different than *Different from* is generally preferred in academic and professional writing, although both of these phrases are widely used. *Her lab results were no different from [not than] his.*

disinterested, uninterested *Disinterested* means "unbiased." *Uninterested* means "indifferent." *Finding disinterested jurors was difficult. She was uninterested in the verdict.*

distinct, distinctive *Distinct* means "separate" or "well defined." *Distinctive* means "characteristic." *Germany includes many distinct regions, each with a distinctive accent.*

doesn't, don't *Doesn't* is the contraction for *does not.* Use it with *he, she, it,* and singular nouns. *Don't* stands for *do not;* use it with *I, you, we, they,* and plural nouns.

each other, one another Use *each other* in sentences involving two subjects and *one another* in sentences involving more than two.

effect See *affect, effect.*

elude See *allude, elude.*

emigrate from, immigrate to *Emigrate from* means "move away from one's country." *Immigrate to* means "move to another country." *We emigrated from Brazil in 1999. We immigrated to the United States.*

ensure See *assure, ensure, insure.*

every day, everyday *Everyday* is an adjective meaning "ordinary." *Every day* is an adjective and a noun, meaning "each day." *I wore everyday clothes almost every day.*

every one, everyone *Everyone* is a pronoun. *Every one* is an adjective and a pronoun, referring to each member of a group. *Because he began after everyone else, David could not finish every one of the problems.*

except See *accept, except.*

explicit, implicit *Explicit* means "directly or openly expressed." *Implicit* means "indirectly expressed or implied." *The explicit* *message of the ad urged consumers to buy the product, while the* **implicit** *message promised popularity if they did so.*

farther, further *Farther* refers to physical distance. *How much* **farther** *is it to Munich? Further* refers to time or degree. *I want to avoid* **further** *delays.*

fewer, less Use *fewer* with nouns that can be counted. Use *less* with general amounts that you cannot count. *The world needs* **fewer** *bombs and* **less** *hostility.*

firstly, secondly, etc. *First, second,* etc., are more common in U.S. English.

former, latter *Former* refers to the first and *latter* to the second of two things previously mentioned. *Kathy and Ana are athletes; the* **former** *plays tennis, and the* **latter** *runs.*

further See *farther, further.*

good, well *Good* is an adjective and should not be used as a substitute for the adverb *well. Gabriel is a* **good** *host who cooks* **well***.*

hanged, hung *Hanged* refers to executions; *hung* is used for all other meanings.

herself, himself, myself, yourself In general, do not use these reflexive pronouns as subjects or as objects. *Jane and I* [not *myself*] *agree. They invited John and me* [not *myself*].

hopefully *Hopefully* is often used informally to mean "it is hoped," but its formal meaning is "with hope." *Sam watched the roulette wheel* **hopefully** [not *Hopefully, Sam will win*].

hung See *hanged, hung.*

illusion See *allusion, illusion.*

immigrate to See *emigrate from, immigrate to.*

implicit See *explicit, implicit.*

imply, infer To *imply* is to suggest indirectly. To *infer* is to guess or conclude on the basis of indirect suggestion. *The note* **implied** *they were planning a small wedding; we* **inferred** *we would not be invited.*

inside of, outside of Use *inside* and *outside* instead. *The class regularly met* **outside** [not *outside of*] *the building.*

insure See *assure, ensure, insure.*

irregardless, regardless *Irregardless* is a double negative. Use *regardless*.

is when, is where These vague expressions are often incorrectly used in definitions. *Schizophrenia is a psychotic condition in which* [not *is when* or *is where*] *a person withdraws from reality.*

its, it's *Its* is the possessive form of *it. It's* is a contraction for *it is* or *it has. It's important to observe the rat before it eats its meal.*

know, no Use *know* to mean "understand." *No* is the opposite of *yes*.

later, latter *Later* means "after some time." *Latter* refers to the second of two items named. *Juan and Chad won all their early matches, but the latter was injured later in the season.*

latter See *former, latter* and *later, latter*.

lay, lie *Lay* means "place" or "put." Its main forms are *lay, laid, laid*. It generally has a direct object, specifying what has been placed. *She laid her books on the desk. Lie* means "recline" or "be positioned" and does not take a direct object. Its main forms are *lie, lay, lain. She lay awake until two.*

leave, let *Leave* means "go away." *Let* means "allow." *Leave alone* and *let alone* are interchangeable. *Let me leave now, and leave* [or *let*] *me alone from now on!*

less See *fewer, less*.

let See *leave, let*.

lie See *lay, lie*.

like See *as, as if, like*.

literally *Literally* means "actually" or "exactly as stated." Use it to stress the truth of a statement that might otherwise be understood as figurative. Do not use *literally* as an intensifier in a figurative statement. *Mirna was literally at the edge of her seat* may be accurate, but *Mirna is so hungry that she could literally eat a horse* is not.

loose, lose *Lose* is a verb meaning "misplace." *Loose* is an adjective that means "not securely attached." *Sew on that loose button before you lose it.*

lots, lots of Avoid these informal expressions meaning "much" or "many" in academic or professional discourse.

may See *can, may*.

may be, maybe *May be* is a verb phrase. *Maybe* is an adverb that means "perhaps." *He may be the head of the organization, but maybe someone else would handle a crisis better.*

might of See *could of.*

moral, morale A *moral* is a succinct lesson. *The moral of the story is that generosity is rewarded. Morale* means "spirit" or "mood." *Campus morale was low.*

myself See *herself, himself, myself, yourself.*

no See *know, no.*

nor, or Use *either* with *or* and *neither* with *nor.*

number See *amount, number.*

off, of Use *off* without *of.* *The spaghetti slipped off* [not *off of*] *the plate.*

one another See *each other, one another.*

or See *nor, or.*

outside of See *inside of, outside of.*

passed, past Use *passed* to mean "went by" or "received a passing grade." *The marching band passed the reviewing stand.* Use *past* to refer to a time before the present. *Historians study the past.*

per In formal writing, use the Latin *per* only in standard technical phrases such as *miles per hour.* Otherwise, find English equivalents. *As mentioned in* [not *As per*] *the latest report, food insecurity among college students is at an all-time high.*

percent, percentage Use *percent* with a specific number; use *percentage* with an adjective such as *large* or *small.* *Last year, 80 percent of the members were female. A large percentage of the members are women.*

precede, proceed *Precede* means "come before"; *proceed* means "go forward." *Despite the storm that preceded the ceremony, the wedding proceeded on schedule.*

principal, principle When used as a noun, *principal* refers to a head official or an amount of money; when used as an adjective, it means "most significant." *Principle* means "fundamental law or belief." *Albert went to the principal and defended himself with the principle of free speech.*

proceed See *precede, proceed.*

quotation, quote *Quote* is a verb, and *quotation* is a noun. *He quoted the president, and the quotation [not quote] was preserved in history books.*

raise, rise *Raise* means "lift" or "move upward." (Referring to children, it means "bring up.") It takes a direct object; someone raises something. *The guests raised their glasses to toast. Rise* means "go upward." It does not take a direct object; something rises by itself. *She saw the steam rise from the pan.*

real, really *Real* is an adjective, and *really* is an adverb. Do not substitute *real* for *really*. In academic and professional writing, do not use *real* or *really* to mean "very." *The old man walked very [not real or really] slowly.*

reason is because Use either *the reason is that* or *because*—not both. *The reason the copier stopped is that [not is because] the paper jammed.*

reason why Avoid this expression in formal writing. *The reason [not reason why] this book is short is market demand.*

regardless See *irregardless, regardless*.

respectfully, respectively *Respectfully* means "with respect." *Respectively* means "in the order given." *Zara and Felix are, respectively, a juggler and an acrobat. The children treated their grandparents respectfully.*

rise See *raise, rise*.

set, sit *Set* usually means "put" or "place" and takes a direct object. *Sit* refers to taking a seat and does not take an object. *Set your cup on the table, and sit down.*

should of See *could of*.

since Be careful not to use *since* ambiguously. In *Since I broke my leg, I've stayed home*, the word *since* might be understood to mean either "because" or "ever since."

sit See *set, sit*.

so In academic and professional writing, avoid using *so* alone to mean "very." Instead, follow *so* with *that* to show how the intensified condition leads to a result. *Aaron was so tired that he fell asleep at the wheel.*

some time, sometime, sometimes *Some time* refers to a length of time. *Please leave me* <u>some time</u> *to dress. Sometime* means "at some indefinite later time." <u>Sometime</u> *I will take you to London. Sometimes* means "occasionally." <u>Sometimes</u> *I eat sushi.*

subsequently See *consequently, subsequently.*

supposed to, used to Be careful to include the final -*d* in these expressions. *He is* <u>supposed to</u> *attend.*

sure, surely Avoid using *sure* as an intensifier. Instead, use *certainly. I was* <u>certainly</u> *glad to see you.*

than, then Use *than* in comparative statements. *The cat was bigger* <u>than</u> *the dog.* Use *then* when referring to a sequence of events. *I won, and* <u>then</u> *I cried.*

that, which A clause beginning with *that* singles out the item being described. *The book* <u>that</u> *is on the table is a good one* specifies the book on the table as opposed to some other book. A clause beginning with *which* may or may not single out the item, although some writers use *which* clauses only to add more information about an item being described. *The book,* <u>which</u> *is on the table, is a good one* contains a *which* clause between the commas. The clause simply adds extra, nonessential information about the book; it does not specify which book.

then See *than, then.*

they, them The pronouns *they* and *them* have traditionally been used to refer to plural antecedents. However, when the gender of a singular antecedent is not known or is nonspecific, *they* or *them* is an acceptable and appropriate choice over singular pronouns such as *him* or *her* or combinations such as *he or she* and *his or her. Someone left* <u>their</u> *jacket on the bus.* Also, an individual may choose *they/them/their* as pronouns for themself. *Lise was prepared for the speech, but* <u>they</u> *looked nervous when the cameras turned on.*

thorough, threw, through *Thorough* means "complete." *After a* <u>thorough</u> *inspection, the restaurant reopened. Threw* is the past tense of *throw,* and *through* means "in one side and out the other." *He* <u>threw</u> *the ball* <u>through</u> *a window.*

to, too, two *To* generally shows direction. *Too* means "also." *Two* is a number. *We, too, are going to the meeting in two hours.* Avoid using *to* after *where*. *Where are you flying* [not *flying to*]?

two See *to, too, two.*

uninterested See *disinterested, uninterested.*

unique Some people argue that *unique* means "one and only" and object to usage that suggests it means merely "unusual." In formal writing, avoid constructions such as *quite unique.*

used to See *supposed to, used to.*

very Avoid using *very* to intensify a weak adjective or adverb; instead, replace the adjective or adverb with a stronger, more precise, or more colorful word. Instead of *very nice*, for example, use *kind, warm, sensitive, endearing,* or *friendly.*

well See *good, well.*

where In formal writing, use *where* alone, not with words such as *at* and *to*. *Where are you going* [not *going to*]?

which See *that, which.*

who, whom In formal writing, use *who* if the word is the subject of the clause and *whom* if the word is the object of the clause. *Monica, who lives in Tucson, is my godmother.* (*Who* is the subject of the clause; the verb is *lives.*) *Monica, whom I saw last winter, lives in Tucson.* (*Whom* is the object of the verb *saw.*) Because *whom* can seem excessively formal, some writers rephrase sentences to avoid it.

who's, whose *Who's* is a contraction for *who is* or *who has.* *Who's on the patio? Whose* is a possessive form. *Whose sculpture is in the garden? Whose is on the patio?*

would of See *could of.*

your, you're *Your* shows possession. *Bring your sleeping bag along. You're* is the contraction for *you are. You're in the wrong sleeping bag.*

yourself See *herself, himself, myself, yourself.*

Index

with Glossary of Terms

Words in **blue** are followed by a definition. **Boldface** terms in definitions are themselves defined elsewhere in this index.

A

a, an, 315, 316–17, 395, 396
abbreviations, 368, 387–89
abilities and disabilities, 259–60
"about" page, evaluating, 98, 102
absolute concepts, 329
abstract
  citing
    in APA style, 195
    in CSE style, 235, 240
  evaluating, 104
abstract language, 273
Academic Search Premier, 126, 148
academic writing
  active, respectful reading and listening, 5–6
  authority in, 4
  claim, 5
  design decisions, 17, 18, 19–20
  directness and clarity, 5
  editing, Twenty Tips for, 27–36
  expectations for, 4, 67–69
  genres of, 67–80
  rhetorical analysis, 48–51
  sharing and reflecting, 38–40
  standardized English for, 262–65
  subjunctive mood, 310
  thesis, 5
  who, whom, 404

writer positioned for, 3–6
  See also writing projects
accept, except, 395
accessibility of presentations, 259–60
acknowledgments of sources, 117
active listening, 5–6

active voice, 289, 294 The form of a **verb** when the **subject** performs the action: *Lata sang the chorus.* Contrast with **passive voice**.

  for conciseness, 289
  passive voice vs., 289, 302
  shifts to passive voice, 294, 302
AD, CE, 388
addresses and place names
  abbreviations, 362, 363
  commas for, 345
  numbers in, 363

adjective, 35, 325–29, 357, 388, 393 A word that modifies, quantifies, identifies, or describes a **noun** or words acting as a noun.

  abbreviation as, 388
  absolute concepts, 329
  after linking verb, 326–28
  capitalization, 32, 385
  clause, commas with, 345
  comparatives and superlatives, 328–29
  compound, 33, 371
  coordinate, 360
  hyphens with, 35, 392
  place names, abbreviated, 363
  with plural nouns, 327
  proper, 32, 385
  See also modifier

adverb, 325–29, 346 A word that qualifies, modifies, limits, or defines a **verb**, an **adjective**, another adverb, or a **clause**, frequently answering the question *where? when? how? why? to what extent?* or *under what conditions?*

absolute concepts, 329
after linking verbs, 326–28
clause, commas with, 345
comparatives and superlatives, 328–29
conjunctive, 346, 361, 365
hyphens with, 392
See also modifier
adverbial particle, 344
advertisements, citing
in APA style, 201
in MLA style, 160
advice, advise, 395
affect, effect, 395
afterwords, citing
in *Chicago* style, 220
in MLA style, 144

agreement, 319 The correspondence between a **pronoun** and its **antecedent** in **person**, number, and gender (*Mr. Fox and his sister*) or between a **verb** and its **subject** in person and number (*She and Moe are friends*).

pronoun-antecedent, 34–35, 333, 339
subject-verb, 319–21
alignment, in design, 18
all. See indefinite pronoun
all ready, already, 395
all right, alright, 395
all together, altogether, 395
allude, elude, 395
allusion, illusion, 395
along with, 319
a lot, 396
already, all ready, 395
alright, all right, 395

alternative ("alt") text, 259
altogether, all together, 395
AM, a.m., 388
AmericanPressInstitute.org
(fact-checker site), 97
American Psychological Association
(APA) style. *See* APA style
Americans with Disabilities Act,
259
among, between, 396
amount, number, 396
an, a, 315, 316, 395, 396
analogies, 57, 274
analysis, 7–9, 47–48. *See also*
critical reading and listening;
evaluating sources; synthesis
and, 283, 322. *See also* coordinating
conjunctions
and/or, 396
Angelou, Maya, 284–85, 383
annotated bibliography, 111–12.
See also working bibliography
annotating, 45–46, 111

antecedent, 30, 323, 333, 338 The **noun** or noun **phrase** that a **pronoun** replaces.

agreement with pronouns, 34, 323, 339
agreement with verbs, 323–24
ambiguous, 340
collective-noun, 338
compound, 338
implied, 341
indefinite pronoun, 34, 339
pronoun reference to, 30, 333, 340–41
anthologies, works in, citing
in *Chicago* style, 220
in MLA style, 133, 142
any. See indefinite pronoun
any, some, 315
any body, anybody, any one, anyone, 396
anyway, anyways, 396

Anzaldúa, Gloria, 249, 261

APA style, 115, 174–211 The citation style guidelines issued by the American Psychological Association.

  authors, 179–80, 183, 185–86
  books, 186–89, 197
  combining parts of models, 184
  content notes, 176
  database sources, 174–75
  digital sources, 180–81, 192–98
  format, 176–77
  in-text citations, 175, 177–82,
      183, 378
    list of examples, 178
    parts of, 175
  long quotations, 177, 178, 374
  other sources, 198–201
  parts of citations, 175
  print periodicals, 189–91
  references, 182–201
    formatting, 184
    list of examples, 182–83
    models for, 185–201
    sample, 210–11
  sample student writing, 201–11
  signal phrases in, 115, 177–78, 183
  source maps
    articles from databases, 194
    articles from print periodicals,
      190
    books, 187
    works from websites, 196
  sources without models, 192
  types of sources, 174–75
  understanding, 174–76
  verb tense in, 115, 177, 308
  visuals and media, 177, 181–82,
      197, 199–201
apostrophes, 33, 370–73
appeals, in argument
  emotional, 52, 57, 62
  ethical, 52, 55–56
  identifying, 52–53
  logical, 52–53, 56–57, 63

appositive, 359, 380 A **noun** or noun **phrase** that adds identifying information to a preceding noun or noun phrase: *Zimbardo, an innovative researcher, designed the experiment.*

arguable statements, 55

argument, 51–67 A **text** that makes and supports a **claim**.

  alternative, 56, 58, 61, 63
  appeals, 52–53, 55–57, 62–63
  Classical, 57, 58
  elements of, 53
  evidence in, 53, 55, 56, 252–53
  invitational, 54, 59
  listening and reading purpose-
      fully and openly, 52
  making an, 54–57
  organizing, 57–59
  purpose of writing, 53–54
  Rogerian, 54, 57, 59
  sample student essay, 60–67,
      162–73
  stance and tone, 9
  statements making, 54–55
  thesis or claim, 55, 60–65
  Toulmin, 53, 57
articles (*a, an, the*), 315, 316, 395,
      396
articles from databases
  citing
    in APA style, 174–75, 193–94
    in *Chicago* style, 212–13,
        222–25
    in CSE style, 242
    in MLA style, 148–49
  searching for, 93
articles in periodicals
  capitalizing titles, 386
  citing
    in APA style, 189–91, 192–93
    in *Chicago* style, 221–25
    in CSE style, 240–41, 242
    in MLA style, 145–47, 150

articles in periodicals (*continued*)
 evaluating, 104–5
 online, 92
 popular and scholarly, 91
artwork
 capitalization of titles, 386
 citing
  in *Chicago* style, 230–31
  in MLA style, 159
 italics for titles, 390
as, as if, like, 274, 396
assignments. *See* writing projects
assumptions
 about abilities and disabilities, 259–60
 about gender and pronoun preferences, 255–57
 about race and ethnicity, 257–59
 for arguments, 53, 55
 audience and, 89, 252, 259–60
 in conditional sentences, 312
 cultural, 251
 examining, 9, 252, 254–59
assure, ensure, insure, 396
as to, 396
as well as, 319
attention, 44
attitude. *See* stance
audience
 analyzing, 8–9, 89, 252, 259–60
 appeals to, 52–53, 55–57, 62–63
 expectations of, meeting, 252–53
 informal vs. formal writing for.
  See formal writing; informal writing
 for presentations, 81
 public writing for specific, 72
 for research projects, 89, 117
 sharing and reflecting with, 36
 of sources, 98
 stance and tone for. *See* stance; tone
 varieties of English language, 262–68

audio clips
 citing
  in APA style, 200, 201
  in *Chicago* style, 229–30
  in MLA style, 158
 italics for titles, 389
 as visuals and media, 20, 23, 117. *See also* visuals and media
Austen, Jane, 373
authority
 in academic writing, 4
 in argument, 57
 audience expectations, 252
 in sources, 91, 92, 98, 104
 See also credibility
authors
 citing
  in APA style, 179–80, 183, 185–86
  in *Chicago* style, 218–19
  in CSE style, 237, 238–39, 241
  in MLA style, 125, 129–30, 131–33, 138–40
 credentials, evaluating, 98, 100, 104
auxiliary verb, 300–301. *See also* helping verb
awhile, a while, 396

B
bad, badly, 326, 397
bar and line graphs, 21
base form, 298, 301, 319 The form of a **verb** listed in a dictionary (*go*).
 conditional sentences, 312
 forming auxiliary verbs, 300, 303
 infinitive from *to* with, 303
 present subjunctive with, 311
 -s, -es added to, 319
BC, BCE, 388

been as auxiliary verb, 301
Bell, Martha (student writer), 75,
    201–9
beside, besides, 397
between, among, 396
be verbs
    agreement with subjects, 298,
        319, 325
    as helping verbs, 301
    as irregular verbs, 298, 319
    as linking verbs, 326, 397
    and passive voice, 301, 302
    subjunctive mood, 310
    in varieties of English, 325
    wordiness and, 289
bias, 9, 98, 99, 113
bibliographies
    annotated, 111–12
    in APA style, 182. *See also* APA
        style: references
    in *Chicago* style, 213, 215–31,
        234
    colons in, 381
    evaluating, 104
    as library resources, 94
    in MLA style, 127–28. *See also*
        MLA style: works cited
    research project, 94, 106, 107,
        111–13, 118, 121
    working, 106, 107, 111, 121
block quotations. *See* quotations:
        long
blogs or discussion groups
    citing
        in APA style, 197
        in *Chicago* style, 227
        in MLA style, 155
    low-stakes writing, 42–44
    reflective, 39
    sharing writing, 38
books
    capitalizing titles, 386
    citing
        in APA style, 186–89, 197

    in *Chicago* style, 218–19
    in CSE style, 238–40, 243
    in MLA style, 140–45, 150
    italics for titles, 390
both . . . and, 291. *See also* correla-
        tive conjunctions
brackets, 107, 116, 378–79
brainstorming, 11, 96
brochures, citing. *See* pamphlets,
        citing
Brown, Eugene, 290
Bryan, L.J. (student writer), 60–66
business terms, abbreviations, 387
but, 275. *See also* coordinating
        conjunctions

C

can, may, 397
capitalization, 32, 137, 374, 384
captions for visuals, 20–21, 117,
        129, 135
case, 334 The form of a **noun** or
    pronoun that reflects its grammatical
    role: *He ate* (subjective). *His food
    was cold* (possessive). *I saw him*
    (objective).
catalogs, library, 92–93
CE, AD, 388
cf., compare (*confer*), 388
charts
    citing
        in APA style, 198
        in MLA style, 160
    as visuals or media, 20. *See also*
        visuals and media
checklists
    analyzing and fact-checking
        texts, 47–48
    citing digital sources
        in APA style, 192
        in MLA style, 151
    citing sources without models
        in APA style, 192

checklists (*continued*)
  citing sources without models
    (*continued*)
      in *Chicago* style, 217
      in MLA style, 138
  class blogs, wikis, and forums
    participation, 43
  commas, 355
  drafting, 14
  editing
    for commas, 355
    pronouns, 336
    subject-verb agreement, 322
    Top Twenty Tips, 28
    verbs, 302
  formatting references, 184
  paragraphs, strong, 17
  presentations, 83
  pronouns, 336
  reference models, combining
    parts of, 184
  search techniques, 93
  subject-verb agreement, 322
  Top Twenty Tips for Editing, 28
  U.S. academic writing expecta-
    tions, 4
  verbs, 302
  visuals and media, 23
chemistry lab report, 72–74
Chicago style, 115, 212–34
Citation guidelines based
on *The Chicago Manual of Style*.
  authors, 218–19
  books, 218–21
  digital sources, 212–13, 218–30
  format, 213–16
  in-text citations, 213, 214–15
  notes and bibliographic entries,
    214–31
    formatting, 214–16
    list of examples, 216–17
    models for, 217–31
    parts of, 213
    sample, 233–34
  other sources, 230–31

parts of citations, 213
print and digital periodicals,
  221–25
sample student writing, excerpts
  from, 231–34
signal phrases in, 115, 215
source maps
  articles from databases, 224
  works from websites, 228
sources without models, 217
types of sources, 212–13
understanding, 212–13
verb tense in, 115, 215
visuals and media, 214, 229–31
citation-name format, CSE style,
  236, 237, 238–42
citations. *See* documentation;
  in-text citations
citation-sequence format, CSE
  style, 236, 237, 238–41
claim, 5, 53, 55, 100 An arguable
statement.
clarity
  in academic writing, 5
  of language meaning, 251–52
  necessary words for, 292
class discussion forums, 42, 44
classroom materials, citing in MLA
  style, 161
clause, 34, 310, 313, 332, 345 A
group of words containing a **subject**
and a **predicate**. An **independent
clause** can stand alone as a **sentence**,
while a **dependent clause** must be
attached to an independent clause.
  adjective and adverb, 357–58
  in comma splices, 34, 345–48
  commas with, 29, 33, 346, 347,
    354
  dangling modifier, 332–33
  dashes linking, 347–48
  fragments, 351
  fused sentences, revising, 34,
    345–46
  if clause, 311

introductory elements, 29, 354–55

subjunctive mood, 310

that clause, 311, 355

truths and facts, and present tense, 308

clichés, 274

close reading of poems, 72–80

clustering, 11

coherence, 15–16 Also called "flow," the quality that makes a **text** seem unified.

collaboration, 6, 45

collections, works in, citing in MLA style, 133

collective nouns, 313, 327

colloquial language, 260, 269, 377

colon, 31, 367, 377, 380–81, 384

color
in design, 17, 18
perceptions of, 259
in storyboarding, 14

comics. *See* graphic narratives or comics; web comic

commas, 354–64
with adjective clauses, 345
with adverb clauses, 345
with appositives, 359
with contrasting elements, 361–62
with dates and addresses, 362
in direct address, 361
editing for, 29–36, 355
with independent clauses, 355
with interjections, 361
with introductory elements, 29–30, 354
with items in a series, 32, 359–60, 366
with nonrestrictive elements, 33, 356–59
with parenthetical and transitional expressions, 361, 378
with quotation marks, 31, 376
splices, 34, 345–48

with tag questions, 361
unnecessary, 31–32, 363–64

comma splice, 34, 345–48 An error in formal writing resulting from joining two **independent clauses** with only a comma.

comment on topic
dashes setting off, 377
in paragraph, 15
in thesis statement, 11

common errors. *See* Top Twenty Tips for Editing

common ground, building, 254–59

common knowledge, 117

communication, cross-cultural, 250–53

communities
connecting with, 264
evoking sense of place or, 263
writing across, 250–53

comparative, 328–29 The *-er* or *more* form of an **adjective** or **adverb** used to compare two things (*happier, more quickly*).

compare to, compare with, 397

comparisons, complete, 282–83

complement, compliment, 397

complements. *See* object complements; subject complements

complete sentences, 280

compliment, complement, 397

compose, comprise, 397

compound adjectives, 34–35, 392

compound antecedents, 338

compound constructions, 30, 364

compound nouns, 371, 392

compound numbers, 393

compound predicates, 351, 364

compound sentences, 32–33, 355–56

compound structures
avoiding unneeded commas, 363–64
commas with, 355
and pronouns, 335

compound subjects, 320, 364
compound words, 31, 392
comprise, compose, 397

conciseness, 287–89 Using the fewest possible words to make a point effectively.

of poster message, 78
in sentences, 287–89
in summarizing, 46–47
conclusions
of arguments, 54, 64
planning and drafting, 13, 121
of presentations, 81
of research projects, 121
concrete language, 273
conditional sentences, 312
conference proceedings, citing
in APA style, 199
in CSE style, 240
in MLA style, 161
confirmation bias, 9

conjunction, 386 A word or words joining words, **phrases**, or **clauses**. *See also* **coordinating conjunctions**; **correlative conjunctions**; **subordinating conjunction**

conjunctive adverb, 346, 361, 365 A word (such as *moreover* or *nevertheless*) that modifies an **independent clause** following another independent clause. A conjunctive adverb generally follows a semicolon and is followed by a comma: *Thoreau lived simply at Walden; however, he regularly joined his aunt for tea in Concord.*

connotation, 271
conscience, conscious, 397
consequently, subsequently, 397
consistency, in sentences, 281
containers, in MLA style, 125–26
content notes. *See* endnotes; footnotes

context
for argument, 51–67
correctness dependence on, 27
cultural, 47, 251
discipline as, 67–80
genre appropriate to, 67–80
for presentations, 81–85
reading and listening, 44–51
in research, 89
of sources, MLA style, 124–28
for writing, 42–44, 67–80
See also Language, Culture, and Context; rhetorical situation
continual, continuous, 397
contractions, 372
contrast, in design, 17–18
contrasting elements, commas with, 361
convince, arguing to, 54
coordinate adjectives, 392

coordinating conjunctions, 32, 283, 346, 355, 365 The words *and, but, for, nor, or, so,* and *yet,* which give the same emphasis to both the elements they join: *Restaurants are expensive, so I cook.*

commas unnecessary with, 32, 355
commas with, 33, 355–56
to fix fused sentences, 34, 346
to link clauses, 346
parallel ideas, 291
semicolons with, 366–67
coordination and subordination, 283–87
copyrighted materials, 114, 117. *See also* intellectual property rights
corporate authors. *See* organizations as authors, citing

correlative conjunctions, 32, 291
Paired **conjunctions** (*both . . . and,
either . . . or, neither . . . nor, not
only . . . but also*) used to connect
equivalent elements.

*could of, would of, should of, might
of,* 397
Council of Science Editors (CSE)
style. *See* CSE style
counterarguments, 56
count noun, 314, 316 A **noun**
referring to something that can
be directly counted: *women, trees.*
Contrast with **noncount noun.**

court cases, citing in MLA style, 162
Creative Commons license, 114
credibility, 13, 97, 264, 280. *See
also* evaluating sources
criteria, criterion, 397
critical reading and listening, 5–6,
44–51, 97–100
CSE style, 115, 235–45 The citation
style guidelines issued by the Council
of Science Editors.

authors, 237, 238–39, 241
books, 238–40, 243
digital sources, 241–43
format, 235
in-text citations, 236
periodicals, 240–41, 242
references, 237–43
formatting, 235
list of examples, 238
models for, 238–43
sample, 245
sample student writing,
243–44
signal phrases in, 115–16
cultures
academic writing styles, 5
cultural context, 47, 251
interviews appropriate to, 94
listening to and reading from, 6
"normal" in, 251
openness to, 2
writing across, 250–53
See also Language, Culture, and
Context
currency, of source, 98, 104

D

-d, -ed endings, 298
dangling modifiers, 332–33
Dart, Justin, 79
dashes, 347, 377, 379–80
data, 397
databases, 92, 93–94, 174–75,
212–13. *See also* articles from
databases
dates
commas in, 362
numbers in, 389
of source publication, 98
deadlines
for collaborating, 7
for research projects, 120
defensive reading strategies, 44, 88
definite article, 317, 318
definitions and quotation marks,
373
delivering a presentation, 84
denotation, 271–72
dependent clause, 279, 281, 310,
335, 347, 351, 366 Sometimes
called a "subordinate clause," a
word group that contains a **subject**
and a **predicate** but can't stand alone
as a **sentence** because it begins with
either a **subordinating conjunction**
(*because, although*) or a relative
pronoun (*that, which*).

commas with, 366
fixing clause fragments, 351
fixing comma splices, 347
in sentence openings, 279

dependent clause (*continued*)
subjunctive mood and, 310
subordination of, 284
with *who, whom*, 335
design decisions, 17–23. *See also*
formatting; visuals and media
details, in paragraphs, 15
determiners, 315–16. *See also*
articles
development in paragraph, 15
diagrams, 21
dialects, regional, 261
diction. *See* word choice
dictionary entries, citing in MLA
style, 134
different from, different than, 398
digital and nonprint sources
citing
in APA style, 180–81, 192–98
in *Chicago* style, 212–13,
218–30
in CSE style, 241–43
in MLA style, 131, 148–56
evaluating, 96–113
keeping track of, 106–7
for research projects, 90–91,
96–113
digital object identifier. *See* DOI
(digital object identifier)
direct address, 361
direct discourse, 295
directness, in academic writing, 5
direct questions, 94, 368
direct quotations, 106, 116, 340,
373–77
disabilities and abilities, 259–60
disciplinary style, studying, 68
disciplines, writing in, 67–80
disinterested, uninterested, 398
disruptive modifiers, 331
dissertations, citing
in APA style, 198–99
in MLA style, 161
distinct, distinctive, 398

diversity of audience, 8
documentation
in academic writing, 5, 30
APA style, 117, 174–209
Chicago style, 115, 212–34
complete, 30
considering, 10
CSE style, 115–16, 235–45
MLA style, 115, 124–73
plagiarism, avoiding with, 30, 117
of visuals and media, 20. *See also*
under specific styles
doesn't, don't, 398
DOI (digital object identifier)
in APA style, 192, 193
in *Chicago* style, 222–23
in MLA style, 148, 150, 151
dots. *See* ellipses
double comparatives and
superlatives, 328
doublespeak, 271
drafting, 10–17
checklist for, 14
paragraphs, 15–16
planning and, 13–14
research project, 120–21
working thesis, 11–12

E

each. See determiners; indefinite
pronoun
each other, one another, 398
e-book, citing
in APA style, 197
in *Chicago* style, 219
in MLA style, 150
-ed, -d endings, 298
editing
commas, 28, 29–30, 31–32, 354
pronouns, 336
proofreading and, 25–26, 31,
32, 121–22
subject-verb agreement, 322

Top Twenty Tips, 28–36
verbs, 302
editions other than first, citing
in APA style, 188
in *Chicago* style, 220
in MLA style, 143
editorials or letters to the editor,
citing
in APA style, 191
in MLA style, 147, 152
editors, citing
in APA style, 186, 188
in *Chicago* style, 219–20
in CSE style, 239
in MLA style, 142
effect, affect, 395
e.g. (for example), 388
either . . . or, 291, 401. *See also*
correlative conjunctions
electronic sources. *See* digital and
nonprint sources
ellipses
in APA references, 185
informal writing, 366, 383
in quotations, 107, 116, 377,
382–83
elliptical constructions, 335
elude, allude, 395
emails or messages
citing
in APA style, 180, 197
in *Chicago* style, 229
in MLA style, 156
informal writing, 268
emigrate from, immigrate to, 398
emotional appeals, 52, 57, 62
emphasis
dashes for, 379
double comparatives and
superlatives, 328–29
italics for, 392
quotation marks for, avoiding, 376
sentence structure for, 349
empty words, eliminating, 287–88

encyclopedia entries, citing
in APA style, 188
in MLA style, 134, 144
endnotes
in APA style, 176
in *Chicago* style, 213, 214–15,
217–31, 233
in MLA style, 128
end punctuation, 367–70
English language, varieties of, 260–68
abbreviations in, 387–90
academic expectations, 67–69
African American or Black, 249,
262, 264, 293, 325
editing, 27
evoking place or community, 263
formal vs. informal, 268
forms of *be*, 325
global varieties, 266
identity and, 248–50, 261
illustrating a point, 264–65
language awareness and, 261–62
other languages, bringing in,
265–67
shifts in, 260–68, 293
standardized, 68, 250, 262–65,
268, 293, 368
enough, some, 315
ensure, assure, insure, 396
equal ideas, relating, 283–84
-er, -est ending, 328
errors, common. *See* Top Twenty
Tips for Editing
-es, -s ending, 319
essays. *See* sample student writing
et al. (and others), 388
etc., 388
ethical appeals, 55–56
ethics
argument with, 51–67
research, 88
social media usage, 3
source usage, 114
visuals and media usage, 22–23

euphemisms, 270
evaluating sources, 96–113
  annotated bibliography, 107–9
  for argument, 53
  fact-checking, 97, 99, 100
  keeping track of sources, 106–7
  quoting, paraphrasing, and
    summarizing, 107–10
  reading and analyzing, 100–101
  source maps, 104–5
  synthesizing, 101
every day, everyday, 398
every one, everyone, 398

evidence, 13, 53 Support for an
argument's claim.

  in academic writing, 5, 69
  analysis of, 48, 53, 58, 69
  in argument, 53, 55, 56, 252–53
  audience and, 8
  in the disciplines, 69
  fact-checking, 47–48
  firsthand and secondhand, 53
  gathering and researching, 13,
    55, 106
  in paragraphs, 15–16
  persuasive, 252–53
  planning and drafting, 13–14
  in research projects, 13, 88, 106
  Toulmin argument, 53
  See also sources
except, accept, 395
exclamation points, 369, 376
explanatory notes, in MLA style, 128
explanatory words, in brackets, 378
expletives, 289
explicit, implicit, 398
exploring a topic, 10–11

F
Facebook, 44
FactCheck.org, 97
facts
  fact-checking, 47–48, 88, 97,
    99, 100

and use of gerunds, 304–5
  verb tense with, 308
  widely known, 118
"fair use," 117
fake news, 44, 88
farther, further, 399
faulty predication, 281
a few, many, 315
fewer, less, 399
field research, 94–96, 118
figurative language, 26, 57, 274–75
figures (images). *See* visuals and
  media
figures (numerical). *See* numbers
films
  capitalization of titles, 374
  citing
    in APA style, 201
    in *Chicago* style, 231
    in MLA style, 162
  italics for titles, 390
  See also video clips
firstly, secondly, 399
first person (*I, we, us*), 294
fonts, 19, 26
footnotes
  in APA style, 176
  in *Chicago* style, 213, 214–15,
    217–31, 233
  in MLA style, 128
  numbers of, with quotation
    marks, 376
for, 283. *See also* coordinating
  conjunctions
foreign words/language, 265–68, 391
forewords, citing
  in *Chicago* style, 220
  in MLA style, 144
formal writing
  word choice and, 268–71
  in writing process, 253
formatting
  in APA style, 176–77
    references, 184
  in *Chicago* style, 213–16

in CSE style, 235
for genre, 70
IMRAD organization, 70
in MLA style, 128–29,
     135, 137
for writing projects, 10,
     18–20
former, latter, 399
forums, class discussion, 43, 44

fragment, 36, 281, 349–52 A
group of words that is not a
complete **sentence** but is punctuated
as one. Usually a fragment lacks a
subject, a **verb**, or both, or it is a
dependent clause.

freewriting, 11, 43
further, farther, 399

**fused (run-on) sentence, 34,
345–48** Sometimes called a
"run-on," a **sentence** in which
two **independent clauses** are run
together without a **conjunction** or
punctuation between them: *My dog
barked he woke me up.*

future perfect, 307
future perfect progressive, 307
future progressive, 307

future tense, 307 The **tense** of
a **verb** that indicates an action or
condition has not yet happened:
They will arrive next week.

G
García-Muñiz, Paola (student
     writer), 266
gathering evidence, 13, 55, 106
gender
     gender-related terms, 257–58
     pronoun-antecedent agreement,
          338–40

gender-neutral pronouns, 26, 256
Alternatives to gendered third-
person **pronouns**. For example, *they*
is a gender-neutral pronoun that

refers to plural **antecedents** and can
also be used as an alternative to
he/she in third-person singular.

     agreement with antecedents,
          34–35, 339
     sexist language, 255
generalizations, no article for,
     317–18
general vs. specific language, 273

genre, 10, 70 A form of communication used for a particular purpose
and incorporating certain conventional features. Some common examples include lab reports, researched
essays, brochures, invitations, etc.

     academic writing, 67–80
     considering, 10
     formatting for, 70
     headings in, standard, 19–20
     organization for, 70
     in public writing, 72, 78–80
     sample student writing,
          72–80
     understanding and using, 70

gerund, 304, 334 A verbal form that
ends in *-ing* and functions as a **noun**:
Sleeping is a bore.

     infinitives and, 304–6
     pronouns and possessive case,
          334
good, well, 326, 399
Google Drive, 7, 45
Google Images, 23
Google Scholar, 92
Google searches, 93
Google Slides, 82
government sources
     citing
          in APA style, 179, 198
          in *Chicago* style, 231
          in CSE style, 243
          in MLA style, 134,
               160–61
     for research projects,
          92, 102

government terms, abbreviations
for, 387
grammar
adjectives and adverbs, 326–28
comma splices and fused
sentences, 345–48
modifier placement, 329–33
nouns and noun phrases,
313–17
prepositions and prepositional
phrases, 342–45
pronouns, 333–41
sentence fragments, 349–52
subject-verb agreement, 319–25
verbs and verb phrases, 298–313
See also specific parts of speech
graphic narratives or comics, citing
in MLA style, 143, 160

H

habits of mind, 2
handouts, for presentations, 83
hanged, hung, 399
Hauer, Cameron (student writer),
49–51
have
agreement with subject, 319
as auxiliary verb, 300–304
Hays, Joanna (student writer),
243–45
headings
in APA style, 177
in *Chicago* style, 214
in CSE style, 235
formatting, 19–20
in MLA style, 129
organization (IMRAD), 70
parallelism in, 291

helping verb, 300–303 A **verb**
such as a form of *be, do,* or *have* or a
modal combined with a main verb.

herself, himself, myself, yourself, 399

he/she, his, her, 256–57
high-stakes writing, 42
himself, herself, myself, yourself, 399
historical sources, 91
homonyms, overlooked by spell
checkers, 31
hopefully, 399
however, therefore, 346, 358, 365
hung, hanged, 399
hyphens, 35, 390–93
hypothesis, 89–90, 96

I

I, me, my, 334–35
ideas, main. *See* main ideas,
distinguishing
identities
language and, 248–50, 261
writing across, 250–53
i.e. (that is), 388
if clauses, 311–12
illusion, allusion, 395
illustrations. *See* visuals and media
immigrate to, emigrate from, 398
imperative mood, 310
implicit, explicit, 398
implied antecedents, 341
imply, infer, 399
in, on, 342–43
in addition to, 319
inclusive pronouns, 339
in contrast, 279
indefinite articles, 316–17

**indefinite pronoun, 34, 322, 339,
370** A word such as *each, everyone,*
or *nobody* that does not refer to a
specific person or thing.

possessive case, 370
pronoun-antecedent agreement,
34–35, 339
subject-verb agreement, 322
you, it, and *they*, 341

indenting
    in APA style, 176, 177, 183
    in *Chicago* style, 214–15
    in CSE style, 237
    long quotations
        in APA style, 176
        in *Chicago* style, 214
        in MLA style, 129, 374
    in MLA style, 128
    in MLA works cited, 135
    poetry quotations, 374

independent clause, 281, 284, 345, 365 A word group containing a **subject** and a **predicate** that can stand alone as a **sentence**.

    commas used with, 33–34, 355–56
    fused sentences and, 34, 345–47
    semicolons used with, 34, 346–47, 356, 365–66
    in sentence structure, confusing, 281
    subordination to, 284–86
indexes, for research, 93–94
indicative mood, 310
indirect discourse, 295
indirect questions, 368, 369
indirect quotations, 295, 376
indirect sources, citing
    in APA style, 180
    in *Chicago* style, 221
    in MLA style, 134
infer, imply, 399

infinitive, 303, 304, 331, 386
To plus the **base form** of a **verb** (*to go, to run, to hit*), which can serve as a **noun**, an **adverb**, or an **adjective**: *One option is to leave* (noun). *We stopped to rest* (adverb). *He needs time to adjust* (adjective).

    gerunds and, 304–6
    split, 331
    to preceding, not capitalized, 382

informal outlines, 13–14
informal writing
    ellipses with, 369–70, 383
    end punctuation, 369–70
    fragments in, 349
    letters or emails, 268
    low-stakes writing as, 42–44
    slang and colloquial language, 263, 269
    subjunctive mood, 310–11
    word choice and, 268–71
    in writing process, 253
-ing words, 298, 301, 303, 305
inside of, outside of, 399
Instagram, 38, 56
insure, assure, ensure, 396
integrating sources, 113–20
    acknowledgments, 117–18
    ethical use of sources, 114
    quotations, paraphrases, and summaries, 114–16
    visuals and media, 117
intellectual property rights, 114, 124, 174, 212
intentions and infinitives, 304–5
interjection, 361
Internet sources. *See* digital and nonprint sources; web sources
interviews
    citing
        in APA style, 180, 191
        in *Chicago* style, 229, 230
        in MLA style, 156, 157–58
    in field research, 94–95, 118
in-text citations
    abbreviations in, 388–85
    in APA style, 175, 177–83, 378
    in *Chicago* style, 214–17
    in CSE style, 236
    ellipses and periods with, 383
    in MLA style, 124, 126–35, 138

in-text citations (*continued*)
  parentheses for, 129–30, 138, 378
  reasons for, 124
  signal phrases, 129–30, 138
intransitive verbs, 306
introductions
  in arguments, 58
  to chemistry reports, 75
  citing
    in *Chicago* style, 220
    in MLA style, 144
  in IMRAD organization, 70
  planning and drafting, 13, 120
  in presentations, 81
  in research projects, 120
introductory elements, commas with, 29–30, 354
invitational argument, 54, 59
irregardless, regardless, 400
irregular verb, 298–300, 319 A **verb** that does not form the **past tense** and past **participle** by adding -*ed* or -*d* to the **base form**.
is, are, was, were, been (*be* verbs). See *be* verbs
is when, is where, 282, 400
it, this, that, and *which,* vague use of, 340–41
it, you, they, indefinite use of, 341
italics, 31, 137, 390–93
items in a series. See series of items
its, it's, 33–34, 372, 400

J
jargon, 68, 269–70
journals. See articles in periodicals
JSTOR, 148
just as . . . so, 291. See also correlative conjunctions

K
Karas, Zack (student writer), 80
key words and phrases
  annotating, 45–46, 111, 112
  in disciplinary vocabularies, 68
  for paragraph coherence, 15–16
  in presentations, 82
  repetition of, 15–16, 18, 83
keyword searches, 93, 94
know, no, 400
Kung, James (student writer), 40

L
labels
  identity and, 248–49
  stereotypes and, 254, 255
  for visuals and media, 22–23, 117, 129, 177, 214
lab report, 70, 75–77
language
  on abilities and disabilities, 259–60
  audience and, 8
  avoiding stereotypes, 254, 255, 257
  awareness of, practicing, 261–63
  building common ground, 254–60
  cross-cultural communication and, 250–53
  doublespeak, 270–71
  euphemisms, 270
  examining assumptions, 252, 254–59
  figurative, 57, 274–75
  formal vs. informal. See formal writing; informal writing
  gender and pronoun preferences, 255–57
  general and specific, 273
  identity and, 248–50, 261
  jargon, 68, 269–70

meaning of, clarifying, 251–52
other (non-English), 265–67,
    391
pompous, 270
of power, 27, 250, 262–63
on race and ethnicity, 257–59
sexist, 255
signpost, 81–82
slang and colloquial, 263, 269,
    377
topic exploration in familiar or
    useful, 10–11, 43
varieties of, 27, 67–68, 260–68,
    266, 325
See also word choice
Language, Culture, and Context
adjectives with plural nouns,
    327
Black language, 262
English, global varieties, 266
fancy language, avoiding, 270
grammar flexibility, 301
plagiarism, 119
sentence length, 346
sources, identifying, 111
thesis, review by peers, 121
thesis, stating a, 12
verb usage, checking with search
    engines, 305
visuals, using, 22
*See also the directory of boxed tips
    on p. 444*
later, latter, 400
lateral reading, 47, 99–100, 102
Latin terms, abbreviations for, 388
latter, former, 399
latter, later, 400
lay, lie, 302, 306–7, 400
leave, let, 400
lectures. *See* presentations
length of sentences, 278, 346
less, fewer, 399
let, leave, 400

letters
    citing
        in APA style, 191
        in *Chicago* style, 229
        in MLA style, 162
    colons after salutations, 381
    informal and formal, 268–69
    in portfolio, 38, 39
    See also editorials or letters to
        the editor, citing; newsletter
letters (alphabetical), as terms,
    391
librarians, reference, 92
Library of Congress, 92, 93
library research, 92–94
lie, lay, 302, 400
like, as, as if, as though, 274, 396
limiting modifier, 330
line and bar graphs, 21
line spacing. *See* margins and
        spacing
linguicism, 262
linking verb, 323, 326, 393 A **verb**
that suggests a state of being, not
an action.
    adjectives and adverbs after,
        326–28
    subject agreement with, 323
    subject complement following,
        not hyphenated, 393
links to audio and visual sources,
    20, 22, 78
list
    colon introducing, 367, 380
    numbers in, parenthetical, 378
    parallel form, 290
    See also series of items
listening
    active and respectful, 5–6
    analytically, critically, and
        respectfully, 44–51
    beginnings and endings of
        presentations, 81

listening (*continued*)
and collaboration, 6–7
and reading purposefully and
openly, 52
list of references. *See* APA style;
CSE style
list of works cited. *See* MLA style:
works cited
literacy narrative, 265–66
literally, 400
literary present tense, 308
literary works
citing, in MLA style, 133
verb tense, 302
See also books; plays; poetry
literature review, excerpts from,
243–45
a little, much, 315
live performances, citing in
MLA style, 159. *See also*
presentations
logical appeals, 52–53, 56–57, 63
long quotations. *See* quotations:
long
loose, lose, 400
lots, lots of, 400
low-stakes writing, 42–44
-ly adverbs, 325, 393

M

magazines. *See* articles in
periodicals
main clause. *See* independent
clause
main ideas, distinguishing,
284–87. *See also* thesis; topic
sentence
main verbs, 300. *See also* verb
manuscript format. *See* formatting
manuscripts or unpublished works,
citing in MLA style, 162
many, a few, 315

maps
citing, in MLA style, 160
as visuals or media, 22
margins and spacing
in APA style, 176
in *Chicago* style, 214
in CSE style, 235
design decisions, 18. *See also*
formatting
in MLA style, 128
in poetry, 374
may, can, 397
may as modal verb, 301
may be, maybe, 401
me, my, I, 334–35
meaning, clarifying, 251–52
measurement, units of, 388
medium, 10. *See also* visuals and
media
metaphors, 57, 61, 274
*might of, could of, would of, should
of*, 397
misinformation, 44, 88
misplaced modifiers, 330–31
missing words, 32
mixed metaphors, 274

mixed structure, 280–81 A
common writing problem in which
a **sentence** begins with one grammatical pattern and switches to
another.

MLA style, 115, 124–71 The
citation style guidelines issued by the
Modern Language Association.

authors, 125–27, 129, 131–32,
138–40
books, 140–45, 150
context of sources, 124–28
digital written-word sources,
128, 148–56
elements of citations, 125–26
explanatory notes, 128
format, 128–29

in-text citations, 126–27,
129–35, 138
list of examples, 130
parts of, 126–27
long quotations, 129, 374
other sources, 160–62
parts of citations, 126–27
print periodicals, 145–47
sample student writing, 49–51,
62–65, 72–74, 126, 163–71
signal phrases in, 115, 130–31, 138
source maps
articles from databases, 149
articles in print periodicals, 146
books, 141
works from websites, 154
types of sources, 126
understanding, 124
verb tense in, 115
visual, audio, media, and live
sources, 129, 135, 156–62
works cited, 135–62
formatting, 135, 137
in-text citations and, 126–27,
138
list of examples, 136–37
models for, 139–62
sample, 51, 74, 170–71

modal, 301–3 A kind of **helping verb** that has only one form and shows possibility, necessity, or obligation: *can, could, may, might, must, shall, should, will, would, ought to.*

Modern Language Association (MLA). *See* MLA style

modifier, 287, 325 A word, **phrase,** or **clause** that acts as an **adjective** or an **adverb,** qualifying the meaning of another word, phrase, or clause.

dangling, 332–33
disruptive, 331
limiting, 330
misplaced, 330
placement of, 329–33
and split infinitives, 331
squinting, 330
vague, 287
See also adjective; adverb

mood, 310–11 The form of a **verb** that indicates the writer's attitude toward the idea expressed. The indicative mood states fact or opinion (*I am happy*); the imperative gives commands (*Keep calm*); and the **subjunctive** refers to a condition that does not exist (*If I were rich . . .*).

moral, morale, 401
more. See indefinite pronoun
most. See indefinite pronoun
much. See indefinite pronoun
much, a little, 315
multimedia presentations, 81–85.
See also presentations

multimodal text, 67 A **text** that may include oral, visual, or audio elements in addition to (or instead of) words on a printed page. *See also* visuals and media

multivolume works, citing
in APA style, 188
in *Chicago* style, 220
in MLA style, 132–33,
143–44
musical compositions
capitalization of titles,
386
citing, in MLA style, 158
italics for titles, 390–91
my, me, I, 334–35
my, our, your, his, her, its, their,
315
myself, yourself, himself, herself,
399

N

name-year format, CSE style, 236, 237–41
narratives
in argument, 58
literacy, 265–66
as sources, 91
N.B. (note well), 388
n.d. (no date), in APA style, 181
necessary words, 292
neither . . . nor, 291, 320. *See also* correlative conjunctions
nevertheless, 279
newsletter, 18, 19
newspapers. *See* articles in periodicals
Nguyen, Thanh (student writer), 39
no, know, 400
noncount noun, 314, 316–17 A **noun** referring to a collection of things or to an idea that cannot be directly counted: *sand, rain, violence.* Contrast with **count noun.**

none. See indefinite pronoun
non-English words/language, 391
nonprint sources. *See* digital and nonprint sources
nonrestrictive element, 33, 356–59 A word, **phrase**, or **clause** that provides more information about, but does not change, the essential meaning of a **sentence.** Nonrestrictive elements are set off from the rest of the sentence with commas: *My instructor, who is perceptive, liked my introduction.*

adjective and adverb clauses, 357–58
appositives, 359
commas setting off, 33, 356–59
nor, or, 283, 346, 355, 401. *See also* coordinating conjunctions

"normal," judgments about, 251
not . . . but, 291. *See also* correlative conjunctions
notes
abbreviations in, 388–89
in APA style, 176
in *Chicago* style, 213, 214–15, 217–31
in MLA style, 128
See also footnotes
note-taking
annotated bibliography, 111–13
annotating, 45–46, 106
in field research, 94
paraphrasing, 108–10
quoting, 107–8
sources, keeping track of, 106–7
summarizing, 110–11
synthesizing sources, 101
translingual, 266–67
not only . . . but also, 291. *See also* correlative conjunctions
noun, 31, 287, 290, 313–18, 325, 333, 359, 370, 385, 388 A word that names a person, place, thing, or idea.

abbreviation as, avoiding, 388
and adjectives, 325
antecedents for pronouns, 333. *See also* antecedent
appositives, 359, 380
articles with, 316–18
capitalization, 32, 385
collective, 321, 338–39
compound, 371, 392
count and noncount, 314–16
determiners, common, 315–16
parallelism, 290
possessive, 34, 315, 370
pronouns replacing, 333. *See also* pronoun

proper, 31, 32, 385
sexist, 255
vague, 287
we and *us* before, 336–38
words between subject and verb,
   319–20
noun phrases, 313–17, 359
number (singular or plural)
   apostrophes and plural forms,
     372–73
   count and noncount nouns,
     314–16
   determiners, 315–16
   pronoun-antecedent agreement,
     34–35, 323, 338–40
   subject-verb agreement, 319–25
   See also plurals
number, amount, 396
number of, a vs. *the*, 321
numbers, 388–89
   abbreviations and, 387
   colons with, 381
   figures for, 389–90
   hyphens with, 393
   in parentheses, 378
   plural of, 372–73
   slashes in fractions, 382
   spelling out, 389
   as terms, italicizing, 391

O

**object, 32, 306, 334, 342, 344,
364, 381** A **noun** or **pronoun** receiving the action of a **verb** (*We mixed
paints*) or following a **preposition**
(*on the road*).
   avoid colons, 381
   avoid commas, 364
   of preposition, 342
   pronouns as, 334–36, 344
   transitive verbs, 306, 344
object complements, 32

objective case, 334–35
observation, in field research,
   95–96
off, of, 401
on, in, 342–39
one another, each other, 398
one of the, 323
online sources. *See* digital and
   nonprint sources
openings, sentence, 278–80
openness, as habit of mind, 2
opinion, personal. *See* stance
opinion surveys, 96
opposing points of view, 50, 56,
   59, 114, 168
or, nor, 283, 320, 338, 401. *See also*
   coordinating conjunctions
oral presentation. *See* presentations
organization
   in academic writing, 5
   of arguments, 57–59
   audience expectations, 253
   for genre, 70
   IMRAD, 70
   of paragraph, 15
   planning and drafting, 13–14
   of presentations, 81
   of writing project, 10
organizations as authors, citing
   in APA style, 179, 185
   in *Chicago* style, 218
   in CSE style, 239
   in MLA style, 132, 139
outlines, 13–14, 122, 291
outside of, inside of, 399

P

page numbers
   in APA style, 176
   in *Chicago* style, 214
   in CSE style, 235
   in MLA style, 128–29, 130

paired ideas, 291–92
pamphlets, citing
    in *Chicago* style, 231
    in MLA style, 160
paragraphs, 15–17
parallelism, 290–91
    with conjunctions, 291
    necessary words for clarity, 292
    paired ideas, 291
    for paragraph coherence, 15
    for sentence structure, 32–33,
      290–91
    in series or list, 290
paraphrasing
    citing, in APA style, 178
    integrating, 116
    plagiarism in, 109, 118–19
    present tense in, 308
    of sources, 108–10, 116
parentheses, 377–78, 383
parenthetical citations. *See* in-text
    citations
parenthetical expressions,
    361, 378
participial phrases, 358
participle, 298 A word formed
from the **base form** of a **verb**. The
present participle always ends in
-ing (*going*). The past participle ends
in *-ed* (*ruined*) unless the verb is
irregular. A participle can function
as an **adjective** (the *singing* frog, a
ruined shirt) or form part of a **verb
phrase** (*You have ruined* my shirt).

particles, adverbial, 344
parts of speech. *See* adjective;
    adverb; conjunction; interjec-
    tion; noun; preposition;
    pronoun; verb
passed, past, 401
passive voice, 289, 310 The form
of a **verb** when the **subject** is being
acted on, not acting: *The batter*
was hit by a pitch. Contrast with
active voice.

    and forms of *be*, 300–302
    shifts from active voice, 289,
      310
    wordiness of, 289
past participles, 298–99, 301, 303,
    306
past perfect, 307
past perfect progressive, 307
past progressive, 307
past subjunctive, 311
**past tense, 115, 177, 298–99,
306–9, 319** The **tense** of a **verb**
that indicates an action or condition
has already happened: *They arrived*
yesterday.

per, 401
percent, percentage, 401
perfect progressive, 307 The
form used when the **perfect tense**
of a **verb** shows an ongoing action
completed at some point in the past,
present, or future, with the main
verb in the *-ing* form: *The workers*
had been striking for a month
before the settlement. He has been
complaining for days. The construc-
tion will have been continuing for a
year in May.

perfect tense, 301–3, 308 The
tense of a **verb** showing a completed
action in the past, present, or future:
They had hoped to see the parade
but got stuck in traffic. I have never
understood this equation. By then,
the governor will have vetoed the
bill.

periodicals. *See* articles in
    periodicals
periods
    with abbreviations, 368
    comma splices, fixing with, 34

with ellipses, 383
end punctuation, 368
in informal writing, 369–70
with parentheses, 377–78
with quotation marks, 376
with source citations, 383

person, 319, 338 The point of view of a **subject**. The first person refers to itself (*I*); the second person addresses *you*; the third person refers to someone else (*they*).

pronoun-antecedent agreement, 34–35, 323, 338–40
pronoun preferences, 256. *See also* singular *they*
shifts in, 294
subject-verb agreement, 303, 319–25
personal experience, as source, 91
personal opinion. *See* stance
persuasive writing. *See* argument
photographs
citing
in APA style, 201
in MLA style, 159
as visual or media, 21. *See also* visuals and media
phrasal verbs, 344

phrase, 29–30, 270, 281, 284, 288, 290, 314, 332, 350, 354, 358, 366 A group of words that lacks a **subject**, a **verb**, or both.

appositives, 359
commas with, 29–30, 354, 354, 366
dangling modifier, 332–33
fragments, 349
introductory elements, 29–30, 354–55
noncount nouns with preceding, 314
noun, 313–18, 359

participial, 358
prepositional. *See* prepositional phrases
sentence openings, 279
signal, 115, 129–30, 138, 177–78, 183, 215
subordination, 284
wordy, replacing, 288, 289
pie charts, 21
place names. *See* addresses and place names
plagiarism
avoiding, 30, 113–20
deliberate, 119
documentation to avoid, 30, 118
paraphrase, unacceptable, 109, 118
unintentional, 47, 107, 119
planning
drafting and, 13–15
for presentations, 82–84
for research, 90
plays
capitalization of titles, 386
citing in MLA style, 133
italics for titles, 391
plurals
adjectives with, 327
apostrophes, 372–73
collective nouns, 321, 339
compound. *See* compound entries
count nouns, 314–17
determiners with, 316
gender and pronoun preferences, 255–56
nouns, possessive case, 371
pronoun-antecedent agreement, 338–40
See also number (singular or plural)
PM, p.m., 388

podcasts
  citing
    in APA style, 201
    in *Chicago* style, 229
    in MLA style, 159
  italics for titles, 391
poetry
  capital letters, use of, 374, 384, 385
  citing, in MLA style, 133, 151
  close reading of, 72–75
  italics for titles, 391
  quoting and quotation marks, 374–75, 382
  slashes used with, 374, 382
  spacing, 374
  titles of, 375, 386, 391
point of view
  opposing, 50, 56, 114, 168
  shifts in, 294
  See also stance
PolitiFact (fact-checker site), 97
pompous language, 270–71
popular sources, 91
portfolios, 38–39, 40

possessive form, 34 The form of a **noun** or **pronoun** that shows possession. Personal pronouns in the possessive case don't use apostrophes (*ours, hers*), but possessive nouns and **indefinite pronouns** do (*Harold's, everyone's*).

  apostrophes for, 34, 370
  indefinite pronouns, 370
  its and *it's*, 34, 372, 400
  joint possession, 371
  nouns and phrases, 34, 315, 371
  plural nouns, 371
  pronouns, 34, 334, 370, 372
postal abbreviations, 368
posters
  citing, in APA style, 199
  as visuals or media, 78. *See also* visuals and media

precede, proceed, 401

predicate, 32, 281, 308, 351 The **verb** and related words in a **clause** or **sentence**. The predicate expresses what the **subject** does, experiences, or is. The simple predicate is the verb or **verb phrase**: *We have been living in the Atlanta area.* The complete predicate includes the simple predicate and its **modifiers, objects**, and complements: *We have been living in the Atlanta area.*

  compound, 351, 364
  matching with subjects, 281–82
  truths and facts, and present tense, 308
prefaces, citing
  in *Chicago* style, 220
  in MLA style, 144

preposition, 29, 32, 292, 306, 342–45, 364, 381, 386 A word or word group that indicates the relationship of a **noun** or **pronoun** to another part of the **sentence**: *From the top of the ladder, we looked over the rooftops.*

  capitalization, omitting, 386
  choosing correct, 342–43
  for clarity, 292
  colon following, avoiding, 381
  commas, unneeded, 32, 364
  gerunds following, 306
  idiomatic use of, 29
  object of, 342
  omitted, 32
  phrases. *See* prepositional phrases
  relating to space and time, 343
  two-word verbs with, 344–45
  wrong, 29
prepositional phrases, 342–45
  commas with, 358
  parallelism, 290

in sentence openings, 279
and sentence structure, 281
wordy, replacing, 288
presentations
accessibility of, tips for, 259
checklist for, 83
citing
in APA style, 200
in MLA style, 158
creating, 81–85
delivering, 84
introduction and conclusion, 81
practicing or rehearsing, 83–84
sample excerpts, 84–85
script for, 82
signpost language and structure,
81–82
task, purpose, and audience, 81
visuals, 82–85
present participles, 298–99, 301,
303, 306
present perfect progressive, 307

present perfect tense, 115, 308
The **tense** of a **verb** that indicates
an action or a condition has been
completed before the present: *The
team has worked together well.*

present progressive, 308
present subjunctive, 311

present tense, 115, 307–9, 319
The **tense** of a **verb** that indicates a
general truth or a current action or
condition: *Things fall apart. We live
off campus.*

previewing, 45

primary source, 90 A research
source that provides firsthand
knowledge of raw information.
Contrast with **secondary source**.

principal, principle, 401
proceed, precede, 401

progressive, 301–3, 307 The *-ing*
form of a **verb** showing a continuing
action in the past, present, or future:
*He was snoring during the lecture.
The economy is improving. Business
schools will be competing for this
student.*

projects. *See* writing projects

**pronoun, 30, 323, 325, 333–41,
344, 370, 372** A word used in place
of a **noun**.

and adjectives, 325
agreement with antecedents, 34,
323, 338–40
agreement with verbs, 322
antecedent reference, clear, 30,
333, 340–41
and compound structures, 335
and elliptical constructions,
335
gender-neutral, 26, 34–35,
256–57, 339–40
gender of, and preferences,
257
gerunds and possessive case of,
334
inclusive, 339–40
indefinite, 34, 322, 339, 341,
370
as object, 334–36, 344
possessive, 34, 334, 370, 371
reference, checking, 30, 333,
339–40
relative, 323
role in sentence, 334–38
sexist, 255–56
singular *they,* 35, 256, 339, 341,
403
subject complements, 334–36
we and *us* before nouns,
336–38
who, whom, 334–36, 404
pronoun-antecedent agreement,
34–35, 338–40
collective-noun antecedents,
338–39
compound antecedents, 338

pronoun-antecedent agreement
(*continued*)
indefinite pronoun antecedents,
34, 339
singular *they*, 35, 339, 341
subject-verb agreement, 323–24
proofreading, 25–26, 31, 32,
121–22
proper adjectives, 32, 385
proper names with titles, 385
proper nouns
capitalization, 32, 385
spelling, 31
ProQuest, 148
proximity, in design, 18
pseudonym for author, citing in
MLA style, 140
psychology research essay, 75
publication date, sources, 98
public speaking. *See* presentations
public writing, 72, 78–80, 349
publisher or sponsor
citing multiple, in MLA style,
150
evaluating, 98, 99–100, 102,
104
punctuation
apostrophes, 33–34, 370–73
brackets, 107, 116, 378–79
colons, 31, 367, 376, 380–82,
384
commas, 29–33, 345–48,
354–64, 376, 378
dashes, 347–48, 376, 379–80
ellipses, 107, 116, 185, 369–70,
374, 382–84
end, 367–70
exclamation points, 369, 376
hyphens, 35, 392–93
parentheses, 377–78, 387
periods, 34, 365, 368, 378, 383
question marks, 363, 368–69
quotation marks, 31, 107, 129,
138, 362, 376–77, 383

semicolons, 34, 283, 346, 356,
365–67, 376
slashes, 377, 382
purpose for writing
analysis of, 7
for argument, 53–54
in field research, 94, 96
listening and reading with, 52
for presentations, 81
for public writing, 72, 78–80
for research projects, 89, 90, 94,
96, 97
of sources, 101, 102

Q

qtd. in, MLA style, 134
qualifiers, in arguments, 53
question marks, 363, 367–69
questionnaire, 53, 96, 176, 257
questions
for analyzing, 47–48
annotating, 45–46
commas with, 362, 363
direct, 94–95, 368
exploring topics, 10–11
indirect, 368
in introduction, 120
opinion surveys, 96
research, and working hypothesis, 89–90, 96
tag, 361–62
quotation, quote, 402
quotation marks, 373–77
capital letters, use of, 384
commas with, 31, 362–63, 376
conventional use, 31
definitions, 375–76
long quotations without, 129,
374
misused, avoiding, 376–77
note-taking including, 107–8
with other punctuation, 376
poetry, 374–75

single, 373
titles of short works, 31, 137, 375–76
quotations
  in arguments, 57
  block, 374. *See also* long *subentry*
  brackets in, 107, 116, 379
  capitalization in, 384
  citations
    in APA style, 177–78, 374
    in MLA style, 131
  colons before, 381–82
  commas with, 31, 362–63, 376
  direct, 106, 116, 295, 373
  ellipses with, 107, 116, 377, 382–84
  emotional appeal, 52
  indirect, 295, 376
  integrating, 35, 114–16
  long
    in APA style, 177, 178, 374–75
    in *Chicago* style, 214
    integrating, 115
    in MLA style, 129, 374
  missing words, avoiding, 32
  note-taking and, 107–8
  plagiarism, avoiding, 118–20
  of poetry, 374–75
  present tense in, 308–9
  "selective," avoiding, 114
  sic (so), use of, 379
  signal phrases for, 115, 177–78
  synthesizing, 101

R

race and ethnicity, 257–59
radio
  citing, in MLA style, 157
  italics for series title, 390–91
raise, rise, 306–7, 402
readers. *See* audience
reading
  aloud, 25, 36
  analytically, critically, and respectfully, 5–6, 44–51, 97–101
  close, of poetry, 72–75
  collaboratively, 45
  defensive strategies, 44, 88
  and evaluating sources, 96–101
  lateral, 47, 99–101
  purposefully and openly, 52
  vertical, 97–99
  See also proofreading
reading responses, 44
real, really, 402
reason is because, 283, 402
reasons, in argument, 53, 55, 56, 58, 61
reason why, 402
rebuttal, 61
redundant words, 287
references, list of. *See* APA style; CSE style
reference works
  citing
    in APA style, 188, 197–98
    in *Chicago* style, 227
    in MLA style, 134, 144, 152
  as research source, 94
reflecting, 39–40, 42
regardless, irregardless, 400, 402
regular verb, 298 A **verb** that forms the **past tense** and past **participle** by adding *-d* or *-ed* to the **base form** (*care, cared, cared; look, looked, looked*).
relative pronouns, 323
relevance of sources, 97, 99, 101, 104
repetition
  in design, 18
  of key words or phrases, 16, 18, 83
reports
  citing
    in APA style, 195–96, 199

reports (*continued*)
  citing (*continued*)
    in *Chicago* style, 231
    in MLA style, 160
  lab, 70, 75–77
  verb tense in, APA style, 308
republications, citing
  in APA style, 189
  in MLA style, 144
research and research projects
  acknowledgments, 117–18
  audience, 89, 117
  bibliography, 94, 106, 107,
    111–13, 118, 121
  challenges to, 88
  citing and documenting sources.
    See also documentation
    APA style, 115, 174–209
    Chicago style, 115, 212–34
    CSE style, 115, 235–44
    MLA style, 115, 124–71
  conclusion, 121
  conducting, 88–96
  context, 89
  determining needed, 13
  drafting, 120
  editing and proofreading, 121–22
  ethical, 88
  evaluating sources, 96–101
  evidence in, 13, 89, 106
  fact-checking, 47–48, 88, 97,
    99, 100
  field research, 94–96, 118
  integrating sources, 113–20
  library, 92–94
  note-taking, 96–113
  outline, 122
  paraphrasing and paraphrase
    integration, 108–10, 116
  plagiarism, 107, 109,
    113–20
  planning, 90
  process, beginning, 88–90
  purpose for, 89, 90, 94, 96, 97

  quoting and quotation integra-
    tion, 107–8, 115
  research question and hypoth-
    esis, 89–90, 96
  reviewing and revising, 121
  sample student writing, 76,
    162–71, 201–9, 231–32,
    243–44
  sources, 89–121
  stance or attitude, 89, 121
  summarizing and summary
    integration, 110–11, 116
  synthesizing sources, 101, 106
  thesis, 90, 121, 122
  topic, 89
  visuals and media, 89, 117
  working title and introduction,
    120
  writing, 120–22
respectfully, respectively, 402

restrictive element, 32, 357, 363
A word, **phrase,** or **clause** that
changes the essential meaning of a
sentence. A restrictive element is not
set off from the rest of the sentence
with commas or other punctuation:
The tree <u>that I hit</u> was an oak.

reviewing and revising, 24–25, 121
reviews
  citing
    in APA style, 191
    in *Chicago* style, 225
    in MLA style, 148, 152
  literature, excerpts from,
    243–45
  peer review of thesis, 121
rhetorical analysis, 48–51

rhetorical situation, 7–10 The
whole context for a piece of writing,
including the person communicating, the topic and the person's
attitude toward it, and the intended
audience.

rise, raise, 306–7, 402

Rogerian argument, 54, 57, 59
run-on sentences, 34, 345–48

S
-s, -es ending, 306, 319
sacred texts
 citing
  in *Chicago* style, 221
  in MLA style, 133, 145
 colons with chapters and verses,
  380–81
 titles, not italicized, 391
Sakowitz, Julia (student writer),
 16, 122, 127, 162–71
sample student writing
 annotated bibliography, 112–13
 argument essay, 60–65, 162–71
 chemistry lab report, 75–77
 close reading of poetry, 72–75
 documentation
  in APA style, 202–9
  in *Chicago* style, 232–34
  in CSE style, 243–44
  in MLA style, 49–51, 60–65,
   72–74, 126, 162–71
 literacy narrative, 265–66
 literature review, excerpts from,
  243–45
 outline of a research project,
  122
 paragraph, 16, 17
 poster, 78
 presentation, excerpts from,
  84–85
 psychology research essay, 75
 reflective blog post, 39
 reflective cover letter, 40
 research-based argument, 162–71
 research-based history essay,
  excerpts, 231–32
 research projects
  in APA style, 201–9
  in *Chicago* style, 231–34

  in CSE style, 243–44
  in MLA style, 162–71
 rhetorical analysis, 48–51
 web comic, 80
 web page, 79
scholarly sources, 91
sciences, writing in
 abbreviations for, 387
 lab reports, 70, 75–77
 passive voice for, 310
 verb tense for, 115, 307
 See also research and research
  projects
screen name for authors, citing in
 MLA style, 140
searches and search techniques,
 92–94, 305

secondary source, 90 A research
source that reports information from
research done by others. Contrast
with **primary source**.

second person (*you*), 294
semicolons, 365–67
 avoiding misuse of, 366–67
 comma splices, fixing with, 34,
  346
 equal ideas, relating, 283–84
 independent clauses, 34, 347,
  355, 365–66
 items in a series, 366
 with quotation marks, 376

sentence, 30, 277–95 A group of
words containing a **subject** and a
predicate and expressing a complete
thought.

 capitalization, 32, 384
 comparisons, complete, 282–83
 compound structures, 33, 364
 conciseness, 287–90
 conditional, 312–13
 confusing, editing/revising,
  32–33, 281
 consistency and completeness,
  280–83

sentence (*continued*)
coordination and subordination, 283–87
elliptical construction, 335–36
equal ideas, relating, 283–84
fused or run-on, 34, 345–48
length, 278, 346
main ideas, distinguishing, 284–86
openings, 278–80
parallelism, 33, 290–92
pronoun role in, 334–38
separating into two, 345
shifts, revising, 293
simplifying structure, 289
topic, 15, 16
See also sentence structure
sentence fragments. *See* fragment
sentence structure
adapting to genre, 71–72
compound, 33, 364
confusing, editing/revising, 32–33, 281
consistent and complete, 280–83
emphasis with, 349
parallel, 33, 290–92
paraphrasing, 108–10
in presentations, 83
simplifying, 289
varying, 278–80
series, books in, citing in MLA style, 144
series of items
colons preceding, 367, 376
commas with, 32, 356, 360
parallelism and, 290–91
semicolons with, 360
set, sit, 306–7, 402
sexist language, 255
sharing writing, 38
shifts, 293–95
in discourse, 295

between general and specific ideas, 15
in point of view, 294
in style, and plagiarism, 120
in varieties of English, 260–68, 293
in verb tense, 32, 293
in voice, 294, 310
short works and quotation marks, 31, 137, 375–76
should of, might of, could of, would of, 402
sic (so), 379
signal phrases, 115, 129–30, 138, 177–78, 183, 215
signpost language, 81–82
Sillay, Bonnie (student writer), 72–74
similes, 57, 274
simple tenses, 307 Past (*It happened*), present (*Things fall apart*), or future (*You will succeed*) forms of **verbs.**
since, 402
single quotation marks, 373
singular nouns, 338, 370
singular *they,* 35, 256, 339–40, 403
sit, set, 306, 402
slang and colloquial language, 263, 269, 377
slashes, 377, 382
slides, 82–83, 85
Snopes.com (fact-checker site), 97
so, 283, 402. *See also* coordinating conjunctions
social media
acknowledgments, 117–18
citing
in APA style, 197
in *Chicago* style, 229
in MLA style, 155–56
cross-cultural communication with, 250

ellipses on, 383
low-stakes writing, 44
sharing writing, 38
unreliability, 88
using wisely, 2–3
software
    italics for titles, 390–91
    for presentations, 82
some, any, 317
some, enough, 315
some time, sometime, sometimes, 403
Song, Shuqiao (student writer),
    84–85
sound recordings. *See* audio clips
source maps
    APA style
        articles from databases, 194
        articles from print periodi-
            cals, 190
        books, 187
        works from websites, 196
    Chicago style
        articles from databases, 224
        works from websites, 228
    evaluating articles, 104–5
    evaluating web sources, 102–3
    MLA style
        articles from databases, 149
        articles from print periodi-
            cals, 146
        books, 141
        works from websites, 154
sources
    acknowledging, 117–18
    audience of, 98
    author, sponsor, publisher
        credentials, 98, 100, 102
    browsing, 11
    choosing, 90–91
    citing and documenting.
        See also bibliographies;
        documentation
        APA style, 115, 174–209

Chicago style, 115, 212–34
    CSE style, 115, 235–44
    MLA style, 115, 124–71
date of publication, 98
in the disciplines, 68
ethical use of, 114
evaluating, 53, 96–101
exploring topic, 11
fact-checking, 47–48, 88, 97,
    99, 100
field research, 94–96, 118
government. *See* government
    sources
historical, 91
identifying, 111
integrating, 113–20
keeping track of, 106–7
library, 92–94
list of, preparing, 121
note-taking and, 96–113
older and current, 91, 98
online. *See* digital and nonprint
    sources
personal experience and narra-
    tives, 91
popular, 91
primary, 90
purpose of, 101, 102
quoting, paraphrasing, and
    summarizing, 107–11,
    114–16
reading and analyzing, 97–101
relevance of, 97, 99, 101, 104
for research project, 89–120,
    121
scholarly, 91
secondary, 90
specialization, 98
stance and tone, 97, 98, 102,
    104
synthesizing, 101, 106
web, 92–94, 96–103. *See also*
    digital and nonprint sources

spacing. *See* margins and spacing; white space

specialization, source, 98

specificity
in paragraphs, 15
specific vs. general language, 273
of working thesis, 11–12

speeches. *See* presentations

spell checkers and spelling, 29, 31

split infinitives, 331

squinting modifiers, 330

stance
considering, 9–10, 68
evaluating, of source, 97, 98, 102, 104
research project, 89, 121
See also point of view

standardized English, 67–68, 250, 261–65, 268, 293, 368

state names and abbreviations, 368

stereotypes, avoiding, 254–55

storyboarding, 14

structure. *See* organization; sentence structure

student writing. *See* sample student writing

subject, 32, 281, 309, 319, 326, 332, 334, 335, 336, 350, 351, 354, 364 The **noun** or **pronoun** and related words that indicate who or what a **sentence** is about. The simple subject is the noun or pronoun: *The timid gray mouse ran away.* The complete subject is the simple subject and its **modifiers**: *The timid gray mouse ran away.*

active and passive voice, 309–10
adjectives describing, 325
agreement with verbs, 303, 319–25
comma between verb and, avoiding, 364

compound, 320–21, 364
dangling modifier revised with, 332–33
following verb, 324
fragments without, 35–37, 350–51
introductory elements preceding, 354–55
matching with predicates, 281–82
pronouns as, 334–36
words between verb and, 319–20
See also topic

subject complements, 35, 323, 334–36, 393

subjective case, 334–35

subject-verb agreement, 319–25
with auxiliary verbs, 303
with *be* verbs, 303, 319, 325
with collective nouns, 321
with compound subjects, 320–21
with indefinite pronouns, 322
with linking verbs, 323
with relative pronouns, 323
with subjects ending in -*s*, 323–24
with subjects that follow the verb, 324
with titles of works, 324–25
with words between subject and verb, 319–20
with words used as words, 324–25

subjunctive mood, 310–13 The form of a **verb** used to express a wish, a suggestion, a request or requirement, or a condition that does not exist: *If I were president, I would change things.*

subordinate clause. *See* dependent clause

subordinating conjunction, 283, 285, 347, 351 A word or **phrase** such as *although, because,* or *even though* that introduces a **dependent clause**: *Think carefully before you answer.*

excessive use of, 286
linking clauses, 347–48
list of common conjunctions, 285
and sentence fragments, 351
sentence openings, 279
subordination and coordination, 283–87
subsequently, consequently, 397
summarizing texts, 46–47
present tense in, 308
research projects, 110–11, 116
See also paraphrasing; quotations

summary, 110 A brief retelling of the main points of a **text**.

citing, in APA style, 178
evaluating, 104
integrating, 116
note-taking and, 110–11
present tense for, 308

superlative, 317, 328–29 The *-est* or *most* form of an **adjective** or **adverb** used to compare three or more items (*happiest, most quickly*).

supposed to, used to, 403
sure, surely, 403
surveys, 96
symbols, with numbers, 388

synthesis, 101, 106 Grouping ideas and information together in such a way that the relationship among them is clear.

T
tables
in APA style, 177, 181–82
in *Chicago* style, 214

in CSE style, 235
in MLA style, 129, 135
as visuals and media, 20. *See also* visuals and media
tag questions, commas with, 361–62
technical language, 68, 269–70
television
citing
in APA style, 200, 201
in MLA style, 157
italics for series title, 390–91

tense, 33, 298, 302, 307–9 The form of a **verb** that indicates the time when an action takes place — past, present, or future. Each tense has **simple** (*I enjoy*), **perfect** (*I have enjoyed*), **progressive** (*I am enjoying*), and **perfect progressive** (*I have been enjoying*) forms.

text, 45 Traditionally, words on paper, but now anything that conveys a message.

alternative, 259
genres, 10. *See also* genre
multimodal, 67
reading analytically, critically, and respectfully, 44–51
than, then, 403
that, this, it, and *which,* vague use of, 340–41
that, this, these, those, 315
that, which, 357–58, 403
that, who, and *which,* subject-verb agreement, 323
that clauses, 311, 357
the, a, an, 315–17, 386
then, than, 403
therefore, however, 346, 361, 365
there is, there are, 289, 324
these, those, 315

thesis, 5, 11–12 A statement that indicates the main idea or **claim** of a piece of writing. Thesis statements should include a topic—the subject matter—and a comment that makes an important point.

  in academic writing, 5
  or claim, in arguments, 53, 60–63
  paragraph coherence by returning to, 15
  peer review of, 121
  for research projects, 90, 121, 122
  working, 11–12, 90
they, singular pronoun, 35, 256, 339–40, 403
they, them, 403
they, you, it, indefinite use of, 341
third person (*he, she, it, one, they*), 298, 319
this, that, it, and *which*, vague use of, 340–41
this, these, that, those, 315
thorough, threw, through, 403
those, these, 315
titles
  abbreviations of, 387
  in APA style, 176
  of arguments, 60
  capital letters in, 32, 137, 386
  in *Chicago* style, 213–14
  colons in, 381
  in CSE style, 235, 237, 241
  evaluating, 104
  italics for, 31, 137, 390–91
  in MLA style, 125, 128, 137
  of poems, 375, 386, 391
  with proper names, 385
  quotation marks for, 31, 137, 375
  subject-verb agreement, 324–25
  within title, books or articles with, 145, 189, 221
  working, 120

to, too, two, 404
together with, 319
tone, 9–10, 97, 252
topic
  choosing, 8, 11
  exploring, 10–11
  low-stakes writing on, 42–44
  paragraph identifying, 15
  research projects, 89
  stance and tone toward, 9. *See also* stance; tone
  in working thesis, 11
topic sentence, 15, 16
Top Twenty Tips for Editing, 27–37
  apostrophes, checking, 33–34
  capitalization, checking for, 32
  commas, unnecessary, 31–32
  commas after introductory element, 29–30
  commas in compound sentence, 33
  comma splices, 34
  commas with nonrestrictive elements, 33
  documentation, confirming complete, 30
  hyphens, unnecessary or missing, 35
  missing words, looking for, 32
  pronoun-antecedent agreement, 34–35
  pronoun reference, checking, 30
  quotation marks, conventional use, 31
  quotations, integrating smoothly, 35
  sentence fragments, checking for, 35–37
  sentences, fused (run-on), 34
  sentence structure, confusing, 32–33
  spelling, checking, 31

verb tense, shifts, 33
wrong words, checking for, 29
Toulmin argument, 53, 57

transition, 16, 346, 361, 365 A
word or **phrase** that signals a
progression from one **sentence** or
part of a sentence to another for
coherence.

adapting to genre, 71
in arguments, 62
commas with, 361
to fix fused sentences, 346, 347
fragments beginning with,
    350–51
in paragraphs, 16
semicolons with, 365
sentence openings, 279
in summaries, 46
transitional expressions, 361

transitive verb, 306, 344 A **verb**
that acts on an **object**: *I posted my
review online.*

translations, citing
in APA style, 188
in *Chicago* style, 220
in MLA style, 142–43
truths or scientific facts, and
    present tense, 308
tweets, citing in MLA style, 155
Twitter, 2–3, 38, 155, 287, 349
two, to, too, 404
two-word verbs
hyphens, unnecessary, 35, 393
idiomatic use, 344–45
missing words, 32
type size and typeface, 18, 19

U

understand, arguing to, 54
uninterested, disinterested, 398
unique, 404
unity in paragraph, 15

unknown authors, citing
in APA style, 179, 181, 185
in *Chicago* style, 219
in MLA style, 132, 139
U.S., as abbreviation, 388
U.S. academic writing expecta-
    tions, 4
us and *we,* 336–38
used to, supposed to, 403

V

varieties of English. *See* English
    language, varieties of

**verb, 32, 115, 289, 290, 293, 298,
300, 302, 319, 325, 331, 344, 350,
364, 381** A word or **phrase**, essential to a **sentence**, that expresses the
action of a sentence or **clause**. Verbs
change form to show **tense**, number,
voice, and **mood.**

and adverbs, 325
agreement with subject, 303,
    319–25
auxiliary or helping, 300–304
colon following, avoiding, 381
commas, avoiding unneeded, 364
conditional sentences, 312
editing, checklist for, 302
fragments without complete,
    36, 350
gerunds, 304–6, 334
infinitives, 303, 304–6, 331,
    386
linking, 323, 326–28, 393
mood of, 310–12
parallelism, 290
phrasal, 344
regular and irregular forms,
    298–300, 319
-*s* form of verbs, 306, 319
signal, 115
strong, 289

verb (*continued*)

tenses. *See also specific tenses*
    in APA style, 115, 177, 308
    in *Chicago* style, 115, 215
    in MLA style, 115
    sequencing, 309
    shifting, 33, 293
    of signal verbs, 115
    using, 307–9
transitive and intransitive, 306,
    344
two-word
    hyphens, unnecessary, 35, 393
    idiomatic use, 344–45
    missing words, 32
verb phrases, 33, 298–313
voice, active and passive. *See*
    voice
words between subject and,
    319–20

verb phrase, 33, 298–313 A main
verb and one or more **helping verbs**,
acting as a single verb.

vertical reading, 97–99
very, 404
ve/ver/vis, 256
video clips
  citing
    in APA style, 200
    in *Chicago* style, 229–30
    in MLA style, 157
  as visuals and media, 20, 22, 78,
    82, 83. *See also* visuals and
    media
video games, citing in MLA style, 158
visuals and media
  in APA style, 177, 181–82,
    198–201
  in argument, 55, 63
  audience for, 117
  audio or video clips, 20, 22, 78,
    82, 83
  bar and line graphs, 21
  captions, 20, 117, 129, 135

  in *Chicago* style, 214, 229–31
  choosing, 20
  in CSE style, 235
  design decisions, 17–23, 78
  diagrams, 21
  documentation, 20. *See also
    under specific styles*
  emotional appeal, 57
  ethical appeal, 55–56
  ethical use of, 23
  handouts, 83
  integrating, 117
  labeling, 20, 117, 129, 177, 181
  logical appeal, 56–57
  maps, 22
  in MLA style, 129, 135, 156–60
  permission to use, 20, 117
  photographs, 21
  pie charts, 21
  position and identification, 20–22
  on posters, 78
  in presentations, 82–84
  in research projects, 88, 117
  slides, 82–83, 85
  storyboarding, 14
  tables, 21
  tone with, 9

voice, 289, 309 The form of a
verb that indicates whether the
subject is acting or being acted
on. In the **active voice,** the subject
performs the action: *Parker* <u>*played*</u>
the saxophone. In the **passive voice,**
the subject receives the action: *The
saxophone* <u>*was played*</u> *by Parker.*

  active and passive, 289–90, 294,
    301–3, 309–10
  shifts in, 294, 310

W

warrant, 53 An assumption,
sometimes unstated, that connects
an **argument**'s **claim** to the reasons
for making the claim.

Warren, Hebron (student writer), 78
we and *us*, 336–38
web comic, 80
web page for fundraising, 79
websites
  accessibility of, 259
  citing
    in APA style, 195–96
    in *Chicago* style, 226–28
    in CSE style, 243
    in MLA style, 151, 152–54
  design decisions, 18, 20
  evaluating, 96–113
web sources, 92–94, 96–103. *See also* digital and nonprint sources
well, 326–28, 399
what, whose, which, 315
where, 404
whether . . . or, 291. *See also* correlative conjunctions
which, that, 357–58, 403
which, that, this, and *it,* vague use of, 340–41
which, whose, what, 315
white space, 18
who, which, and *that,* subject-verb agreement, 323
who, whom, 334–35, 404
who's, whose, 404
whose, which, what, 315
Wikipedia, 38, 92, 197
wikis
  citing
    in APA style, 197–98
    in MLA style, 152
  as class discussion forum, 43
  as research sources, 92
  sharing writing on, 38
word choice, 268–75
  for abilities and disabilities, 259–60
  clichés, 274–75

denotation and connotation, 271–73
doublespeak, 271
euphemisms, 270–71
figurative language, 57, 274–75
formal vs. informal, 260, 268–71
gender-related terms, 255
general and specific language, 273
jargon, 68, 269–70
metaphors, similes, and analogies, 57, 61, 274
mixed metaphors, 274–75
pompous language, 270
for race and ethnicity, 257–59
sexist, 255
signpost, for presentations, 81–82
slang and colloquial language, 263, 269, 377
standardized English, 67–68, 250, 261–65, 268, 293, 368
wrong, 29
See also key words and phrases; language
word pictures, 11
words used as words, 324–25, 391
wordy phrases, replacing, 288
working bibliography, 106, 107, 111, 121
working thesis, 11–12, 89, 90
working title and introduction, 120
works cited. *See* MLA style
world audiences, expectations of, 253
would, in conditional sentences, 312
would of, should of, might of, could of, 397
writing process
  analyzing the rhetorical situation, 7–10
  assignment and purpose analysis, 7–8

writing process (*continued*)
  audience, 8–9. *See also* audience
  choosing a topic, 8, 11
  design decisions, 17–23, 78
  developing a working thesis,
    11–12
  developing paragraphs, 15–17
  drafting, 10–17, 120–21
  editing and proofreading, 25–26,
    121–22. *See also* editing
  evidence and research, 13. *See
    also* evidence; research and
    research projects
  exploring a topic, 10–11
  formal vs. informal style. *See*
    formal writing; informal
    writing
  genres and disciplines, 10, 67–80
  organizational patterns. *See*
    organization
  planning, 13–15, 82–83, 90
  reviewing, 24, 121
  revising, 24–25, 121
  sentences. *See* sentence;
    sentence structure
  sharing and reflecting, 38–40
  stance and tone, 9–10. *See also*
    stance; tone
  time, genre, medium, and
    format, 10. *See also* format-
    ting; genre
  writer's choices, 7–10
  writer's opportunities, 2–7
writing projects
  analyzing assignments for, 7–8
  arguments, 51–65
  collaborative, 7
  in the disciplines, 67–80
  genres and, 67–80
  high-stakes, 42
  language for. *See* language
  low-stakes, 42–44
  presentations, 81–83
  public writing, 72, 78–80, 349
  reflection, 39–40, 42
  sharing, 38
  See also academic writing;
    research and research pro-
    jects; sample student writing
writing to learn, 42
wrong words, 29

Y

yet, 283. *See also* coordinating
    conjunctions
you, it, they, indefinite use of, 341
your, you're, 404
yourself, myself, himself, herself, 399
YouTube, 38, 200

Z

ze/hir/hirs, 256
ze/zir/zirs, 256
Zoom sessions, 43, 82

Revision Symbols

Numbers in bold refer to sections of this book.

abbr	abbreviation **47a**	*para*	paraphrase **13g, 14b**
ad	adjective/adverb **34**	*pass*	inappropriate passive **30b, 31f**
agr	agreement **33, 36b**	*ref*	unclear pronoun reference **36c**
awk	awkward		
cap	capitalization **46**	*run-on*	run-on (fused) sentence **38**
case	case **36a**	*sexist*	sexist language **22b, 36b**
cliché	cliché **24d**	*shift*	shift **30**
com	incomplete comparison **26c**	*slang*	slang **24a**
concl	weak conclusion	*sp*	spelling
cs	comma splice **38**	*sum*	summarize **8d, 13g, 14b**
def	define	*trans*	transition
dm	dangling modifier **35c**	*verb*	verb form **31**
doc	documentation **16–19**	*vs*	verb sequence **31e**
emph	emphasis unclear	*vt*	verb tense **31e**
ex	example needed	*wc*	word choice **24**
frag	sentence fragment **39**	*wrdy*	wordy **28**
fs	fused sentence **38**	*wv*	weak verb **28d**
hyph	hyphen **48e–f**	*ww*	wrong word **24**
inc	incomplete construction **26**	. ? !	period, question mark, exclamation point **42a–c**
it	italics **48a–d**	,	comma **40**
jarg	jargon **24a**	;	semicolon **41**
lc	lowercase **46**	'	apostrophe **43**
lv	language variety **23**	" "	quotation marks **44**
mix	mixed construction **26, 30**	( ) [ ] —	parentheses, brackets, dash **45a–c**
mm	misplaced modifier **35a**	: / …	colon, slash, ellipses **45d–f**
ms	manuscript format **16c, 17b, 18b, 19a**	^	insert
no ,	no comma **40i**	∿	transpose
num	number **47b**	⌣	close up
¶	paragraph	X	delete
//	faulty parallelism **29**		

Language, Culture, and Context (Multilingual)

 Look for this icon to find advice of special interest to international students, speakers of multiple English dialects, or anyone else curious about language and culture.

- Positioning yourself as an academic writer **1c**
- Adapting genre structures **10c**
- Meeting audience expectations **21c**
- Building verb phrases **31b**
- Using infinitives and gerunds **31c**
- Using conditional sentences appropriately **31h**
- Understanding count and noncount nouns **32a**
- Using determiners **32b**
- Using articles **32c**
- Choosing the right preposition **37a**
- Using two-word verbs idiomatically **37b**

Boxed Tips Related to Language, Culture, and Context

Stating a Thesis 12

Using Visuals 22

Identifying Sources 111

Thinking about Plagiarism as a Cultural Concept 119

Asking Experienced Writers to Review a Thesis 121

Respecting Black Language 262

Recognizing Global Varieties of English 266

Avoiding Fancy Language 270

Seeing Grammar as Flexible 301

Checking Usage with Search Engines 305

Using Adjectives with Plural Nouns 327

Judging Sentence Length 346

Contents

QUICK START MENU i

How This Book Can Help You v

WRITING PROCESSES

1 A Writer's Opportunities 2
a Engaging difference
b Using social media wisely
c Positioning yourself as an academic writer
d Collaborating

2 A Writer's Choices 7
a Assignment and purpose
b Topic
c Audiences
d Stance and tone
e Time, genre, medium, and format

3 Exploring, Planning, and Drafting 10
a Exploring a topic
b Developing a working thesis
c Gathering credible evidence
d Planning and drafting
e Developing paragraphs

4 Making Design Decisions 17
a Design principles
b Appropriate formats
c Visuals and media
d Ethical use of visuals and media

5 Reviewing, Revising, and Editing 24
a Reviewing
b Revising
c Editing and proofreading

 Top Twenty Tips for Editing Your Academic Writing 27

6 Sharing and Reflecting on Your Writing 38
a Sharing with audiences
b Creating a portfolio
c Reflecting on your own work
d STUDENT WRITING: REFLECTION

CONTEXTS FOR WRITING, READING, AND SPEAKING

7 Learning from Low-Stakes Writing 42
a The value of low-stakes writing
b Types of low-stakes assignments

8 Reading and Listening Analytically, Critically, and Respectfully 44
a Reading collaboratively

b Previewing
c Annotating
d Summarizing
e Analyzing
f STUDENT WRITING: RHETORICAL ANALYSIS

9 Arguing Ethically and Persuasively 51
a Listening purposefully and openly
b Identifying basic appeals
c Analyzing the elements of an argument
d Arguing purposefully
e Making an argument
f Organizing an argument
g STUDENT WRITING: ARGUMENT ESSAY

10 Writing in a Variety of Disciplines and Genres 67
a Expectations of academic disciplines
b Understanding and using genres
c Adapting genre structures
d Choosing genres for public writing
e STUDENT WRITING: SAMPLES IN A VARIETY OF DISCIPLINES AND GENRES

11 Creating Presentations 81
a Task, purpose, and audience
b Memorable introduction and conclusion
c Structure and signpost language
d Script
e Visuals
f Practice
g Delivery
h STUDENT WRITING: PRESENTATION EXCERPTS

RESEARCH

12 Conducting Research 88
a Understanding challenges to research
b Beginning the research process
c Choosing among types of sources
d Using web and library resources
e Doing field research

13 Evaluating Sources and Taking Notes 96
a Checking facts
b Reading vertically
c Reading laterally
d Reading and analyzing sources
e Synthesizing sources
f Keeping track of sources
g Quoting, paraphrasing, and summarizing
h Creating an annotated bibliography
i STUDENT WRITING: ANNOTATED BIBLIOGRAPHY ENTRIES

Contents, continued

14 Integrating Sources and Avoiding Plagiarism 113
a Using sources ethically
b Integrating source material
c Integrating visuals and media
d Knowing which sources to acknowledge
e Avoiding plagiarism

15 Writing a Research Project 120
a Drafting your text
b Reviewing and revising
c Preparing a list of sources
d Editing and proofreading
e STUDENT WRITING: OUTLINE

DOCUMENTATION

16 MLA Style 124
a MLA citation style
b Context of sources
c MLA format
d MLA in-text citations
 ● List of examples 130
e MLA list of works cited
 ● List of examples 136
f STUDENT WRITING: MLA STYLE

17 APA Style 174
a APA citation style
b APA format
c APA in-text citations
 ● List of examples 178
d APA list of references
 ● List of examples 182
e STUDENT WRITING: APA STYLE

18 *Chicago* Style 212
a *Chicago* citation style
b *Chicago* format
c *Chicago* notes and bibliographic entries
 ● List of examples 216
d STUDENT WRITING: *CHICAGO* STYLE

19 CSE Style 235
a CSE format
b CSE in-text citations
c CSE list of references
 ● List of examples 238
d STUDENT WRITING: CSE STYLE

STYLE: EFFECTIVE LANGUAGE

20 Language and Identity 248
a How language shapes identity
b Language to shape your own identity

21 Writing across Cultures, Communities, and Identities 250
a Thinking about what seems "normal"
b Clarifying meaning
c Meeting audience expectations

22 Language That Builds Common Ground 254
a Assumptions and stereotypes
b Assumptions about gender; pronouns
c Assumptions about race and ethnicity
d Abilities and disabilities

23 Language Varieties 260
a Practicing language awareness
b Understanding "standardized English"
c Bringing in other languages

24 Word Choice 268
a Levels of formality
b Denotation and connotation
c General and specific language
d Figurative language

STYLE: EFFECTIVE SENTENCES

25 Varying Sentences 278
a Sentence length
b Sentence openings

26 Consistency and Completeness 280
a Revising sentence structure
b Matching subjects and predicates
c Making complete comparisons

27 Coordination and Subordination 283
a Relating equal ideas
b Distinguishing main ideas

28 Conciseness 287
a Eliminating redundant words
b Eliminating empty words
c Replacing wordy phrases
d Simplifying sentence structure

29 Parallelism 290
a With items in a series or list
b With paired ideas
c Words necessary for clarity

30 Shifts 293
a In tense
b In voice
c In point of view
d Between direct and indirect discourse

GRAMMAR

31 Verbs and Verb Phrases 298
a Regular and irregular verb forms
b Verb phrases
c Infinitives and gerunds
d *Lie* and *lay*, *sit* and *set*, *rise* and *raise*
e Verb tenses
f Active and passive voice
g Mood
h Conditional sentences